Social Science Research on CAD/CAM

Results of a First European Workshop

Michael Rader · Bernd Wingert
Ulrich Riehm (Eds.)

Social Science Research on CAD/CAM

Results of a First European Workshop

With Contributions by
J. Bessant, P. Berckmans, O. Brivio, D. Buschhaus
G. C. Cainarca, A. Clauwaert, E. R. Eriksen, H. Finne
M. Fodgaard, E. Frydendal Pedersen, H. Gottschalch
F. Hansen, B. Haywood, P. Higgins, H. Hirsch-Kreinsen
D. Hoß, J. Huys, P. L. Jensen, W. Jonas, A. Kjellberg
G. Kovács, F. Manske, I. McLoughlin, N. Møller
M. Mutinelli, J.-P. Poitou, M. Rader, L. B. Rasmussen
M. Resch, U. Riehm, C. Roveda, K. Spors, M. van Wagenberg
Y. Waern, B. Wingert, W. D. Zinkl

With 41 Figures

Physica-Verlag Heidelberg

Dr. Michael Rader
Bernd Wingert
Ulrich Riehm

Kernforschungszentrum Karlsruhe
Abteilung für Angewandte Systemanalyse
Postfach 36 40
7500 Karlsruhe 1, FRG

ISBN 978-3-7908-0392-1 ISBN 978-3-642-52380-9 (eBook)
DOI 10.1007/978-3-642-52380-9

CIP-Kurztitelaufnahme der Deutschen Bibliothek

Social science research on CAD-CAM: results of a ...
European Workshop. - Heidelberg: Physica-Verl.
1(1988)
ISBN 978-3-7908-0392-1

Cover: Erich Kirchner, Heidelberg

7100/7130-543210

PREFACE

Computer Aided Design (CAD) and Computer Aided Manufacture (CAM) are but two of the more recent examples of computer applications in domains previously dominated by human labour. The use of computers in such areas has increasingly attracted social science research. There are several reasons one could suggest for this, not least of them being the simple fact that public money is being provided for such research. Of course, some of the interest may be due to the wish to prove that technology is being used to inhuman ends, but undoubtedly there is also some degree of fascination involved. Can you really do all the things with computers that people claim you can? There is certainly satisfaction to be had from smugly pointing out its shortcomings, but many of the few sociologists in our own organisation are also among the most avid users of modern technology. Needless to say, they also belong to the most critical users of the technology! A new strain of motivation for social science research which appears to be gaining significance, is the desire to "re-direct" technology, or at least - and probably more realistically - to play a part in shaping future technology.

The entire range of motives may be recognised in the collection of papers contained in this volume. They are all original contributions prepared for a workshop on social science studies dealing with CAD/CAM which took place at Karlsruhe Nuclear Research Centre from the 28th to the 30th of October 1985. Rather than simply collecting the pre-prints, writing an intelligent-sounding introduction and putting a more or less durable cover around the set, we decided to take the job of editing seriously. This meant a certain amount of correction of the English in order to ensure intelligibility while retaining certain national idiosyncracies, re-typing (word-processing, actually) the whole collection, and listening to the tapes of the discussions in order to preserve the most important points for posterity. This latter proved a most daunting task, for although modern stereo microphones were purchased especially for the workshop, we made the mistake of not taking a sound-check before recording. Although participants close to the microphone were recorded remarkably well, those more distant or not blessed with powerful voices are scarcely audible. To be more exact, they sound as if they are standing under a shower. Although one of us has had over twenty years' experience listening to ancient jazz recordings including some sung in heavy Southern US dialects, these sometimes seemed of very high fidelity in comparison with the pianissimo passages of the workshop's discussions. So apologies are due to anyone who feels they made a valid point in the discussions not included in the transcripts. We shall try to find a vintage Edison cylinder recorder for our next workshop.

For various reasons, editing and word-processing took longer than we had originally anticipated. Since we urged the participants in the workshop to submit their final contributions by the end of 1985, or else, we owe a further apology to anyone who took our threats seriously. In the event, we were very lenient and actually received the final contribution (in German, so it still had to be translated) in the second half of 1986. While in the apology department, we should point out that our text processing system has an option for checking spelling, but this is for American English, so anyone who submitted a paper in British English might be in for a shock when reading his or her paper.

Despite the delay, we feel the papers are well worth reading, even if some of the projects have progressed enormously since. One of our intentions in publishing this volume is to expand the network which served to bring the various projects together for the workshop. Readers conducting or considering their own project on a topic related to those covered by the volume, are encouraged to contact either us or any institution in their own country doing work of a similar nature. There is promise of a second workshop in 1988, so we look forward to meeting anyone there who was able to profit from the information included in this volume.

Finally, we would like to thank everyone who made the workshop and this volume possible. Foremost, this applies to the participants who provided contributions of a very high standard indeed. We also owe a great debt of gratitude to our department head, Dr. Herbert Paschen, for smoothing the way and to the executive board of Karlsruhe Nuclear Research Centre, in particular to Professor Dr. Wolfgang Klose, for a generous grant without which the whole event would not have been possible. Thanks also to various staff of the Nuclear Research Centre for providing meals and getting the participants to events on time, and particularly to our lady caretaker, Marie-Luise Störtzer for keeping things running smoothly. Finally, we wish to express our gratitude to our typing staff here at the Department of Applied Systems Analysis, in particular Charlotte Neu-Thoss, Gabriele Kaufmann and Gabriele Rastätter, for their patience in successive typing and correction of various drafts and the final manuscript. We feel that the result was well worth the effort and trust that readers will also.

Michael Rader, Bernd Wingert, Ulrich Riehm
Leopoldshafen, November 1987

Contents

EDITOR'S INTRODUCTION: A PERSONAL HISTORY OF THE EUROPEAN CAD/CAM SOCIAL STUDIES NETWORK

Michael Rader
Kernforschungszentrum Karlsruhe
Abteilung für Angewandte Systemanalyse (AFAS)
7500 Karlsruhe, Postfach 3640

1. The pre-history

Whenever a researcher starts an empirical project, he or she usually looks first at which previous work has been done on the subject. In the case of technologies like CAD/CAM, this is all the more important since technologies have certain properties which may not be visible at first glance, particularly to researchers from non-technical fields such as the social sciences. Otherwise there might be a tendency to assume that one computer-based technology is much like the other and that any effects one technology may have will also be produced by applying another similarly based technology.

When we *) started our own CAD project in 1977, to our knowledge, no other empirical project on the subject had been completed or, indeed, was in hand. There had been a great deal of debate on the use of computers in the printing industry and in office work with forecasts of enormous loss of jobs. CAD was touched on in Buschhaus' examination of future skill requirements of draughtspeople [1]), but otherwise mention of CAD in industrial sociology was usually marginal. It was invariably mentioned as one of the technologies most likely to have great effect in the future, especially where job loss or deskilling were concerned. In fact our project came into existence as a result of the concern about possible negative effects of CAD, mainly because people realized that computers had been having such effects elsewhere, with the result of resistance on the part of those likely to be affected. As a measure to help develop a German CAD industry and to encourage the adoption of the technology by industry, a government funding and project management agency (Projektträgerschaft CAD) had been set up at Karlsruhe Nuclear Research Centre and it was this agency which requested the original study. This study ran from 1977 to 1979 and resulted in the publication of the book "Mechanisierung geistiger Arbeit" [2]). The original project team included an economically oriented engineer ("Wirtschaftsingenieur") to provide the technical expertise required and it has been a matter of policy since then to include in our projects at least one member with some background in engineering.

---

*) When I write "we", this applies strictly only to Bernd Wingert. Gotthard Bechmann, Richard Vahrenkamp and Raimund Werle belonged to the original project group, but left between 1979 and 1980. Ulrich Riehm and I joined the project in 1979 and Werner Duus was with it from 1981 to 1985.

Although ours was among the first three projects specifically on CAD in Germany at the time *), there was of course, a great deal of work being done on other computer-based technologies, both for white-collar work and in production. The German metal workers' union, IG-Metall, was concerned about possible negative effects of CAD for its members, particularly draughtspeople, and staged a seminar on the subject for some of its works councillors with a number of social scientists in attendance. A guest speaker at this seminar was Mike Cooley, then in the middle of his involvement with the corporate plan at Lucas Aerospace, his employer at the time. COOLEY's 1972 booklet on CAD 3) had been translated into German the year before and was to be very influential in Germany as, indeed, it must have been throughout Western Europe. His hypothesis, borrowed from Blauner, on the bi-polarization of skills, i.e. deskilling of the greater part of design-office staff leaving an elite with the more demanding, creative and strenuous parts, received a great deal of attention and was to influence the course of research and discussion on the effects of CAD for the years to come. Besides his own work in the field, Cooley helped to make known the writings of Howard Rosenbrock. Rosenbrock is a highly-respected control scientist and since the mid 1970s has concerned himself increasingly with technology designed to take advantage of and enhance skills, due mainly to his belief in the superiority of human skills over any machine. These writings have exerted great influence on social scientists and "enlightened" technologists. This has particularly been the case in Scandinavia and in the Federal Republic of Germany where the IG-Metall has translated and published a selection of ROSENBROCK's writings 4) and certain ideas were picked up by the Federal Ministry for Research and Technology's Manufacturing Technology Programme's management team.

In view of the fact that both Cooley and Rosenbrock are what may be termed socially-minded engineers, it is hardly surprising that the unionists present at the IG-Metall seminar expected more from this quarter than from social scientists!

2. First contacts

At the end of 1979, a small party from our project visited Great Britain 5) to collect information on developments there, particularly as there was thought to be 5 years' more experience with CAD due largely to the more prominent role of the British aerospace industry. Once again, the most significant contributions towards the debate on CAD were coming from engineers: Cooley, Rosenbrock, the ABACUS-group at Strathclyde University and people linked with the CAD Centre in Cambridge (particularly Malcolm Sabin and Arthur Llewelyn). Although we met Peter Senker at S.P.R.U, this was before any work had been done there on CAD. Viewed in retrospect, we had difficulty in finding any people actively involved in the social side of CAD/CAM. If the visit had taken place a few years later, we would probably have had difficulty in finding time to visit *all* the people in the field.

---

*) The other two projects were one by Rolf Thärichen and the study run at the Technical University of Berlin (cf. Contribution by Wingert et al. in this Volume).

A first European Conference on CAD in medium sized and small industries (MICAD) was held in Paris in September 1980 [6]). This included a session on the social and economic consequences, once again with Mike Cooley as an invited speaker. It is interesting to look at the topics covered in this session:

- The economics of CAD systems, a subject always of great interest to firms considering the adoption of the technology, although tangible economic effects have proved highly elusive.
- The integration of computer aided processes into the design and production cycle.
- Overcoming resistance toward computer aided design. Significantly, the problem of how well CAD was suited to the tasks for which it was being employed was not yet regarded as important an issue.
- Personnel selection, again implying that the computer was more important than existing skills.
- The solution of design office problems through the use of CAD, and
- The impact of automation on productivity, also a subject of great interest to company decision-makers despite the difficulty in relating theory to reality.

The session also included two papers with a genuine social science background by Jean-Pierre POITOU [7]) and ourselves [8]). At the time, Poitou was unable to report any results from his own work on the subject, but since then has worked continuously on CAD. The 1982 version of MICAD dropped the session on social and economic consequences, although there were a single-paper session on training and one on investment strategies. A solitary paper by Rader [9]) on the subject of problems encountered in the introduction of CAD into the design office was relegated to the "other applications", i.e. "miscellaneous" division.

In the course of work on the project, we became aware of other studies which had been set up on CAD. Contacts took the shape of letter-writing, meetings at conferences and visits. Occasionally, there were small seminars or discussions specifically on CAD, but no recognized forum for general social science discussion on the subject. Perhaps the best opportunity for such discussion, albeit on the more general subject of computer-based production technology, were regular specialist meetings held by the government project management agency in Karlsruhe, now re-named "Projektträgerschaft Fertigungstechnik" (PFT) to mark the new program it was handling. These meetings take place when supported projects are presented and discussed with peers of those conducting the projects and interested industrialists. Most of the institutions involved in industrial sociology are invited to these meetings and almost all are now involved with CAD/CAM in one way or the other (see their contributions to this volume). Although they themselves have not been able to engage actively in research [*]), the members of the project management agency have played an important part in encouraging social science research and the diffusion of its results.

----

*) One exception is Peter Brödner, another example of the breed of socially-minded engineers, who was given leave to write a book "Fabrik 2000" (Berlin: Edition Sigma 1985). The book is being widely read and discussed in Germany.

3. The network takes shape

In February 1983, Håkon Finne, of the Institute for Social Research in Industry at the Technical University of Norway, a researcher with qualifications in both sociology and engineering who had spent some time with Rosenbrock in England, circulated a list of researchers he knew were engaged in social studies on CAD. His intention was to establish an informal network of contacts between these individuals and groups in order to exchange information and experience. Something similar had been in our minds here at Karlsruhe for some time and we picked up Finne's lead and went a step further by suggesting a workshop to bring all the people involved in social studies on CAD together. At the same time, we started distributing irregular newsletters containing the latest information available to us and offered to act as a clearing house for all forthcoming information of the kind. An initial attempt was made to convene the social science researchers attending the CAPE'83 conference in Amsterdam.

The conference itself was remarkable in the respect that the conference chairman, Jakob VLIETSTRA, devoted a considerable proportion of his opening address to social issues [10]. In addition, there was a panel discussion on social problems, marred by poor organization. The papers included several of interest to social scientists:

- A state-of-the-art presentation titled "Dreams, Nightmares and Reality" by Joe HATVANY, a remarkably cosmopolitan Hungarian CAD pioneer fully aware of the social implications of technology [11];
- A case study on user participation in systems development by the late Fred MARGULIES, a highly influential trade-unionist/engineer also a one-time Secretary General of the International Federation of Automated Control [12]. In fact the project was terminated before actual systems development could be completed;
- Theoretical deliberations on "Social and Engineering Design of an FMS" [13] by Howard ROSENBROCK, who was reporting on a project which was to give him the opportunity to put his theory into practice, although by some accounts he was not entirely successful.

Our own project was represented with two papers [14], [15], but for several reasons this conference demonstrated again the need for a separate meeting for social scientists:

- The marginal status of social studies in such technical meetings;
- The divergent interests of technologists and social scientists, at the same time acknowledging the importance of exchange of ideas between these disciplines (see the final section of this volume);
- The lack of opportunities to "talk shop";
- The lack of a conference specifically aiming to involve all the significant social scientists working in the field.

Another factor which may seem trivial is that of participation fees which are often prohibitive for non-industrial organizations, serving to filter out most social scientists.

In the event, attempts to meet social scientists at CAPE were not entirely successful, although we did establish a fleeting contact with a new organization being set up in Ann Arbor, close to the heart of the American automobile industry in Detroit. This organization, the Industrial Technology Institute, was to employ social and political scientists among other people, but attempts to draw it into the network failed despite a professed eagerness to establish links with social scientists in Europe. Throughout our entire project we did not find one reference to actual social science research work done in the USA, although we refused to believe that none had been done. A character claiming to be from the Congressional Research Service of the Library of Congress turned up at an EC conference on Information Technology in Dublin [16]). His review on human considerations in the implementation of CAD systems turned out to be a summary of the papers from the social and economic issues session of the 1980 MICAD conference with a couple from the references of those papers thrown in for luck, and his actual presentation was a blatant plug for a CAD journal whose staff he had recently joined. We were later visited by a well known American industrial psychologist who had been instrumental in introducing participative approaches to job design to the States, but by then he was interested in finding out why US firms seemed reluctant to adopt new technologies in which the US otherwise had a leading edge. So much for our attempts to trace US studies!

4. Planning for the workshop

In the Autumn of 1983, IFAC staged a workshop on "The Design of Work in Automated Manufacturing Systems" [17]) chaired by Tom Martin of PFT in Karlsruhe and this gave us the opportunity to meet Håkon Finne and draw up a proposal for the present workshop, which was duly circulated to people on our joint mailing lists. The aims are worth repeating here:

- The workshop should contribute towards firmly establishing the network and to making it known to all social scientists in Europe working on CAD and related technologies. Results will be diffused more widely and cooperative relationships may be instigated.
- This exchange of information should include not only actual results and research instruments, but also discussions on research methods. As an effect of this, some future projects could be better aligned and results would readily be more comparable. This again could help to reveal comparable trends in the kind of applications and with regard to effects.
- Similar aims regard *theoretical approaches*, especially in the discussion of the social sciences' perception of technology.

  We wish the existing breadth of methodological approaches to be exposed for possible cross-breeding effects. This would include, for example, consequence research, "Begleitforschung", action research, participative design of organizations and technology, social scientists involved in CAD systems design.

- The workshop should also aim to give an overview of experience in the various European countries on the *design of CAD* (Work stations, technology, organization). It should thus also be possible to contribute to
- the *professionalization* of efforts of the social sciences directed towards technological problems.

5. The workshop takes place

The workshop was originally scheduled for the Autumn of 1984, but for various reasons was postponed for a year. In the meantime, several new projects got off the ground while others were completed and their authors went on to other subjects, in some cases with the unfortunate effect that they were unable to contribute their knowledge to the workshop. The people attending the workshop were a mixture of established researchers in the field and of others just starting out, sometimes with valuable prior experience in a related field. Although we had intended to restrict attendance to social scientists or engineers working in socially oriented projects with social scientists, several engineers with practical experience did take part - we hope to the mutual benefit of those involved.

If we look at the original aims of the workshop and compare them with the programme, it is easy to recognize that some had already been dropped in planning the event, mainly due to the interests of those who were willing to contribute. For instance, there was no session on methods although it was obvious that participants were using a wide variety of them just as they came from a variety of scientific disciplines. Maybe this is a topic for a subsequent workshop, since both social science research and the technology itself are still in the process of consolidation, so there is yet time for comparative studies.

The papers cover a wide range of topics, some of them being of a more theoretical nature while others report actual results from ongoing or completed projects. Some of the Scandinavian projects in particular seem very ambitious since they intend to influence the course of technology. It will be interesting to see how they fare. Apart from the training project [18]), most of the other projects are in the less exposed position of merely reporting and analyzing changes effected by the decisions of others. A common theme which appears to be emerging from almost all of these is the re-discovery of skilled work and of ways and means in which technology may be employed to take advantage of it [19]), [20]). Here, it will be interesting to observe whether this lead is taken up by engineers and the industry - there certainly are indications that this may be so.

After a session to set national "scenes", there were four sessions on selected topics:

- The nature of design work, including an interesting discussion on the role of "tacit knowledge";
- Implementation of CAD and training for use;
- Organizational effects and CAD/CAM integration;
- Utilization of results from research and cooperation between the disciplines.

This division has been retained for these proceedings except that a 2-paper section on the development of CAD systems has been added. Some of the most interesting points from the discussions are mentioned in the introduction to each chapter, but no attempt has been made to summarize them in their entirety.

The workshop was certainly successful in that it helped to establish contracts and enabled informal exchange of experience, questionnaires and so forth. Perhaps this will lead to joint projects at later stages or at least to directly comparable studies. Håkon Finne and Lauge Rasmussen have undertaken to organize a second workshop. It is then that the results of this first European Workshop on Social Science Studies on CAD/CAM will become truly visible.

References

1) Buschhaus, D.:
Problemanalyse zur Neuordnung der Berufsausbildung für Technische Zeichner, Teil 2, Berichte zur beruflichen Bildung, Heft 8, Berlin 1978

2) Bechmann, G., Vahrenkamp, R., Wingert, B.:
Mechanisierung geistiger Arbeit. Frankfurt, New York: Campus 1979

3) Cooley, M.J.E.:
Computer Aided Design - Its Nature and its Implications. AUEW-TASS, 1972 translated as: Computer Aided Design, Sein Wesen und seine Zusammenhänge. Stuttgart: Alektor 1978

4) Rosenbrock, H.H.: Technikentwicklung: Gestaltung ist machbar. Arbeitsheft 9 der IG Metall zur Humanisierung des Arbeitslebens. Frankfurt a. Main: IG Metall 1984.

5) Rader, M., Wingert, B.:
Computer Aided Design in Great Britain and the Federal Republic of Germany - Current Trends and Impacts. Karlsruhe: KfK 3065, March 1981

6) Mermet, J. (Ed.):
CAD in Medium Sized and Small Industries. Amsterdam et al.: North Holland 1981

7) Poitou, J.P.:
CAD and Working Conditions, in reference /6/ above.

8) Wingert, B., Rader, M., Riehm, U.:
Changes in Working Skills in the Field of Design caused by the Use of Computers, in reference /6/, above.

9) Rader, M.:
Managing the Introduction of CAD into the Design Office. In Texts of the Conferences, 2nd European Conference on Computer Aided Design in Small and Medium Size Industries. MICAD'82

10) Vlietstra, J.:
Computer Applications in Technology - Opportunity and Problems, in: Warman, E.A. (Ed.): Computer Applications in Production and Engineering. Amsterdam, New York, Oxford: North Holland 1983

11) Hatvany, J.:
Dreams, Nightmares and Reality, in Warman, E.A. (Ed.): op. cit. (see reference 10, above)

12) Margulies, F.:
User Participation in Systems Development - A Case Study, in Warman, E.A. (Ed.): op. cit. (see reference 10, above)

13) Rosenbrock, H.H.:
Social and Engineering Design of an FMS, in Warman, E.A. (Ed.): op. cit. (see reference 10, above)

14) Riehm, U., Wingert, B.:
Technology Induced Morphogenesis of Skills: The Case of CAD, in Warman, E.A. (Ed.): op. cit. (see reference 10, above)

15) Duus, W., Rader, M.:
The Tightrope Act of Proving Effectiveness - Some results on CAD, in Warman, E.A. (Ed.): op. cit. (see reference 10, above)

16) Bannon, L. et al. (Eds.):
Information Technology - Impact on the Way of Life. Dublin: Tycooly 1982

17) Martin, T. (Ed.):
Design of Work in Automated Manufacturing Systems. Oxford et al: Pergamon 1984

18) See Papers by Buschhaus and Gottschalch in this volume.

19) Kern, H., Schumann, M.:
Das Ende der Arbeitsteilung? Rationalisierung in der industriellen Produktion. München: Beck 1984

20) Schröder, K.T. (Ed.):
Arbeit und Informationstechnik. Berlin, Heidelberg et al.: Springer 1986

CHAPTER 1: NATIONAL REVIEWS

This chapter requires little or no explanation. Researchers from 11 European countries took part in the workshop in addition to one Australian. This latter circumstance was not the result of deliberate planning on our part. We have the happy coincidence that Peter Higgins of the Swinburne Institute of Technology was visiting Scandinavia to investigate industrial relations there to thank for the chance to learn a little about the Australian scene. A brief note based on his oral contribution is included in this chapter.

Erik Arnold included a short section on "Studies on the effects of CAD in Europe" in his booklet on "CAD in Europe" [1]). In fact, these are all covered again by the reviews in this chapter. In some cases, the project represented at the workshop is the only one in a country. This applied to smaller and lesser industrialized countries, where both CAD applications and social studies on them are rare and recent. Such countries are usually covered by a brief note, in some cases edited out of a longer contribution on the project. There had been a meeting of people involved in social science projects on CAD/CAM at Aix-en-Provence just prior to the workshop. So, rather than duplicating the results of that meeting, interested readers are urged to obtain a copy of its proceedings [2]).

Two of the reviews cover groups of countries. German-speaking countries (i.e. Austria, the Federal Republic of Germany and part of Switzerland) and Scandinavian countries (i.e. Denmark, Norway and Sweden). Considering the sizes of these latter countries, it is truly remarkable how much research is being done. Håkon Finne's contribution on Scandinavia also throws some light on the history of CAD/CAM research in Europe.

It may be unfair to single out any particular country, but George Kovacs' piece on Hungary (edited out of a longer paper) may be of particular interest, since his is the only contribution from political Eastern Europe and thus sheds a little light on what would otherwise be a dark spot on the map. Although there are probably no fully-fledged social science studies on CAD/CAM going on and George himself is an engineer, his paper does show that the situation faced by would-be users of technology there is completely different from that in Western industrialized countries, with the result that systems are put together for a single application. Perhaps this means that there will be fewer social problems, but it is to be hoped that social scientists from Eastern European countries will be able to report on actual empirical research at subsequent workshops.

References

1) Arnold, E., 1984:
Computer-Aided Design in Europe, Sussex European Research Centre, University of Sussex: Sussex European Paper No. 14, 1984

2) Actes du colloque "Espace graphique, Dessin technique, C.F.A.O." Aix-en-Provence, 23 - 24 octobre 1985; Technologies, Idéologies, Pratiques. Volumes V n° 4 et VI n° 1 1986. Publication de l'Université de Provence.

CAD/CAM AND SOCIAL SCIENCE IN SCANDINAVIA

Håkon Finne
Institute of Social Research in Industry (IFIM)
N-7034 Trondheim, NTH

1. Introduction

In this paper I will first give some rough estimates of the diffusion of CAD/CAM technology in Denmark, Sweden and Norway. Then I will give an overview over current and completed social science research projects on CAD/CAM in these countries. Finally, some issues of trade union involvement will be discussed.

During the preparation of this paper I learned about a number of new relevant activities in the field. Without the cooperation of many Scandinavian colleagues this paper would not have been possible.

The historical development of working life research in Scandinavia has of course been decisive in forming our activities in the CAD/CAM area. The field is dominated by problem oriented case studies (and less by wider surveys), qualitative methodology flourishes. The theoretical framework is often adapted from social psychology, there is a strong socio-technical tradition, and worker participation as prescribed by law and collective agreement is the cutting edge of many projects. Finally, many of the larger institutions doing this kind of research belong to, or are affiliated with, technical universities.

CAD/CAM here covers a large variety of CAD and CAM applications. Clearly many findings should be related to a more specific typology. For the sake of brevity I have largely refrained from a more detailed classification in this overview paper even where it had been possible to link findings with properties of particular systems.

2. The diffusion of CAD/CAM technology

CAD/CAM has a long history in Scandinavia. First out was Norway with the Autokon CAD system for shipbuilding developed by the SI research institute and the Aker group. The first industrial installation was in 1964 and two years later the first delivery was made to the USA (ARNOLD 1984). For a comparison, Computervision - which used to be the world market leader - was not even formed at that date.

The first Swedish CAD system, named Styrbjorn and developed in-house by the Kockum shipyards, was in use from 1969 (ARNOLD 1984). Both these early developments were batch systems, interactive graphics was still far ahead.

The early start was followed up in different ways. In Norway, CAD/CAM development became a substantial research area and a small but advanced industry grew up. Norwegian firms are now making and customizing software for mechanical, electronic and construction industries as well as some advanced hardware. In Sweden, some important work that has been carried out as in-house development in a few of the larger firms, is now partly commercialized. CAD is presently a research area of high priority in both Sweden and Denmark. In Denmark, however, there appears to be no truly national CAD development yet beyond the research stage.

The pattern of diffusion into industry deviates from what could be expected from the development of the national supply industry. Figure 1 shows estimates of numbers of systems (excluding systems for personal computers) in use in the three countries over time. The estimates should he interpreted with care. There are problems connected both with delimiting a CAD or a CAD/CAM system and with counting the kind of units one has decided to count. Furthermore, some sources limit themselves to certain branches of industry. The figure is meant to cover all kinds of applications.

Figure 1 shows that Swedish industry has adopted the new technology rapidly after 1979. By 1982, more than 200 systems had been installed (LINDEBERG 1983), a number that according to an official prognosis made two years earlier should not have been reached until 1985 (SOU 1981). Unfortunately no later counting exists but there is agreement that the revised prognosis of 35 % annual market growth (made by Lindeberg in accordance with international figures) has not been met.

While Norwegian industry was first, the diffusion has been slower. Figure 1 shows absolute numbers but even when corrected for the larger volume of industrial production in Sweden, Norway is at least three years behind. In Denmark again the numbers are significantly smaller. The systems on sale are considered to be two years behind the German market.

The grand explosion in the Scandinavian CAD/CAM market was expected to come in 1983, then in 1984, then in 1985. The basis of these predictions was the falling price level of the systems and a tremendous interest at exhibitions and in the press. Why predictions were too conservative until 1981 and too optimistic later is of course a topic of future investigation for social scientists.

There is a correlation between the number of systems in use, the number of firms using systems, and the number of persons involved. Lindeberg found averages of almost two systems per firm, four workstations per system and three users per workstation. In Denmark and Norway one finds closer to one system per firm. A very rough estimate for 1985 would yield that some 2000-4000 people in 300 Scandinavian firms have hands-on experience with the new technology. With the advent of systems on personal computers, however, this number may easily double within a year.

Since the future growth is expected to be largest in small systems, there will be more systems per firm and fewer users per system. These figures therefore need separate counting.

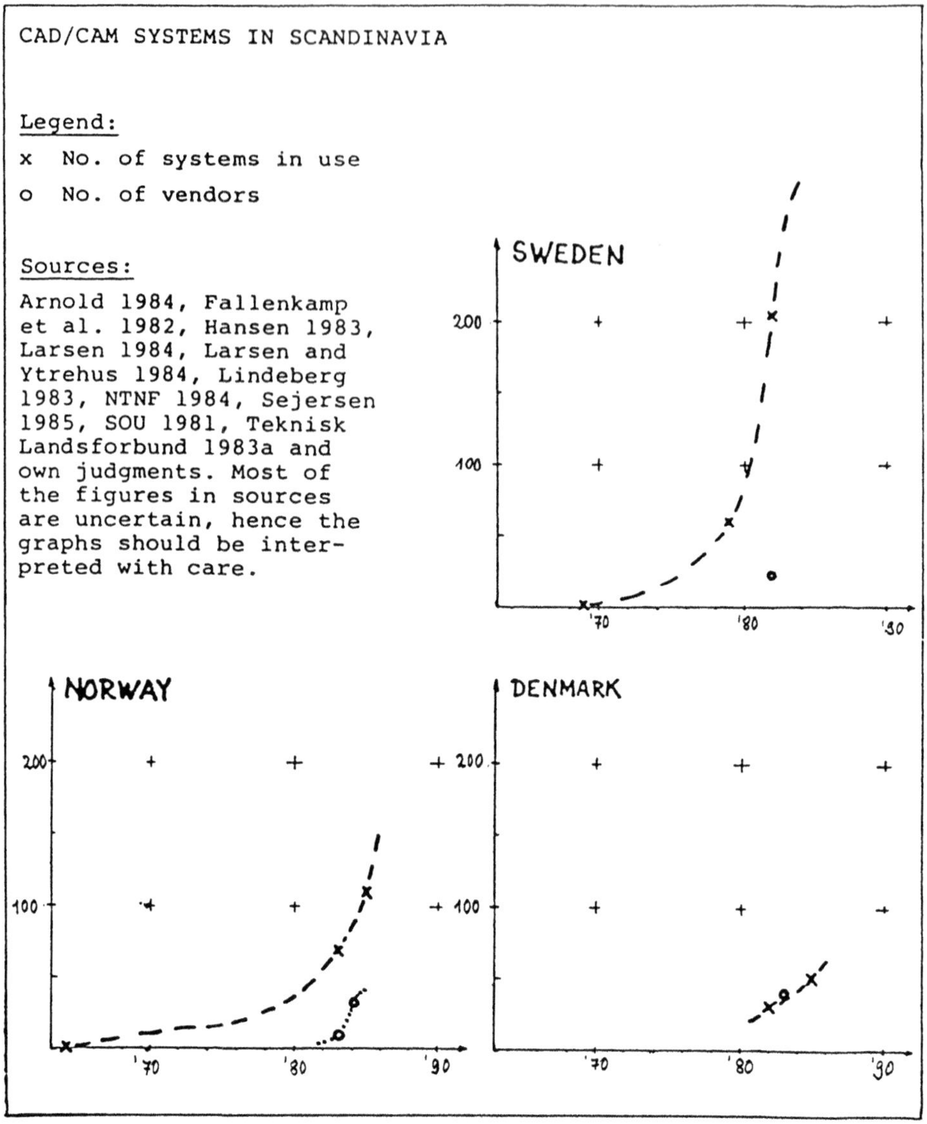

Figure 1: CAD/CAM diffusion in Scandinavia

Figure 1 also shows estimates of the number of systems vendors in the three countries. I venture the claim that until 1981 there were more Scandinavians developing the technology and trying to sell it than there were people actually using it. Even today the number of vendors is impressively high compared to the number of systems sold. All three governments also fund national programs for speeding up CAD/CAM diffusion into industry. Hence in Scandinavian history I don't think there is any stronger case of technology push in industrial development.

3. Social science research into CAD/CAM

General remarks

Given the strong technology push, one would think that economists were the first social scientists to be drawn towards studies of CAD and CAM. But this has not been the case in Scandinavia. Rather, sociologists and psychologists have been in the fore-front. Why are these groups showing such an interest in CAD/CAM?

I can think of several reasons for that. In the first place, we are drawn towards CAD and interactive graphics for the same reason as other people: the fascination of creative work with a visual medium. While other factors are decisive for investments in this kind of systems, the visual effects are the first that attract people in general and the systems vendors know it.

The second reason is more related to social science than to social scientists. CAD is the first attempt to rationalize by mechanical means engineering labour. Not only mental work is here affected by automation but CAD even goes into the heartland of creativity. Both in terms of social class and in terms of the kind of work involved mechanization has reached new levels and this alone is a very good reason for studying the CAD/CAM phenomenon. Ironically, the actions of the engineering profession may now turn back onto themselves. Mike Cooley speaks of the "deskiller deskilled".

A third reason concerns the organizational repercussions of integrating disparate activities in the firm by means of computers. Is CAD/CAM the opportunity to overcome dysfunctions of specialization or are organizations so rigid that only new strains will be created?

A fourth reason lies in the social organization of our work and concerns funding. By and large those agencies that fund social science research into causes and effects of technology have strong affiliations to those who promote specific technologies at the national level. Given the current interest in promoting CAD/CAM in Scandinavia and elsewhere, it is no surprise that social science research into this area is easier to fund than, say, work on knitting machines used in paid home work.

Early projects

The earliest social science project in CAD/CAM started in 1979 in Sweden but was little known outside CAD/CAM development circles until recently. This project will be discussed in a section below (cf. social science influence on design of CAD/CAM systems).

The first works on CAD/CAM appeared fairly early in all three countries. Simultaneously and independently of each other one Danish and one Norwegian project were undertaken in 1981. The first Swedish project of this kind came one year later. I will present these projects before I proceed to subsequent work in the field.

The first *Danish project* was undertaken by the engineering students Fallenkamp, Hansen and Jessen at the Technological University of Denmark (DTH) (Department of Social Science), and in close cooperation with the Danish Technicians' Union (Teknisk Landsforbund, TL). The project title was "CAD/CAM - technology, economy and work environment". The reports (FALLENKAMP et al. 1982b) show a fascination with the possibilities of the technology and a strong concern about the possible negative effects for the users (designers and draftspeople). Seven Danish and four foreign small case studies were made, thus they must have covered about one third of the Danish installations at the time.

There is a strong influence from the German analytical tradition in this work. In particular, the early work of BECHMANN et al. (1979) is used as a standard of reference for empirical findings and also for analyzing changes in skill requirements. This German influence is largely absent elsewhere in Scandinavia due to cultural and political factors.

Their findings may seem commonplace today but aroused considerable interest at that time. They found that the work of technicians became more abstract and required a higher degree of pre-planning, they foresaw a strong degree of polarization of skill requirements, they feared negative effects on employment, and the ergonomic arrangements at the workplace were appalling. They also launched an interesting analysis and critique of the CAD training available in as much as it was a narrow *training* for particular jobs with particular systems and did not give the *education* necessary to understand the technology, its social and economic background and how to use it as a tool for problem-solving.

The first *Norwegian project* was part of a larger undertaking by my institute (IFIM) in collaboration with the Production Engineering Laboratory at SINTEF in Trondheim in contract with the Mechanical Engineering Employers' Association and the Iron- and Metalworkers' Union. The "Future environment of mechanical engineering" concentrated on social effects and organizational patterns of CNC adaptation (RASMUSSEN 1984), but CAD/CAM was studied separately and reported as "Between the drawing board and the terminal" (FINNE 1982).

The main influence in this report was the work of Mike Cooley in England, who has been producing both speculative and empirical work on CAD since the late sixties. As is probably well known, Cooley's central message is that although there are great possibilities of making CAD systems that enhance skills and creativity, the economic incentives lie in using CAD to deskill designers and taylorize their work, and CAD also makes it easier to do this.

The empirical basis of this first Norwegian project was one case study and a couple of shorter visits to other installations. The case chosen was a lucky one though in the sense that it shed light on a large number of aspects. One of those aspects was CAD/CAM integration, which is considered separately in another paper in this volume (FINNE 1986a).

The study found a large number of negative effects for designers such as mental overload, fatigue, higher reported stress level, and an inability to think creatively in front of the screen, leading to a need to preplan the design exercise more than before. Ergonomic conditions were generally poor. These negative effects were partly masked, however, by the novelty of the situation and either ignored or rationalized as beginners' problems. Furthermore, a strong reduction in the ratio of drafting assistants to designers was predicted and later verified. Skill requirements were found to depend on the nature of the systems and the organization of design work, but a polarization hypothesis was considered the most probable. Many interesting new patterns of work organization within the design department were envisaged.

The report compared the actual work of designing through interactive graphics with manual work at the drawing-board. This analysis largely explained some of the negative effects. The main point was that the interaction with the system required constant attention to the impediment of thinking design.

The first *Swedish work* of this kind definitely had the largest empirical basis of the three. Lindeberg, an independent consultant in contract with the Swedish white collar industrial union SIF, tracked down practically all the 205 installations at the time and developed a good basis for understanding why and how CAD/CAM systems were introduced. The effects on design work and designers were studied from interviews with SIF representatives in about 10 firms and a similar number of experts.

Lindeberg' s report (LINDEBERG 1983) is much larger than the two previous ones and covers more aspects. No specific analytic tradition can be found as his work is largely descriptive. The emphasis is on describing the areas of CAD/CAM application within different branches of industry. As for introduction strategies, he found a shift from narrow drawing office productivity justifications towards more strategic considerations of systemic effects. He also found lack of active management support to be an important factor in unsuccessful cases of introduction.

Interestingly, his findings concerning effects for CAD personnel are in general positive except for the question of ergonomics. No redundancies were found, and designers were largely enthusiastic both in terms of getting less routine work and increased scope for creativity.

How can the differences between the Norwegian and Danish reports on one side and the Swedish report on the other be explained?

There is a methodological difference between the works. Lindeberg reports what designers' representatives tell him to be the experience of their fellow designers while the other works analyze the work situation and relate this to the admittedly varying statements from the people affected. Thus Lindeberg' s interviews may be masking the negative side while Finne and Fallenkamp et al. may be doing the screening themselves, but in the opposite direction. In either case the technology itself is in its infancy and there is too little use of it for any particular effects to have stabilized. Even in 1985 and even in Sweden, where the diffusion has come near to establishing preferred patterns, I would still think the situation is malleable. In my opinion this is good because it leaves us scope for influencing development. As we shall see below, a number of projects aim at doing just that.

Other completed projects and work in progress

Very few projects have been completed after these initial ones but a number of interesting activities are in progress. I shall try to discuss them thematically below although some projects then will be mentioned several times because many of them typically cover a wide range of questions.

Reasons for introducing CAD/CAM

FALLENKAMP et al. (1982b) distinguish two rationalization strategies behind CAD introduction: rationalization in (or of) design itself and through design. The former strategy relates to cost- and time-cutting in the design office and was predominantly found in small firms. The latter strategy, found in larger firms, is concerned with improving design and drawings in order that product quality increase and production cost and time decrease. Löwstedt (at Stockholm School of Economics) has found both strategies in large firms. He also reports that reasons given by management vary widely in terms of refinement and realism. There are also great differences in how these large firms pre-calculate the return on their investment (LÖWSTEDT 1984). In a follow-up in-depth study nearing completion no manager was found who would unambiguously state that the investment had been profitable (LÖWSTEDT 1985a). This may be an indication of the strategic nature of many decisions to implement CAD.

Norrgren (at Goteborg University, department of psychology) is presently studying how goals were developed before investment and later adjusted. A preliminary analysis (NORRGREN 1985) suggests that the levels of ambition and width of CAD application are progressively diminishing as more and more problems are encountered during the introduction of the new systems. Similar problems of introduction, leading sometimes to rejection, are reported by Remoe and Rasmussen at the Rogaland Research Institute, Stavanger (REMOE and RASMUSSEN 1985).

A related question concerns how managers are influenced before deciding on CAD/CAM investment. Norrgren is presently studying this in Sweden and there are bound to be evaluations of the national CAD/CAM promotion campaigns in all three countries. In Denmark, Fodgaard (at DTH, department of construction management) found large influence of organizational, social, and structural constraints on CAD investment decisions in building consultancy firms (FODGAARD 1985, 1986). Møller and Jensen (at DTH, department of work environment) are evaluating the effects of the activities of TL in promoting certain CAD/CAM utilization patterns (MØLLER and JENSEN 1985, 1986).

Organizational aspects

Organizational aspects are studied at a number of levels: the organization of CAD work, the organization of design and product development, the organization of integrated CAD/CAM activities, and the organization between firms.

Due to the technical expertise required and the size of investments - which until recently averaged almost NOK 1 million per workstation - CAD is a scarce resource in many firms. This has generally resulted in a low number of people being trained and two main variants of access to CAD: designers either queue up or some of them specialize in CAD within particular areas of design (LÖWSTEDT 1985a, 1985b). There has been little evidence of specialized CAD operators who perform 'electronic tracing' with design drafting content (FALLENKAMP 1984), although some instances exist (FINNE 1982).

Interactive graphical modelling allows new relations to develop within design departments between analysts, designers and detail draftspeople (FINNE 1982), but too little can be said yet as to development patterns. The more people that get involved, the stronger the tendency towards standardization of design (LÖWSTEDT 1985a). In very small firms, however, design is organized extremely flexibly and care should be taken not to introduce systems that would require more rigidity than the firm can live with (FINNE 1984b).

While CAD/CAM integration certainly creates organizational strains across departmental boundaries most firms shun all organizational changes that would endanger their functional organization. Although many scenarios are cast for the future (FINNE 1982, 1984a), a lack of competence in organizational development in industry seems to prevent anything but marginal change. Even the simple case of letting skilled operators do their own CNC programming turns out to be difficult (GUSTAVSEN et al. 1985) and the solution to this question in the individual firm is determined by product, product market, labour market and company traditions, not by free management choice (RASMUSSEN 1984).

In fact, unawareness of and inability to handle the organizational issues - including inadequate training - is probably one of the main reasons for the high number of disappointing CAD/CAM experiences. Some consultants label 80 % of all the 75,000 CAD workstations in the USA unprofitable investments, largely due to a mismatch between system capabilities and organizational capabilities (AGERMAN 1985).

In Scandinavia there is therefore a growing interest in bringing the issues of organization of CAD and CAM beyond the research stage and so far two or three development programs have been initiated. The largest of these is a Swedish undertaking including four CAD/CAM projects. The program totals 30 projects with various technologies so far and has a budget of SEK 55 million. Funded publicly by the Work Environment Fund (Arbetarskyddsfonden, ASF) in Stockholm, these projects aim at influencing and documenting patterns of introduction, organization and job design with new technology. Hence the funds do *not* cover investments. This remarkable program, whose CAD/CAM activities are coordinated by Tedenfors, is a result of the Scandinavian culture of participative systems design and introduction(STEEN 1985, ASF various).

A similar background caters for the much smaller attempts at organizational development around CAD/CAM in Norway and Sweden undertaken by Gustavsen and colleagues at the Work Research Institute (AFI) in Oslo (SVERIGES VERKSTADFÖRENING 1985). They are also summing up current experience in a report to the ILO.

At the inter-organizational level, possibilities and problems are yet poorly researched. Subconsultants to the same construction project, e.g. architects, builders, electrical and piping consultants planning the same building or offshore installation may benefit from using a common CAD system. But problems arise as to which profession will dominate the introduction of CAD (KREINER 1983) and due to conflicting interests in general. In the mechanical engineering industries, large firms may control smaller subcontractors by requiring them to apply certain CAD/CAM routines as has been shown in the USA (NOBLE 1985).

The design process and education for CAD

Since design is largely intellectual work and also has a strong and important content of creativity, the nature of the design process in relation to computer aids has spurred the interest in understanding how designers work. In FINNE (1982) a brief analytic comparison was made between designing at the drawing-board and the terminal. CAD work was found to yield a cognitive overload resulting in the need to solve the design problems *before* sitting down at the terminal. Reference was also made to KOESTLER (1964) who sees a person's routine submersion into the details of a problem as a prerequisite to creative solutions. This would speak against a division of labour where creative designers sketched ideas that CAD operators then documented. KJELLBERG and KJELLBERG (1984) from a foundation of cognitive psychology stressed the possibilities of overcoming the designer's insufficient short term memory when handling complex problems. This could be done by creating a three-dimensional product model in the computer with other kinds of relevant data connected to it and displaying it in various perspectives on the screen. In their view, CAD would be an aid in creative work.

The contradiction between Finne and Kjellberg may rest upon differences in the systems (or the user interfaces) studied. However, the Norwegian findings are more in line with continental results. The Swedish study relates to not yet existing applications and may point more towards the future.

Later approaches also try to understand design (or problem solving) in organizational terms. This holds for the current work of Finne and Nilssen on CAD/CAM in small firms (FINNE 1984b) and the proposed project of Rasmussen et al. (at DTH) (RASMUSSEN et al. 1986) on human-centred systems. A crucial turning point in the analysis of the latter is the application of Polanyi's concept of tacit knowledge which will require an elaboration from the personal to the organizational level.

Complementary to these rather basic research activities there is quite some interest in education for CAD. Hansen and Rasmussen (at TL and DTH) are mapping and evaluating educational efforts in Denmark (TEKNISK LANDSFORBUND 1983). The same will be done on a smaller scale at IFIM in Norway. A more psychological approach is taken by Waern (at Stockholm University, department of psychology) who studied how individuals learn to interact with CAD systems (WAERN 1986a). The span of data-gathering methods in the project is impressive and should allow for good triangulation of data. She found that once test subjects had developed a new set of rules for attacking a class of drawing problems, they were able to solve them faster at the terminal than at the drawingboard, and less pre-planning was required at the terminal (WAERN 1986b). However, no designers were subjected to the test and the problem was one of drawing (not design), which would clearly limit the significance of this finding.

Effects of CAD on people

Under this heading come questions of health and safety, physical and psycho-social work environment, skill requirements and employment.

Elsebet Pedersen (at DTH, department of construction management) is working on a unique project about unintended side effects on worker safety at the construction site when CAD is used in construction management (PEDERSEN et al. 1986). No results have been published yet.

Only one proper study has been made of the physical work environment of designers who are using CAD but many reports mention the problem. The one study concerns CAD use in cartography and shows little difference from conventional work which is also very vision intensive (PAPE 1982). It is not surprising that this aspect has been given a scant treatment as there are so many other issues more interesting to working life researchers. TL have found it sufficiently important to produce detailed guidelines that are of high quality and relevance in lack of suitable material from the national worker protection inspectorate (FALLENKAMP 1981, TEKNISK LANDSFORBUND 1983b). As for psycho-social work environment, only one project has had this as its primary focus. Ann Kjellberg (at The Royal Institute of Technology in Stockholm, dept. of manufacturing systems) is working on how new technology can be used to promote personal development through the job. Her hypothesis is that the existence of problem solving tasks (e.g. design) and powerful tools (e.g. CAD systems) will provide for this goal (KJELLBERG 1986a, 1986b).

Psycho-social work environment considerations are also dealt with explicitly or implicitly in a large number of the other projects listed. Scandinavian working life research is brought up on psycho-social variables like skill requirements, control over work and social contact in the job. It seems hard not to say at least something about effects of technology and organization on health (e.g. stress) and satisfaction in our projects. I find it difficult to give a good overview of this aspect, however, without repeating too much of what has been said already.

Employment issues are seldom covered but often mentioned. We have to my knowledge no case of redundancies due to CAD/CAM introduction. The situation is of course more complex than that. Scandinavian industrial relations are such that natural wastage is preferred whenever possible and hence technological unemployment is very difficult to trace at all. This is however a field that needs further attention.

Social science influence on design of CAD/CAM systems

Interestingly enough , social scientists in all three countries are presently engaged in influencing the design of CAD/CAM systems and their utilization pattern in industry. Development projects where the organization is adapted to technology have been commonplace for 20 years now but there have been few occasions - and little willingness among both social scientists and engineers - to try to develop new technology on the basis of a social science input. User participation in systems development is fairly widespread but its influence on the design is still marginal (NILSSEN 1984).

The Swedish large scale activities funded by ASF and the AFI projects belong to the former category. In this section I shall concentrate on the attempts to influence technology in a more fundamental way.

In Sweden, the principal CAD/CAM research centre has an in-house social scientist and also collaboration with university-based cognitive psychologists. This remarkable constellation has been in operation since before 1980. In a first phase, the social scientists had a rather missionary task of making the technology developers aware of the importance of psycho-social factors in the design and introduction of new technologies (KJELLBERG 1983). From the subsequent work, I will concentrate on two main aspects.

On a theoretical level, systems requirements were specified that would enhance personal development in the job for future users. These included that the user be the problem solver and that (s)he handle an optimum quantity of problems, that the computer be the user's extended memory, and that the physical handling of the computer system be such that it can be handled with a minimum of conscious attention (KJELLBERG 1986b).

The second aspect that has been pursued in more detail is the development of a method for testing the ease of learning how to work with a CAD system (WAERN 1986b). This method could be used to develop training programs contingent on the previous knowledge of future CAD learners, but also to test individual CAD interfaces and identify their weak spots and perhaps also any inappropriateness of their internal logic.

As far as I can judge, the principal influence of social science in these ongoing activities is on the future development of user interfaces to 3D modelling that facilitate the user's creation of such models in a time-efficient manner without overloading the operator mentally. It is too early to see, however, to what extent CAD systems with these user interfaces will be better to use than similar systems that have been developed without the assistance of social scientists.

In Denmark, social scientists and technologists at DTH have prepared a research proposal for ESPRIT in collaboration with the University of Bremen and a joint British effort between Howard ROSENBROCK of UMIST (Manchester) and Mike COOLEY of GLEB (London). The ESPRIT funds will go towards the creation of humancentered systems. In Britain, it is an FMS, in Bremen, a computer-aided planning system, and in Denmark, an electronic full size drawing board. Important social science work on tacit knowledge in design work will be an input to the design of the actual drawing board. (See RASMUSSEN et al. 1986, as approved project descriptions do not yet exist.)

In Norway, a joint effort is set up between social scientists and technologists in SINTEF in Trondheim to develop low cost CAD/CAM systems for small firms. Social science work in this project will concentrate on analyzing the organization of design and the planning of manufacturing in small mechanical engineering firms. A hypothesis is that small firms survive partly due to their flexibility in organizing this kind of work, and CAD/CAM systems should be designed in such a way that it allows profitable use without adopting the more rigid organizational patterns of larger CAD/CAM user firms, for whom the systems were developed in the first place (FINNE 1984b.)

It is too early to say anything about the success of these undertakings. All social scientists in question seem to share both expectations and a certain degree of skepticism. Some of the problems inherent in this approach are discussed in another paper in this volume (Finne 1986b).

Trade Union activities

In Scandinavia, industrial relations are such that trade unions engage continuously in questions of new technology, both nationally and locally, both on their own and in cooperation with the employers and their organizations. The number of jobs is of course an issue but only rarely one of conflict, and hence the discussion tends to center on work organization, job content, participative design, and work environment.

The Danish Technicians' Union (Teknisk Landsforbund, TL) have been very active in CAD/CAM questions. One of the authors of the first Danish work has been working full time since 1982 with TL on the questions of CAD/CAM and related technologies. They have produced a number of booklets and visual aids on CAD/CAM and ergonomics, psycho-social work environment, social impact of technology, etc., that have been distributed widely. They are also designing a whole series of courses that aim at providing an education (not training) for CAD/CAM. Significantly, they have landed a collective agreement in at least one large firm where CAD work in front of screens in practice is limited to 50 % of the workday (Fallenkamp, personal communication). This may seem a defensive measure but on the other hand, it forces management to think twice about work organization. They keep close contact with social science research and have, amongst other things, commissioned a project to evaluate the impact at the local level of their own central activities (see MØLLER and JENSEN 1985).

The sister organization in Sweden (Svenska Industritjänstemannaförbundet, SIF) commissioned the first Swedish investigation performed by Lindeberg but after that there has been little interest in developing a strategy towards the new technology other than to adopt it and adapt to it as quickly as possible (AVNER, personal communication). Recently, however, SIF organized a meeting with TL and Scandinavian social scientists to see if anything new ought to happen in this area.

In Norway, the Metalworkers' Union is far more concerned with CAD (and CAM, of course) than any of the unions of engineers and technicians. The Metalworkers' Union and their counterpart on the employers' side have jointly sponsored some researcher-guided organizational development in this area (GUSTAVSEN et al. 1985), and they were also behind the first project (FINNE 1982, RASMUSSEN 1984).

4. Concluding remarks

What is the future of social science research on CAD/CAM in Scandinavia ? I shall try to list some possible trends and comment on them.

The technology itself is coming into a new phase. Many CAD systems have now become so versatile and inexpensive that the technico-economical barrier to its diffusion has been broken down. This means that systems, in particular those running on personal computers, will be installed in large numbers. Hence the organizational problems will be felt by very many firms, but these problems may not be the same ones that we researched for the pioneer users of large systems. For one thing, a PC CAD system is much more likely to be the instrument of designers than to require specialized CAD operators. Large systems for large and specialized firms will still pose some of the old questions, however.

The point here is that there will be an incentive in the research councils to look for organizational solutions to problems of utilizing CAD. These will be questions on the level of the organization of design work, the organization of design and manufacturing departments, and the organization between firms linking up with the same system. Undoubtedly social scientists will be asked to look at these problems in cooperation with technologists, in order that the technology be utilized to its fullest potential.

There is also an urgent need for educational efforts geared towards the new technology but whether this will be an area of social science research is less evident. Also, some research will always be directed towards working conditions. Furthermore, there are national promotion programs for CAD/CAM in all three countries and at least some of these will be evaluated by social scientists.

It is less evident that social science will play an important role in the design of the technology itself. The efforts towards this end are at an experimental stage and by the time they might have reached maturity, so will also CAD/CAM and hence there is only scope for marginal changes.

References

Agerman, Erik:
CAD CAM tekniken - en del av ASEA:s produkt och produktionsstrategi. Paper, Teknik Front 85, Goteborg 1985. Available from author, ASEA Västerås

Arnold, Erik:
Computer-Aided Design in Europe. Report, Sussex European Research Centre, Falmer 1984

ASF:
"The Development Programme" and other pamphlets (largely in Swedish). Arbetarskydds-fonden, Stockholm 1978-85

Bechmann, G., R. Vahrenkamp, B. Wingert:
Mechanisierung geistiger Arbeit. Campus-Verlag, Frankfurt a.M. 1979

Fallenkamp, Bernt:
Arbejdsmiljøet ved CAD/CAM arbejdspladsen. Teknikernes krav til indkøb og anvendelse af CAD/CAM-udstyr. Pamphlet, Teknisk Landsforbund, København 1981.

Fallenkamp, Bernt:
The experience of Teknisk Landsforbund (Danish federation of technicians, designers etc.) in the field of CAD/CAM in Denmark. Mimeo, Teknisk Landsforbund, København 1984

Fallenkamp, Bernt, Finn Hansen, Karl Erik Jessen:
Hvad er CAD/CAM? Teknikken bag CAD/CAM og EDB. Pamphlet, Teknisk Landsforbund, København 1982a

Fallenkamp, Bernt, Finn J. Søderman Hansen, Karl Erik Jessen:
CAD/CAM - teknologi, økonomi og arbejdsmiljø. Partial reports 1-6 and main report, Dept. of Social Science at the Technological University of Denmark, Lyngby 1982b

Finne, Håkon:
Mellom tegnebrett og terminal. Report, IFIM, Trondheim 1982

Finne, Håkon:
The designer and his job in the face of integrated CAD/CAM systems. In Tom Martin (ed.): Design of Work in Automated Manufacturing Systems. Pergamon Press, London 1984a

Finne, Håkon:
IFIMs plass i NTNF-programmet Lavkost EDB-verktoy for SMB. Mimeo, IFIM, Trondheim 1984b

Finne, Håkon:
Organizational alternatives in the integration of CAD/CAM. Paper in this volume, Karls-ruhe 1987a

Finne, Håkon:
How do we feed our findings back into the design process? Paper in this volume, Karlsruhe 1987b

Fodgaard, Marianne:
CAD - beslutninger, teknologi, konsekvenser. Report, Dept. of Construction Management at the Technological University of Denmark, Lyngby 1985

Fodgaard, Marianne:
Decision-making on CAD in consulting firms in Denmark. Paper in this volume, Karlsruhe 1987

Gustavsen, Bjørn et al.:
Teknologi/organisasjon rapport fra kartleggingskonferanse "organisasjonsmessige konsekvenser av DAK/DAP". Work Research Institutes, Oslo 1985

Hansen, Finn:
CAD/CAM-markedet. Mimeo, Teknisk Landsforbund, København 1983

Kjellberg, Ann:
Beteendevetenskap i verkstadteknisk tillämpning. Pedagogiska processer i teknikutformning. Dissertation, Dept. of Manufacturing Systems at the Royal Institute of Technology, Stockholm 1983

Kjellberg, Ann:
Psychosocial aspects treated in a CAD/CAM research project. Paper in this volume, Karlsruhe 1987

Kjellberg, Ann:
Psychosocial factors in CADCAM. Report, Dept. of Manufacturing Systems at the Royal Institute of Technology, Stockholm 1986

Kjellberg, Torsten and Ann Kjellberg:
CAD/CAM for engineering problem solving and communications - human engineered systems. Paper, 9th World Congress of IFAC, Budapest 1984. Available from authors, Dept. of Manufacturing Systems at the Royal Institute of Technology, Stockholm

Koestler, Arthur:
The Act of Creation. Macmillan, New York 1964

Kreiner, Kristian:
CAD og arbejdsdelingen i bygge- og anlaegssektoren. Paper, 12. Nordiske Sociologkongres, Stavanger 1983. Available from author, Dept. of Construction Management at the Technological University of Denmark, Lyngby

Larsen, Knut Agnar:
Markedsoversikt. DAK/DAP-systemer til under 600.000 kroner. Teknisk Ukeblad, Vol. 131, No. 22, 1984

Larsen, Knut Agnar and Anne-Marie Ytrehus:
DAK/DAP - Behovs- analyse. Report, SI, Oslo 1984

Lindeberg, Sten:
Datorstött konstruktionsarbete. Report, SIF, Stockholm 1983

Löwstedt, Jan:
Teknik och organisation - datorstödd konstruktion (CAD) i nio verkstadsföretag (del I). Research Paper No. 6277, EFI/Stockholm School of Economics, Stockholm 1984

Löwstedt, Jan:
Automation or cognition in the design office? Paper, EGOS colloquium on 'Challenges for organizational authority', Saltsjöbaden 1985a. Available from author, EFI/Stockholm School of Economics

Löwstedt, Jan:
Automation eller kunskapsproduktion? Om ingenjörsarbetets organisation och innehåll vid införande av CAD. Final report, EFI/Stockholm School of Economics, 1985b (forthcoming)

Møller, Niels and Per Langaa Jensen:
TA-FAT: Teknologiske Alternativer og Faglig Aktivitet vedr. Teknologi. Mimeo, Dept. of Work Environment at the Technological University of Denmark, Lyngby 1985

Møller, Niels and Per Langaa Jensen:
Utilization of research results by the employees. Paper in this volume, Karlsruhe 1987

Nilssen, Tore:
Brukermedvirkning: Holdninger og praktisering. Report, IFIM, Trondheim 1984

Noble, David:
Forces of Production. New York: Knopf, 1985

Norrgren, Flemming:
(1st project report on CAD/CAM decision making.) Göteborg Universitet, Göteborg 1985 (forthcoming)

NTNF:
Strategi for CAD/CAM i Norge. Report, Royal Norwegian Council for Scientific and Industrial Research, Oslo 1984

Pape, Arne:
Teknologi og arbeidsforhold for kartkonstruktører i privat virksomhet. Report, Norwegian Computing Center, Oslo 1982

Pedersen, Elsebet Fryendal et al.:
Consequences on the working conditions on site with increased use of CAD/CAM in construction. Paper in this volume, Karlsruhe 1987.

Rasmussen, Bente:
Fagarbeid og ny teknologi. Report, IFIM, Trondheim 1984

Rasmussen, Lauge Baungaard, Erik Rask Eriksen, Finn Hansen:
Tacit knowledge versus system knowledge. Paper in this volume, Karlsruhe 1987

Remoe, Svend Otto and Hilde Rasmussen:
Innføring av datateknologi i små og mellomstore bedrifter: En analyse av fem eksempelstudier. Report, Rogaland Research Institute, Stavanger 1985

Sejersen, Ib:
En raekke danske CAD-systemer. Memo, Technological Institute, Taastrup 1985

Steen, Roland:
Utvecklingsprogrammet för ny teknik, arbetsorgaisation och arbetsmiljö. Lägesrapport 2. Report, Arbetarskyddsfonden, Stockholm 1984

Sveriges Verkstadsförening:
En utvärdering av datorstödd konstruktion vid SAAB-SCANIA SCANIA-divisionen. Report, Verkstadindustrins forskningsnämnd, Stockholm 1985

SOU 1981 :
Datateknik i verkstadsindustrin. Rapport från data- och elektronikkomittén. Report SOU: 10, Sveriges Offentliga Utredninger, Stockholm 1981

Teknisk Landsforbund:
CAD/CAM - teknologiudvikling og uddannelse. Project description, Teknisk Landsforbund, København 1983a

Teknisk Landsforbund:
Ergonomien ved CAD/CAM-arbejdspladsen. Slides and text, Teknisk Landsforbund, København 1983b

Teknisk Landsforbund:
Anvendelse og planer for EDB-teknologigi i private virksomheder. Mimeo, Teknisk Lands forbund, København 1983c

Waern, Yvonne:
Previous knowledge and learning. Paper in this volume, Karlsruhe 1987

Waern, Yvonne:
Problem solving in CAD/CAM. Report, Dept. of Manufacturing Systems at the Royal Institute of Technology, Stockholm 1986

SOCIAL SCIENCE RESEARCH ON CAD/CAM IN THE UK

Ian McLoughlin
Kingston Polytechnic
Kingston upon Thames, Surrey KT2 7LB
United Kingdom

1. Introduction

Social science research on CAD/CAM technologies in the UK cannot readily be disentagled from the more general interest amongst social scientists in the implications of the new microelectronics-based Information Technology 'revolution'. Since the late 1970s a number of research units and individuals have been exploring the social implications of a range of new technologies. Whilst the focus of this review will be on CAD/CAM it will also be useful, in so far as they inform this work, to point to the more general themes that have emerged in the social analysis of new technologies. Before reviewing social science approaches to CAD/CAM I will briefly outline available evidence of the diffusion of the technologies and the main issues that they have raised.

2. The diffusion of CAD/CAM technologies in the UK

The most recent comprehensive data on the diffusion of CAD technologies is provided in a survey by NORTHCOTT & ROGERS (1983) of the Policy Studies Institute (PSI) on a representative sample of 1200 manufacturing establishments employing more than 20 people. Of the 737 firms utilising CAD/CAM technologies, 17 % (124 establishments) had one or more CAD work stations and 30 % anticipated using the technology by 1985. This suggests a figure of 9000 CAD workstations in use througout UK manufacturing as a whole in 1983, and a projected 14 000 work stations by 1985. Most current users (50 %) had between two and ten work stations, whilst a significant minority (31 %) had only one workstation. Eleven per cent of users had large installations of between 11 and 50 work stations. Thirty per cent of current users were establishments of over 1000 employees and the principal sectors of industry involved were electrical engineering (37 %) and vehicles (39 %). Unfortunately, the PSI survey did not cover non-manufacturing users of CAD where the technology appears to be diffusing at an increasing rate in the architecture and civil engineering sectors.

The PSI survey also provided data on CAM technologies. Computer Numerical Control (CNC) machines were used by 29 % of establishments and robots by 5 %. Projecting these figures for UK manufacturing as a whole suggests a total of 17 000 CNC machine tools were in use in 1983 and around 1000 robots. Based on the respondent's anticipated usage, a five-fold increase in the number of robots was predicted in UK manufacturing by 1985, with the number of CNC machine tools in use rising to 27 000. Use of both CNC and Robot technologies was concentrated in larger establishments but with greater diffusion to smaller users anticipated.

The PSI data suggests that little attempt has been made by UK CAD/CAM users to develop integrated CAD/CAM systems. Most installation seems to have occured on an 'island automation' basis. The majority of users reported applications of microelectronics for the control of individual machines or processes, and only a minority for the centralised control of groups of machines or several stages in processes. Only 3 % reported applications which integrated manufacturing processes with test, design or automated handling. These results confirm ARNOLD & SENKER's (1982) earlier finding in the UK engineering industry that, outside of the special case of electronics applications, the integration of CAD and CAM technologies using digital CAD output as a direct input to CAM systems is very limited. A more recent survey of the use of Flexible Manufacturing Systems suggests a similarly slow rate of diffusion with only 60 current users in the UK, although a more rapid uptake by smaller firms is anticipated in the next five years (see BESSANT &HAYWOOD , 1985).

Issues raised by CAD/CAM

As in most European nations, the 'discovery' of microelectronics based information technologies in the late 1970s has resulted in considerable public debate in the UK. Three related issues have predominated: the question of whether British industry will adopt the new technologies quickly enough to combat foreign competitors; the implications of the technology for employment; and the consequences of technological change for industrial relations.

In relation to the first issue, considerable attention has focused on CAD/CAM technologies by the observation in a number of recent influential reports that design is a critical 'non-price' factor in industrial competitiveness (see eg. FINNISTON REPORT, 1980; ALDINGTON REPORT, 1985; SCIENCE AND ENGINEERING RESEARCH COUNCIL, 1985), and that advanced manufacturing technologies such as CAD/CAM are central to the 'design-led' regeneration of British industry (ADVISORY COUNCIL FOR APPLIED RESEARCH AND DEVELOPMENT, 1980; 1983). The UK government has provided around £ 24 million of aid to promote the adoption of CAD/CAM technologies but there appears to be increasing scepticism with the use of CAD/CAM as a 'technological fix' (ARNOLD, 1983).

In particular, there is growing evidence that the limitations of existing graphics software and management approaches to CAD/CAM utilisation, seem to have restricted current users to deploying CAD interactive graphics for 'electronic drafting', rather than 'upstream' in design or for realising 'downstream' benefits in manufacture (see eg. ARNOLD & SENKER, 1982; CARNALL & MEDLAND, 1984; McLOUGHLIN, 1986). Further, recent research suggests that whatever the technical possibilities for integrating CAD and CAM (which again may at present be overstated), there are considerable problems relating to organisational integration which arise. These problems may not only act as an effective 'barrier' to diffusion but also raise considerable doubt as to whether computer integrated manufacturing is the 'one best way' forward for every organisation (see eg. WINCH, 1983; PARTRIDGE et al. 1984; MUCCI, 1984).

In relation to the second issue, public concern with the employment effects of new technology has to some extent been subsumed by a more general disquiet with the continuing high levels of unemployment in the UK economy. Indeed, survey data - again produced by the PSI - suggests that the dramatic predictions made in the late 1970s in relation to the adverse employment implications of new technologies have, as yet, little evidence to support them. Indeed, the introduction of new technologies in manufacturing was estimated to result in one job loss per factory per year, or less than 0.5 % of total manufacturing employment, and 5 % of the manufacturing jobs lost through other causes (NORTHCOTT et al. 1985). Evidence on the employment implications of CAD/CAM technologies is sparse, compounded by the methodological difficulties of establishing a direct causal link between changes in technology and changes in employment levels. For example, ARNOLD & SENKER (1982 p. 36) could only point in general terms to an association between increased use of CAD interactive graphics and falling levels of employment amongst draughtspeople, not least because of management reluctance to attribute redundancies to productivity increases derived from the technology.

Finally, the implications of the diffusion of new technology for industrial relations have emerged as a major issue in the UK - in some cases, as in the national newspaper industry, with dramatic results. Initial interest in the area of CAD/CAM has been stimulated by the attempts of the principal union organising drawing office staff - TASS - to establish 'New Technology Agreements' (NTAs) as the basis for the joint regulation of the introduction of interactive graphics systems (see TASS, 1978). The success of NTAs in general in Britain has been limited (see eg. WILLIAMS & STEWARD, 1985). In terms of TASS's original objectives, the NTAs concluded with employers have also fallen some way short of the hoped for extension of union control over technological change (for a review of the content of agreements that have been reached, see INCOMES DATA SERVICE, 1982; 1983; and 1985). Nevertheless, some influence over managerial decisions has been achieved - in particular in relation to selection of staff for retraining, payments for using the new technology, and health and safety (see ARNOLD & SENKER, 1982; BALDRY & CONNOLLY, 1986). However, whether NTAs offer a sufficient procedural means of shifting the 'frontier of control' towards the unions in the joint regulation of technological change in the context of industrial relations in Britain in the 1980s, must be doubted. Similarly, whether NTAs can address in practice the broader issues relating to skill and work organisation raised by new technologies such as CAD/CAM also remains to be demonstrated.

4. UK social science research on CAD/CAM

Generally speaking UK social science research on CAD/CAM has been conducted from within two research traditions. First, that of science and technology policy studies. Here the primary focus has been on survey-based studies of the development of CAD/CAM as an innovation and the factors determining the diffusion of CAD/CAM amongst adopting organisations. Second, that broadly based on industrial sociology, here the focus of research interest has been on case studies of the processes and outcomes of change within adopting organisations. Attention has focused mainly on questions such as the role of management strategy in the organisation and control of the labour process, and the deskilling of work. What follows is a brief review of some of the material that has emerged from various research programmes on CAD/CAM.

One of the most interesting conceptual discussions of the role of CAD/CAM in the context of automation in general, has been provided in two books by Raphael KAPLINSKY (1982; 1984). According to Kaplinsky, interactive graphics represents the latest stage in the 'electronification' of manufacture, building on other CAD and CAM innovations since the mid-fifties. Further, interactive graphics technology has a number of characteristics which suggest it is the 'key piece in the electronic jigsaw that will allow for the development of the automated factory' (1982, p. 35). That is, by allowing the creation of a single data-base at the design stage which can communicate information in graphical form and allow designers to interact in 'real-time' with the data-base in constructing designs, interactive graphics provides the basis for a qualitative change in the nature of automation. This involves the electronic linking together of the previously separate design, management control and production elements in manufacturing. What KAPLINSKY terms 'inter-sphere automation' (1984, p. 26). However, whatever the potential capabilities of an innovation, it does not follow, as Kaplinsky notes, that these are necessarily achieved in practice.

From the 'science policy' perspective explanations of the outcomes of technological change rest on identifying the factors which variously promote and act as barriers to innovation. The best known study of CAD/CAM based on this approach is the survey of 34 establishments drawn from the UK engineering industry by ARNOLD & SENKER (1982) of the Science Policy Research Unit (SPRU) at Sussex University. The principal concern of this survey - which was conducted for the UK Engineering Industry Training Board (EITB) - were the implications of the use of CAD interactive graphics systems for employment and skill requirements.

Perhaps the most pertinent observation in the survey's findings was that the use of CAD had no single 'impact' on skill and employment common to all establishments in the study. The actual effects of the new technology depended in large measure on the stage in the 'learning curve' that establishments - in particular management - had reached in using the technology. It was only at the third stage of the learning process, reached after about two years of system operation, that CAD was exploited to its fullest potential in terms of improvements in draughting productivity.

A major 'barrier' to the successful adoption of CAD/CAM therefore appeared to be weaknesses in managerial skills in the actual use of the technology (see also ARNOLD, 1983; SENKER, 1984). Indeed, whilst Arnold & Senker anticipated major long term employment implications in the adoption of CAD, in particular in relation to the career structure within the drawing office, the skill implications for CAD operators compared to those required of managment, were 'relatively trivial' (ARNOLD, 1983, p. 39).

The 'science policy' perspective has been criticised for an overly deterministic conception of technological change which is concerned with management strategy and skill only in so far as they act as constraints on the innovation and diffusion process, or, are themselves changed by the 'impact' of an innovation (WILKINSON, 1983, p. 11). Researchers approaching the study of CAD/CAM from an industrial sociological perspective have been at pains to avoid what they see as 'technological determinism' - although what is really meant by 'technology' and 'determinism' is rarely clear (see ROSE et al. 1986). Wilkinson, for example, argues that technological change must be seen as a political process within adopting organisations involving a 'contest for control' between management and labour. In 'science policy' studies, he suggests, the idea of 'barriers' to technological change begs the question of why the technology is being introduced in the first place and whose objectives are being 'designed' into new systems.

The biggest stimulus to this kind of approach was provided by BRAVERMAN's (1974) thesis on deskilling and the degradation of work through the application of modern technology as part of a managerial strategy to extend control over the labour process. Braverman, in fact, cites both CAD and Numerical Control (NC) technologies as examples of this process. The notion that CAD deskills the work of the draughtsperson and design engineer is of course a major theme in the widely read work of Mike COOLEY (see e.g. 1980; 1981). Not surprisingly, the deskilling hypothesis has provided the main focus for social science studies of CAD/CAM from an industrial sociological perspective.

JONES (1982) has conducted a frequently cited study of the introduction of NC machine tools in six UK engineering firms. His conclusions presented a major challenge to crude exponents of the deskilling thesis, suggesting that there were no 'inherent tendencies' towards deskilling in the utilisation of NC. In fact, variations existed in the precise division of tasks and skills in each firm according to product market, organisational and trade union influences. Indeed, in some circumstances this could enable an extension of the range of operator skills. This latter point has been taken further to suggest that there is scope to 'upskill' operator jobs in 'human centred' applications of CAD/CAM technologies as 'computer aids' rather than as a means of replacing human labour (see e.g. WILKINSON, 1983; BUCHANAN & BODDY, 1983; SACKETT & EVANS, 1984; BUCHANAN, 1985).

Despite Cooley's longstanding assertion that CAD will lead to a deskilling of work in the drawing office in much the same way as it is assumed to have been taking place on the shop floor, there have been few studies of the implications of interactive graphics for the skills of design and drawing office staff. BALDRY & CONNOLLY (1986) report the results of a study of seven companies using CAD. Their conclusions would seem to support the view that a deskilling of drawing office work is taking place, with work being more routine, repetitive, machine-paced, intensified, and fragmented. The latter effect was particularly evident in the way the traditional working environment of the drawing office was changed from one which allowed for the free and easy interaction between draughtspersons, to one in which the requirement of the technology for controlled environments in separate areas also created a social division within the drawing office. This division was accentuated by the emergence of a small group of higher paid regular CAD users and the introduction of shift working.

Evidence from four case studies conducted by the author (McLOUGHLIN 1986a; 1986b) suggests that it is perhaps premature to label CAD interactive graphics as a 'classic case of deskilling' (BALDRY & CONNOLLY, 1986). For example, the actual changes to the skill content of draughting work may not be as comprehensive as is often assumed. Most respondents interviewed pointed to changes in the skills required for drawing (e.g. the addition of the ability to use a light pen and digitising tablet to the traditional skill of using a pencil and T-square), but all stressed that the basic engineering skills in order to use these new tools were unaltered. Further, an examination of management objectives and changes in management organisation suggest considerable internal division and potential for conflict within the management function itself. In these circumstances it is difficult to attribute a unitary commitment to deskilling - or anything else for that matter - in the introduction and utilisation of CAD on the part of management.

It was noted above that one finding from 'science policy' studies was that management organisation and skills in the exploitation of CAD/CAM are far from highly developed. Unfortunately, many of the hypotheses that have guided existing industrial sociological research on new technology have assumed management to be far more competent and unified than they are in practice! The realisation that management strategy is neither immutably fixed by the 'laws of capitalist accumulation' nor determined by the capabilities of the technology, at least opens up the possibility for considering ways in which the range of choices open to all organisational practitioners might be broadened.

5. Conclusions

There is now a growing body of social scientific evidence on the implications of new technology for work and employment in the UK. Studies of CAD/CAM have taken place within this broader concern with the 'Information Technology' revolution. These studies have pointed to considerable deficiencies in the approach of both management and unions to the introduction of CAD/CAM. It has also pointed to the scope for choice in the way the technology can be used and the potential for developing more 'human centred' applications of CAD/CAM. It is by no means inevitable - even just left in the hands of management - that a deskilling of work results from the introduction of CAD/CAM. However, exactly what the alternatives to deskilling are, and by what means employee participation in their development may be extended, remain open questions. Little research on alternatives in the actual design of CAD/CAM technologies has been conducted. The most famous attempt by Rosenbrock at UMIST has yet to publish results, although reports on progress suggest more limited success than was originally hoped (ROSENBROCK, 1985).

One major problem here is that this kind of work requires collaboration between social scientists and engineers - something which in the UK is still in its infancy. Perhaps more fundamental is, that even if alternative options in the design and use of CAD/CAM can be specified, it is by no means certain that management and unions would embrace them. The present stress on the managerial prerogative in British industrial relations would appear to make innovations in human resource management which stress employee participation in such areas as job redesign even more difficult than they were before. Moreover, the current preoccupation of trade unions with the high level of unemployment and the restriction on their power by new labour legislation, means that collective bargaining over new technology - where it can take place at all - has been restricted to the traditional issues of pay and jobs, rather than the more central questions of skill and work organisation that new systems pose.

Existing social science research on CAD/CAM in the UK has raised many issues which require further exploration. It is quite clear, for example, that the implications of technological change for skill require both a far more elaborate conceptual understanding of 'skill', and more detailed and rigorous empirical studies of the effects of technological change on the content of jobs. In the case of CAD interactive-graphics, for example, far more needs to be understood about the nature of design and drawing work, and exactly how far electronic drawing aids really do transform the skills required. Further, social scientists in the UK have stated countless times that technology does not determine, and that social actors can choose the way work is organised and controlled. However, what does this mean in practice in relation to the options that are available in the design of jobs for using CAD/CAM systems? Few answers have been provided in this respect, in particular, in relation to how management at present go about choosing system designs and forms of work organisation and control. A better understanding of these processes, and their inadequacies, could well provide the basis for developing alternative human resource strategies which enable the participation of those who will use the new technology to ensure that the likes of CAD and CAM are deployed as aids rather than substitutes for human labour.

References

Advisory Council for Applied Research and Development, 1980:
Computer Aided Design and Manufacture, HMSO

Advisory Council for Applied Research and Development, 1983:
Advanced Manufacturing Technology, HMSO

Aldington Report, 1985:
House of Lords Select Committee on Overseas Trade, HMSO

Arnold, E. & Senker, P., 1982:
Designing the Future. Engineering Industries Training Board

Arnold, E., 1983:
'Information Technology as a technological fix: computer-aided design in the United Kingdom', in Winch, G. (ed.)

Baldry, C. & Connolly, A., 1986:
'Drawing the Line: computer-aided design and the organisation of the drawing office', New Technology, Work and Employment, Vol. 1, No 1

Bessant, J. & Haywood, B., 1985:
The Introduction of Flexible Manufacturing Systems as an Example of Computer Integrated Manufacturing, Brighton Polytechnic

Braverman, H., 1974:
Labour and Monopoly Capital, Monthly Review Press

Buchanan, D., 1985:
'Canned cycles and dancing tools; who's really in control of computer aided machining?', paper presented at the 3rd Annual Conference on the 'Organisation and Control of the Labour Process', April 9th to 11th

Buchanan, D. & Boddy, D. (ed), 1983:
Organisations in the Computer Age , Gower

Carnall, C.A. & Medland, A.J., 1984:
'Computer-aided design: social and technical choices for development', in Warner, M. , Microelectronics, Manpower and Society, Gower

Cooley, M., 1980:
Architect or Bee? - The Human/Technology Relationship, Langley Technical Services

Cooley, M., 1981:
'Some social implications of CAD' in Mermet J. (ed), CAD in Medium Sized and Small Industries, North-Holland

Finneston, Sir Monty, 1980:
Engineering Our future, HMSO

Incomes Data Services, 1982:
'CAD: agreements and pay', Study 276

Incomes Data Services, 1983:
'Draughtsmen and CAD', Study 302

Incomes Data Services, 1985:
'CAD and Draughtsmen', Study 347

Jones, B., 1982:
'Destruction or redistribution of engineering skills? The case of numerical Control', in Wood, S. (ed), The Degradation of Work? Hutchinson

Kaplinsky, R., 1982:
Computer-Aided Design, Pinter

Kaplinsky, R., 1984:
Automation: the Technology and Society, Longman

McLoughlin, I.P., 1986a:
'Management strategies for the introduction and control of Interactive Computer Graphics systems', Proceedings of Social Science Studies on CAD/CAM in Europe

McLoughlin, I.P., 1986b:
The Changing Role of the Engineer in High Technology Enterprises, Research report to the Economic and Social Research Council

Mucci, P., 1984:
'The selection, installation and operation of CAD systems', Computer-Aided Engineering Journal, December

Northcott, J. & Rogers, P., 1984:
Microelectronics in British Industry, Policy Studies Institute

Northcott, J., Fogarty, M. & Trevor, M., 1985:
Chips and Jobs, Policy Studies Institute

Partridge, J., Clark, J. & Mucci, P., 1984:
'The integration of design and manufacturing through Computer-Aided Engineering systems', Computer Aided Engineering, Proceedings of International Conference organised by the Institution of Electrical Engineers, University of Warwick, November

Rose, H., McLoughlin, I.P., King, R. & Clark, J., 1986:
'Opening the black box: the relation between technology and work', New Technology Work and Employment, Vol. 1, No 1

Rosenbrock, H.H., 1985:
'Engineering design and social science', Discussion paper delivered at ESRC/SPRU Workshop on new technology, Cumberland Lodge, Windsor, May 28-9

Sackett, P.J. & Evans, S., 1984:
'Computer Aided Engineering, productivity and quality of working life', Paper delivered at conference on 'Human Factors in Manufacturing', London, April

Science and Engineering Research Council, 1985:
The Needs of Engineering, SERC

Senker, P., 1983:
'Some problems in implementing computer-aided engineering - a general review', Computer-Aided Engineering Journal, November

Senker, P., 1984:
'Implications of CAD/CAM for management', Omega, Vol. 112, No 3

TASS, 1978:
New technology: A Guide for Negotiators, TASS

Wilkinson, B., 1983:
The Shop Floor Politics of New Technology, Gower

Winch, G., 1983:
'Organisation Design for CAD/CAM', in Winch, G. (ed)

Winch, G. (ed), 1983:
Information Technology in Manufacturing Processes, Rossendale

SELECTED RESULTS FROM GERMAN LANGUAGE STUDIES IN THE SOCIAL SCIENCES ON THE EFFECTS OF CAD-TECHNIQUES

Bernd Wingert, Ulrich Riehm, Michael Rader

Karlsruhe Nuclear Research Centre
Department for Applied Systems Analysis
7500 Karlsruhe, Postfach 3640

1. Introduction

When one has worked for several years in a certain area, in an interdisciplinary project with an expanding network of contacts to similar studies, to current projects or to studies at the planning stage, the impression of a mainstream of research will gradually emerge. In the preparation of this contribution which will attempt a content analysis of several German language studies on CAD it became apparent that there are in fact not all that many *completed* or truly *empirical* studies. Therefore, we shall first refer to studies whose central theme was not CAD although they dealt with CAD as one aspect of their subject. These studies will not be included in the following analysis. As a rule, they are dealt with in separate publications and several of the researchers whose projects are mentioned attended the workshop so that they were able to present results and details in the discussion. Despite the heterogeneity of approaches, methods selected and cognitive interests, an attempt will be made in the section after the next to point out similarities - or in some cases discrepancies - with regard to certain theses.

2. Brief description of studies excluded from the present analysis

Although we shall not focus our attention on them later, several studies deserve mention at this point (where we are dealing with the impact of technologies related to CAD). This may be justified by the fact, among others, that the patterns of introduction, the innovation processes and also the actual effects do not vary that much from one stage of technology to the next or from one area of application to the other. One of the aims of any researcher starting up in this area should be to preserve the orientation towards a broad range of issues and to keep an eye on the historical context. Viewed in such a broad historical perspective, the changes currently taking place in design and draughting activities would appear to mark the beginning of a new historical phase, precisely on account of new forms of representation of the objects designed with CAD while at the same time there is a break in the means employed for production (cf. WINGERT, RADER, RIEHM 1980).

To start off, deserving mention is a study by Siegfried ROTH which examined the application of CAD/CAM in the automobile industry, as yet unpublished and thus unfortunately not available. The automobile industry is viewed by many experts as the outrider to test technical feasibility. In our own study, we excluded this industry after the pilot study because plant organization differs substantially from the remainder of mechanical engineering. In his diploma thesis at the Ludwig-Maximilians-University Munich, Hans MEIER dealt with "Industrial Rationalization Strategies in Design and their Impact on Employees" (1985). This is mainly an evaluation of the available literature but does include in its appendix two interesting case studies from the automobile industry. Only two findings from these case studies will be emphasized here. CAD is not yet suitable for non-standard tasks. Unusual special design work would still be done at the drawing board. In addition, in both firms there was an awareness of a danger that frequent work with CAD and the "simple" use of libraries of standards and design macros could threaten innovative and creative thinking.

Next, we must mention the work of MARGULIES who, with his colleagues, set out to achieve a specially intensive form of user participation. His two projects were unfortunately not completed, but it is to be hoped that these threads will be picked up again despite the recent death of Fred Margulies (cf. MARGULIES 1983; BROCKHAUS et al. 1985) *). It was shown that participative approaches may rely on the interest, collaboration and competence of those affected even if there are barriers to be found in the shape of conflicting internal interests.

CAD is dealt with only marginally in the study "New technology and alternative design of work" by the Institute for Social Research in Frankfurt (cf. BENZ-OVERHAGE et al. 1982). However, the thesis of a change in the economy of time connected with new technologies may also prove fruitful for CAD. In our own study, we found certain evidence pointing in this direction (cf. WINGERT et al. 1984, p. 158 ff.). The results from several projects at the Ruhr University in Bochum have been incorporated in a booklet written as a problem description for trade unionists (cf. BURR 1984 and ANGERMAIER et al. 1983).

WILDEMANN took an entirely different perspective to examine 25 firms using CAD in various industries. He centered his research on strategic investment planning using CAD as an example, naturally incorporating questions of the organization for introduction and application in addition to economics and accounting costs. For those people who like to juggle with reduction factors and calculations of economic feasibility, this is certainly a useful study since it relativates the presumably objective world of times and costs (cf. WILDEMANN 1986).

Finally, mention should be made of several pieces of work done at the *Federal Institute for Vocational Training* which also refer to CAD and its associated changes and effects, however with strong emphasis on the conclusions to be drawn for future vocational training in the

---

*) There were in fact 2 studies with the same approach. The goals were "CAD for all" and comprehensive training. The concept of a group of experts for the introduction and running of CAD was rejected. Users' subjective expectations were recorded and two interesting results are reported here. The first is that they complained about limited opportunities to communicate with colleagues although close cooperation and some agreement are absolutely necessary. The second is that 35 % feared further specialization because of CAD.

area, especially for technical draughtspeople. Among other reasons, these studies deserve special mention since they dealt with changes in work content and vocational skills caused by CAD at a very early point in time (cf. BUSCHHAUS 1978; BUSCHHAUS et al. 1980).

Within a large evaluation project, the *Fraunhofer Institute for System Technology and Innovation Research (ISI)* is currently researching firms supported by the Federal Government's "indirect specific CAD support programme" with regard to actual organizational, economic and qualificational effects, among other things. The project will run until 1988, but first results were recently reported in a presentation at Karlsruhe (cf. LAY et al. 1986). Table 1 provides a brief overview of these and other studies not analyzed in the following.

Table 1: Studies excluded from present overview

(1)	Siegfried Roth	automobile industry, results not published at time of the workshop
(2)	Hans Meier	diploma thesis, 2 empirical cases
(3)	Fred Margulies	pilot project on "CAD for all"
(4)	Institut für Sozialforschung Frankfurt	concentrated on FMS (flexible manufacturing systems), CAD marginal
(5)	Technologieberatung Oberhausen (Angermeier/Burr)	problem descriptions for unionists, own empirical data somewhat vague
(6)	Wildemann	economics of CAD, introduction process; not available at time of the workshop
(7)	ISI Studie	impacts analysis on CAD/CAM programme of German Government, in hand
(8)	Buschhaus, BiBB	Bundesinstitut für Berufsbildung, Berlin, requirements for education and vocational training
(9)	awfi-Studie	Arbeitswissenschaftliches Forschungsinstitut Berlin, consultant study, data not yet available
(10)	Sofi-Studie	Soziologisches Forschungsinstitut, Göttingen in cooperation with GH Kassel, focus on CAD and CAP, in hand
(11)	Institut für Sozialwissenschaftliche Forschung, München	CAD/CAM and qualification, just starting
(12)	SFB Berlin	Sonderforschungsbereich, CAD and expert systems, starting
(13)	Institut für Angewandte Organisationsforschung, Karlsruhe	Processes for the introduction of CAD, just completed, report available

3. General description of studies included in the analysis

Let us now turn to brief descriptions of those studies we are including to come to empirical generalizations on the effects of CAD-techniques (cf. Table 2):

- The *AFAS* study which is mentioned first because of alphabetical order and, we may add, because it appears to be one of the first and longest running studies in Europe. In the last phase of our study, we concentrated on mechanical engineering, analyzed fourteen cases and interviewed CAD experts, heads of design departments, CAD users and representatives of the works council. The range of persons included is comparable throughout the following studies.
- The next one is the study by *Planconsult* and Professor Studer from Switzerland with a project report now available (cf. MUGGLI and ZINKL 1985). This is especially noteworthy for its comparison of CAD/CAM in different branches of industry, namely mechanical engineering, chemicals and architecture, although chemicals were excluded from the final report.
- The third study was performed within the framework of an interdisciplinary project at the *Technical University of Berlin*, hence the abbreviation TUB, authored by Klaus BEDNARZ, Günther HEITMANN and Peter KEMPIN. Unfortunately they didn't participate in this workshop. In their recent publication (1984), they report four case studies in mechanical engineering, automobile design and electrical design.
- Next is the study by the *VDI-Technology Centre* in Berlin, which is interesting since it covered small and medium-sized companies. We were unsuccessful in our attempts to get one of the authors, Werner KNETSCH or Thomas BAAKEN, to attend the workshop.
- The study by Professor Klaus ZINK of the University of Kaiserslautern, gathered questionnaire data on some seventy firms, one third of them using CAD.
- We also wish to include a diploma thesis by Uwe KEIL of the University of Mannheim who has performed a fine piece of empirical research, although he interviewed only representatives of works councils.

Table 2: Empirical studies included in overview

Sectors of industry; firm size; persons					
Study	Sector	Firm Size			persons interviewed/ observed
		< 1000	- 5000	> 5000	
AFAS	- mechanical engineering	4	6	4	CAD experts head of des. dept. CAD users works council
PLAN-CONSULT	- mechanical engineering - chemistry - architecture	no figures available	no figures available	no figures available	CAD experts CAD users
TUB	- mechanical engineering - automobile - electric engineering	4 in all 2 for explorative analysis			CAD experts CAD users works council
VDI	- mechanical engineering - electric engineering - optical & precision engineering	3	3	-	CAD experts CAD users management head of des. dept. works council
ZINK	- mainly mechanical engineering	71 in all, mainly large firms			CAD experts
KEIL	- mechanical engineering - automobile - electric engineering - plant construction	4	8	2	works council representatives

Fields of application in the studies

In the next passage we shall characterize in a little more detail the fields of application and the CAD programmes analyzed (cf. Table 3). The information on the programmes is rather sparse and this is certainly one of their shortcomings although it must be admitted that there is some danger in identifying a specific programme too closely.

In our study there were two calculation programmes, three applications for drafting, two programmes for automatic variant design and five graphics packages with applications both in mechanical and in electrical design. Besides mechanical engineering tasks, the Planconsult study examined two very interesting fields in the R&D sector of the chemical industry, namely CAD as an aid for the visualization of the structure of chemical compounds and CASP, which stands for Computer Assisted Synthesis Planning. Planconsult also analyzed various applications in the sector of architectural design.

Tasks involved in the layout and routing of circuit boards were examined in the TUB study as well as those by the VDI and Keil.

A very interesting area of CAD programme application in the automobile sector is styling car bodies and the development of tools for pressing machines and this is also included in the TUB study.

If we take all these studies together and look at their fields of application, we see that they provide us with quite a representative selection of tasks which are among the most important present and future applications of CAD and CAM techniques.

Table 3: Fields of application and CAD programmes

AFAS	- users in mechanical design (10) and electrical design (2) - 1 non user - 1 ex-user	- calculation (2) - drafting (9) - automatic variant design(2) - interactive graphics (5)
PLAN-CONSULT	- mechanical design mainly, (compl. R&D, production planning) - CAD as visualization of chemical compound structure - CASP - different applications in architectural design	- no details available
TUB	- layout & routing of circuit boards - styling of automobiles & development of tools for pressing - programming & control of machine tools (without CAD)	- no details available
VDI	- tasks in wind-up of sheet metal - electrical design - circuit boards - 1 non user	- no details available
ZINK	- 24 CAD users - 27 non users	
KEIL	- electrical design - circuit boards - plant construction - mechanical engineering	- calculation (15) - drafting (13) - interactive graphics (6)

Perspectives of studies

The studies chosen for closer examination not only have their own selection of variables - which makes comparisons between them a real task - but every study its own focus and perspective as well (cf. Table 4). The PLANCONSULT study selected *typical applications* in three fields of industry as objects of the study, whereas our own study restricted itself to only one branch of industry but assessed the *complete innovation process* in order to get an understanding of the process of change at the level of individual action and organizational design. The TUB study had as well a clear theoretical focus and conceptualized the *technological variable as "implemented theories"*. The VDI, ZINK and KEIL studies have in common a focus on practical measures and utilization of the research (which applies as well to the PLANCONSULT study, esp. as to options for the introduction process). KEIL concentrated on *factors of non-acceptance* of the new technology whilst exploring the introduction processes within companies. The VDI study had a special interest in transforming the results of the investigation into *training and education measures* for the whole company, and ZINK was looking for fields which are likely to become objects of *ergonomic design*.

Given all these diversities we nevertheless tried to extract communalities in the results of the six studies. We will report both on trends supported by the majority of the studies and on those which are controversial.

Table 4: Perspectives of the studies

AFAS	- Analyzing and observing the *complete innovation process* through the different stages of implementation; paradigm according to industrial sociology with heavy emphasis on design theory and psychological action theory
PLAN-CONSULT	- Describing the CAD *applications typical of respective sectors* of industry and aiming at options of shaping the introduction, organization, technology, and education / training of CAD techniques
TUB	- Conceiving machines and software as "implemented theories" and analyzing this *technological variable* as determinant for changes in work situations and job *qualifications*
VDI	- Analyzing the situations of using CAD and *transforming* and applying the results *in training* and education programmes for *whole companies*
ZINK	- Identification of fields which may become objects of *measures of ergonomic design*
KEIL	- Diploma thesis; exploring processes of introduction of CAD, especially conditions and *factors of non-acceptance* of new technology

4. Selected empirical findings

Work load

The first issue is the *question of work load* (cf. Table 5). According to extant research it is beyond question that CAD techniques are especially accompanied by an *increase in work load*. In our own study, almost all of the experts interviewed acknowledged that the screen is a critical factor for the increase in work load, that this increase is linked with concentration during work and with the diligence required for operation and manipulation. Aspects of work load and of intensification of work are intricately mixed (cf. WINGERT et al., 1984, p. 160).

The Planconsult study also reports the general acknowledgement of an intensification of performance by all their interview partners, while half of the persons interviewed stated the opinion that work load would be greater at the beginning of work with CAD although the process of habitualization could lead to a long-term subjective decrease in work load (cf. MUGGLI and ZINKL 1985, p. 87). A critical condition for the increase in work load, especially for vision, is the extension of single CAD working sessions beyond four hours. In addition, the VDI study reports fatigue and pains in the eyes, head and back.

A comparison of results shows that the increase in the work load is reported more definitely by the CAD experts than by the CAD users themselves. For the individual user, specific factors and conditions may alleviate this general trend, foremost factors of motivation. Work performed with interest and intrinsic motivation is likely to be less fatiguing and stress inducing. Thus it follows that retaining interesting work content may also be a critical factor for the question of work load in future CAD work. This should not be taken to mean that measures taken to reduce work load are without importance.

Table 5: Results from studies

WORK LOAD - increase - individual factors modify trend
WORK ORGANIZATION - software expert groups developing - for users: mainly closed shop
CAD-CAM-INTEGRATION - few examples, growing trend - competing factors
"ABSTRACTIFICATION" - real trend - more thorough studies needed
QUALITY OF RESEARCH - report empirical results explicitly! - do not confuse technical potential with empirical fact!

Work organization

There are at least two main aspects having to do with work organization:

- The first is the emergence within firms of a specialized *CAD expert group* whose task it is to select CAD software, to prepare and implement it, to train the users and to assist in helping to keep operations running etc. Naturally, this CAD team grows with the size of the firm and with the size of the CAD application. For the time being, it is still an open question whether such expert teams are of a transitional nature or whether they develop into permanent groups or departments. Even Margulies, who in his work conceived a system of "CAD for all" designed to prevent a further division of labour between "thinking" and "acting" and between trained "CAD experts" and taught "CAD operators", was forced to acknowledge the necessity of a "CAD manager" with a whole range of central tasks in preparation and coordination (MARGULIES 1983, p. 103f.). According to our own results and those of the TUB study it would seem to be a rare exception for those people preparing software for the actual users to have comprehensive or indeed any knowledge at all on the actual work processes.
- The second aspect is that of *actual work organization* in the area of application. One may find a variety of situations depending on the amount of specialization introduced along with the CAD programme, the amount of work suitable for CAD, the qualification levels in the departments concerned etc. Both the closed shop model and the open shop model may be found, with a bias towards the closed shop model. This is interesting in view of the fact that experts - in the ZINK study over 90 % - voiced their willingness to create so called "mixed jobs" (combining CAD use with other tasks) and that about 70 % were willing to integrate CAD work in the departments involved. Similarly in our own study, experts with systems at early stages of implementation would talk about decentralized work organization while in fact at later stages of implementation, we found not one single example of a truly decentralized application, meaning the CAD work station at an individual work place. The conclusion to draw from this is to be wary of claims made about decentralization and to look closely at the real situation. It may well be that the advent of the powerful PC-workstation endows the issue of centralization with a new quality since circumscribed tasks, at least, may be performed at these machines.

MEIER reports that the CAD users he interviewed in a car factory no longer wished to give up the pool solution as opposed to management, who had a tendency to re-integrate CAD into the specialist departments.

CAD/CAM integration

The next issue we wish to touch on is CAD/CAM integration, to be dealt with in detail in another session of the workshop.

In contrast to the amount of discussion devoted to this topic, the actual situation is characterized by but a few examples of CAD/CAM integration. In our study, we encountered only two examples of CAD-NC integration while another four CAD experts were taking planning steps in this direction (WINGERT et al. 1984, p. 238f.).

Let us point out briefly some of the conflicting factors in the issue of CAD/CAM integration:

- In its section on mechanical engineering, the TUB study argues that in future the designer might also be responsible for CNC programming since he is already designing the geometry of the parts.
- Another question concerns the fate of intermediate groups and departments such as production planning. The Planconsult study argues that this link is so important that it will survive into the future and will not be absorbed into design or production divisions. At the same time, the same authors point out that introducing CAD has taken a long time and that the introduction of CAD/CAM will take even longer, something like 10 or even 20 years. So it would appear that we as researchers still have sufficient time to study this process of integration. In Germany, the Institut für Sozialwissenschaftliche Forschung in Munich has started such a project and Hartmut Hirsch-Kreinsen, who contributed to this workshop, is among the researchers involved (cf. HIRSCH-KREINSEN, SCHULZ-WILD 1986). Another project examining integration from a slightly different perspective involves the Fraunhofer ISI in Karlsruhe and the Institute for Social Research in Frankfurt. A paper by Dietrich HOSS from this project is included in the section on CAD/CAM integration in this volume.

Abstractification

Now for our last point which concerns a question we in Germany like to discuss and which is most certainly important. There is no elegant translation for the term: in our own publication we referred to a trend that CAD work was becoming increasingly abstract, the TUB study uses the term "abstractification" - supposedly a non-expression in English! - and the Planconsult study speaks of a trend towards "dematerialization". Be that as it may, the meaning should be clear: due to the new instruments used for work and to the models behind these, work with CAD programmes is indeed getting more abstract. The *means of work* are no longer concrete objects like the pencil or even paper but rather tablets, menues and command procedures. The *content of work* is no longer a sketch or a drawing, but programmes which, when manipulated, make lines or pictures appear on a screen. Even the *work process* is no longer a flow of action dependent on one's own operations, but now largely dependent upon the fulfillment of definitional requirements of the programme and upon the actual capacity of the computer, which also largely determines the time structure of work.

Bearing this in mind, we feel that we as social scientists, technically minded sociologists or socially minded technologists should go a step further and analyze also tendencies in the opposite direction, for example displaying tension structures with finite element programmes, the possibility of switching one's viewpoint in such things as 3D architecture modeling programmes or the visualization of chemical structures.

These issues will be discussed in more detail in another session, so let us conclude this review with a few remarks on the quality of research.

5. Remarks on the quality of research and reports

While preparing the material for this contribution, we must admit we had difficulties, even with our own study, in re-translating the text of the report into real results. We also found that in the studies reviewed here technological potential is sometimes confused with empirical fact, that data reporting is sometimes implicit and unprecise and that the techniques and time when the technology was examined are insufficiently specified. As you and we all know, empirical research is very valuable but also time and energy consuming. Therefore, we should make every effort to report our results in an explicit and well-stated manner.

References

Angermaier, M., Burr, M., Weber, U.:
Rechnereinsatz in der Konstruktion (CAD). Technologieberatungsstelle beim DGB Landesbezirk NRW. Oberhausen 1983.

Bednarz, K. et al.:
CAD/CAM und Qualifikation. Auswirkungen integrierter Computersysteme auf Arbeitsprozesse in Konstruktion und Fertigung. Frankfurt a.M.: Campus 1984.

Benz-Overhage, K., Brumlop, E., Freyberg, Th. von, Papdimitriou, Z.:
Auswirkungen integrierter Computersysteme auf Arbeitsprozesse in Konstruktion und Fertigung. Frankfurt: Campus 1984.

Brockhaus, M., Margulies, F., Tavolato, P., Ulich, E., Weseslindtner, H.:
Partizipative Gestaltung anwendungsorientierter CAD-Systeme. 1 Teil (Vorstudie), Schlußbericht. Manuskript 1985.

Buschhaus, D.:
Problemanalyse zur Neuordnung der Berufsausbildung für Technische Zeichner, Teil 2. Bundesinstitut für Berufsbildung Berlin: Berichte zur beruflichen Bildung, Heft 8, 1978.

Buschhaus, D. et al.:
Problemanalyse zur Neuordnung der Berufsbildung für Technische Zeichner, Teil 3, Analyse der beruflichen Tätigkeiten. Bundesinstitut für Berufsbildung Berlin: Berichte zur beruflichen Bildung, Heft 28, 1980.

Keil, U.:
Wandel von Angestelltentätigkeit durch Einführung der EDV - eine Fallstudie. Eine Betriebsrätebefragung zu neuen computergestützten Technologien am Beispiel von CAD. Diplomarbeit, Universität Mannheim, Lehrstuhl f. Soziologie III, Wintersemester 1984/85.

Knetsch, W., Baaken, T.:
Veränderungen der beruflichen Qualifikation durch neue Technologien am Beispiel CAD/CAM. VDI Düsseldorf (Hrsg.). VDI Technologiezentrum Berlin, September 1983.

Lay, G. et al.:
Erste Ergebnisse der Wirkungsanalysen der indirekt-spezifischen Förderung zur betriebli-

chen Anwendung von CAD-CAM Systemen. In: Bey, I., Mense, H. (Hrsg.): Bewertung von Entwicklung und Einsatz moderner Fertigungstechnologie. KfK-PFT 119, Karlsruhe 1986.

Margulies, F.:
Individualisierung von Technologieanwendungen: 'CAD für alle'. Psychosozial 6 (1983), Heft 18, S. 90 - 108.

Meier, H.:
Betriebliche Rationalisierungsstrategien im Konstruktionsbereich und ihre Auswirkungen auf die Beschäftigten. Diplomarbeit, LMU München 1985.

Muggli, Ch., Zinkl, W.D.:
CAD in der Maschinenindustrie und im Architekturbüro. VDF 1985.

Wildemann, H.:
Strategische Investitionsplanung für CAD/CAM. Stuttgart: Schäffer 1986.

Wingert, B., Rader, M., Riehm, U.:
Technologie und Tätigkeit. Überlegungen zur Erfassung ihrer Wechselwirkungen. In: Dürholt, E. u.a.: Qualitative Arbeitsanalyse, Frankfurt a.M.: Campus 1984.

Wingert, B. et al.:
CAD im Maschinenbau. Wirkungen, Chancen, Risiken. Berlin u.a.: Springer 1984.

Zink, K.J.:
Arbeitswissenschaftliche Aspekte bei der Einführung neuer Technologien - eine empirische Studie. Zeitschrift für Arbeitswissenschaft 37 (9 NF) (1983), Heft 3, S. 134 - 137.

CAD APPLICATIONS IN ITALY - A REVIEW

Olimpio Brivio - MAIN S.r.l.
Via G.de Grassi 3, 20123 Milano, Italy
GianCarlo Cainarca - University of Padova and MAIN S.r.l.
Marco Mutinelli - Politecnico di Milano,
Piazza Leonardo da Vinci 32, 20133 Milano, Italy
Claudio Roveda - Politecnico di Milano and Cestec S.p.A.

1. Introduction

Aim of this paper is to present a general overview of the actual state of CAD applications in Italy.

This overview is based both on quantitative and qualitative elements. First of all, some data are provided on CAD systems installed so far, on their evolution in recent years and on short-term trends; this analysis of the CAD market is combined with a brief description of the vendors of CAD (hardware, software) operating in Italy.

2. Diffusion of CAD/CAE systems in Italy*

The introduction of CAD/CAE systems in Italy started somewhat later than in the other industrialized countries of Europe, but in very recent years, the rate of introduction has greatly increased so that now the level of diffusion is not far from the situation in these countries.

This is true both in terms of number of users (with at least one CAD/CAE workstation) and of number of installed workstations, as is shown in Tables 1 and 2: it appears that 1982 was a turning point in the diffusion of CAD/CAE in Italy. Since then, the annual rate of growth in the number of users has approximately increased by 50 %.

At the level of industries, the highest rates of growth in the period 1980-84 are shown by the mechanical engineering and construction engineering sectors (with ratios over 10).

Similar conclusions are drawn when considering the number of workstations, with the exception of the electronics industry which shows a rate very similar to the top ones.

The distribution of CAD/CAE applications among industries shows a well defined pattern: at the beginning of the period, workstations are concentrated in the automobile and

(*) The data reported in this paragraph are mainly taken from a statistical investigation carried out in 1984/85 by the consulting firm RESEAU: it involved mailing more than 5.000 questionnaires to potential users and more than 100 questionnaires to CAD/CAE vendors (systems, hardware, software, services) operating in Italy. From the answers to the questionnaire some extrapolations have been made for the overall Italian situation.

Table 1: CAD/CAE Users in Italy

Industry	1980	1982	1984
Automobile + Aircraft	11	16	35
Mechanical Engineering	10	27	110
Electro-Mechanics	3	10	24
Electronics	15	19	35
Plant Building	6	16	70
Construction Engineering	19	40	180
Land Management + Services	15	32	60
Textile	12	20	60
Others	5	10	65
Total	96	190	610

Source: Reseau

Table 2: Installed CAD/CAM Workstations

Industry	1982	%	1984	%
Automobile + Aircraft	134	25,5	350	18,6
Mechanical Engineering	74	14	300	16
Electro-Mechanics	20	3,8	70	3,7
Electronics	80	15,2	300	16
Plant Building	60	11,4	260	13,8
Construction Engineering	46	8,8	240	12,7
Land Management + Services	80	15,2	210	11,2
Textile	22	4,2	75	4
Others	10	1,9	75	4
Total	525	100,0	1880	100,0

aircraft industry, followed at a large distance by the electronic and mechanical engineering industries. At the end of the period, the ranking is almost the same, but differences in relative weight are much smaller.

If one considers the distribution of CAD/CAE applications according to the user's size, the results differ strongly among industries (see Table 3.a,b,c,d): in the automobile, aircraft, electronics and electro-mechanical industries most users are large companies (more than 1.000 employees); on the other hand, in the construction engineering industry most users are very small firms (fewer than 20 employees).

The mechanical engineering industry appears to be in an intermediate situation, with most users being medium size firms (employees between 100 and 500).

Apart from these differences, which greatly reflect the overall structure of these industries, data show a quite definite trend in the period 1980-84: applications involve an increasing number of smaller firms in every industry, with a higher rate of diffusion for medium size firms.

On the vendors' side, it is enough to mention that at the end of 1984 about 100 firms were operating of which 25-30 offered turn-key CAD/CAE systems, 30 offered graphic terminals, peripherals and generally dedicated hardware and more than 50 offered application software and CAD/CAE services.

CAD/CAE market distribution among the principal vendors is shown in Table 4: almost all the Italian market is captured by foreign companies (mostly US) while the share of Italian firms (mostly Olivetti and Selenia) is marginal.

The structure of CAD/CAE supply in Italy is somewhat different than in other European countries: the degree of concentration is lower, as the 4 largest companies cover about 60 % of the overall Italian market and the 8 largest companies cover little less than 80 %, and there is a large number of companies, each with a small market share, that anyway make up altogether a significant percentage.

Competition is very keen, as shown by the fact that some of the companies leading the market in 1984 were not even active in 1982.

3. Review of the investigations into CAD applications in Italy

In recent years increasing attention has been devoted to CAD in technical journals and in the general press in Italy.

Technical topics, both relating to R & D and innovation and to industrial applications, are most frequently dealt with; topics regarding organizational and social effects are mostly mentioned with reference to specific case studies.

In Italy, as in other countries, some sociological studies have been carried out on the various effects of the new automation technologies (specially office automation, industrial

Table 3: Distribution of Users (%) According to Firm Size

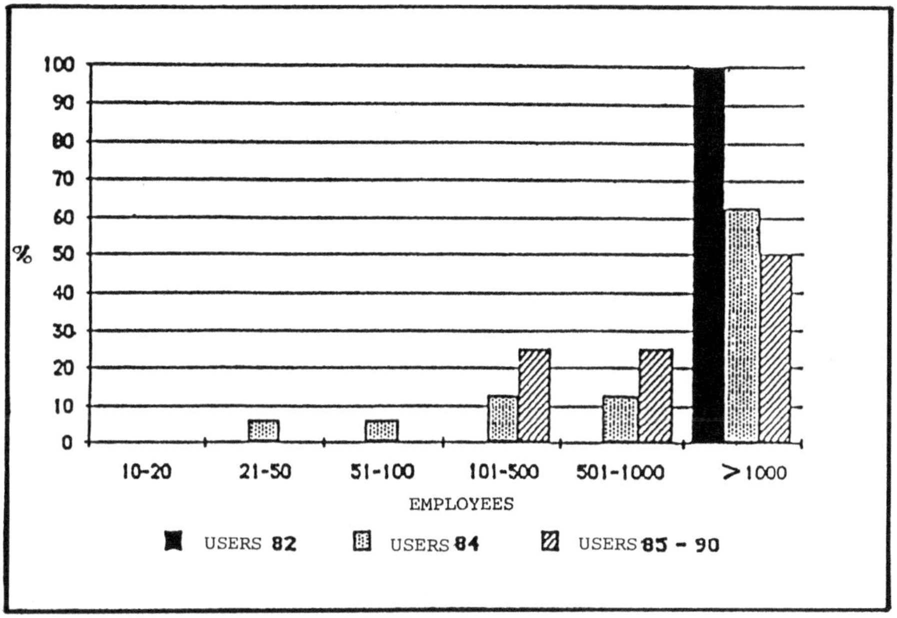

Source: Reseau

(a) AUTOMOBILE + AIRCRAFT

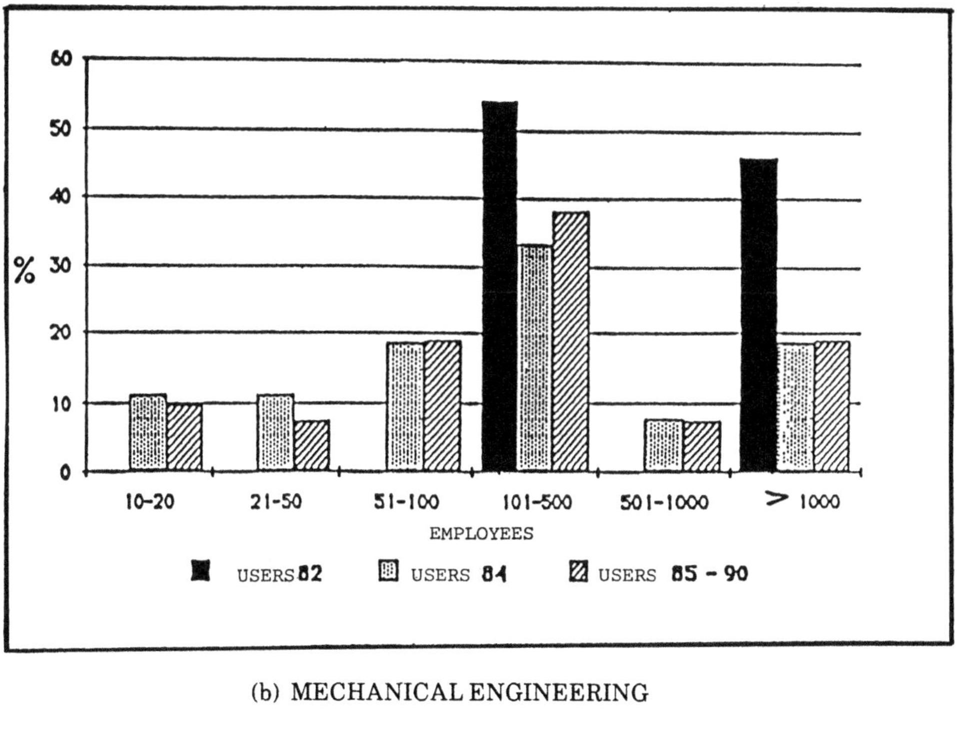

(b) MECHANICAL ENGINEERING

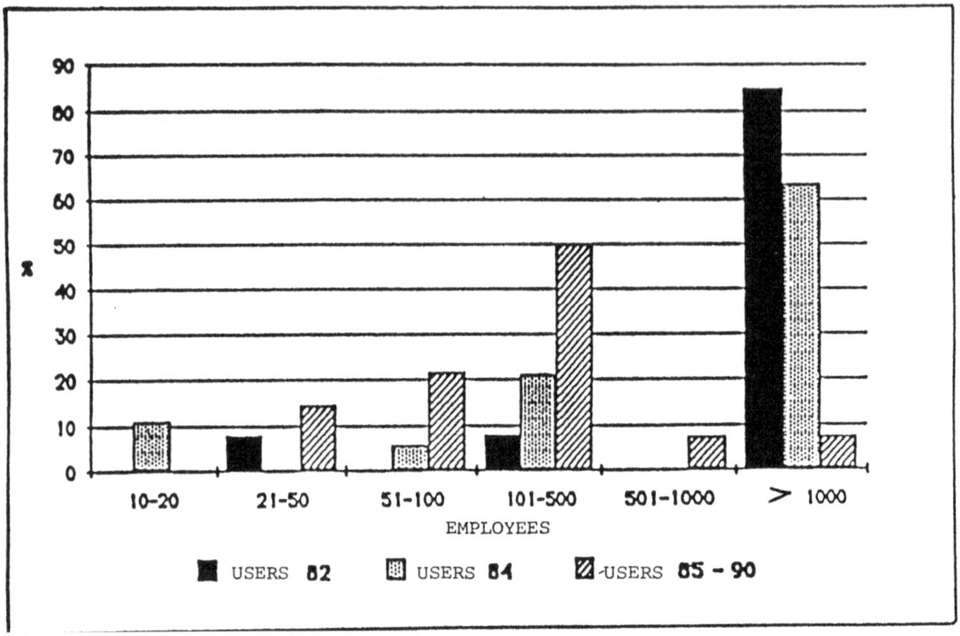

(c) ELECTRONICS

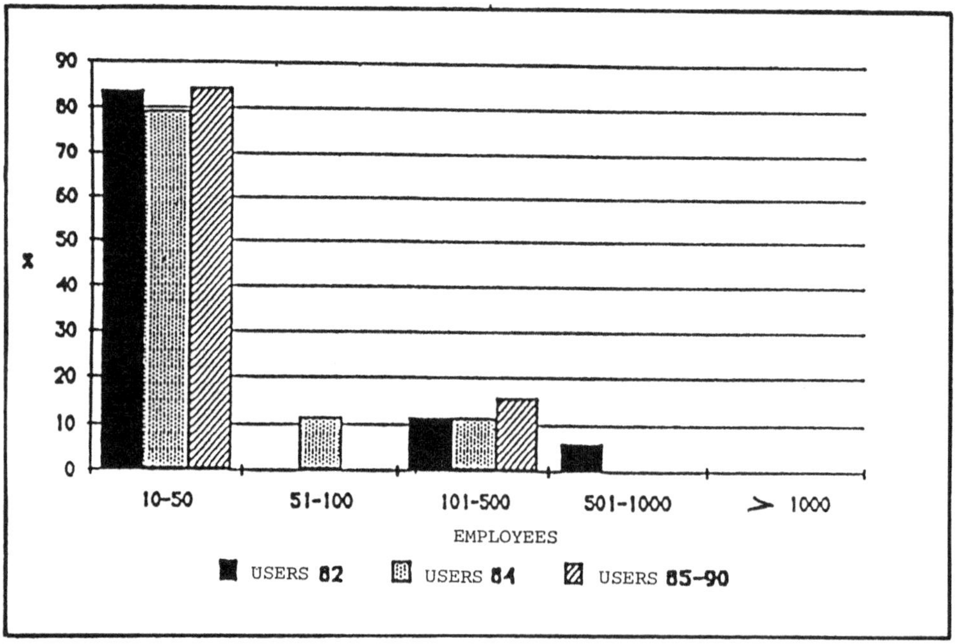

(d) CONSTRUCTION ENGINEERING

Table 4: Market Share of Major CAD/CAE Vendors (1984)

Company	Market Share (in %)
COMPUTER VISION	15 - 20
IBM	15 - 20
CALMA	10 - 15
TEKTRONIX	5 - 10
SELENIA AUTOTROL	3 - 5
DAISY	3 - 5
INTERGRAPH	3 - 5
HEWLETT-PACKARD	3 - 5
APOLLO	1 - 3
APPLICON	1 - 3
CAD LAB	1 - 3
CALCOMP	1 - 3
CGD	1 - 3
EUROBIT	1 - 3
MATRA	1 - 3
OLIVETTI TECNOST	1 - 3
SIEMENS DATA	1 - 3
OTHERS	10 - 15 %
TOTAL	100 % = 130 Bill.Lit

Source: Reseau

robots, CNC machine tools). Up to now, few studies have dealt with the social and organizational effects of CAD, based on a comparative empirical analysis. Among these one can mention:

- a research project, promoted by CESOS (GHERARDI S., MASIERO A., 1983), on the decision-making process for technological innovations, which in 5 case studies (two of which concerned CAD applications), conducted an analysis of the phases of the decision-making process, of the methodologies adopted, and of the roles of the various actors;
- two research projects undertaken by the Foundation "Pietro Seveso", one evaluating the effects of new technologies on industrial relations (NEGRELLI, 1985) on the basis of eight case studies (two of which involved CAD applications), the other (in progress), analyzing the management of employees' working-hours and working-times in some specific situations (including CAD applications).

The consulting firm MAIN has started a research project, sponsored and financed by the European Foundation for the Improvement of Living and Working Conditions, on the effects of new automation technologies on working conditions, organization and personnel management.

The project, just completed, examined 6 cases of CAD/CAM applications, and 1 case of assembly automation, all involving large industrial firms.

In 1985 Cestec, a public agency for the promotion of technological innovation in the small and medium size firms (SME) of Lombardy, started collecting case studies on the application of CAD/CAM within SMEs, focusing on the problems (technical, financial, organizational) encountered at the various stages of the implementation process.

From the results of these last two empirical investigations it is possible to make general statements on the main topics of the implementation of CAD, both in large and in small and medium firms, such as:

- decision-making processes on the introduction of CAD (goals, criteria, actors);
- implementation strategies;
- organization effects (structure, skills, motivations);
- results (as compared with the goals that supersede the decision to introduce CAD);

In the case of SMEs special attention is given to the main factors that today still constrain, or even forbid, the utilization of CAD.

References

Gherardi, S., Masiero A.:
"Technological transformation and decision-making processes", Rapporti Cesos, No. 13, December, 1983

Negrelli, S. (ed.):
"Company Industrial Relations in the Eighties" in Quaderni di formazione ISOFOL, No. 3/85, May-June 1985

THE HUNGARIAN CAD/CAM SCENE

George Kovács

Computer and Automation Institute
Hungarian Academy of Sciences
Budapest, Hungary
H-111 Kende utca 13/17

1. The development of CAD/CAM in Hungary

In Hungary (and in some other Eastern countries) the development of CAD/CAM took a completely different path than in Western countries because of the special circumstances (e.g. import restrictions).

In Hungary, the *first* large *turn-key* CAD System (ISTER) was only developed in the seventies. The programs (about 60.000 instructions) were written in assembly language and sophisticated overlay methods were used as the CPU of the computer was only 28 Kbyte. The hardware units were put together - without system concept - according to availability (Hungarian CPU, American discs, Czechoslovakian plotter, etc.).

The *next generation* of CAD Workstations is based on the PDP - like Hungarian TPA 11/40 computer (64-256 Kbyte) and on our GD'80 graphic display. These, connected with discs, magnetic tapes, plotter and paper-tape units form a good, but expensive CAD/CAM Workstation.

The last years resulted in different CAD/CAM systems developed on this hardware. During the development of these programs a so-called general purpose CAD-monitor became necessary and was developed.

2. Hungarian possibilities

If we had a choice, we should purchase all the necessary CAD/CAM systems from countries with more experience in the technology, but as a matter of fact that has not been a real possibility recently.

Thus if we need CAD/CAM systems we have to develop them, i.e. not only software, but also hardware:

- Some results are achieved developing local area network working on coaxical cable (COBUS).
- IBM PC compatible microcomputers (VTPC, PROPER) are already available with restricted graphics.
- TEKEMU is a raster-graphics display (1024x780) to be used as a TEKTRONIX emulator. Two versions of the GKS standard are available as XGKS (under UNIX) and RGKS (under RSX). Both can be used from FORTRAN and C. The GD'85 TEXPRO is a DIN A4

raster-graphics terminal (1024x800) for text- and picture-processing. A GKS terminal is under development where most GKS functions will be realized in hardware.

- The TEKEMU, TEXPRO and the GKS Terminal are supposed to work with our recently developed 16/32 bit minicomputer, the SUPERMICRO, which works on standard VME bus. This minicomputer will be used either stand alone, or in a computer net, under a Unix operational system.
- The above mentioned displays and computers should result in basic CAD hardware-software systems in 1987/88, with similar capacities to the recent APOLLO DOMAIN system.
- We have to mention that the development of VAX-like computers and different peripheral devices is going on and hopefully will give positive results soon.

Our special system-programming language is specially designed for minicomputers with restricted CPU having a cartridge disc. The language is called GESAL, it is fast and effective, having Algol 68-like structures and Pascal-like data structures.

On the meta-CAD level there is a virtual memory handling system, an interactive graphics system with geometric functions, a CODASYL-like DBMS system, and there are some debug facilities to help fast, reliable and easy programming.

3. CAD-systems using the monitor

The last ten years resulted in some CAD systems which helped to develop the monitor-system and which use its final version.

- ISTER: interactive punch-die design system
- MINDS: minicomputer NC system
- Interactive shaft design system
- Pre- and postprocessor for the GEDMAP 3D modeller
- GRECO: 2D drawing editor
- Gamma: Interactive process-control design system
- HUMBUG: NC path checking
- FFS: Free form shape CAD/CAM system

Most of these systems are detailed in earlier publications (GAÁL, VÁRADY 1984; ANDOR et al. 1984; KOVÁCS 1982) thus now we only have to mention that with the available computers (TPA 11/40 - GD'80) the monitor-system was necessary to be able to finish program developments within finite time limits, to fit the programs into the computers, and to hand over the systems to the end users.

Some of the systems are used as turn-key systems (the user doesn't need any computer science knowledge), others are open, i.e. the user may change them or add new modules. The monitor-system assists in modular programming, new modules can be added without recompiling and re-editing the rest of the programs.

References

Gaál, B.; Váradym T.:
Experiences and further development of the FFS System. Proc. of the 9th IFAC World Congress, Budapest, 1984

Andor et al.:
GRECO, User Manual Computer and Automation Institute, Budapest, 1984

Kovács, G.:
Displaying Tool Paths IKM'82, Vortrag 39, Leipzig, 10-12 March'82

COMPUTER AIDED DESIGN IN SWITZERLAND

Wolf D. Zinkl
PLANCONSULT AG
Peter-Merian-Straße 34
CH - 4002 Basel

1. CAD in Switzerland

In Switzerland, interest in the introduction, application and effects of Computer-Aided-Design Systems has extended beyond the circle of specialists and come to the attention of a broader public. This fact was particularly well illustrated by the interest focused on CAD at recent exhibitions such as 'Swissdata' in Basel, and at union meetings like 'Gewerkschaft Bau und Holz'.

By the end of 1984, according to various estimates, fewer than 100 3-D CAD systems had been installed in Switzerland. Approximately 50 % of them are at present fully operational. Future sales though, will certainly be favourably influenced by the expected decrease in price for CAD.

Since the beginning of the century, Switzerland has practised capital intensive production, and has attained its current position in the world market due to the high quality and standard of its industrial products. In many companies, CAD will be a further aid to maintaining and possibly supplementing the quality of these products.

The majority of the CAD systems functioning at present are employed in the mechanical industry, in companies which retain a staff in excess of 300 workers. Some of the remaining CAD units are either already being utilized, or are in the process of being introduced into architecture. Here too, the users tend to be larger organizations. Similarly, the system has found its place in other fields, particularly in the chemical industry, Computer-Assisted-Synthesis Planning (CASP) and in the design of circuit boards in electronics.

CAD has been in use in the two Swiss technical universities in Zürich and Lausanne for some years now, and in all probability will be adopted by many engineering colleges within the near future. Apprentices at this stage however, have not yet had sufficient formal training in the use of CAD, and subsequently the work has, to some extent, remained the domain of persons of higher education.

The connection between CAD and Computer-Aided Manufacturing (CAM) is actually rather rare in Switzerland. Although it is certainly a goal in many companies, the costs of the implementation of CAD/CAM and the partially unavailable technology, has been hampering CAD/CAM expansion.

2. Social science research

One major social science project, funded by the government, has thus far been conducted on CAD. In 1984, Planconsult investigated, in the mechanical and architectural fields, the qualitative effects that CAD had on the working abilities of its users. The results of this investigation were published at the end of 1985 (cf. MUGGLI, ZINKL 1985).

The project was carried out on an empirical basis, and consisted of some 50 structured interviews with both CAD-users and CAD experts in colleges, universities and German and Swiss companies using CAD. Twenty-six social aspects were evaluated, and these were divided into four main groups:

- Content of work
- Working conditions
- Organization
- Education and training

3. Results and conclusions

The investigation established two main findings:

- Work with CAD has qualitative effects on the working conditions of CAD users.
- In both the mechanical industry and architecture, the qualitative effect of CAD on its users is similar in many respects.

Concerning the contents of work, CAD affects most of the traditional activities. With CAD, a shift from manually orientated activities to intellectually orientated activities can be observed.

CAD also alters general working conditions. It was observed that users were exposed to a more selective stress. The move from the person-to-person communication to a man-machine communication can therefore affect the social working conditions and relationships within a company.

Further, due to the introduction of CAD, the organization of work and the organization of the various departments of a company are likely to change. Here, generally, the result will be more one of consolidation of the sections than a decentralization of them. CAD often results in more rigid hierarchical pyramids.

For these reasons CAD is of course altering educational and training requirements. Thus to realize the full potential and usefulness of the system, special care needs to be taken in the training of CAD users.

The introduction of CAD is linked to qualitative effects on the working conditions of CAD users. Certainly CAD can increase the productivity of its users, but it can also be the source of social problems. This last aspect will become even more pertinent when it becomes obligatory for certain categories of workers to use CAD regularly.

Most of the social problems that occur with the use of CAD, are however not only part and parcel of the new technology. They are also largely due to the method employed in introducing CAD into a company. For instance, CAD may be used to justify certain organizational changes within a company for which it is not directly responsible. Thus, it must be emphasized, that the social effects are also the result of an interaction between CAD and the environment in which it is situated. Therefore the social effects are likely to vary according to the chosen strategies and goals for the introduction of CAD in a company.

Reference

Muggli, Ch.; Zinkl, W.D.:
CAD in der Maschinenindustrie und im Architekturbüro. Zürich: Verlag VDF 1985

NOTES ON OTHER COUNTRIES

Michael Rader, Based on oral contributions by:

Peter Higgins
The Swinburne Institute of Technology
Hawthorn 3122
Australia

Maurits van Wagenberg
Studiegroep CAD en Organisatie
Singel 159-A
1012 Amsterdam
The Netherlands

Australia

Australia is a federation of 6 states with roughly 15 Million inhabitants. Compared world-wide, the country is in the middle-range with regard to proportion of gross national product spent on research and development. This is mainly from the public sector with little expenditure from private industry. There is also little expenditure on military R&D compared with countries like the USA or Great Britain. In common with British tradition, there is a sharp division between industry and academia. Most industrial equipment is purchased overseas, particularly in the USA.

Because of the federal system of government, a lot takes place at the State level, however certain Federal schemes are worth mentioning:

- Demonstration projects in engineering, including one CAM, one computer-integrated manufacturing, one application of CAD/CAM for learning engineering, one teaching scheme to test cooperation between industry and academia in solving problems.
- The Technology Transfer Council which is designed to enable the transfer of technology from overseas into the country, examples being Flexible Manufacturing Systems (FMS) and Just-in-time delivery.
- The Commonwealth Scientific Industrial Research Organization, which was traditionally responsible for such things as wool and wheat, is now entering research into manufacturing technology.

As for other measures, it is important to realize that these are within the discretion of the individual States which differ widely with regard to policies. When considering CAD/CAM it is important to bear in mind that 80 % of people in industry are employed by firms of up to 20 staff, that a medium-size firm by Australian standards has about 100 employees and a firm with 500 staff is really large. Thus CAD/CAM prices are too high for wide diffusion in Australia. Swinburne Institute is in the State of Victoria and what follows applies to Victoria only. There is a small State CAD centre to demonstrate CAD and a CAD/CAM network has been established to exchange experience. Swinburne Institute has a CAD system and has started offering a master's course in CIM.

From the beginning of the century up to very recently, the Federation and individual States have had Conservative governments. There are now Labour governments in all but 2 States and this has brought about a policy change. About 70 % of the labour force are organized in unions and a system of Industrial Accord has been established between the Government and the Australian Federation of Trade Unions. The Government has been particularly interested in the workings of industrial democracy in Scandinavia and has commissioned a report. Industrial democracy is being put into practice in the public sector. Otherwise the accord means that there is a centralized system for regulating disputes and relations in general. One outcome of this has been the union demanding a socio-technical analysis to be done within the demonstration programme on CIM. This analysis is being funded. Another result is the "Job protection test case", whereby 6 months' notification of redundancy and re-training schemes are required.

The Netherlands

The Netherlands are a small, moderately industrialized country with little really large industry. Until 1983-4, there was no CAD to speak of with the possible exception of 3 industries: Electro-technical (Philips); mould and die making and petro-chemical engineering. Correspondingly, there was no great interest in social research before 1983 and even now it is mainly being backed by the Ministry of Economic Affairs, giving it an appropriate bias.

CHAPTER 2: The Nature of Design and the Effects of CAD/CAM

The papers submitted under this heading sparked off perhaps the most controversial discussions in the entire workshop. An introduction to the role of tacit knowledge in design is provided by RASMUSSEN, ERIKSEN and HANSEN, who in common with authors like Cooley warn against trying to eliminate this kind of knowledge by the application of technology. Erik ARNOLD felt that there was a tendency to romanticize traditional skills and to make over-large claims for tacit knowledge. For instance, there had been some discussion on whether machines incorporating the latest computer control technology should be equipped with traditional hand-wheels or levers just to make operators with traditional skills feel more comfortable. He also pointed out that processes described as "de-skilling" were, in fact, leading to an increase in the average level of skills in that they were removing people from the lowest level in the pyramid-shaped hierarchy of firms. However, Jean-Pierre POITOU pointed out that this lowest level had already been forced out of the design office to a large extent *before* CAD was introduced. Håkon FINNE doubted whether such upgrading of skills was altogether desirable, since routine, which would be edged out of designers' work by CAD, was necessary in order to be creative.

ARNOLD also pointed out what he felt to be a contradiction in the debate on tacit knowledge: on the one hand tacit knowledge was defined as knowledge which defied formalization and thus could not be automated and on the other hand there was concern because people were, in fact, formalizing it and automating it anyway. Other contributions suggested that this apparent contradiction could be due to a lack of precise definition. For instance, RASMUSSEN suggested that tacit knowledge will also be required to operate CAD/CAM systems, but that this will have a new tacit dimension. To this, WINGERT added that tacit knowledge was developed in the interplay between the human and technology. Thus it would be interesting to observe if the development of tacit knowledge is changed by new technology. POITOU saw a problem in locating tacit knowledge: if we knew where it was, it would no longer be tacit. In this respect the architect /bee comparison employed by Marx and COOLEY [1], [2] was not quite correct: while the bee cannot have knowledge outside itself, the architect has access to knowledge on paper or built into products and tools. POITOU felt that the key to tacit knowledge is to be found in the hand rather than in the brain of the craftsman, the leading question being: will the designer who no longer uses his hand for design be less creative? This problem should be dealt with in research on tacit knowledge and on CAD/CAM systems of the future. Poitou was also certain that CAD/CAM could be improved if the hand were retained in the design process. Finally on the subject of tacit knowledge, Finne doubted that tacit knowledge was merely a component of the total sum of an individual's knowledge. He felt that it was a kind of "glue" holding knowledge together.

ARNOLD also criticized that the social sciences' conception of CAD/CAM appeared to be static while the technology was, in fact, developing rapidly. His own experience with a word-processor suggested that they did have technical shortcomings which made using them for certain purposes slightly uncomfortable, but that they helped to enhance the product - his prose. The situation with regard to CAD/CAM might be similar, but since a great deal of effort was being put into the human/machine interface, constraints were likely to be less severe in the future. ZINKL agreed that CAD was developing at an amazing pace and pointed out that, contrary to expectations, CAD did not have entirely negative effects. In his experience, designers enjoyed working with CAD because it gave them higher salaries and more spare time at work. The changes caused by CAD were not particularly dramatic and many were organizational. In some instances CAD had been used as an excuse to instrument changes which had been planned anyway. It was important to explain what CAD was being used for.

Yvonne WAERN cited examples from history to point out that people had always worried about the effects of technology: the ancient Greeks had been concerned about the effect of writing on the memory and currently there was anxiety about the effect of the use of pocket-calculators on childrens' ability in mental arithmetic. WAERN felt that while some abilities or skills had been lost, something else had been gained: writing had provided the ability to distribute knowledge etc. We must therefore ask ourselves what we are trying to do with CAD. Are we trying to preserve skills or what other aspects are we interested in? Dietrich Hoss linked this question with the problem of tacit knowledge by asserting that there were basically two alternative strategies for the application of CAD/CAM. One alternative had the aim of concentrating all available knowledge in a process in a computer integrated manufacturing system, while in the other alternative CAD is seen as a means of providing people from various departments involved in the process with the necessary knowledge and the opportunity to contribute their own particular knowledge. While the principle feasibility of this second approach was not denied, there was some doubt whether it had actually been put into practice, although HOSS claimed he had seen references to examples in the literature.

The paper by Karin SPORS on so-called user-friendly systems served to illustrate differences between engineers trying to provide equipment designers enjoy using and social scientists, who tend to be wary of a wider range of possible effects and have different ideas on the criteria for systems. For instance WINGERT agreed that a number of criteria were indeed meaningful, but disagreed with designing systems that required no EDP knowledge on the part of the user or "self-explanatory" systems which he finds both misleading and dangerous.

Some criticism was also leveled at the very idea of building "user friendly" systems. Langaa JENSEN cited the example of "ergonomic" text-editing systems in Denmark which were so user-friendly that they were defeating their purpose. Because they fascinated the users so greatly, these stuck in front of their screens for hours ignoring regulations designed to protect their health limiting the period of time to be spent at the screen. FINNE added that such systems were being designed for comfort to make them less unbearable.

There was also some controversy on the subject of dialogue. The very term itself was questioned by GOTTSCHALCH who wished to reserve it for interaction between two conscious beings. Thus working around decision-trees could not be described as a dialogue. Although no-one actively disagreed with this argument, the term "dialogue" persistently survived into discussion. Arnold felt that attitudes of users toward "comfortable" dialogues changed over time: while novices with the systems liked this feature, it tended to bore them as they gained experience. This suggested that a truly "comfortable" system would require adaptable software. Wingert proposed systems which gave the user a choice for the selection of a model in the machine while KOVÁCS denied that dialogue was necessary in every application of CAD. He claimed that dialogue was only required if the designer was not sure in advance what he wished to do. FINNE interpreted this as implying that the computer was in command of the process, leading the designer onto the correct path when he had lost his way. He also felt that other requirements would be more important than those mentioned by SPORS. For instance, there was a tendency for CAD systems to shift the designer's attention from the design task in hand to the operation of the system and FINNE was strongly in favour of CAD systems that put design back into the hand of the designer. Finally on this subject, POITOU doubted whether the idea of a general framework for comfortable CAD/CAM equipment was at all useful. He pointed out that there were different types of design, each with their own location and for these to be useful, one would have to be far more specific. In this respect, at least three dimensions were of importance: 1. The relative value added to the product; 2. the size of the series of product; 3. the size of the firm in terms of numbers of employees.

The paper by RESCH was the subject of a small controversy among the psychologists attending the workshop. WINGERT was of the opinion that social science studies should indicate the changes on the collective body of designers and felt that the VERA model was unsuitable for this purpose. He illustrated this by the example of calculations. In conventional work, the designer employed certain algorithms and worked his way through a sequence of calculations making cross-checks as he went along. The mathematical models can be incorporated in a CAD-model having certain pre-conditions. The designer would have to be aware of these preconditions, but WINGERT doubted that the approach taken by RESCH had an equivalent of "being aware" (of conditions or prerequisites). Both GOTTSCHALCH and RESCH, who share the same approach, claimed that action was regulated by internal models which covered the problem mentioned by Wingert.

References

1) Marx, K., 1974:
Capital, Vol. 1, p. 174. London; Lawrence & Wishat 1974.

2) Cooley, M.J.E., 1980:
Architect or Bee? Slough: Hand and Brain 1980.

TACIT KNOWLEDGE VERSUS SYSTEM KNOWLEDGE

Lauge Baungaard Rasmussen, Erik Rask Eriksen
Finn Hansen

Institut for Samfundsfag
Danmarks Tekniske Hojskole
Bygning 301,
DK-2800 Lyngby

1. Introduction

This paper presents some considerations from the Danish part of the project: "Comprehensive Criteria and Exemplary Prototype of a Human-centred Computer-integrated Manufacturing System".

Since 1984, we have cooperated with research-groups at the University of Bremen and UMIST in Manchester. The Greater London Enterprise Board (GLEB) has been the coordinator of this international research cooperation.

The objective of the whole project is to challenge the tendency of rejecting design and skilled abilities, which, at the moment, seem to be the going trend of the dominating system development. In contrast hereto, the project intends to investigate and suggest alternatives using the skills and knowledge instead of destroying them.

In relation to this, we found it fruitful to contrast different views of knowledge in order to be able to specify the constraints of using computer technology in design-work.

In *chapter 2,* we shall try to encircle what system knowledge and constraints are. Discussion moves from the man-machine level to the organizational level. We propose that the Tayloristic approach is to be seen in a dialectical context with the system approach. Different alternative strategies are discussed.

In *chapters 3 and 4,* we introduce the concept of Polanyi: Tacit Knowledge, and how it may influence the design-process. Besides this, we shall discuss some possible consequences for the tacit dimension of designing when CAD-systems become more widely used.

In *chapter 5,* we briefly mention some examples of strategies which Danish firms have until now seemed to use in connection with CAD-systems.

Finally in *chapter 6,* we summarize some theoretical and empirical problems, which we think will dominate in our project in the coming years.

2. System knowledge

System knowledge at the man-machine level

Knowledge-diagrams

It became more and more obvious that Computer-Aided Design technology - mainly developed in the US - cannot encompass all kinds of knowledge.

The following diagram illustrates this in a simplified manner:

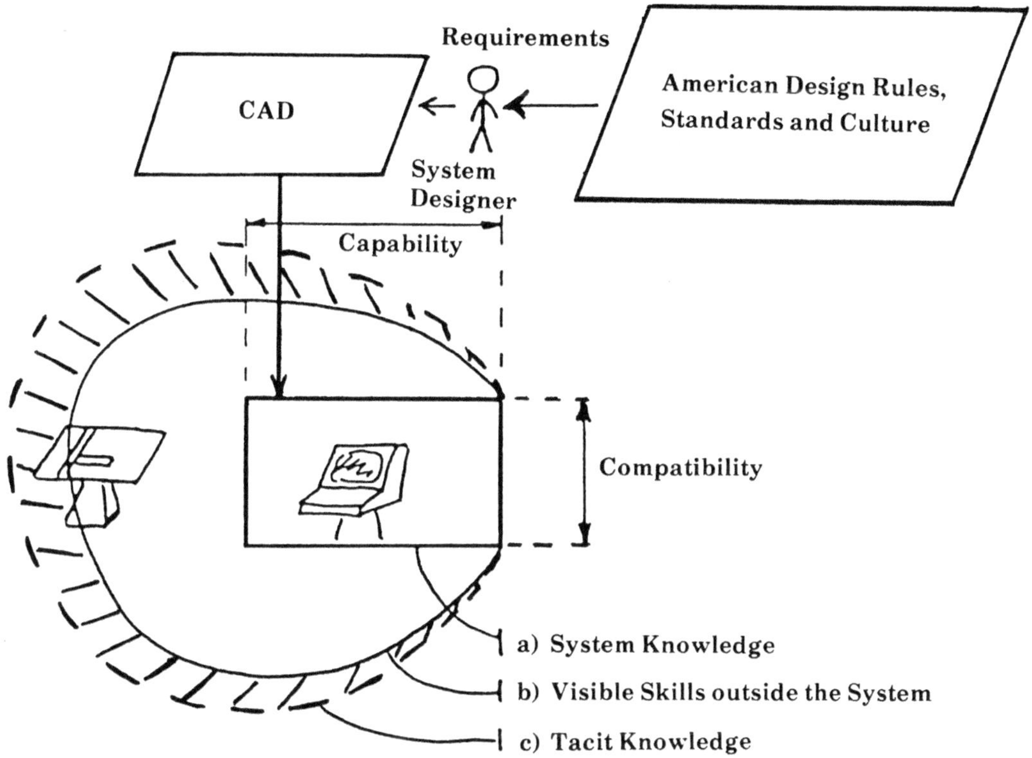

Figure 1: A knowledge diagram

Figure 1 shows a knowledge-diagram. Compatibility is the *vertical* proportion between a) and b). The gap represents the reduced compatibility due to standardization and formalization of skilled knowledge. Reduced compatibility appears when i.e. US-standards and Danish standards are not identical. The capability represents the horizontal ratio between the system (a) and skilled knowledge (b). Not all functions and facilities are possible by means of the system.

Tacit knowledge (c) is an area outside and *behind* the area of both system-knowledge (a) and the explicit skilled knowledge outside the system (b). The tacit dimension is - as we shall discuss in more detail later - very difficult to encircle in the design-process, but nevertheless of vital importance.

The constraints of the design-job

The constraints of system knowledge also mean constraints of the design-job when a certain system is applied.

The constraints differ, depending on the type of design-work. This is illustrated in the following figure.

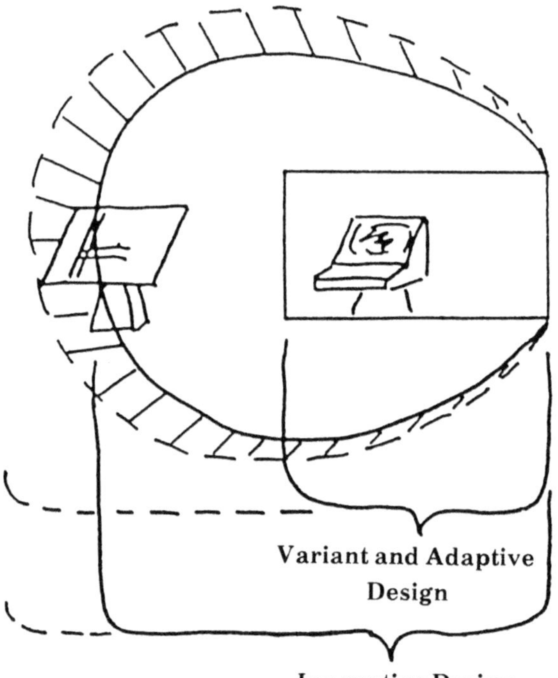

Figure 2: Constraints according to type of design work

When the geometry is already in the CAD-system, variant and adaption design can be done very effectively by means of the system. It is on the other hand evident that it is difficult to do innovative design without using skilled and tacit knowledge.

The figure illustrates that both variant adaption and innovative design contain all three kinds of knowledge. However, innovative design in particular is much more dependent on tacit knowledge than the other two.

Alternative strategy at man-machine level

We have interviewed Danish engineers and designers and based on these preliminary studies, we can report the following conclusions from the Danish project of the Danish Council of Technology (ERIKSEN, E.R., 1983 [1]).

Design work at a CAD-work station is restricted in several senses with regard to the creative parts of the work. The most significant ones are insufficient vision ("you are looking through a keyhole all the time") and limits caused by standardization.

The advantages of CAD-work stations comprise efficiency as a result of the multiplication of details, modification ("the electronic eraser"), automation of routine work such as automatic hatching and dimensioning.

The above limits do not include a number of problems dealing with health and safety, for instance that a human cannot work at a screen for more than a maximum of 4 hours a day. Therefore, you still cannot do without the conventional drawing board. It would be a step forward if the drawing machine were interfaced to the computer system. This increases the probability of maintaining the drawing board in future CAD-systems. This strategy of using both the electronic or non-electronic drawing machine and the CAD-system is aiming at a new system-concept. Is it possible to find new ways to combine the drawing machine and the CAD-system?

System knowledge at the organizational level

The immanent organizational system knowledge

It is becoming more and more evident that system design and system integration are going to influence not only the man-machine relationship but also the organizational level.

Our hypothesis is that complex and integrated systems mean serious constraints of organizational latitude. In many ways the organizational structure seems to be partly built into the information systems. The constraints are of a different kind, due to the effects of integration, or respectively the tendency for computerized control.

Integrational constraints

As shown in Figure 1, system knowledge is only a part of total knowledge. We, therefore, perceive system knowledge as the limiting bottleneck, not so much where quantities are involved but more in the qualitative dimension.

The pressure of standardization can be observed in the integrated system for several reasons. With regard to CAD/CAM, the problem can be illustrated in the following way.

Figure 3 illustrates the fact that when you integrate more and more job functions into the system, the latitude for allowed and possible acts becomes more and more restricted. Therefore, computer-integrated plants until now seem to be rather specialized (group technology might modify this tendency in the future to a certain extent).

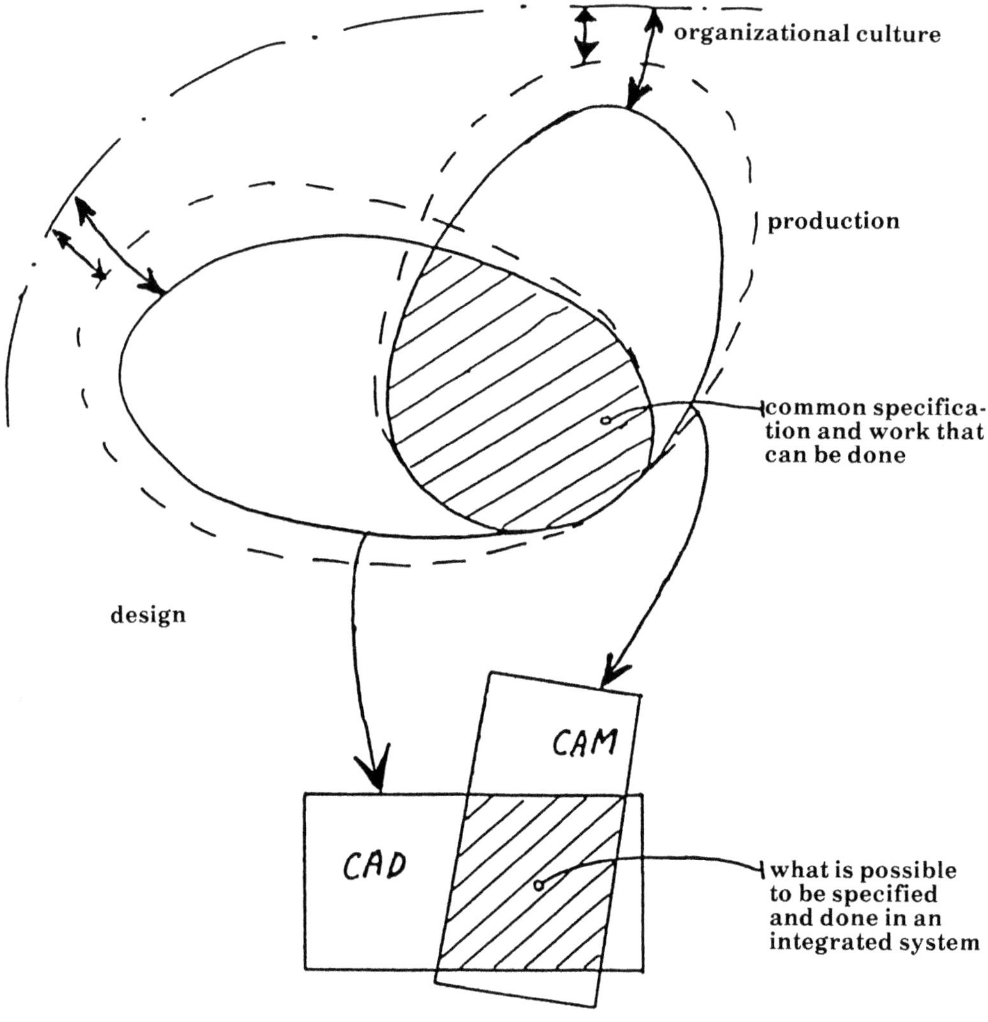

Figure 3: Constraints on integration

Our point of view is that there is more than one solution when transforming skills into system knowledge. Existing skills (and tacit knowledge) and the social context are very important. A high degree of social integration would stimulate the CAD- and CAM-people to find better solutions.

As a matter of fact, we have discovered a *contradiction. When implementing the integrated plant, the multiple intergrational constraints are increasing and the requirement for cooperation is increasing too, but organizational freedom (latitude) is reduced in these complex systems.*

The question is if and how it is possible to develop user-interface to create a larger degree of organizational latitude for the people involved at both the design and production levels in the plant?

Organizational constraints due to computerized control

In some ways, the new technology still seems to follow traditional Tayloristic principles. The point is that the monopoly on knowledge is the decisive condition of control. As Braverman notes: "... the mental labor is first separated from the manual labor and ... then itself is subdivided rigorously according to the same rule" [2].

Tentatively, the *mental work* outside the shop floor could be divided into three categories:

- *development/analysis-work*
  This kind of work is very difficult to formalize and structure. Several attempts have been made to invent methods to control this work (e.g. 'structural design' [3]), but until now no one has yet succeeded in doing so.
- *specification work* (more general than detail design)
  This kind of work is more predictable and to some extent possible to rationalize and automate (e.g. CAD/CAM).
- *Control work*
  This kind of work is also possible to rationalize (Tayloristic methods) and automate (edp, CAP, CIM, etc.).

But though the fundamental principle guiding Taylor in his development of methods still seems to be in force, the concrete strategies have certainly changed a lot. The following figure 4 illustrates some of these changes.

The "ideal" of management is to control the shop floor directly by means of the computer systems. In the system-oriented strategy, control of the shop floor is computerized, because management tries to avoid uncertainty (marketing experience, KOTTLER [4]) and perceives machines as more reliable than human beings. The 'ideal' is to get as much interaction in the organization computerized as possible.

THE OLD "TAYLORISTIC" CONTROL CONCEPT AND STRATEGY

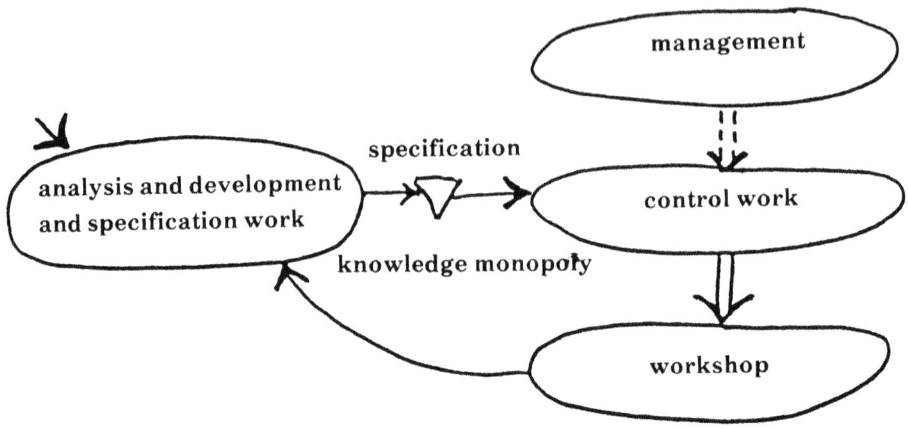

THE NEW "IDEAL" SYSTEM-ORIENTED CONTROL CONCEPT AND STRATEGY

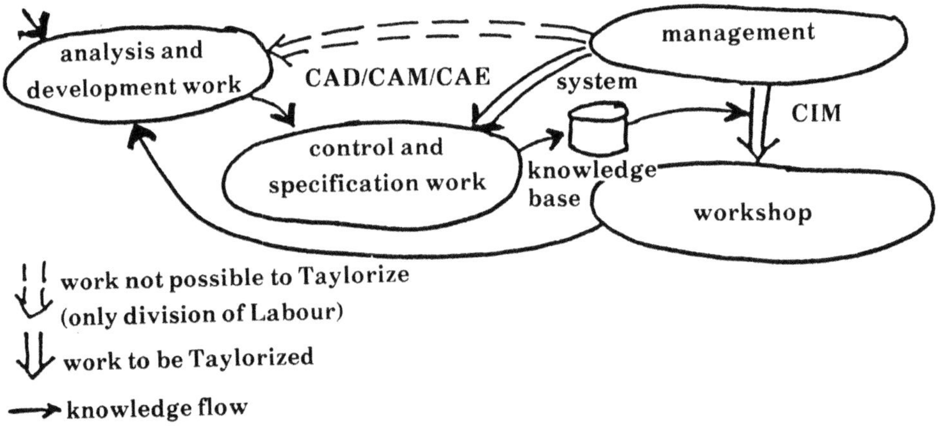

Figure 4: Alternative control concepts and strategies

The differences of the two approaches are sketched in the following table:

Approaches	Traditional Tayloristic Concept	New System-concept
Objective	effective parts	effective cooperation (less lead time and store)
General principle	differentiation	integration
Management principle	management of control	management of cybernetics
Model of human being	effective parts (machine part model)	adapted parts (gear wheel model)

Management of cybernetics is to be considered in a more narrow sense than management of control. The two approaches are complementary in a dialectic context. Though the system concept is still dominated by the Tayloristic principle of centralization of knowledge and power, there are important differences in relation to the traditional Tayloristic strategy.

The system concept is used to systemize and formalize further parts of mental work, especially control and specification work. People outside the system core are considered only as an appendage to the system.

The temptation for management to computerize control nevertheless runs the risk of imposing unforeseen constraints on organizational latitude. *Our hypothesis is that pressure of this kind seems to be heaviest on the control and specification part of the mental work and less on the development/analysis work. But even the last-mentioned work is also influenced to a certain degree, which may* destroy vital elements of the peculiarities of the *design work*. We are going to discuss this more in detail in chapter 3.

How to oppose the constraints?

As mentioned, two types of constraints seem to follow the implementation of integrated computing at the organizational level: integrational and computerized control constraints.

There are at least two ways of overcoming these constraints.

The first way is to systemize and formalize the organization and different sorts of knowledge even more than at present. Besides this, to develop more 'technically advanced' systems. But this strategy still seems to be contradicted by the kind of mental work, at least in the design process and skilled part of the production level.

The other way is to develop and use systems which are capable of assisting the peculiarities of designers' and skilled workers' knowledge.

A step in this direction may be to change the strategy of system development as illustrated in the following figure:

Strategy of Current Technology, Large Degree of Latitude

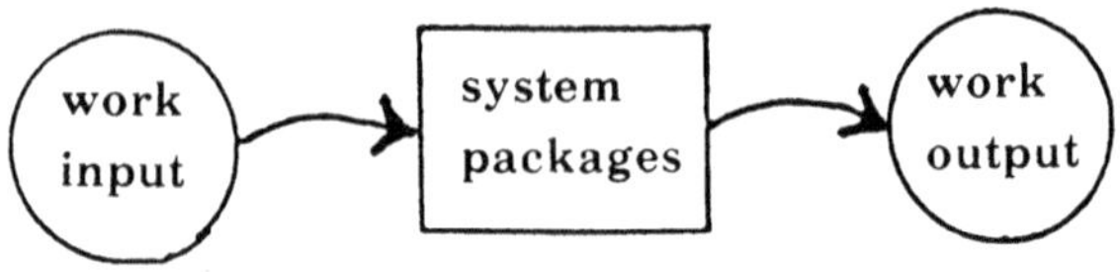

Strategy of Alternative Technology, Large Degree of Latitude

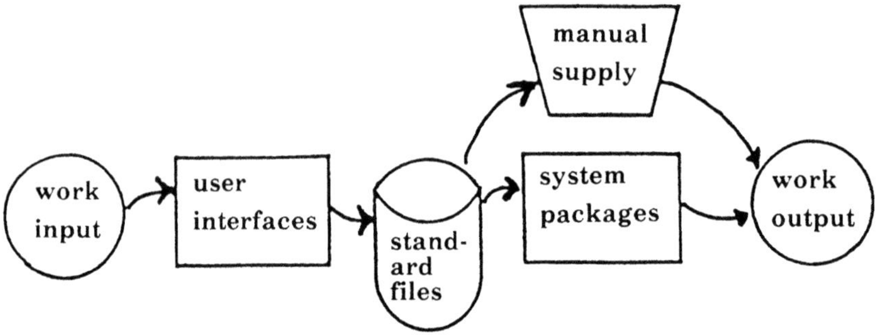

Figure 5: Alternative technology strategies for a large degree of latitude

Instead of developing completely new packages (CAD/CAM, CIM etc.) - which may require several hundreds of man-years - we suggest the following strategy: Try to open up the closed ends of the existing system of software packages by designing interface-software packages. This strategy may be much less expensive and still make it possible to utilize human knowledge and skills in a much more flexible and active manner.

The Technological Institute has succeeded in developing an alternative concept for a new drawing machine enabling the transfer of graphical data (IGES-standard) to the computer system. After the creative process, the drawing board is set to input mode. The basic geometry which is required for transfer to the computer system is drawn. Only very few function keys are used. The drawing is then finished by means of a conventional CAD-system[5].

In order to realize these intentions we think it necessary to get a deeper understanding of the different kinds of knowledge and skills involved in the design process.

The following chapter intends to discuss the concept of tacit knowledge with relation to the design process in more detail.

3. Tacit knowledge and designing

Types of social-psychological accesses to the design process

What is the designer doing when he designs? What should be the ideal working conditions to create the best possible working situation for the designer?

A customary way to investigate the problem is to chart the processes from the start to the end. Several of these flowcharts are available. However, the problem is that such diagrams disguise most of the process, for example, the part which is not obviously visible because it is all in the designer's head, or what the designer cannot/will not explain.

Furthermore, most design problems are *multi-functional* and extremely *interactive*. This property only can be illustrated in a simplified way by flowcharts.

Therefore, you have to ask what the designer is doing in relation to the specific work-conditions. In practice, these two aspects are closely connected. In theory though, we tend to separate them for several reasons. Typically, psychologists focus on the internal mental processes which take place inside the head of the designer, while sociologists and engineers focus on the organization and the technical aspects respectively.

But even within each discipline, there is a surprising amount of disagreement. Psychology holds widely different theories as to how creative thinking is born.

The *Behaviorists* learn to explain thinking solely as a result of direct associative links between stimuli and response. But, when it comes to specifically examining the design process, they have so far only made humble progress.

The *Gestalt Psychologist* has specifically focused on the importance of interpreting the structural relationships of a situation and the ability to reorganize these from various angles, i.e. redefinition of the problem and the applied analogies. They paid particular attention to the way the external world is represented inside our heads.

Some of them (e.g. Barlett, Piaget, Bruner) stress the importance of an internalized mental image, the "Schema". This is thought to be an active organization of past experiences which is used to structure or interpret actual or predict/foresee future problems or events.

The Gestalt Psychologist stresses that human behavior is much more adaptable, unique and complex than the Behaviorists are inclined to assume. As LAWSON (1980) points out the Behaviorists used animals to explain thought, whereas the Gestaltists used animals to show the absence of human-like thought.

Cognitive Psychologists (Neisser, Lawson etc.) build on the Gestalt tradition in many ways. They draw several parallels between thought and perception. They accept the Gestalt theory of information being actively reorganized and reconstructed in memory rather than passively recorded and recalled. Hereby it follows that something must control this process. The executive function has traditionally been denied by both Behaviorists and Gestaltists, but among others, Koestler in his book "Ghost in the Machine" has given this point serious consideration.

Unlike the Behaviorists they are of the opinion that the human being does not only react mechanically to the information received and associate from this. Instead they pick out pieces of this information for closer reflection. Both *primary* and *secondary* processes are postulated as existing in human perception and thinking.

The primary thought process consists of crudely formed thoughts and can be compared with the pre-attentive processes in vision and hearing. They are only brought to our consciousness if chosen against detailed preparation by the secondary processes. It is in these latter processes that all the concrete work is done. These processes depend upon what has already been memorized and the way material has been organized in primary processing.

As mentioned before, Cognitive Psychologists see many parallels between perception and thought. Failure to recall is seen as analogous to a failure to notice something in a visual scene. Thus attention in perception and thought seems important for the direction our thoughts take.

Though these theories are as yet too abstract and underelaborated they, nevertheless, are important as a frame of reference, when you go more into the details of the concept of design. But first we intend to develop more systematically what Michael Polanyi has called "The tacit dimension".

The concept: Tacit knowledge

Tacit knowledge is a concept developed by Micheal POLANYI [6]. We think this concept is worth using to gain a deeper insight into the specific human way of integrating perception, imagination, intuition and logic in the design-process.

Polanyi is clearly influenced by both Gestalt and Cognitive Psychology. He accepts the gestalt point-of-view, that we may know a physiognomy by integrating our awareness of its particulars without being able to identify these particulars. But he also shares the cognitive point of view of an active organization of experiences in the mind during the process of recognition:

> ".. I am looking at gestalt ... as the outcome of an active shaping of experience performed in the pursuit of knowledge. This shaping or integrating I hold to be the great and indispensable tacit power by which all knowledge is discovered and, once discovered, is held to be true" [7].

According to Polanyi all tacit knowledge includes at least three aspects:

- a functional relation
- a phenomenal aspect
- a semantic aspect.

The functional relation means the items' relation to a focal target. That is, the particulars or subsidiaries that we are aware of in the act of focusing our attention on something else. Polanyi also calls it a *from-to knowledge* - a knowledge of them as they appear functionally in establishing the object of focal attention [8].

The phenomal aspect of tacit knowledge means that the coherence may have new sensory qualities not possessed by the sense perceptions from which it is tacitly created. POLANYI exemplified this by the change of appearance which occurs when viewing a pair of stereo pictures transforms them into a stereo image. As opposed to the original pair, the stereo image has a marked depth and also shows firmly shaped "solid" objects [9]. The coherence thus has new sensory qualities.

The semantic aspect of tacit knowing is an act of sense-giving. The subsidiaries do not make sense isolated from each other or from the focal target. On the contrary, the focal target on which they rest is the meaning of the subsidiaries [10].

As seen there are three centers of tacit knowledge:

- the subsidiary particulars
- the focal target
- the knower, who links the particulars to the focal target.

We can think of them as forming a triad. But the knower can dissolve the triad by merely looking differently at the subsidiaries. And we also can paralyze the performance of a skill by turning our attention away from its performance and concentrating instead on the various motions that compose the performance [11].

Polanyi uses this to argue for the existence of two kinds of awareness that are mutually exclusive: a *focal awareness* and a *from-awareness*. That is you can be aware of certain things, either to focus on them directly or to see them as functional parts of a superior target.

Focal awareness is always fully conscious, but from-awareness can exist at any level of consciousness, even at the subconscious level.

Polanyi's thesis of something guiding the active shaping of recognition during the process involves a two- or multi-level structure of higher and lower principles.

He mentions oral communication as including five levels. At the lowest level (1) there is the production of voice sounds. At next higher level (2) these sounds are combined into the utterance of meaningful words. By embedding these words into sentences (3) the words achieve further meaning. In gathering these sentences together into intelligible points (4), you get even further meaning, which the sentences do not have themselves. Finally (5), these intelligible points must themselves be used towards the attainment of the ultimate focal aim of communication [12].

Polanyi's ultimate focal aim is that all knowledge is either tacit or rooted in tacit knowing. Besides he argues that every concept's relation to reality is grounded in personal commitments, which we are unable to specify completely. The reason is that we *dwell* in these basic commitments. Focusing our attention upon them means destroying their subsidiary function. Therefore we cannot spell out this process of tacit integration in explicit steps [13].

Tacit knowledge in the design process

As Bryan LAWSON [14] (1980) points out, design problems are often full of uncertainties. In fact both the objectives and the priorities of these may change during the design process, as the implications of possible solutions begin to emerge.

Many design problems are inevitably value-ladden. In this sense, design problems - like their solutions - remain a matter of subjective perception.

The designer has limited time and resources. Design is often a matter of compromise-decisions made on the basis of inadequate information.

If we look at the design process as a whole, it involves a highly organized mental process, capable of manipulating many kinds of information. Furthermore, these various kinds of information must be integrated into a coherent set of ideas. Finally, the process involves attempts at realizing these ideas in one or the other way.

This design is both a convergent and divergent process.

Convergent thinking will be required as you have to work out the chosen solution of the problem and specify how it fulfills the initial requirements. This is often associated with rational and logical processes.

Divergent thinking will be necessary as design is rarely an optimization procedure leading to only one correct answer. This is often associated with the intuitive and imaginative processes.

Intuition senses the presence of hidden resources for solving a problem and forms our surmises in the course of this pursuit. Furthermore, intuition eventually selects from the material the relevant pieces of evidence and integrates them into a solution of the problem. But intuition cannot work without imagination. And both are highly dependent on the interaction with the world about them. The opportunity to test the ideas, both at the symbolic level and in practice is decisive for the course and the scope of imagination. A closed and preconceived structure may stimulate the imagination much less than an open and experimental, dialogical structure.

As we have mentioned, before, this is one of the risks of using computers in the design process.

Understanding the design process as a whole of both divergent and convergent mental processes, the tacit dimension of this process is vital. The designer as 'the knower' links the 'particulars' to the 'focal target', both in the process of defining and solving the problem. But exactly how he/she does it, is not clear.

Some like LAWSON (1980) even hope, that we:

> "never fully will be able to understand the way designers think, for it is exactly because the designer does not know what he will think next, which makes design such a challenging and satisfying occupation" [15].

Others - like POLANYI - are sure that we never will be fully able to do so, because of the tacit dimension.

In our discussion with designers about their way of working and especially their way of getting good ideas, they often seem to be surprisingly hesitant about describing how they do it. Some of them say that they have a 'sense of spinal cord', which guides them very quickly to limit the possible solutions. Others explain that they try to see the process or even the result in their mind's eye, before they start to work out the solution of the problem at the drawing board or the screen. But exactly how they do it is tacit. In this respect, designing may be related to the handicraft-tradition.

Typically, apprenticeship is traditionally characterized by learning by doing or by showing rather than only by saying. Thomas TEMPTE (1982) has brilliantly illustrated this process with an example from traditional boat-building in Sweden:

> "...When you ask Gösta (the traditional boat-builder) you get a very exact answer. But often not at once. The knowledge is not unconscious or unprepared. But he shows by doing. And during this process he adds small comments. Often he tells a story of a person, who did not do so and therefore was wrong" [16].

The important point is that the transfer of practical skills from one generation to the next in the handicraft-tradition is so closely tied to personal experience, not only with the explicit tool or individual operations, but also with regard to familiarity with materials, the use values of the product and the general set of criteria for "good" work. Much of this knowledge is tacit, guiding the handicraftsman's operations. The same seems to have been, and still is, the case for designers.

Designing with computers

How will the use of computers effect the designer and design-processes?

Bo GÖRANSON (1983) [17] distinguishes between short-term (0-1/2 year after starting point of using computers), medium-term (1/2 - 1 1/2 years) and long-term (4-5 years) consequences.

In the short-term we are typically dealing with technical problems of adaptability of the new system to existing requirements.

The medium-term is related to health- and safety problems (stress, visual problems etc.).

The long-term consequences are related to the change in the way designers use their imagination and logic abilities.

Although we are a bit sceptical about the space of time which GÖRANSON uses to limit the appearance of the three kinds of problem, the distinction between the three seems relevant. In this paper, we will be dealing mainly with the third kind of consequence: the possible change in the mind of designers.

An amazing amount of disagreement exists on how the computer should be used in design.

FRAZER and CONNOR (1978) [18] propose that the computer may be able to play not just the role of calculator, scheduler and checker but also to explore, apparently creatively, possibilities not conceived of by the designer.

Michael COOLEY (1981) [19] fears that the introduction of CAD will produce in design activities similar technical and occupational problems to those which are discernible in the field of skilled manual work, when subjected to technological change (fragmentation, subordination to the machine, further division between creative and non creative components, intensification, limitation of creativity, increased rate of design knowledge obsolescence, etc.) [20].

Cooley finds that the CAD-systems tend to induce passivity and to disconnect the designer from the physical world of machines and equipment and their operational details. The design object is, therefore, increasingly seen in its abstracted, scientific form, rather than in its physical, operation duties [21].

In a broader perspective, this is what Polanyi calls the "modern science-ideal of rigorous objectivity". Following this ideal, all subjective elements should be eliminated or objectified. But if subjective elements are an indispensable part of all knowledge, this tendency results de facto in the destruction of design knowledge, or of the ability to use the knowledge in a reflective way adapted to special or changing circumstances.

Other empirical investigations (FINNE, 1981; WINGERT 1984 etc.) [22] [23] seem to confirm the fears of COOLEY and POLANYI.

In Denmark, the use of CAD-systems is still so new that you cannot observe these tendencies very clearly.

The alternative to FRAZER and CONNER's point of view is then to develop and choose systems which accept the skills and tacit knowledge of the designer and provide them with improved techniques and facilities to exercise their knowledge and skills. The crucial question is then: how much should be left to the *subjective judgment* of the designer? And how much of the design process should be formalized and/or automated?

Following POLANYI, tacit knowledge is bound to subjective judgment. We believe that he is right in his view of the vital importance of the tacit dimension in the design-process. Therefore, the objective of our project is to give suggestions on how qualified subjective judgment could be restored or even improved in the future of designing.

This does not simply mean a quantitative extension of a 'user-friendly' system. The term 'user-friendly' suggests that computers are troublesome machines and that they should be designed and applied in such a way that even the most ignorant person should be able to use them.

The term 'human-centred' is also unfortunate in some respects. It tends to neglect that all technology is human-centred in principle , but differs in relation to where in the power hierarchy the decisive decisions are made. When using the term 'human-centredness', we should not forget the contradictions between various groups and the assymetric relations of power existing in the firm. Nor should we forget that most wage-earner groups lack the knowledge, time and resources to influence technological development in an alternative direction.

If 'human-centred' research overlooks the above-mentioned conditions, it runs the risk of being naive and unrealistic.

Nevertheless, this term is often used as an alternative strategy to secure the subjective judgment of the operator of the machines. Used in this way, naturally, we agree with the intention, although some of the alternative suggestions may be too small in scope to truly deserve the name 'alternative'.

4. Research strategy

How to dwell in the design process?

Since we understand so little about the design process, it may seem foolhardy to attempt a computer-aided design process. How do we use computers in a process that we hardly understand?

In fact, this paradox also explains why computers often function so poorly in connection with creative job functions.

The logical solution of the problem seems to be to investigate the design process more closely. But how? NORDENSTAM (1984) [24] formulates the strategy in the following way:

> "... The objective of the researcher is to help to articulate the already existing tacit knowledge ..., the objective is to change parts of the existing practical (skills) and familiar (close acquaintance) knowledge to theoretical knowledge (declaration)" [25].

But is that possible and is it desirable from the designers' point of view? Is it possible to articulate tacit knowledge without destroying it? And how do we get further understanding if we are not able to articulate it?

We think that it is extremely important to choose the research strategy in such a way that you respect the peculiarity of tacit knowing on the one side and, on the other side, acknowledge that the tacit dimension is of vital importance in design work.

In some ways POLANYI gives a hint on how this could be done.

> "... The fact is, we know other minds by *dwelling* in their acts - as the chess player comes to know the mind of the master, whom he is studying. He does not *reduce* the master's mind to the moves the master takes. He dwells in these moves as subsidiary clues to the strategy in the master's mind, which they enable him to see. The moves become meaningful at last only when they are seen to be integrated into a whole strategy. And a person's behavior, in general, becomes meaningful only when integrated into a whole mind" [26].

Now, chess-playing may be a bad example because it is a relatively closed system compared with most design work. The important point in this quotation from Polanyi is not the specific case: chess-playing, but the concepts "dwelling in their acts" and "meaningful only when integrated into a whole mind".

The objective of the researcher should not be to objectify and formalize these acts, but to show that in some circumstances the attempt at objectification may destroy crucial elements of tacit knowing.

That is, we see it as a primary objective to acknowledge that tacit knowing is still needed and should be given much higher priority than normally is the case, as CAD-systems gain more and more ground.

But which empirical methods are of use for this objective?

The social part of our project intends to use loosely structured interviews to gain deeper insight into the designer's own interpretation of design work. Though a great deal is tacit, we think that it is still possible to get a lot of information from the designers themselves. We assume that we should, thereby, be able to ensure that the tacit dimension influences the course of the design-process. We also assume that a large proportion of the actual difficulties in using computers can be explained by the systems' ignorance of the tacit dimension.

We intend to sketch out suggestions - both at the organization and technical levels - which may improve the physical and social context for the designer to rely on his own qualified, subjective judgment.

This is, for instance, a context which allows quick shifts between divergent and convergent thinking, between imagination/intuition and logic, between holism and detailed analyzing.

Summarizing, the social part of the project will give priority to the following aspects:

- How do designers in various branches and positions experience their own and others' way of designing?
- How conscious are the designers themselves of the tacit dimension?
- How do designers experience the use of computers in relation to their way of thinking?
- What kinds of requirements would experienced designers set for future system-development?
- Which kind of traps should be avoided?
- Is it possible to develop suggestions of contexts that respect the peculiarities of tacit knowing and still use selective developed parts of system-knowledge and the equipment?

5. A preliminary investigation of CAD/CAM use in Danish firms

General background

The following observations are based on visits to about 50 Danish firms of different sizes and branches, mainly concentrated in the metal branch. Since we need to go deeper into the implementation strategy of selected firms, we are only able to sketch some main features of the experience of using CAD/CAM in Danish firms until now.

We estimate that about 250-300 CAD/CAM systems are in use in Denmark at the moment. Most of these are micro-, low-cost or drawing-systems. The size of the firms using CAD/CAM varies from 3000 to 8 persons employed.

As mentioned most Danish firms are only at the beginning of the implementation and adoption of CAD/CAM systems. Therefore, the observed tendencies and experiences may be expected to change in the future.

Different kinds of use of CAD/CAM

Until now we have observed the following ways of using CAD/CAM in the Danish firms:

- as production systems for documentation
- as dedicated systems
- as CAD-tools.

The most common strategy is to use CAD/CAM as a production system for drawing and documentation. The intention is to rationalize the drawing work.

In some big firms we often find a strict division of labor with a special group of employees doing all the CAD/CAM work. This often means a lot of paper communication (as before the use of CAD/CAM). The CAD/CAM draftsmen return drawings to the designer for checking etc.

In other firms, typically smaller ones, the designers produce documentation on the CAD/CAM systems. But the essential design work, for instance the creative process of getting and shaping ideas, still takes place besides the CAD/CAM system. In this case, the designer uses the CAD/CAM system to produce the final documentation, that is as an electronic drawing machine. In reality, the contribution of the system to the essential design process is very modest.

Another strategy is the use of *dedicated systems*. Here the CAD/CAM system is integrated into design work and takes over parts of this work (e.g. in the design of printed boards for electronic circuits). In this case, the CAD/CAM system is doing more than just drawings. It is also used for calculations, optimizations, analysis etc. But the condition is a clearly defined and limited function. It is absolutely necessary to have distinct and unambiguous rules guiding the process. This fact clearly limits the number of functions where it is possible to use dedicated systems.

A *third strategy* is the use of *CAD as a tool*. In recent years, some hundred smaller firms and institutions have bought Micro CAD-systems. This strategy is often rather experimental. The firms intend to gain the possible benefits of knowledge and the use of the technology but they do not have specialized computer staff to deal with it.

Often the designers experiment with the systems themselves. A naval constructor pointed out that he is now using rough drafts from the plotter in the small CAD system. Checking the naval construction etc. was done with the aid of a paper-plot - and not in front of the screen. After working with the plot, he went back and did a better updated drawing on the system (from the drawing to the screen/computer system). You may call this process a man-paper-computer interactive design process.

In some ways, it is a documentation system, but he is not only doing the final documentation on the system. Along the way through the process he is also producing a documentation of his own ideas, sketches etc. But he is himself deciding where in the process the CAD system should be used. He can make use of the system if and when he wants to.

The lack of integration

As in the rest of the Western world, everybody in Denmark is talking about integrated computer systems. Some attempts are being made, some cooperations are taking steps towards systems. *But today it is only data-distribution systems.*

It is a system where computers and equipment are shared (to get cheaper computer systems or distributed computer power). Via local networks etc. the data or programs can be transferred throughout the computer system. *But*, the system is *not* reacting as one integrated system. You have to ask for the data ... as you ask the postman to get your letter.

It is possible to send data directly from design to production through the computer system etc. But this is not done yet, because computer systems are blind to even small errors.

The small firm and human-centred systems

As mentioned previously, designers in small firms seem to have a larger degree of latitude than in big firms. The question is, if the human-centred ideas of qualified, subjective judgment and tacit knowledge have a chance of surviving and even developing in such cases?

At first we wish to specify some characteristics which seem to confirm at least the possibility of such a development. The cases where CAD systems are used as tools are characterized by a decentralized, open and non-integrated computer system.

The designers experiment and play with the system and thereby create their own style of working in front of the CAD system. Often the designer is actively involved in the decision process before and after buying the system. In this process, they learn a lot about the system's capabilities and influence the decision on which programs the firm buys and has installed. In some ways, the designers thereby develop a new CAD based tacit knowledge. Or better: they integrate the CAD system into their total amount of tacit knowledge.

Though these characteristics can be observed in some small firms, it is only half the truth.

The following limitations of realizing human-centredness in full strength may be crucial:

The small firms are very dependent on computer systems existing on the market. They cannot afford the expense of developing their own systems. Their scope of choice is clearly limited by the intentions of the big international producers of computer systems.

Often the small firms are caught by their earlier decisions. They don't have the resources to buy another system. When a system has been purchased they are forced to use it - and get the most out of it. And not to forget: many small firms are very vulnerable towards changes in the market structure, trade conditions etc. Often the daily work of designers is under great pressure just to keep the firm alive or to expand its activities. This time pressure may be a very serious obstacle to playing and experimenting with the computer.

6. Some final remarks and questions

Our preliminary observations of using CAD/CAM systems in Danish firms seem to point to the need for research projects which intend to reflect the possible development and uses of CAD/CAM systems with relation to the different kinds of knowledge and skills of the designer.

If this research succeeds in making the scope of possible technical and organizational solutions more visible, one may hope that the designers themselves could be motivated to be more actively involved in the process of shaping their own work conditions for the future.

The most vital questions seem to be:

- How to conceptualize the constraints of system knowledge in relation to the design process further and in more detail than is done in this paper?
- Is it possible to confirm the hypothesis that constraints are increasing in computer integrated plants which are not dedicated, and how is it possible to overcome these obstacles?
- Is the connection of the Tayloristic and system approach as a new dominating strategy observable in a broader sense with relation to the implementation of computer systems?
- Is it a realistic alternative strategy to open up the ends of the "heavy" systems (software packages) by means of user interfaces?
- Would it be possible to find new ways of combining the drawing machine and CAD systems?
- What kinds of requirements would designers set for future system development?
- What kind of traps should be avoided?
- Is it possible to develop suggestions of contexts that respect the peculiarities of tacit knowing and still use selected developed parts of the system knowledge and equipment?

References

1) "The Future Drawing Office", in Danish. A Danish project of the Danish Council of Technology, Eriksen, E.R. et al., 1984

2) "Labour and Monopoly Capital", Braverman, H., 1974, p. 114

3) Inside the field system development, several attempts have been made to break down and structuralize the system development and establishing division of labour. The latest attempts have been made by Yourdon, E. and DeMarco, T.

4) In the book "Marketing" (1974) the well-known American economist P. Kottler has argued that what the EDP-firms are trying to sell, is not only hardware or problem-solving, but eliminating uncertainties.

5) "Elementary computer science" II (in Danish), 1984, Eriksen, E.R.

6) Polanyi, Michael: "The Tacit Dimension", N.Y. 1966. "Personal Knowledge", N.Y. 1964. Chicago, 1975

7) "The Tacit Dimension", p. 6

8) Polanyi, M.: "Meaning", p. 34

9) Op.cit. p. 35

10) Op.cit. p. 35

11) Op.cit. p. 38

12) Op.cit. p. 50

13) Op.cit. p. 60-61

14) Lawson, Bryan: "How designers think". London, 1980

15) Op.cit. p. 202

16) Tempte, Thomas: "Arbetets ära", Stockholm 1982, p. 88

17) Bo Göranzon: "Datautvicklingens filosofi", Stockholm, 1983, p. 12-13

18) Frazer, J.H./Connor, J.M.: "A conceptual seeding technique for architectural design" in proceedings of PARC 79

19) Cooley, Michael: "The impact of computer aided design on designers and the design process", London, 1981

20) Op.cit. p. 18-19

21) Op.cit. p. 69

22) Finne, H.: Mellom tegnebrett of terminal. Report IFIM, Trondheim 1982

23) Wingert, B.; Duus, W.; Rader, M.; Riehm, U.: CAD im Maschinenbau. Wirkungen, Chancen, Risiken. Heidelberg a.o. 1984

24) In: Göranzon, Bo (ed.): "Datautvecklingens Filosofi", Stockholm, 1984

25) Op.cit. p. 22

26) Polanyi, M.: "Meaning", op.cit p. 48

SELECTED HARDWARE AND SOFTWARE CRITERIA FOR A COMFORTABLE CAD SYSTEM

Karin Spors

RENTACO - Gruppe
Bismarckstraße 17
1000 Berlin 12

1. Introduction

Product descriptions invariably tell us that the system offered is comfortable. This statement may refer to software, hardware or a combination of both. There is no way of telling what is meant.

I would like to present separate criteria for hardware and software which, in my opinion, should be fulfilled by a really comfortable system.

Only the combination of user-friendly software and hardware meeting physiological standards represents a comfortable allround system.

2. Criteria for the software

Programs for design systems must imitate an iterative work process. The use of such a program should not restrict the creativity of the architect.

The program should support the work of the architect in a way that handling the program is not in the foreground.

These requirements may be met only by an interactive dialog program. This dialog should take the form of a human-machine dialog and not vice-versa. Thus, the exclusive use of Y(es)/N(o) statements in a program is not user-friendly and may easily be avoided, as is illustrated in the following example:

Example I: Interactive Dialog using the Program "Wall Input"

machine-human dialog

Wall INPUT Y/N
- Y
PLEASE INPUT DATA
↵ DATA INPUT
DATA CORRECT? Y/N
↵ Y, If program is interactive,
wall will be displayed on monitor
IS THIS CORRECT? Y/N
↵ Y
DO YOU WISH TO INPUT
FURTHER WALLS ? Y/N
↵ Y
and so on.

human-machine dialog (or rather: user-computer dialog)

Selection of routine "Wall INPUT"

↵ INPUT OF DATA FOR 1ST WALL
- WALL IS DISPLAYED ON MONITOR
↵ INPUT OF DATA FOR 2ND WALL
- DISPLAY ON MONITOR
↵ WITHDRAWAL OF LAST INPUT
- LAST WALL IS DELETED FROM MONITOR
↵ INPUT OF DATA FOR NEW WALL

and so on.

After the option "wall input", the user begins directly with input of data for the first wall. The computer reacts and displays the wall on a monitor. Here, the action is by the user and the computer reacts. A wrong input may be corrected with a "delete" function without losing the entire input for the "wall input" section. The user leaves the routine only when he has completed his input. This "interrupt" structure is a requirement for every program.

The dialog should be in the specific language of the architectural profession. A familiar abbreviation such as AVA (Ausschreibung, Vergabe, Abrechnung - Call for Tenders, Ordering, Billing) may be used in the program, but an abbreviation alien to the profession may have a negative effect on comfort. To illustrate this, another example: "The program commands "input GPH", where GPH is the name of a standard graphics module. It means that the disk with program GPH should be inserted into the disk driver and that further instructions should be awaited. The user wouldn't know this. He would ask "what is GPH and where should it be put in ?" It would be a very simple solution to write "Insert program module "GPH" from Diskette 1 into the disk drive." This is an example of the trifles that can cause problems for the user. I have compiled a brief list of criteria to be met by a user-friendly program.

a) The dialog should be in the specific language of the respective trade or profession. If the dialog is in a so-called system language, the user must learn an entirely new language. If the user only works occasionally in this language, he will easily tend to forget it.
b) The program should have the option to interrupt at any point. There are several reasons for this requirement:
   - the choice of the whole program module may have been wrong,
   - there should be an option to leave the program at any point,
   - output lists might have to be terminated before they have reached their designed conclusion.
c) The program should tolerate incorrect input: Incorrect input should not lead to a breakdown of the system. It is extremely annoying for the user when his data are lost due to a system breakdown.
d) The program should make provisions to offset programming errors.
   - Inevitably, all programs include errors, but it is not inevitable that all data be lost after one error. Error messages should be in the user's languages and include instructions on how to return to his first selection. For example, the program should say: "Please press key No. 9 to return to the first selection", rather than:
     "error 19 in line 12345, please don't stop the machine and telephone your software contractor". In this case, the user has no chance of returning to the first selection on his/her own. The software writer cannot expect the user to conduct a time-consuming analysis for the source of his errors. This should be his job.
e) The program should work with a target area for the location of pick points. If the user wishes to add a wall to an existing wall, he must touch the corner of the first wall exactly or there will be a gap between them. If he attempts to find this point with the digitizer, he requires good eyes and even then will not be accurate enough. By defining a target area, it will be sufficient to point roughly to the spot and leave the exact location to the system.

From program descriptions, one would think that this is standard practice - but maybe in the future it will be.

2. Hardware criteria for a physiologically adequate work station

Hardware criteria are the subject of comprehensive discussion, so that I can restrict myself to a brief list:

At a typical CAD work station, the designer may only view his plan in the vertical plane on a static monitor. During conventional work, he may vary the angle of inclination at will.

Computers of the latest generation allow the variation of inclination angles within a limited range. It would be better, if the computer work station were integrated into the customary working plane.

Not like this:

Better like this:

The design of a plan on a monitor is only possible if diagonal screen size is over 69 cm. If the monitor is smaller, the plan is so small one can not recognize all the details. Here, the user may work only with a zoom, but then he has no overview of the entire design.

If the monitor is like this, graphic and character information are superimposed on top of each other. This is not good for clarity.

Here, the monitor is separated into a graphic and an alphanumeric field. If the monitor is of adequate size, it is a real alternative.

In my opinion, the only practical solution is to separate the representation of graphical and alphanumerical information on a monitor each.

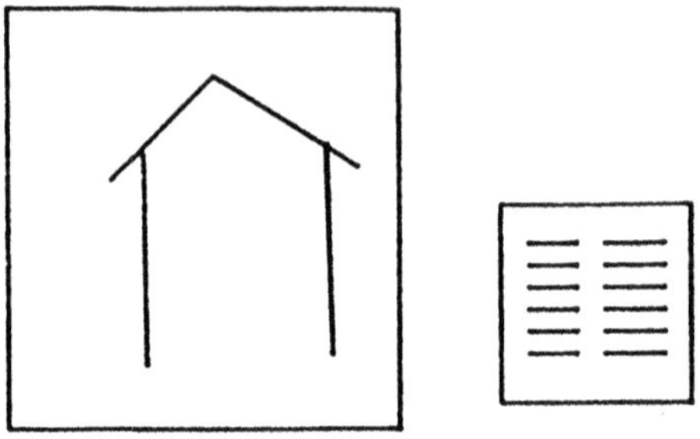

3. The system

The user should have the possibility of using the system without previous knowledge of edp. If it is an interactive dialog program, the user will not know the programming language. However, he does require some knowledge of system language when using peripheral equipment such as plotters etc. For instance he may often be asked "Do you have a V24" (interface)?

Every program should be provided with a manual in the user's native tongue. Everybody having to use one knows the main problem of manuals. Since they are usually written by the software manufacturer, they often do not include sufficient information for the non-expert to use the CAD system on his own. Their correct composition is a subject in its own right.

Control of the program should be possible with or without a digitizer. It is almost a philosophical question whether the user would employ a digitizer or a keyboard for program control. There are arguments for either mode. However, I think it is important that input should be restricted to one mode: either the digitizer or the keyboard. A combination of both forms requires the user to switch input media frequently (thus focusing his attention more on input than on his design task).

The examples described above are but a few criteria for a comfortable CAD system and every user could extend this list. Altogether this would add up to a long catalog of requests for a well-designed CAD-system.

CAD AS MENTAL LABOUR
A THEORETICAL APPROACH AND SOME PRACTICAL CONSEQUENCES

Martin Resch

Institut für Humanwissenschaft
in Arbeit und Ausbildung
Technische Universität Berlin
Ernst-Reuter-Platz 7
D- 1000 Berlin 10

1. What does 'mental labour' mean?

Analyzing the social impact of computer aided design (CAD) requires an idea about what the characteristics of the designer's work are. Many authors have pointed out that the designer performs mental labour and that this argument should influence the social sciences on CAD (cf. BECHMANN et al. 1979, KÜHN 1980, TESCHNER & HERMANN 1981). That raises the question of what mental labour is.

A rather clear idea of mental labour exists. Notions like 'blue collar worker' and 'white collar worker' are commonplace and seem to be precise enough, but it can be shown that they are not sufficient for deeper analysis. BECHMANN et al. (1979) refer to the distinction between 'mental production', i.e. sciences, philosophy, religion, ideology, etc. and 'mental labour'. This distinction seems to be very instructive. The aim of mental labour is to maintain or to improve the production or distribution of material goods. This contrasts mental labour and mental production, but still fails to draw a distinction between manual and mental labour. Some authors define mental labour by saying that it is not manual. However, there is no human work activity which does not comprise any manual parts. Others say that mental labour is information processing (OTTO 1983) or the manipulation of symbols (BECHMANN et al 1979), but these characteristics occur in many work tasks which we would not usually classify as mental labour. Take, for instance, the work task of a printer. Of course, he processes information and, in a way, he manipulates symbols - but this task does not represent what is meant by 'mental labour'.

The problem is that it is on the one hand trivial to say (at least for social scientists) that all work comprises mental and manual components. That means that mental labour has some mental and some manual parts. So does manual labour. But on the other hand the division of labour produces the distinction between mental and manual labour, therefore additional characteristics are required to distinguish between both types of labour. To understand what mental labour is one has to consider its origin. Above all, mental labour is a result of the division of labour. Formerly mental and manual parts had been united in the production of material goods, but with the division the mental processes were separated. To perform these separated processes you need again both mental as well as manual efforts. This is demonstrated in Figure 1. Both types of work result in a material product, but in mental labour the worker produces plans which are executed by *others*. That is the distinctive characteristic of mental labour: to do the planning for other people. In this context planning is used in a wider sense: it comprises all aspects of the regulation of human action, i.e. anticipation of the result, planning of the working procedures, decisions on quality and quantity of production, etc. Formerly, mental labour had been the planning part of a whole work task. Then it became independent as a proper work task of its own.

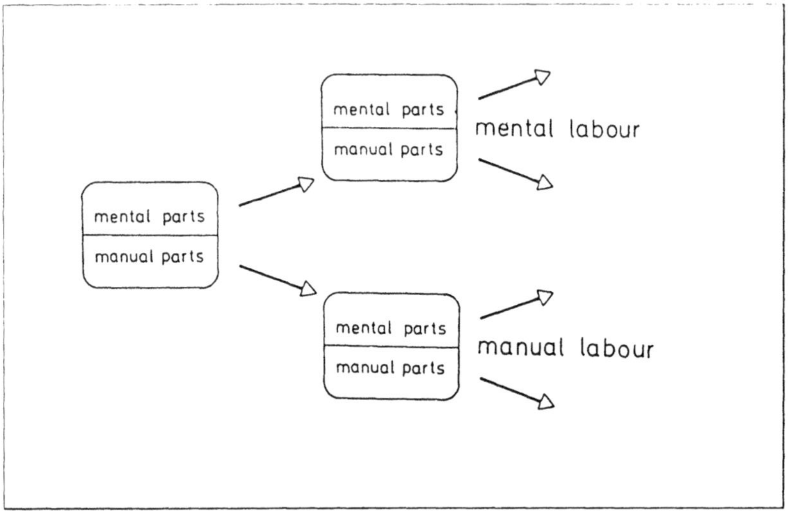

Figure 1: Mental labour as a result of the division of mental and manual parts in work

The division of labour is an ongoing process. Step by step new types of mental labour are being created by separating planning and executing parts in work. If one wants to decide what type of labour a given task is, one has to consider its origins. In general, it can be stated that the division of labour does not totally isolate human functions. Any working task still involves planning and executing processes. That is why I should suggest using the same methods to analyse manual and mental labour. But, first of all, I want to characterize the ongoing change in mental labour.

2. The change in mental labour

Mental labour, too, is permanently divided. The planning processes are again separated from the executing tasks. The means to do so can easily be shown in the design process. Designing is said to be a very creative task. We do not know much about creativity, but it becomes evident how creativity can gradually be eliminated from the design process. Industrial mass production reduces the variability of design tasks. This allows a specialization of the designer. His specialization increases the amount of routine tasks. KÜHN(1980) has convincingly shown that this is the beginning of an increasing formalization of the designer's work. This formalization refers to three components of the design process. There is a difference between the planning processes referring to the design object and those referring to the designer's working process (e.g. EKARDT 1978). These are two separate kinds of planning processes, which can be formalized in a different manner. The design objects are more or less fixed by standards, given ways of calculation, reduced variability of products, etc. If the designer is compelled to use a lot of given standards, the amount of planning and decision making concerning the design object diminishes. Efforts are made even to formalize the planning of the designer's working process, for example by scientific analysis of the design task. This fixation of working procedures is being supported by the hierarchical division of labour. The German system consists of a chief-designer, a designer, a designer for details, a draftsperson, an assistant, etc. The third component subject to formalization is the presentation of the designer's product. Due to the division of labour drawings have to meet a number of given requirements, which have nothing to do with the process and the object of design - therefore the drawing process can easily be entrusted to other workers. If working procedures are extremely formalized they can be written down as an algorithm. Algorithm procedures consist of well-defined working steps. A certain input either leads to a prescribed output or to the end of the procedure (cf. KÜHN 1980, p. 30).

The main question now is: if we consider this process of formalizing working procedures, what happens to mental labour? It has been stated before that mental labour can be characterized as the task of planning for other people. Formalizing the working procedure means that the worker no longer has to produce plans for others. Mental labour will not be changed by formalizing the working processes, it will just be extinguished. If - for example - the work of a designer is totally fixed by forms, standards, etc. he is not performing mental labour any longer. Although his work still includes mental parts, it is no longer his task to do the planning *for others*.

The remaining working steps are mental and manual routines. They can in principle be substituted by machines, i.e. by a computer. This means that a machine or a computer is able to substitute both the mental and the manual parts of a working task. This is the general rule. I want to discuss in the next section how the computer will change the content.

3. The possible change of work content by computer aided design

Thesis about the development of CAD-technology

Before *discussing* the *effects* of new technologies I first want to outline my view of the development of CAD:

In the area of CAD we have to distinguish between short-term and long-term effects. As COOLEY(1973) stated "it is general experience, even where extremely complicated equipment is being designed, that it is at this so-called non-creative design stage that the bulk of development costs are involved, and the greatest amount of project time is required" (p. 18). Up to now CAD is most effective in the production of detailed manufacturing data, e.g. 2 D-drawings, etc. This is the short-term effect.
In the long run the development aims at the integration of CAD and CAM. The division of labour between design office, process planning, shop floor will be affected. The integration is rendered possible by the storage of *geometric data*. This development results in new formalizing processes, which eliminate work tasks.
Whether CAD will be introduced or not is not dependent on the needs of the designer. CAD will be introduced as soon as algorithmic procedures are available.
Just to improve the human-computer interface in CAD-systems does not seem to be the right answer. It could mainly increase the efficiency of the user's performance, while the given work organization is maintained.
More attention should be paid to the possibilities of changing the work organization. Important questions are: How does the division of labour change? Which alternative work organization is possible? Should algorithmic working steps be isolated or integrated into heuristic work?

How to measure the effects on working conditions

The most important consequences of new technologies concern the complexity of work. This dimension of work has a strong influence on the development of personality (e.g. KOHN & SCHOOLER 1983). There are other dimensions of work which are nearly as important, such as mental and physical load. The evaluation of new technologies should start with the analysis of the most important dimension, the complexity of work, but dimensions like physical and mental load should not be forgotten.

'Substantive complexity of work' or 'job decision latitude' can be defined within the frame of the psychological 'theory of action regulation' (see HACKER 1980; VOLPERT 1975, 1982; ÖSTERREICH 1981). This theory implies a general model of the human being. Human action is seen as conscious, goal-oriented and hierarchically - sequentially organized. The hierarchical model of action can be illustrated by a tree-like graph. The top unit indicates a rather general, complex goal. The units one level lower indicate subgoals. The base units consist of the observable sequence of elementary operations (see Figure 2) and are performed sequentially. This is demonstrated by the curved arrows in Figure 2. To reach a certain goal, man must generate such hierarchical, sequentially organized plans. Different work tasks require different amounts of planning. Planning and decision making are called 'processes of regulation' and every working task requires a certain amount of regulation, which we call the 'regulation requirements' of a work task.

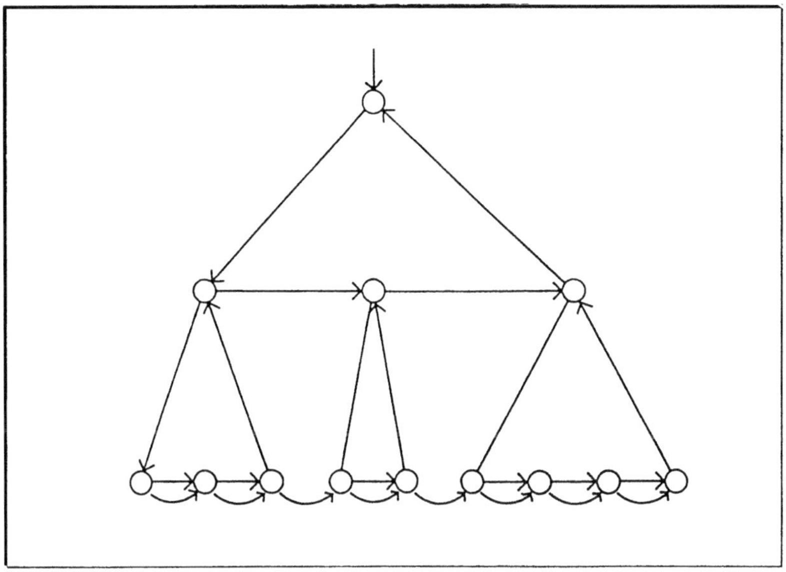

Figure 2: The model of action regulation (from VOLPERT 1975)

We have developed an instrument to measure these regulation requirements (VERA - Verfahren zur Ermittlung von Regulationserfordernissen in der Arbeitstätigkeit, i.e. procedure to assess regulation requirements in industrial work; VOLPERT et al. 1983). With VERA we are able to classify work tasks on a ten-step ordinal-scale based on the five-level-model of regulation by ÖSTERREICH (1981) (see Figure 3). This model can briefly be described as follows:

Level 1: An almost perfectly determined set of work elements are performed. Internal sequence does not change. There is no need to think about the task.

Level 2: The sequence of the work elements changes frequently. The worker has to plan a suitable sequence before he performs the task.

Level 3: The worker must first define a rough sequence of subtasks. Next, he plans in detail and performs on the first subtask. According to the working result he plans and performs the second subtask and so on.

Level 4: The worker has to coordinate two or more separate working processes, each requiring regulation at level 3. Results obtained in one working process influence the planning of the other (and vice versa).

Level 5: The worker has to create a new working procedure with new products. He intervenes in working processes of others.

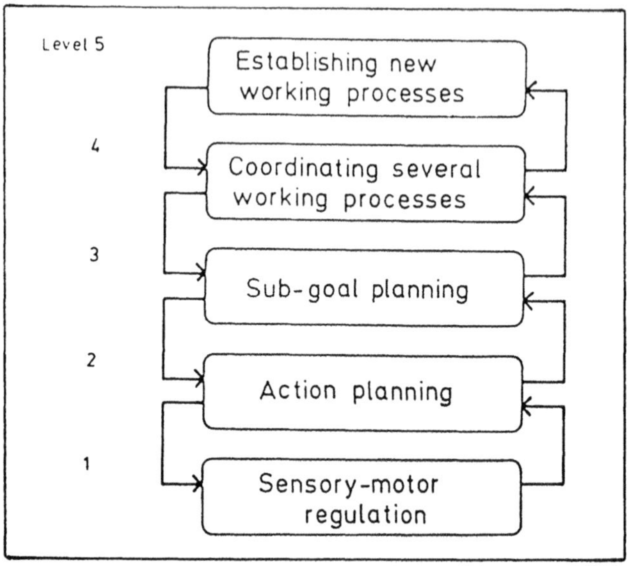

Figure 3: The five levels of action planning in work (by Österreich 1981)

We extended this five-level-model to a ten-step-scale: Each level has an original and a "restrictive form". Restrictive form means that the task does not require original planning at the level in question. The worker must only realize existing plans which are broadly determined either by technology or by instruction. (The restrictive form is marked with an "R", e.g. step 1R, step 2R, etc.).

VERA was first developed in order to classify the tasks of blue collar workers but has recently been adapted to white collar jobs (see e.g. ÖSTERREICH 1986).

How CAD can change the individual working task

One can take different points of view in trying to evaluate technological change. Let us take the case when the new work task can be compared with the former work task of the same person. Judging from the viewpoint of action regulation, the introduction of CAD may alter a work task in three different ways which are shown in Figure 4.

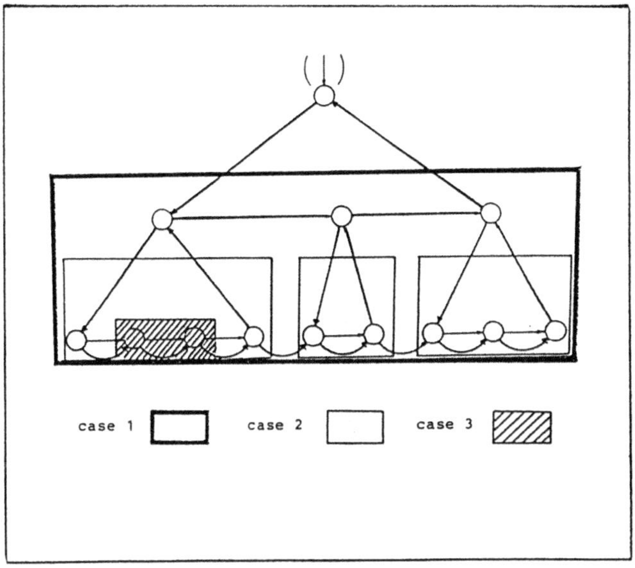

Figure 4: Three cases of working with computers

Case 1:
All parts of the former task are now performed by the computer. If the worker is still needed, his only task is to feed the computer with data. Some CAD-drawing-systems probably function like this.

Case 2:
All the executive operations of the former task are now performed by the computer, but it is still the worker who makes the decision. The computer emancipates him from the routine work, but on the other hand the rate of decisions per unit of time increases. This happens, for example, when CAD is used to design and draw variations of a product.

Case 3:
Only a small part of the executive operations is now performed by the computer. If the computer is a user-friendly one, it can actually emancipate the worker from unpleasant routines. Programs for calculation can be used in such a way.

Many factors determine which of the three cases will be realized. The main factor is work organization, which normally does not exclusively depend on the technological system, the managers' prevalent philosophy being more important. Nevertheless, some technological systems offer more room for alternative work organization than others. The best way to demonstrate this is to evaluate entire structures of work tasks (e.g. in a department) instead of individual work tasks.

How CAD can change overall regulation requirements in the design office

The relation between technological change and work content (i.e. regulation requirements) can be analysed if one examines the regulation requirements of a whole department. There are different ways of analysing the regulation requirements of a structure of work tasks. The usual way is to analyse each work task. The regulation requirements of the whole department then can be displayed in tabulated form. The average of the regulation requirements in the whole department can be computed if each step of regulation requirements is weighted with the relative portion of time. I shall now demonstrate my considerations by giving a fictitious example, which is supposed to explain my ideas, although the model still requires empirical verification. Figure 5 shows the potential distribution of the actual regulation requirements and refers to the following model of a design department:

A design department has nine employees. Six designers, two draftspeople, and one assistant. The characteristics of their tasks are given below in Table 1.

Table 1: Characteristics of Employees' Tasks in a Model Design Department

worker	working task	step of regulation requirements	% of the whole working time in the department
2 designers	designing new parts	4	22.2
2 designers	designing adaptations of known parts	3	22.2
2 designers	designing variants of known parts	2	22.2
2 draftspeople	making the shop drawings	1	22.2
1 assistant	making the parts lists	1	11.1

Next I have chosen a different way of analysis which enables me to show the change in regulation requirements that is brought about by formalization and by the introduction of a computer system. Each working task is divided into several working steps. Of course the work of, say, a designer consists of creative and routine parts. Each working step can separately be classified on the ten-step-scale, as shown in the next table which refers to the same fictitious example.

The potential distribution of regulation requirements is shown in Figure 6. Of course the average is lower now. The Figure indicates the total minimum of required regulations. Even the worst work organization cannot diminish this amount of necessary planning and decisions. The most important question now is: what happens to this minimum if technology changes?

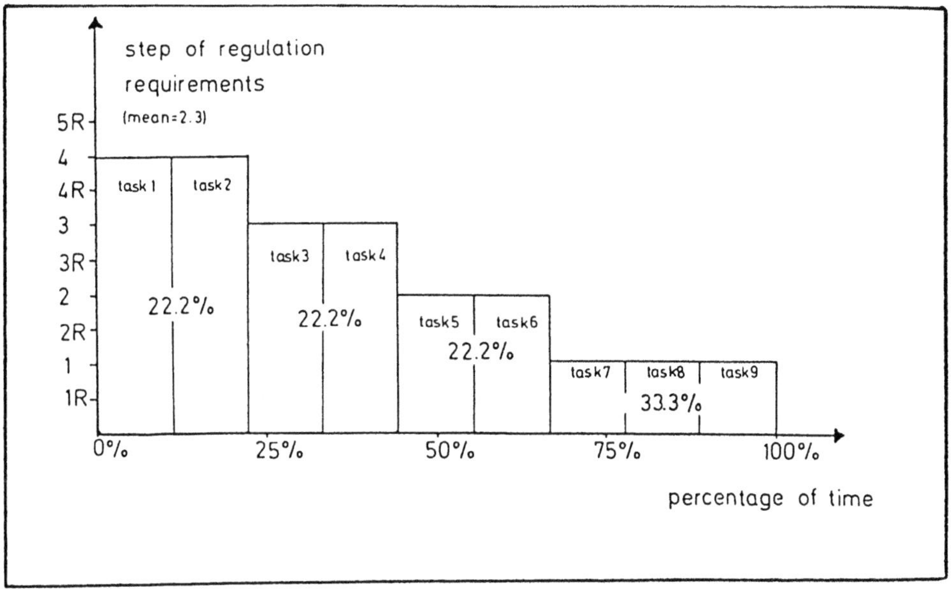

Figure 5: Potential actual regulation requirements in the design department
Note: The average of the actual regulation requirements in the department is 2.3.

Table 2: Ficticious distribution of regulation requirements after the introduction of CAD

Worker	working task	working steps	% of the individual time	step of regulation requirements	% of the whole working time of the department
2 designers	designing new parts	designing detailing drawing	20 60 20	4 2 1	4.4 13.4 4.4
2 designers	designing adaptations of known parts	designing detailing drawing	30 40 30	3 2 1	6.7 8.9 6.7
2 designers	designing variants of known parts	detailing drawing	50 50	2 1	11.1 11.1
2 draftspeople	making the shop drawings	reading the designer's drawing, searching for standards, drawing	10 10 80	1 1 1	2.2 2.2 17.8
1 assistant	making the parts lists	analysing the shop drawing, writing the parts lists	20 80	1 1	2.2 8.9

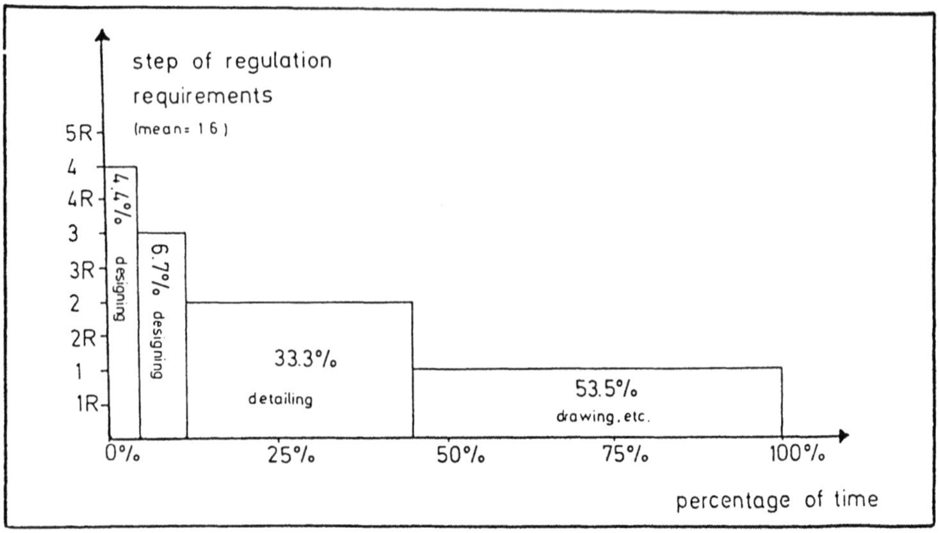

Figure 6: The minimum of regulation requirements in the design department

Further empirical research is required in order to answer this question. I would like to point out that the change in the minimum of regulation requirements - as defined above - is independent of the chosen work organization. Therefore, it is a suitable way of measuring the social impact of CAD.

My hypotheses are that formalization diminishes the step of regulation requirements. On the other hand, the introduction of CAD will reduce the amount of routine work. That means that the overall minimum of regulation requirements increases, whereas the total amount of work needed is reduced. The enhancement of regulation requirements is paid for by the loss of jobs. Increasing overall regulation requirements does not automatically imply that the regulation requirements of one or several work tasks will also increase. That depends only on the *work organization*.

4. Conclusions

Technological change should be evaluated in three steps: In the first place, the change in regulation requirements should be examined. This is the most important step because regulation requirements have a great impact on the development of personality (VOLPERT 1985). Moreover the elimination of regulation requirements is irreversible, if a given task (or e.g. a department) is concerned (see e.g. BEDNARZ et al. 1984). Second, the change in physical and mental load should be examined. In the area of CAD, physical load seems to be of less importance. Mental load can result from working conditions, the special technology or the work organization. An instrument to measure mental load is described in RESCH et al.

(1984) and GREINER et al. (1984). Improving the human-computer interface is one way of diminishing mental load.

Finally, the change in social dimensions should be examined. The most important point seems to be whether work includes the necessity to communicate. A proposal how to assess this dimension was made by ÖSTERREICH & RESCH (1985). Of course it is an important question how many working people must be afraid of losing their jobs. However, this is not a question of work design but of the economic rules in society. Solving this problem is not up to a single factory or branch but to society as a whole.

It was stated before that the most important dimension for the evaluation of technological change is the variation of regulation requirements. It has been shown that the minimum of regulation requirements is determined by the chosen technology. Computer systems should be introduced only if they enhance this minimum.

Apart from that the actual regulation requirements are determined by the work organization. Usually there is a great deal of space to enhance the actual regulation requirements by work design, but in the long run, the minimum regulation requirements will change again. This is due to the fact that the introduction of CAD enables management to share the formalization and standardization between neighbouring departments like process planning or NC part programming. The minimum regulation requirements will decrease again. A reasonable work design must prevent these undesired long-term consequences. There are three ways of attempting this:

a) You can just refuse to introduce CAD. This might not be the worst way but it seems rather utopian.

b) You can try to prevent the separation of routine components from heuristic or creative components. The separation of routine components leads to further standardization and further routine tasks. E.g. you can demand a CAD-system which maintains the traditional sequence of designing. In each phase the computer provides useful help like personal storage (cf. WINGERT et al. 1984), storage of the designer's manual sketches, programs for calculation and simulation, etc. The designer initiates each program and decides when the nest sequence should start. The computer should support the heuristic phases by information, simulation, etc. and perform the routine components. This model claims that the division of labour is almost abolished in the design office, because technology is only a means of supporting work design but not of maintaining it. At present this seems to be the best way.

c) You can try to create totally new structures. CAD supports the integration of different departments, e.g. designing, process planning and NC programming. This is rendered possible by the transfer of geometric data. The new direct link between design office and shop floor can be used to establish working tasks with increased regulation requirements in the design office as well as on the shop floor. It seems to be useful to return some decisions to the skilled metalworker, but this will wipe out the separate job of the process planner. This way runs the risk of eliminating even the need for a skilled metal-worker in the long run. It can accelerate integration instead of controlling it.

References

Bechmann, G., Vahrenkamp, R. & Wingert, B., 1979:
Mechanisierung geistiger Arbeit. Eine sozialwissenschaftliche Begleituntersuchung zum Rechnereinsatz in der Konstruktion. Frankfurt a. Main: Campus

Bednarz, K., Heitmann, G. & Kempin, P., 1984:
CAD/CAM und Qualifikation. Auswirkungen integrierter Computersysteme auf Arbeitsprozesse in Konstruktion und Fertigung. Frankfurt a. M.: Campus

Cooley, M.J.E., 1973:
Computer aided design - it nature and implications. Richmond: AUEW (TASS)

Ekardt, H.P., 1978:
Entwurfsarbeit. Organisations- und handlungstheoretische Ansätze zur soziologischen Analyse der Arbeit von Bauingenieuren im Tragwerksentwurfsbereich. Darmstadt: Technische Hochschule Darmstadt (Dissertation, Photodruck)

Greiner, B., Krogoll, T., Leitner, K., Österreich, R., Resch, M. & Volpert, W., 1985:
Forschungsprojekt "Entwicklung eines Verfahrens zur Ermittlung kognitiver Arbeitsbelastung". 1. Präsentationsbericht an den Projektträger "Humanisierung des Arbeitslebens". Berlin (West): Technische Universität Berlin (Photodruck)

Hacker, W., 1980:
Allgemeine Arbeits- und Ingenieurpsychologie. Psychische Struktur und Regulation von Arbeitstätigkeiten. Berlin (DDR): Deutscher Verlag der Wissenschaften.

Kohn, M.L. & Schooler, C., 1983:
Work and personality. Norwood: Ablex

Kühn, M., 1980:
CAD und Arbeitssituation. Untersuchungen zu den Auswirkungen von CAD sowie zur menschengerechten Gestaltung von CAD-Systemen (=Brauer, W. (Ed.) Informatik-Fachberichte, Band 32). Berlin (West): Springer Verlag

Österreich, R., 1981:
Handlungsregulation und Kontrolle. München: Urban & Schwarzenberg

Österreich, R., 1986:
Veränderungen von Arbeitsinhalten durch Rechnereinsatz. In: Nullmeier, E. & Rödiger, K.-H. (Ed.) Dialogsysteme in der Arbeitswelt. Berlin (West): De Gruyter (in prep.)

Österreich, R. &Resch, M.G., 1985:
Zur Analyse arbeitsbezogener Kommunikation. Zeitschrift für Sozialisationsforschung und Erziehungssoziologie 5, pp. 271-290

Otto, P., 1983:
Voraussetzungen der Automatisierung von Hand- und Kopfarbeit. In: Sonntag, P. (Ed.) Die Zukunft der Informationsgesellschaft (= Harms, J., Leipert, C. & Sonntag, P. (Ed.) Arnoldshainer Schriften zur Interdisziplinären Ökonomie). Frankfurt a.M.: Haag und Herchen, pp. 142-165

Resch, M., Volpert, W., Leitner, K. & Krogoll, T., 1984:
Regulation requirements and regulation barriers - two aspects of partialized action in industrial work. In: Martin, T. (Ed.) Design of work in automated manufacturing systems with special reference to small and medium size firms. Proceedings of the IFAC Workshop,

Karlsruhe, Federal Republic of Germany, 7-9 November 1983. Oxford: Pergamon Press, pp. 29-32

Teschner, E. & Hermann, K., 1981:
Zur Taylorisierung technisch-geistiger Arbeit. In: Institut für Sozialforschung (Ed.) Gesellschaftliche Arbeit und Rationalisierung. neuere Studien aus dem Institut für Sozialforschung in Frankfurt a.M. (= Leviathan Sonderheft 4). Opladen: Westdeutscher Verlag, pp. 118-135

Volpert, W., 1975:
Die Lohnarbeitswissenschaft und die Psychologie der Arbeitstätigkeit. In: Groskurth, P. & Volpert, W. Lohnarbeitspsychologie. Berufliche Sozialisation: Emanzipation zur Anpassung. Frankfurt a.M.: Fischer Taschenbuch, pp. 11-196

Volpert, W., 1982:
The model of the hierarchical-sequential organization of action. In: Hacker, W., Volpert, W. & von Cranach, M. (Ed.) Cognitive and motivational aspects of action. Amsterdam: North-Holland Publishing Company, pp. 35-51

Volpert, W., 1985:
Work and personality development from the viewpoint of the action regulation theory. Paper prepared for the "International Symposium on Learning Processes in Workplace" Stockholm, September 17-19, to appear in: Leymann, H. & Kornblum, H. (Ed.) Learning processes in workplaces (in prep.)

Volpert, W., Österreich, R., Gablenz-Kolakovic, S., Krogoll, T. & Resch, M., 1983:
Verfahren zur Ermittlung von Regulationserfordernissen in der Arbeitstätigkeit (VERA). Handbuch und Manual. Köln: Verlag TÜV Rheinland

Wingert, B., Duus, W., Rader, M. & Riehm, U., 1984:
CAD im Maschinenbau. Wirkungen, Chancen, Risiken. Berlin (West): Springer Verlag

CAD/CAE: ANALYSIS OF TECHNOLOGICAL INNOVATION WITH SPECIAL ATTENTION FOR THE CONSEQUENCES AS TO THE QUANTITY AND QUALITY OF LABOUR

Annick Clauwaert, Jan Huys, Paul Berckmans
Sociaal-Economische Raad von Vlaanderen
Foundation Technology Flanders
Antwerp Tower, De Keyserlei 5
2018 Antwerpen

1. Introduction

This research project forms part of the first STV-research program, commenced at the very end of 1984. The staff comprises an engineer and a social scientist, attended by a project leader, who is also a social scientist *). The final research report may be expected in August 1986.

The motivation for this subject of research is sixfold:

- Within the framework of the "new industrial revolution", CAD is considered to be one of the most promising innovations, its introduction being one of the decisive steps towards the final integration of the different parts of the production process by means of the computer.
- Although the initial celebration a few years back of the explosive growth of the CAD-market has failed to prove entirely appropriate, this new technology none the less is slowly but firmly progressing throughout industrial society.
- CAD, as a technological phenomenon, in Flanders still being limited in its diffusion enables one to study its introduction and consequences as a totally integrated project.
- The introduction of CAD implies the automation of an aspect of the production process which has, so far, practically been spared any form of technological innovation. As a matter of fact, the technical means by which design and drafting work until not so long ago were carried out, have essentially remained the same throughout many decades.
- Besides that, CAD directly affects the group of highly qualified personnel, and it is very much the question how this new technology will affect these qualifications. Will CAD take over routine tasks and enable the designer to employ more fully his creative skills, or will, on the contrary, the design and drafting process be partially automated, reducing man to a mere element in a predescribed logical scheme?
  It might be naive to assume that the Tayloristic principle of organization will stop at the door of the design office, and thus avoid a repetition of the problems which affected blue collar workers when confronted with automation of the production process!

---

*) Respectively: Mrs. A. Clauwaert, Mr. J. Huys, Mr. P. Berckmans

- Finally, we have not been able to track down any study, carried out in Belgium, concerning the social implications of CAD. It is high time, taking into account the expected expansion of CAD-technology, to have a better view, supported by scientific facts, on this field of technological innovation.

2. A research project in 3 stages

The research project can broadly be divided into three stages.

During the first stage an attempt was made to get a fairly accurate overall picture of the diffusion of CAD/CAE in Flemish industry. For this purpose a short, written survey was held amongst some 700 companies in Flanders. The second stage was devoted to a more thorough "X-raying" of those companies which appeared to make use of CAD/CAE-systems. This was carried out by means of a structured questionnaire, partly written, partly oral. At the time of writing, the results of this enquiry are being processed. In a third and final stage it is our intention to select, from the group of CAD/CAE-user companies, a few relevant, representative cases which will be involved in detailed case studies. The latter should enable us to analyze more thoroughly eventual quantitative and qualitative shifts caused by the introduction of CAD/CAE. The first two research stages, however, should provide the base for a justified "generalizability" of the results from the case-studies.

Apart from this research work which is focused on the "CAD/CAE-users", we also intend to take stock of those companies which can be classified as "CAD/CAE-producers". In order to get a more shaded view of the quantitative shifting in employment caused by CAD/CAE, the eventual positive employment effects, due to the production and distribution of software and hardware, were tracked down by means of a written survey amongst these "CAD/CAE-producers".

Stage 1: An enquiry on the use of CAD/CAE in Flanders

Organization and purpose of the enquiry

The enquiry was designed as a "directed search" for those companies in the Flemish region, which make use of CAD/CAE-systems. It was our intention to obtain a rapid and accurate overall view of the diffusion of CAD/CAE in all industrial sectors. The adjective "directed" stands for the method by which the companies to be contacted were selected. Since it was hardly realistic to try to question all Flemish companies as to their eventual use of CAD/CAE-systems, we selected some 700 companies on the basis of size and industrial activity. These companies were approached with a short, written enquiry in terms of "Do you have ....", "Operational or experimental ...", "If you don't, will you in the near future...".

In an accompanying letter we tried to clearly define our field of interest, by explicitly quoting our description of CAD/CAE, a "working definition" which is also our guideline throughout the whole research project:

"CAD includes every system by which the conventional drawing and design work, carried out by a designer, draughtsman or related qualification, is supported or replaced by a computerized drawing and design process".

"CAE includes the execution of 'engineering tasks', such as testing, simulations, calculations, planning, etc.... with the help of an extensive, graphically based computer-system".

Let it be noted that our definition embraces both "computer aided drafting", a simple automation of the drafting work, as well as "computer aided design", the more sophisticated support system for design work.

Computer aided design and computer aided engineering being closely related and - in some sense - overlapping notions, and taking into account the confusion of thought in this field, we decided to unite both notions into one: CAD/CAE, this being our ultimate field of interest.

It should be mentioned that we deliberately do not take into account the "CAM" part of CAD/CAM, although the division between CAD and CAM is sometimes difficult to make.

Results

A total of 691 companies were approached with a mailed questionnaire. The response rate was 60 %. In this way and via information provided by other sources, the number of CAD/CAE-using companies - the use of CAD/CAE being in an operational stage - amounts to 81. Table 2 divides these CAD/CAE-users between sectors and company size (number of employees). Architecture and civil engineering firms being a somewhat special case since they do not include production activities, are tabled separately (cf. Table 1 below).

Table 1: Architecture and civil engineering firms

size	arch. & civ. eng. firms
0 - 10	-
10 - 20	4
20 - 50	2
50	1
not known	3
	10

Table 2: CAD / CAE users, division between size and sector of industrial activity

Sector \ Size	0 - 99	100 - 199	200 - 499	500 - 999	1000 or more	unknown	total
Electricity, electronics	4	-	6	3	5	2	20
Other metal working industry	-	5	1	6	6	-	18
Clothing industry	1	6	6	2	-	-	15
Building trade	-	-	2	3	-	-	5
Automobile industry	-	-	-	-	3	-	3
Textile industry	-	-	-	1	1	-	2
Ship-building	-	-	1	-	1	-	2
Other chemical industry	-	-	-	1	1	-	2
Wood-working industry	-	-	-	1	-	-	1
Pharmaceutical industry	-	-	-	-	1	-	1
Plastics, rubber industry	-	-	1	-	-	-	1
Others	-	-	-	-	-	1	1
total	5	11	17	17	18	3	71

To this list, however, have to be added a number of companies which do not individually possess (a) CAD/CAE-system(s), but which have established so-called "CAD-co-operative societies". A "CAD-co-operative" numbers up to 5 participating companies, which make use of and pay for the CAD-infrastructure on a time and cost sharing basis.

Adding these 24 companies, which are all part of either the textile or the clothing industry, to the 81 individual CAD/CAE-users, a total number of 105 CAD/CAE-users is obtained.

We want to point out the fact that - at least in the Flemish part of Belgium - the clothing industry is the leading CAD/CAE-using industry, in terms of the number of companies involved. However, this does not automatically imply a similar preponderance in the number of CAD/CAE-systems installed, nor in the number of people working with and affected by

CAD/CAE. It is in fact the sector of electricity and electronics which can claim leadership in both cases.

Table 3 illustrates the novel character of this technology, by distributing the individual operational CAD/CAE-users by years of introduction of the system(s).

Table 3: CAD/CAE-users: Year of introduction

Year	Number of Companies
1976	1
1977	1
1978	0
1979	7
1980	3
1981	3
1982	14
1983	16
1984	18
1985	13
not known	5
	81

In addition to the 105 "operational CAD/CAE-users", 22 companies have installed (a) CAD/CAE-system(s), but have not yet introduced it (them) into the everyday activity of the drawing office. These "experimental CAD/CAE-users" are listed below (Table 4).

Table 4: Experimental CAD/CAE-users divided between sector of industrial activity

Sector	Number
Electricity/electronics	1
Automobile industry	2
Other metal working industry	9
Plastics/rubber industry	1
Other chemical industry	1
Archit. & civil eng. firms	5
Building trade	1
Textile industry	1
Clothing industry	1
Total	22

When questioned on their involvement in CAD/CAE, a group of 30 companies replied, that they were planning the introduction of CAD/CAE within the next year (Table 5).

Table 5: New CAD/CAE-users within one year; division between sectors of industrial activity

Sector	Number
Electricity/electronics	9
Other metal working industry	10
Building trade	3
Archit. & civil eng. firms	2
Plastics/rubber industry	2
Pharmaceutical industry	1
Textile industry	1
Clothing industry	1
Wood working industry	1
total	30

Summary

At present, at least 105 companies are actually working with CAD/CAE; within one year this number will have increased to 157. These companies are predominantly located in 3 sectors of industrial activity: metal working, electricity/electronics and clothing. CAD/CAE can be found in small companies as well as in very large ones. The introduction of CAD/CAE in Flemish industry is, save some exceptions, of recent date.

Stage 2: The CAD/CAE-users reviewed

The second stage in this research project was dedicated to "X-raying" the 105 operational CAD/CAE-users. This was carried out by means of extensive questioning in each company, partly in the form of a written questionnaire, partly through a more elaborate oral interview. A standard procedure was applied to all participating companies, although the contents of the questionnaire varied slightly according to the type of company: architecture and civil engineering firm (no questions on the products and production process), CAD-co-op member (additional questions on the organization of work in the co-op) and "conventional CAD/CAE-user" (the standard group).

The raw material of this inquiry is at present still being processed, so definite statements cannot be given on results or tendencies. However, it may be interesting to give a brief outline of the topics dealt with in the questionnaires.

3. Topics dealt with in the questionnaires

Organization of work - mechanization/automation

The definition of the topics to be studied and the formulation of the ensuing questions was carried out on the basis of a literature review on foreign social science work in the field of CAD/CAE.

Proceeding from this review, a number of hypotheses have been formulated as to the possible effects of CAD/CAE on the quantity and quality of work. Some of these hypotheses are elaborated below.

Starting-point is the recurring drive for rationalization, which is a co-responsible factor for the introduction of new technologies into a company. The advances, which are daily being made in the field of electronic data-processing, have triggered the evolution of this rationalization process into a new stage: the "industrialization of the non-material production process".

A number of intellectual jobs such as planning, design and coordination are increasingly affected by this technical evolution and are directly linked with the tangible needs of the material production process. As a result, these jobs lose their independent character and are absorbed into an overall efficiency-strategy. The final aim of this process is C.I.M.: "Computer Integrated Manufacturing", i.e. the complete integration and linkage of the various "computer aided domains" in the company. At present, this tendency is in reality restricted to the establishment of "islands of automation", the links with other "domains" not yet having been made.

One of those "islands of automation" is the area covered by CAD/CAE. The question arises which concrete form the drive for rationalization assumes in this CAD/CAE-area and which are the consequences for employment and quality of work. Rationalization usually assumes two concrete forms: either by acting upon the work organization and/or mechanization and automation. Applied to CAD/CAE, this means the way in which design and drawing work is organized and the potential and limitations of the CAD/CAE-system. In consequence, both aforesaid aspects are carefully examined in the enquiry.

It should be mentioned that work organization and mechanization/automation cannot be considered two independent phenomena; there is mutual influence and interaction which makes it all but impossible to separate both subjects.

Management policies in relation to CAD/CAE

The type of the CAD/CAE-system and the nature of the work organization in the drawing office are the result of the so-called management policy towards CAD/CAE, the term "policy" covering a series of decisions resulting from choices to be made. The extent to which there exists a freedom of choice as far as this CAD/CAE-policy is concerned, depends on the weight of a number of determining factors of this policy.

The following factors can be quoted:

1. *Economical situation of the industrial sector and of the company itself*

On the one hand the introduction of CAD/CAE implies, especially in the case of small companies, a considerable investment; on the other hand the competitiveness of the company may, in the long run, be improved by it.

2. *The nature of the production process*

Not all types of industrial activity are suitable for the application of CAD/CAE.

3. *The structure, in particular the qualification structure, of both the internal and the external labour market*

The qualification structure of available manpower can considerably determine the structure of work organization for the new technology.

4. *Management strategy*

Is it based on a cost-benefit analysis in the short or the long run?

5. *The social and power relations within the company*

e.g. possible resistance to technological innovation; the negotiation strategy of trade unions and works councils; the awareness and militancy of the personnel involved in the introduction of new technologies; the employment and personnel policy pursued by the company.

6. *The existing organization of work*

7. *The extent to which computerization has already penetrated into the company*

8. *The hardware and software market*

The selection of a CAD/CAE-system is co-influenced by the market supply. The producer thus indirectly shapes the form of work organization, the latter indeed being influenced by the structure of the CAD/CAE-system. However, the producer's influence should be considered relative, since the needs and requirements of the clients prevail in the construction of the product (i.e. the CAD/CAE-system).

As far as a standardized questionnaire permits, the above mentioned factors are being touched upon, taking into account the objective, non-interpretative character of the data to be obtained. A more complete analysis of the management policy will be conducted at the next research stage, in the form of case studies.

These factors - which are, by the way, not independent of each other - influence to a greater or lesser extent management policy on CAD/CAE.

The smaller this influence is, the greater is the number of degrees of freedom in the choice-making processes, hence entirely different results can occur. As a consequence, the introduction of CAD/CAE in similar environments does not necessarily result in similar effects. One of the aims of this research project is to trace the possible choices and to predict the consequent, most probable effects on various aspects of labour conditions.

Bibliography - *Only references as to the work hypotheses are listed below*

Angermaier, M.; Burr, M.; Weber, U.:
Rechnereinsatz in der Konstruktion (CAD). Technologieberatungsstelle beim DGB Landesbezirk NRW, Oberhausen, 1983, 104 pp.

Arnold, E.:
Computer-Aided Design in Europe. Sussex European Paper, No 14, Sussex European Research Centre, University of Sussex, 1984, 69 pp.

Burr, M.:
CAD-Systeme. Entscheidungshilfen für Auswahl und Gestaltung. Weiterbildungszentrum, Ruhr-Universität Bochum, 1984, 375 pp.

Cooley, M.:
Computer Aided Design - Its Nature and Implications. A.U.E.W., London 1972.

Encarnacao, J.; Schlechtendahl, E.G.:
Computer Aided Design. Fundamentals and System Architectures. Springer-Verlag, Berlin 1983, 318 pp.

Kühn, M.:
CAD und Arbeitssituation. Untersuchungen zu den Auswirkungen von CAD sowie zur menschengerechten Gestaltung von CAD-Systemen. Informatik-Fachberichte, Springer-Verlag; Berlin-Heidelberg-New York 1980, 215 pp.

Fraunhofer-Institut, Karlsruhe:
Die sozialen Auswirkungen der Integration von CAD und CAM. Teilprojekt I: Technische Entwicklung, Diffusion und betrieblicher Einsatz von integrierten CAD/CAM-Systemen. Fraunhofer-Institut, Karlsruhe, 1983.
Teilprojekt II: Wirtschaftliche und soziale Auswirkungen des Einsatzes von integrierten CAD/CAM-Systemen. Institut für Sozialforschung, Frankfurt a.M.

Margulies, F.:
Is there space for human design of production - technologies and what factors are determining the use that is made of the space available? Workshop on technological choice; Den Haag, 26-27 maart, 1984, 15 pp.

Poitou, J.P.:
Les conséquences psychologiques et sociologiques d'une nouvelle form d'informatisation: les techniques de conception assistée par ordinateur C.A.O., 114 pp. Groupe d'Etudes des technologies, idéologies et pratiques, CREPCO, Université de Provence (Aix-en-Provence).
L'évolution des qualifications et des savoir-faire dans les bureaux d'étude face à la conception assistée par ordinateur, in: Sociologie du Travail, No 4-85, 14 pp.

Appendix: Stichting Technologie Vlaandern (STV)
- Foundation technology Flanders -

As a consequence of a decision within VESOC (Flemish Economical and Social Consultation Committee), the Foundation Technology Flanders was constituted in July 1984.

In the meantime the STV has become operational within the structure of the "Sociaal-Ecomomische Raad van Vlaanderen" (Social Economic Council of Flanders).

Among the tasks assigned to the STV, i.e. the establishment of an information and documentation center on social aspects of technological innovation, the coordination of research in this field, the formulation of policy advice, the support of social partners, the diffusion of results of research projects and the execution of social research programs, the last mentioned has, until now, been the focal point of activity.

A first - limited - research program, started at the end of 1984 and has recently been followed by a more extended one spanning the field of social scientific research on technological innovations. Plans for the near future include the diffusion of research results in a - to the public - more accessible form and a further extension of the documentation center.

One of the intentions of STV being the multidisciplinary approach to social phenomena related to technological innovation, the current research staff includes members from various disciplines such as social sciences, economics, engineering and pedagogy.

PSYCHOSOCIAL FACTORS IN CAD/CAM RESEARCH AND DEVELOPMENT ACTIVITIES

Information about a research project

Ann Kjellberg

Royal Institute of Technology
PS-Lab IVF/KTH
Midskogsgränd 5
S-100 44 Stockholm

1. Introduction

This paper is aimed at providing information about the psychosocial research work in a technical research group in the program for Design and Planning, sponsored by the Swedish Board for Technical Development. The work is carried out at the Unit for Computer Aids in Production at KTH. Identification of psychosocial factors of importance for work-satisfaction and a systematic consideration of human factors as well as analyzing methods for these are the main aims of the project.

The project is one of about ten projects in a research program aimed at testing and verification of ideas applicable in the future engineering office. It deals with how to raise possibilities for visualisation of basic programming work for 3D solid models of products. It is a project of knowledge developing character.

The technical work is based on the unique possibility of creating 3D solids of products in the computer in an engineering oriented, interactive, graphics dialogue. A so-called complete product model contains also all relevant technical information. This combination gives new advantages which increase the possibilities of understanding and of improving creativity as well as facilitating the information representation of the product in design. The designer interprets these data and transfers his knowledge to other designers and thus the computer supported design situation can be stressed for its importance for communication in a new type of computerized interaction network. Computer aided design questions are good examples of future man/machine-interaction, primarily of interest here because of the 3D modelling possibilities.

2. The research situation

The research situation is unique in the respect that future ways of working are developed in a multidisciplinary way. It was not until quite recently that application programs could be made and thus could verify the obtained level of the technical, programming work. Through development of application programs necessary conditions have been created to study how different representations of 3D models will affect the design process. This can be studied while technical specifications are successively formalized. By doing this, efforts are made in defining a way of working in unique research and development environments. The technical as well as the "social" work will aim at giving Swedish industry an idea of coming technique. It will not result in commercial or ready-to-use-systems but rather hint at possibilities - partly demonstrated in application programs.

The basic ideas for the psychosocial research work as well as its concentration on human problem solving processes were formed in 1978 but they were not put into print until 1982 in a doctoral thesis (KJELLBERG, T.). This interest led to a focus on cognitive psychology and the starting of a complementary project on Psychosocial Factors ..., carried out in our research environment. That work has been guided by Yvonne Waern from the University of Stockholm (the problem solving project).

From our research work, it is obvious that these projects of knowledge developing character have a built-in concentration on the establishment of theories, and the level of abstraction is high. As the application programs which are developed are made for research work, no problems for practical use are yet available. This problem is treated by testing potential users as well as researchers, thus summing up practical difficulties in working. The human factors specialists also have to work with the systems and learn the applications from manuals, as well as from learning by doing and in this way make additions to practical aspects of the work.

3. Research areas and theories in focus

By now about two man-years of work have been devoted to the project. It was prepared by an introductory study of 1.5 man-years work on "Man's role in future manufacturing systems", treating different aspects of automation of the production process, looking at examples of future man/machine interactions. The projects concern communication in research environments as well as communications man-to-man and group-to-group for solving problems in the manufacturing process.

The areas of interest are

- information transfer
- human problem solving activities
- design of new technique

and thus also possible effects on (initial) knowledge levels; creativity; mental processes; perception; mental work load and on the man/computer interface. The work is based on the assumption that overall satisfaction is needed in the working situations that we now are in the process of creating for our future society. The necessary ingredients for making work - satisfaction possible have to be identified! Different ways of attacking the problem of gaining satisfaction have been treated, and finally - for the present - we are now concentrating on the following statement:

- "The existence of problem-solving tasks is crucial for work-satisfaction!"

This was examined in the introductory project and reported in 1983 in a lic. thesis (KJELLBERG, A.).

We thus focus on intellectual processes for design work - often characterized as innovative, creative work!

Some hypotheses and basic principles presenting the designer as a processor of information have been formed and strictly guided the work in the research program for Design and Planning, eg.

- The computer as a work tool should be treated as an "extension of man's arm";
- Man is to be regarded as an information handling system;
- Computer support will affect productivity and quality of human thinking (KJELLBERG, T. 1982).

The following statements will then be essential and require consideration for the work of introducing computer supported work tools in the companies (KJELLBERG, A., 1983):

- IF man is given such tools that performance as well as presentation of work-results are facilitated and the quality of the work-results is essentially enhanced. THEN this will form a good basis for well-being at work.
- Positive, long-term work experience is reached when a good problem-solving situation has been formed (from a cognitive point of view).
- The knowledge of having achieved a good work result, its feedback and controlling possibilities is of greater importance for work satisfaction than many other factors.

For the design situation this means that

- COMPUTER AIDS FOR QUALIFIED DESIGN WORK IN 3D "COMPLETE" PRODUCT MODELS WILL GIVE A SUPPORT, QUALITATIVELY AS WELL AS QUANTITATIVELY TO THE PERSONAL RESOURCES AND CAPABILITIES OF THE DESIGNER. FURTHERMORE THEY WILL HAVE A SIGNIFICANT IMPACT ON WORK SATISFACTION.

4. Practical research work

Lectures and project seminars have been the proper forum for mutual exchange of ideas and information. The applications set-up has been another forum. From these, a long term, strategic development of the future engineering office has been set up.

The practical and theoretical research work has concentrated on applications. Designers, researchers and students have been confronted with the different systems and, in one case, one application study was followed by a company study. The company specializes in the selling of conveyor belts for transportation purposes. The study was carried through from the initial discussions about computer supported aids for lay-out work.

One practical result of the theoretical work is the existence of a framework (doctoral thesis, KJELLBERG, T.) for technical as well as for human factors work. Furthermore, we have achieved such a multidisciplinary way of working that human factors are needed and actively asked for. External contacts are increasing as well as external cooperative work, primarily with the Psychological Department at the Stockholm University in the Problem Solving Project. Problem solving tests, from a cognitive point of view, have been made in the specific Problem Solving project guided by Yvonne Waern.

The Introductory Project dealt with the work contents on the shopfloor for manufacturing in production cells, flow based groups, and in flexible automated manufacturing systems. Also from these studies it can be concluded that a concentration on intellectual processes in the development of the contents of new work tasks proved to be of significant importance in order to achieve long-term work satisfaction!

References

Gardell, B.:
Underload and overload in working life; outline of a multi-disciplinary approach. In: Journal of Human stress, Volume 2, No. 3, 1976.

Kjellberg, A.:
Behavioural research in technical application research. Pedagogical processes in design of new techniques. Information transfer, problem-solving and communication in research work concerning development of automation in production research. (In Swedish). Licentiate thesis. The Royal Institute of Technology, Dept. of Manufacturing Systems, Stockholm, 1983.

Kjellberg, A.:
Computer supported aids for human thinking. (In Swedish). Paper for the conference The Nordic CAD/CAM-days, STF, Stockholm, 1984.

Kjellberg, A.:
Psychosocial factors in CAD/CAM-research and -development activities. Draft to final report in the Research Program for Design and Planning, September, 1985. The Royal Institute of Technology, Dept. of Manufacturing Systems, Stockholm, 1985.

Kjellberg, T.:
Integrated computer aids to support human problem solving and human communication for mechanical production within the limits of product development, production planning, design and planning for manufacturing. A system approach based on product models. (In Swedish). Doctoral Thesis. The Royal Institute of Technology, Dept. of Manufacturing Systems, Stockholm, 1982.

Kjellberg, T.:
The integration of CAD/CAM based on product modelling for better human communication. Paper for the conference Utilization of Artificial Intelligence and Pattern Recognition Techniques in Manufacturing Engineering, Tokyo, 1984.

Kjellberg, T.:
Solid modelling R&D in Europe. Paper from the 1985 European Conference on Solid Modelling, London, 1985.

Kjellberg, T. & A.:
CAD/CAM for engineering problem solving and communication - human engineered systems. Paper for 9th World Congress of IFAC, Budapest, 1984.

Sohlenius, G.:

Integrated computer supported production systems for manufacturing engineering companies - possibilities and objectives. PS-Lab IVF/KTH, Stockholm, 1985.

Waern, Y., Möller, C.:
Problem solving in computer aided design. Draft to final report in the Research Program for Design and Planning, September 1985. The Royal Institute of Technology, Dept. of Manufacturing Systems & Stockholm University, Psychological Dept., Stockholm, 1985.

CHAPTER 3: Implementation of CAD and Training

This session dealt with two aspects of the introduction of CAD/CAM into the firm:

- Implementation, i.e. the action taken after the system has been purchased to enable the productive application in everyday work;
- Training in its various aspects including training of existing staff, reform of vocational training for draftspeople, university training of engineers.

Implementation includes the design of the organization into which the application is embedded and thus the division between this and the next session is to some extent arbitrary.

The chapter includes contributions by Yvonne WAERN on prior knowledge and its effects on learning to use CAD/CAM systems, by Dieter BUSCHHAUS on German plans to reform the curricula for technical draftspeople to come to grips with CAD and by Holm GOTTSCHALCH, who reports on one of three experiments in companies to provide just such training for apprentice draftspeople. On the subject of implementation, there is a paper by MCLOUGHLIN. Marianne FODGAARD's contribution goes back a step further and examines the decision-making process with respect to CAD in the smallish building consultant firms currently on the threshold of establishing themselves as a promising market for CAD systems. She also remarks on the implementation process and on resistance towards technology from people inside the firm.

This session apparently produced little fuel for heated discussion, although some participants felt that the method employed by WAERN and her resultant findings covered only part of the picture. For instance, POITOU found it problematic to study prior knowledge since it was necessary to know what kind of knowledge was meant. From his own studies on designers, he would identify at least 3 different kinds of knowledge: First, and most important technology, i.e. how well the people know the trade they are in; second, drawing, although it is uncertain how important this will be in the future; third, a little knowledge of edp. POITOU felt that people with good knowledge of technology but bad at drawing were likely to feel comfortable with CAD. On the subject of the method employed by WAERN, POITOU pointed out the difficulty in finding meaningful indicators for learning and effectiveness. He doubted that the number of operations for a skilled designer was a good criterion and felt that highly-skilled people might feel perfectly at ease with CAD/CAM but use it less than less skilled people, because they thought their designs out more thoroughly while other people didn't think much and tended to try things out at the screen.

Yvonne WAERN remarked that research of this kind provided meaningful information if a particular task and a particular system are considered. Her work with the method proved that such analysis was possible. She argued that prior knowledge is very specific, so that it will be interesting to see what happens when people change systems. Measurement is not restricted to counting operations; the type of operation and the time required are also considered.

FINNE felt that although it might seem that differences were attributable to prior experience with CAD, there could be other causes such as discovery of errors, trying out alternatives or personal characteristics such as conscientiousness (which Karl-Gustav WAERN confirmed). FINNE also noted that the experimental set-up dealt with routine tasks whose solutions were known beforehand. He suggested experiments with creative, non-routine tasks would be useful. GOTTSCHALCH reported that his group was using a certain cross-hatching task to teach distrust of the system. The point was that a draftsperson or designer had full control over his task model while working conventionally, whereas CAD provided a finished model beyond the control of the user. WINGERT remarked that while it was important to do research at the operational level, it was also important to observe the overall situation.

The contributions by BUSCHHAUS and GOTTSCHALCH provoked few questions and little discussion. Participants from other countries briefly reviewed CAD training programmes in their countries, which revealed a distinct bias towards university training rather than re-training of existing staff or reform of training curriculae for draftspeople and other professions likely to be affected by the widespread use of CAD. Some participants were rather surprised that government sponsored training schemes provided the opportunity to discuss the social aspects of technology as in the case described by GOTTSCHALCH.

PRIOR KNOWLEDGE AND LEARNING IN COMPUTER AIDED TASKS

Yvonne Waern
Department of Psychology
University of Stockholm
S-10691 Stockholm, Sweden

In this paper I shall present a frame of reference for analyzing qualitative aspects of prior knowledge in learning, with reference in particular to learning to perform old tasks in a computer aided situation. I shall also present some empirical data to illustrate the analysis.

The relationship between prior knowledge and learning is bidirectional: prior knowledge affects learning as well as learning affects prior knowledge. I will consider these two effects separately.

1. The prior knowledge - learning effect matrix

The frame of reference consists of crossing different levels of prior knowledge with the different effects, which gives the matrix presented in Table 1.

Table 1: Prior knowledge - learning effect matrix

Level of prior knowledge	From prior knowledge to learning	From learning to prior knowledge
Declarative	Metaphors Analogies	Insight
Functional	Selection of concepts and functions	Restructuring of concepts and functions
Procedural	Using procedural rules	Changing procedural rules

I explain this matrix below by first presenting the ideas behind the rows and columns and then analyze and give examples in each cell of the matrix.

Levels of prior knowledge (rows)

During learning, task-specific knowledge may be used on different levels of detail. This is necessary in order to cope with the restricted capacity of short-term memory. The degree of detail is related to the scope of the task to be attended to. The greater the scope, the less detailed the prior knowledge to be used. To simplify matters somewhat, I distinguish here between three different levels of prior knowledge: a general level, which is called the "declarative level", a somewhat more specific level, which will be called the "functional level", and a very specific level, which will be called the "procedural level".

Declarative level

When a learner has to get a full overview over the task to be learned, prior knowledge on a general level will be used, with not many details. This level may be called declarative because no specifications about the procedures to be performed are given.

Functional level

On a more specific level, prior knowledge related to the actual objects to be manipulated may be invoked. This knowledge includes the characteristics of the objects as well as the characteristics of the functions which may be used to manipulate the objects, therefore it is called the "functional" knowledge. This knowledge most often contains too many elements to be useful for covering the entire task, but will rather be used in planning, as in dividing the task into different subgoals.

Procedural level

When the actual procedure to perform the task has to be considered, prior knowledge in terms of procedures will be relevant. This knowledge can be described in terms of rules, which specify the actions to be performed when a particular goal has been posed, given that particular conditions are fulfilled.

Learning effects (columns)

During learning, prior knowledge will affect the learning process. At the same time the learning process itself will affect prior knowledge.

When and how will prior knowledge affect learning? First it should be noted that the degree of use of prior knowledge is related to the degrees of freedom in the learning situation. Prior knowledge will be more freely used when the situation allows the person to reflect over the learning, like for instance in learning by doing. It will be used to a much more restricted extent, if the learning situation requires the person to learn without reflection, as in rote learning (even if we know that prior knowledge will be used here, too). Second we should note that even in a free situation only a selected part of the prior knowledge will be used. The elements of prior knowledge which are most similar to elements in the new situation will most probably be invoked. We may also suggest that some prior knowledge is more vivid than other, like automated rules or well-elaborated ideas and may therefore get activated even though the relevance to the particular situation might seem far-fetched.

I also proposed that learning may affect prior knowledge. If it is held that learning just adds to prior knowledge, this suggestion would be false. Old prior knowledge would continue to exist, beside (or behind) the added new knowledge. However, I want here to stress the irreversible effect of learning. By getting experiences in new situations people may learn to regard things in new ways or to perform actions differently. This is evidenced in learning which restructures a set of ideas, like in the paradigmatic shifts in physics, but it is also true for more modest changes, like reorganizing pieces of knowledge to form a better "gestalt".

Levels and effects crossed

To fill in the matrix with further expansions and examples I will concentrate on a situation which is rather common when people start to learn computerized systems: People are given a more or less extensive introduction to the system and are then to a great extent left on their own. The introduction will seldom be enough to cope with the whole system, nor with the always unexpected errors which occur (if they, for instance, make typing errors or other slips when typing commands to the system). In this situation, then, learning can be characterized as "learning by doing" or problem solving. I argued above that this kind of situation will be most applicable to the effect of prior knowledge on learning and vice versa.

2. The effect of prior knowledge on learning.

Expansion at the declarative level

Knowledge at the declarative level is used to comprehend the problem. By finding general or abstract similarities between the present situation and other previously encountered situations, the learner is helped in defining a problem space, in which to perform the search which is connected to problem solving (cf. NEWELL & SIMON, 1972).

Declarative knowledge can only be used by means of metaphors or analogies. The metaphoric use of prior knowledge is always uncertain, since declarative knowledge per se does not tell which characteristics in prior knowledge are relevant to the new situation. The same applies to the use of prior knowledge as analogies: only structural relationships can be transferred, but it is not quite clear what relations are permissible for transfer (cf. GENTNER & STEVENS, 1983; CARROLL & MACK, 1985). The metaphoric use of prior knowledge is helpful if the metaphor used is relevant and if adequate characteristics are transferred, harmful if the metaphor comes into conflict with the characteristics of the situation to be learned (cf. HALASZ & MORAN, 1982).

Example 1 (effect at the declarative level)

The example here is taken from an investigation on people learning a word-processing system (WAERN, Y. & RABENIUS, 1985). In this study, novices in computer use were given two different models of a word-processing system. One model compared the word processing system to a type-writer, the other compared it to building rows of blocks of letters. These different models can be considered to evoke different kinds of declarative prior knowledge. It was found that the type-writer model led to quicker performance on the task (which mainly was evident in the time taken to read the manual). However, the difference in performance time disappeared after a while. When the subjects had performed about 14 different tasks, the groups given different models performed the tasks in about the same time. This example then shows that declarative knowledge has effect in learning a new task, but that the effect soon disappears when the user can learn through own problem solving. We can suppose that after a while the learner builds up some knowledge which is more detailed and can be more helpful in further problem solving.

Expansion at the functional level

At the functional level learners will try to find concepts in the new task which relate to concepts already familiar from the experience of old, similar tasks. An effect of prior knowledge at this level may thus hinder the learner from seeing new concepts, since their attention is directed towards concepts they already know. It may also keep them from appreciating differences between the well-known prior concepts and the new concepts to be learned. In a problem solving situation, this will mean that the problem space constructed by the prior knowledge at the functional level will be inadequate and hinder the problem solving process. At the same time, of course, learning will be facilitated if the new concepts and functions correspond to those which are well-known from prior experience. In that case, the prior knowledge at the functional level can be used to construct a relevant problem space, and the remaining learning then consists in attempts to remember the search in that problem space. When an attempt at solving the problem fails, this will be remembered so that this particular path in the problem space will be avoided in a renewed attempt at the problem (ANZAI & SIMON, 1979). It is also possible that the learner during the problem solving attempts detects unnecessary "loops" in the attempts to solve the problem, i.e. paths which are repeated without any further success at approaching a solution of the problem. In both cases, the prior knowledge from previous tasks is used to define the problem space, whereas the prior knowledge from the particular task worked with is used to refine the knowledge down to the next level of specificity.

Two examples of effects of prior knowledge of the functional level are given, one illustrating the effect of inadequate functional knowledge, the other illustrating the effect of adequate functional knowledge.

Example 2

The first example refers to a study of people learning Jackson's structured programming technique as a part of a Cobol programming course (SAAF, 1984). In this study a simple task was given, i.e. to specify a program (in terms of a structured diagram) which could identify a particular record on a magnetic tape. This particular task was solved in about 4 minutes by two novices at computer programming. The same task took an experienced programmer about an hour and a half. By careful analysis of the problem solving process used by the experienced programmer, it was possible to show that this person started to work in an inadequate problem space, due to his prior knowledge of programming. Since he was not familiar with the structuring technique, he tried to solve the task with those techniques he knew, i.e looking for an already written program (which did not exist) and drawing a flowchart. After these vain attempts at the problem, he ultimately came up with a structured solution, which was perfect.

Example 3

Next example is taken from a study on CAD workers working at a task, that consisted of sectioning of detail which had previously been defined in the CAD database (WAERN, K.G. & HAGLUND, 1985). The example refers to one CAD operator, who had about a year's experience with the CAD system used. Since this particular example has not been presented before, I will present it here in somewhat more detail than the other examples. In Figure 1 a graph is given of this person's problem solving attempts.

Each circle (node) represents a particular state in the interaction between the operator and the system. The graph should be read from left to right and from top to bottom. The lines going horizontally between the nodes indicate the actions performed by the operator. A node with no lines leaving it indicates either a failure or a success in achieving a goal. The lines going vertically indicate that the operator has backtracked and started over again with a new action from a previously reached state.

We now see that the operator has made seven vain attempts at sectioning the detail. The graph nicely illustrates the nature of a search in a problem space. If we look closer at the reasons for failing, we find that the original figure given in the database is not precise enough; it contains tiny line gaps that render the final sectioning command ineffective. The operator certainly shows that he knows the functions possible to perform with the system: he enlarges the drawing, and he displays the information of different levels, he rescales the drawing and he deletes unnecessary lines. Ultimately he solves the problem by increasing the tolerance of the sectioning command (in the four last attempts). It is however interesting to note that he does not attempt to fill out the gaps in the original figure found in the database.

Filling in lines is an operation which, of course, is familiar to him. Still, in this particular task it did not seem to occur to him as a relevant action, and was thus not included in his problem space. The figure indicates how he learns from his experience in the task: during the first four attempts he uses four different actions before trying the sectioning procedure. At his fifth attempt, he finds the action which he apparently believes will lead him towards the solution of the task. As we will see later there are other actions which may equally lead to a solution.

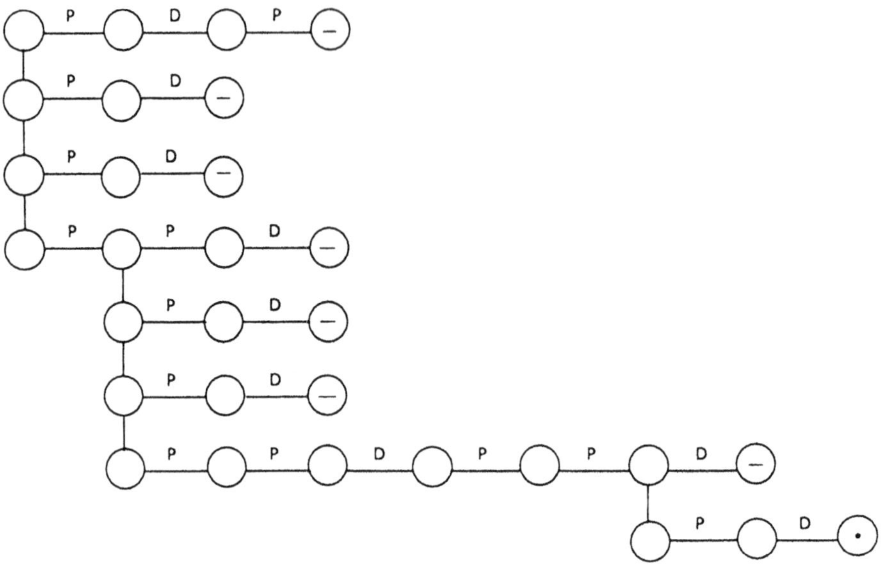

Figure 1

Expansion at the procedural level.

The knowledge at the procedural level can be described as rules in the following way:

IF GOAL X
AND CONDITION Y
THEN ACTION Z

The knowledge is now used in the new situation by matching the condition side (the IF and AND), which then triggers the action Z. This means that the old action will be triggered, as soon as the learner perceives the condition sides as being similar enough. Given that we may define what conditions are similar enough, it is possible to predict learning difficulties (as well as learning facilitation) by comparing old and new rules. When the old rules contain condition sides which are objectively similar to the condition sides of the new rules, but the action sides of old and new rules differ, negative transfer effects should be expected. I will give below one example of how learning difficulties may be predicted.

When old procedures correspond to those needed in the new situation, we might hesitate to call the learning "problem solving". Here the prior knowledge makes it possible for the learner to perform the task according to the rules already acquired without having to perform any search. However, it has been suggested that this situation could be regarded as a contrived problem solving situation, where the search has been reduced to just one single path in the problem space (CARD, NEWELL & MORAN, 1983). I give an example of a proceduralized problem solving below.

Examples of effects of prior knowledge at the procedural level

Example 4

The first example illustrates how prior procedural knowledge may be used to predict difficulties. The tasks concerned were drawing simple figures with the support of a simple computer aided drawing system. The system's interface was designed to be as similar to an ordinary drawing board as possible. It was possible to invoke a ruler in order to draw lines, and to turn that ruler in different directions (WAERN, Y. 1984). This similarity makes it possible to compare the rules necessary to draw lines on a drawing board and in the computer aided system. Some crucial differences were found: First, the computer aided system required the user to start the line at the origo of the drawing ruler. This is of course not necessary on an ordinary drawing board. Second, the computerized system allowed the draughtsman to draw lines by a simple "connect" command, by pointing to two endpoints of already drawn lines. This is, of course, not possible to do on an ordinary drawing board. Finally, the feedback from the computer aided system differed from that from an ordinary drawing board. When the system did not show the effect of the action quickly enough, two reasons could be responsible: Either the action had not been noted by the system or the system's response was delayed due to overload. On an ordinary drawing board, the line drawn is of course always visible at the same time as it is drawn. It was now found that most difficulties encountered by novices working with the computer aided system could be related to these differences in the procedures to produce lines. The results from this investigation show that it is possible to predict difficulties in learning computerized tasks from a thorough analysis of prior knowledge of the procedural level.

Example 5

The next example is taken from the same study of real CAD operators working with the same sectioning task as presented above (WAERN, K.G. & HAGLUND, 1985). Here I take as example the processes used by a CAD worker with four years of experience with the particular system investigated. The graph of the problem solving episode is given in Figure 2. This graph differs radically from the graph presented in Figure 1. We see that the operator does not perform any search in the problem space. The few backtrackings evidenced are due to minor emissions. The interesting thing in this graph is the conscentious preparative activities performed before attempting the main sectioning command sequence. The operator enlarges the picture and completes the drawing in the database, where she finds deficiencies. When one line has been completed, she reflects it to the other part of the (symmetric) figure. She checks round the whole figure before giving the sectioning command. When that command finally is given, it immediately succeeds.

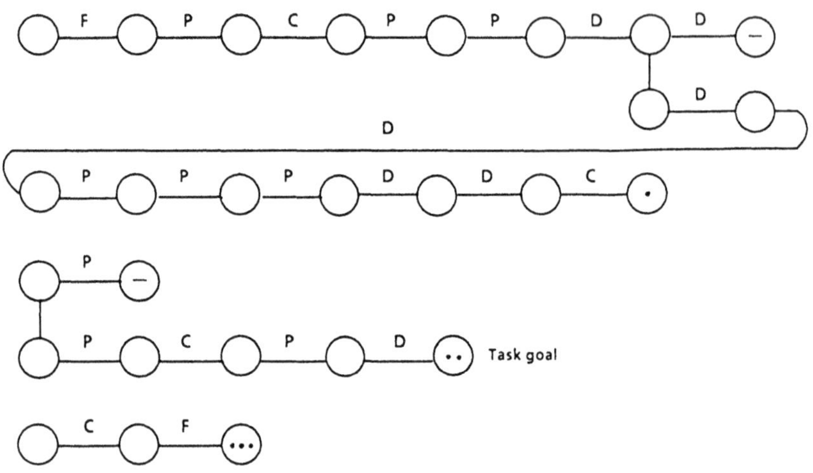

Figure 2

3. Effects of learning on prior knowledge

Learning is not only affected by prior knowledge, it also affects prior knowledge in an integrative way. These effects represent something else than additive learning effects. In additive learning, new knowledge may coexist with old knowledge. In integrative learning, new knowledge changes the old knowledge in a way which is irreversible.

Effects on prior knowledge at the declarative level.

Expansion

At the declarative level, the new situation may give rise to new ways of looking at problems. This new way can be something totally different, like in getting "insights" into problems, but it can also be something more modest, like seeing new aspects to which attention was not directed before. Such changes are probably irreversible, as is evidenced by the solution of gestalt problems: Once we have found for example that Maier's two-string problem can be solved by swinging one of the strings. It will probably be very difficult to exclude this possibility from the representation of the problem.

I have no example from the area of human-computer interaction to illustrate the effect of restructuring. In a study on word-processing I had hoped that a "building block" model might give users the idea that blanks were also valid signs, to be treated in a similar way as letters. This did not succeed, however, which shows that it may be difficult to induce restructuring at the declarative level. Studies of people working with gestalt-type problem solving suggest that restructuring does not happen until the subjects have experienced extensive failure with other approaches to the same task.

Effects of learning on prior knowledge at the functional level

At the functional level, learning may result in new definitions of objects and adding of new functions which were not considered before. This means that the problem space will differ. This difference may show up in the size of the problem space. "Good" learning should result in the problem space getting more comprised, for instance by chunking operations and knowledge states. As we saw in another example above (the programming example), the experience may also result in an expansion of the problem space, since the learner learns that several different alternatives exist. If no good heuristics exist to search an expanded knowledge space, learning will lead to slower rather than quicker problem solving. Bad experience during problem solving may also lead the learner to add operations to the problem space which would not be necessary if the problem situation was different. In computerized tasks, certain characteristics of the computer system may lead the user to add operations which would not be necessary if the system was flawless. This will be illustrated with the example below.

Example of effects on functional knowledge

<u>Example 6</u>

The example is taken from the CAD study, referred to above, where CAD operators with different degrees of experience with the system performed the same standardized tasks (WAERN, K.G. & HAGLUND, 1985). It was found here that one of the operators, the most experienced one, used many more operations to perform a task which consisted of a qualified assembly of existing details than did the less experienced operators. We encountered that CAD operator before, in example 5 above. After a closer analysis of the kind of actions performed by this operator it was found that she used many more checking operations than did the other operators. Table 2 below shows an overview over the number of operations of different types performed in the task for the four operators studied.

The results suggest that the problem space of the experienced operator (No. 3 in the table) differs from the problem space used by the other operators. This impression is consistent through all of the five main tasks and subtasks in the study and is supported by her spontaneous comments while doing the extra checks of the sectioning task referred to in example 5 above: "I must make sure that this really is correct", "You never now what may happen". Together, the quantitative data and her comments indicate that her problem space includes states which contain possibilities that the system makes errors or that errors exist in the existing designs to be worked with.

Table 2: **Number of operations used by different CAD operators in a given assembly task**

	Operator			
Operation	1	2	3	4
Preparative	61	39	52	38
Data changing	34	47	45	38
Checking	14	21	51	20
Others	7	6	12	7
Sum	116	113	160	103

Expansion of effects at the procedural level.

At the procedural level, the revision of prior knowledge concerns the content and format of the rules. We know that learning tends to combine rules into greater chunks, which then are difficult to separate into their original parts. Learning also changes the content of the rules, by means of generalisation, where conditions which are applicable to several different situations are treated as equivalent. Learning may also occur by discrimination, when it is found that different conditions must be treated differently (ANDERSON, 1983).

I have no own examples from systematic studies regarding changes at the procedural level in computer aided situations. The effects at the procedural level have, however, been extensively studied both with regard to motoric and intellectual skills. One interesting example concerning the work of a skilled electronic designer designing an electronic circuit has been described by CARD, MORAN & NEWELL (1983).

4. Conclusion

The present analysis takes its point of departure in the suggestion that learning is something more than just adding facts to some kind of memory database. I have here attempted to show how learning interacts with knowledge in a way that requires a quite different view of acquisition of knowledge.

In recent research on learning in computer aided situations, prior knowledge has not been neglected. However, it has been treated in a quantitative way. Prior knowledge is acknowledged to the extent that it coincides with the facts to be learned: the more "new" facts to be learned (in relation to prior knowledge), the longer time it will take to learn these new facts (POLSON & KIERAS, 1985).

Of course, it cannot be denied that prior knowledge also has this quantitative effect. However, for designing systems to fit people's prior knowledge, the qualitative aspect is at least as important. Also, in designing instructions and information about systems for new users, a qualitative analysis of their prior knowledge may suggest new ways of solving the well-known communication problems.

The above frame of reference can be used for such a qualitative analysis of prior knowledge. First, it can be asked, at what level the prospective users' prior knowledge can be used to facilitate learning. If users have got no detailed knowledge related to the system's functioning at all, the system (and information about it) should be designed keeping in mind that the users will be reminded of some similar situation and use this situation in a metaphoric way. It is then essential to design the new system in a way which evokes the best fitting similar situation, and to make the differences to that situation clear.

At the more detailed levels of prior knowledge, the problem space and possible rules evoked by the new situation are of particular importance. Again, the design of the system and the information about the system can be made to capitalize as much as possible upon similarities. At the same time, care should be taken that the problem space or set of rules to be invoked is not unnecessarily large. The risk of getting similar conditions to evoke different actions (the classical negative transfer effect) should also be considered.

The present analysis has one further aspect to add to the design of computer systems as supports for other, "main" tasks. I pointed out that learning might lead to irreversible changes. When new concepts and rules are integrated in for prior knowledge, restructuring and tuning may radically change the conception of the task to be performed with computer support. In designing a new system, it should thus be considered what kind of changes are desirable. In the examples above, we found on experienced CAD operator, who had included a lot of checking operations in her rules to handle the task just in order to prevent errors from occurring. A CAD system provides opportunities to prepare a drawing in much greater detail than would be feasible on an ordinary drawing board. A change towards greater precision may be desirable in the situation investigated. In other situations, for instance those requiring new conceptualizations, other features of the CAD system might be needed to change the users' approach to the task.

References

Anderson, J.R.:
The Architecture of Cognition. Harvard University Press, Cambridge, Mass., London, 1983.

Anzai, Y. & Simon, H.A.:
A theory of learning by doing. Psychological Review, 1979, 86, pp. 124-140.

Card, S.K., Moran, T.P. & Newell, A.:
The Psychology of Human-Computer Interaction. Lawrence Erlbaum, Hillsdale, New Jersey, 1983.

Carroll, J.M. & Mack, R.L.:
Metaphor, computing systems, and active learning. International Journal of Man-Machine Studies, 1985, 22, pp. 39-57.

Gentner, D. & Stevens, A.L.:
Mental models. Lawrence Erlbaum Ass., Hillsdale, N.J. 1983.

Halasz, F. & Moran, T.P.:
Analogy considered harmful. Human Factors in Computing Systems. Proceedings, Gaithersburg, Maryland, 1982.

Newell., A. & Simon, H.A.:
Human problem solving. Englewood Cliffs, New Jersey: Prentice-Hall, 1972.

Polson, P., Kieras, D.:
An Approach to the Formal Analysis of User Complexity. Intern. Journal of Man-Machine Studies, Vol. 22, 1985, pp. 365 - 394.

Sääf, J.:
Can experience be a disadvantage in computer programming? A study of the problem solving approaches of experienced and inexperienced programmers. B.A. thesis. Department of Psychology, University of Stockholm, 1984.

Waern, K.G. & Haglund, N.:
Manuscript in preparation. 1985.

Waern, Y.:
To predict difficulties in using a computerized drawing system. PS-Info, Production system laboratory, The Royal School of Technology, Stockholm, 1984, No. 16.

Waern, Y & Rabenius, L.:
On the role of mental models in instructing novice users of a word processing system. Paper presented at the MACINTER meeting, Stuttgart, September 23, 1983.

MANAGEMENT STRATEGIES FOR THE INTRODUCTION AND CONTROL OF INTERACTIVE COMPUTER GRAPHICS SYSTEMS

Ian McLoughlin

Kingston Polytechnic
Kingston upon Thames, Surrey KT2 7LB
United Kingdom

1. Introduction

This paper presents some preliminary observations from a study of the introduction of interactive computer graphics (ICG) systems into the drawing offices of companies in England [1]. The subject of this research has been the management strategies developed to introduce and control the operation of ICG systems. This focus arises from a concern that at present most attention is being given to the patterns of adoption and diffusion of this technology and to the 'impact' on the workforce. In contrast, little research has been done on the managerial aspects of change, and in particular the questions of strategy and control raised by ICG systems.

The data to be presented derives mainly from interviews with senior managers and CAD managers in four organisations. These were: 'ConsultantCo', a small private civil and structural engineering consultancy employing around 55 people, of whom about 40 were engaged on technical projects; 'BuildCo', a privately owned firm designing, manufacturing and building specialist private dwellings, which employed about 1500 people nationwide of whom around 20 were employed in a headquarters design department; 'ShipCo', part of the nationalised British shipbuilding industry, employing about 2000 employees of whom around 150 were employed in the drawing office; finally 'MechCo', an American owned subsidiary, designing and manufacturing process plant, with a workforce of about 650, of whom around 40 were employed in the drawing office.

The paper will look at three aspects of management strategies for introducing ICG systems. First, the reasons for adoption; second, approaches taken to implementation, in particular in relation to industrial relations questions; third, changes in management organisation to accommodate ICG systems, in particular the creation of CAD departments and CAD managers responsible for controlling their use. Before turning to a discussion of these issues it is worth making some clarificatory points in relation to the technology itself.

2. Interactive computer graphics

The use of the acronym 'CAD' has caused considerable confusion in the debate over the current wave of new technologies being introduced into drawing offices. First, as a general term it does not adequately distinguish between the various computer-aids that have been available and in use in the design process for many years which, 'assist in the creation, modification, analysis or optimisation of a design', and the more recent widespread use of interactive computer graphics' to create, transform and display data in the form of pictures and symbols' [2]. It is this latter application which is the subject of this paper, and indeed, most of the current social scientific interest in 'CAD'. Second, the acronym can be taken to refer to both 'design' and 'drafting' processes. This can lead to misleading impressions about the current utilisation of interactive computer graphics systems in drawing offices.

One of the CAD managers interviewed in this study usefully distinguished between two main types of ICG systems. The first, using a word processing analogy, are essentially 'shape processors'. Here a computer aid is used to replace what before was essentially a manual process. In this limited application ICG systems are little more than electronic drawing boards, in much the same way that wordprocessors are essentially electronic means of producing text. Of course, there are distinct advantages in both cases over manual methods, not least in streamlining the production of repetitive material and in making corrections - 'the best rubber known to man' as another CAD manager put it. Moreover, the ability of ICG systems to allow the 'layering' of drawings suggests a greater sophistication which goes beyond the 'wordprocessing' analogy.

The second type of ICG systems are those which allow the creation of virtual models of a three dimensional object either in a $2\frac{1}{2}$D or 3D presentation. Whilst modelling systems can, and usually are, used for the production of drawings, the real benefits come from 'upstream' advantages in the design process, and 'downstream' benefits in the manufacturing process. 'Upstream' benefits include making a wider range of design choices possible and the optimisation of existing choices. 'Downstream' benefits include the automatic production of manufacturing data in digital form for computer aided manufacture [3].

In using ICG systems as 'shape processors' the emphasis rests on their capabilities as drafting systems, or electronic drawing boards. Their use as 'modellers' on the other hand points to what are at least potential applications in the design process. Existing evidence on the actual use made of ICG systems in Great Britain, suggests that current applications have concentrated on the drafting rather than design capabilities of the technology [4].

This emphasis in utilisation was reflected in the four cases studied. ConsultantCo, on their own admission, used their four workstation system as a drafting tool whose main advantages were found to be the faster production of 'cleaner' drawings which could be up-dated with far greater ease. The main benefit of this was a reduction in the cost of producing finished drawings for clients and in making alterations to these drawings after they had been issued to the construction site. BuildCo, who had a three workstations system and had just taken delivery of three more workstations, also used the system as an 'electronic drawing board'. Along with the advantages noted by ConsultantCo in producing finished drawings BuildCo, because of the highly standardised nature of their product, were also able to gain benefits from compiling a data base of standard layouts and components. One potential 'downstream' benefit of such a data base was seen to be in the production of a bill of materials. However, in practice the amount of data input required and software problems had made this potential use so far unrealisable.

MechCo also used their system primarily as a drafting tool. According to the senior engineering manager their six workstation system was a 'workhorse' not a 'racehorse', and its main advantages lay in shortening lead times. However, one potential 'upstream' benefit was demonstrated to the author in the form of a software programme which was being developed to 'automate' the design of standard components. Similarly, potential 'downstream' benefits were being explored in relation to integrating the production of drawings with a computer-based manufacturing planning system. However, at the time of interview the ultimate goal of complete integration from the point of sale, through design to manufacture was seen as some years off.

Finally, ShipCo provided the only clear example of the use of an ICG system for modelling with both 'upstream' and 'downstream' benefits as longterm goals. Here a 30 workstations system with 3D capability was being used to construct a three-dimensional model in space of a proto-type design. It should be noted that the basic conceptual design of the ship had been accomplished by conventional means. The ICG system was being used for the detailed design of the internal workings of the ship. Once completed an infinite number of drawings could be generated. One major advantage of the system was a facility which automatically updated drawings if any modification is made to the model, thus providing much tighter control over design information. At the time of interviews, most 'downstream' benefits had yet to be realised as the ship was still awaiting firm orders for manufacture. However, benefits from 'clash detection' in the routing of the complex pipework, electrical wiring and ducting that comprise much of the detailed design work in shipbuilding, had already been realised. It was also anticipated that in future more of the basic conceptual design of the ship would be accomplished using the ICG system, although here it was envisaged that the drafting rather than modelling capability of the system would be used.

3. Management strategies for introducing ICG

It is possible to distinguish three kinds of objectives which underlay management strategies for introducing new technology [5]). These are: 'strategic' objectives, concerned with improving the position of the company in relation to its external environment; 'operating' objectives, concerned with improving the internal efficiency and performance of the company; and 'control' objectives, concerned with day-to-day supervision of work operations. Previous research by the author has suggested that management strategies are best regarded as a series of 'sub-strategies' developed at different stages in the process of technological change [6]). It can be hypothesised that at different stages in introducing new technology - for example, the decision to adopt, implementation, and operation - varying importance will be attached to 'strategic', 'operating' and 'control' objectives. In so far as different management groups may be involved in each stage of change, there is also potential for conflict or tensions between the objectives being pursued. For example, between the cost-oriented 'strategic' and 'operating' concerns of corporate and financial management, and the 'control' objectives of supervisory management [7]). As we shall see, the cases studied here reveal some evidence of tensions between the demands for quantitative productivity gains from senior management and the control problems this induced for CAD managers responsible for the operation of ICG systems. Interestingly, one consequence of the emergence of CAD managers and CAD departments was also a tension between them and the supervisory management responsible for the control of existing manual drawing offices.

The decision to adopt ICG systems

Both ConsultantCo and BuildCo had computer-oriented managing directors who owned the major share of the business. Both companies had been established in the early 1970s and were growth-oriented. The adoption of new technology was seen as an essential part of their plans to expand market share and continue growth in the future. In the case of ConsultantCo, a number of CAD technologies had been in use for some time. The move into ICG was seen as a natural development out of this experience, in particular as it meant that 'in-house' expertise existed to evaluate the potential of the various ICG systems on the market. As far as ConsultantCo was concerned, it was not a question of 'if' to invest in ICG, but more one of 'when' as finance became available. As is apparently typical in engineering and architectural practices, investment funds eventually became available 'on the back' of a large contract, and in the case of ConsultantCo a government grant. According to the senior partner, no rigorous attempt was made to 'cost-in' the system, it was just expected that the investment of £ 150,000 should 'pay back' in five years. In the view of the CAD manager cost justifications for ICG systems were 'somewhat fictitious' as many of the benefits that were being achieved were intangible. Moreover, measureable productivity gains were variable according to the type of drawing involved. After a year of utilisation the operators were currently achieving up to 6:1 improvement in time on complex drawings but doing little better than by manual methods on routine drawings.

In BuildCo the ICG system was introduced as part of a company five year plan to continue its phenomenal growth. In 1984 BuildCo was rated the fourth most profitable company in Britain by a leading management journal, and as part of a strategy for further expansion the company had just developed a regional organisation to provide a nationwide market for its specialist dwelling product. This organisational change led eventually to the creation of a central ICG department at headquarters to service architects departments located in the regional offices. A total investment of £ 150,000 had initially been made two years previously, with a similar sum just about to be paid to expand the system. The principal objective in introducing ICG was to reduce lead times between the granting of planning permission and the start of construction on a site. According to the CAD manager savings of up to 50 % were being achieved with user productivity improvements of between 1.3:5 and 1:5.

MechCo had been a user of NC machine tools for 15 to 20 years. In the early 1980s they invested in CNC machines. At this time engineering management became aware of developments in ICG technology and looked for possible applications in their drawing office. A management consultant was commissioned to carry out a feasibility study and 20 potential benefits were identified. Corporate management demanded a rigorous cost justification for the investment in an ICG system which ultimately totaled around £ 500,000 with an expected 'pay back' in three years. After about one year of operation a productivity improvement of about 3:7 was being achieved with a pay back period then estimated at 2.5 years. The CAD managers also pointed to other intangible benefits that could not easily have a monetary value placed upon them, such as the capability to show a potential customer how the process plant they wished to purchase could be laid out.

ShipCo's decision to invest £ 4 million in an ICG system was heavily influenced by the corporate policy of British Shipbuilders of which it was a constituent company. In British Shipbuilders as a whole it was planned to invest £ 30 million over four years in CAD/CAM systems. The principal objective in this investment programme was to improve the competitiveness of the British shipbuilding industry which has been in decline for many years in the face of intensive foreign competition. There was some resistance amongst some ShipCo managers to the investment in an ICG system, as to some extent it was a decision that was imposed upon them. However, top level support from the board encouraged the adoption of the system based on the perception that the only way to win new ship orders would be to offer the latest design and manufacturing technologies. Operational improvements were envisaged in relation to drawing office productivity, less re-working because of design errors during construction, better information management, and a more flexible flow of information to the shop floor. At the time of interviews, after about three years of operation, the CAD manager claimed no cost evaluation was possible because no production drawings had, as yet, been produced.

Implementation of ICG systems

Sub-strategies developed in the implementation stage of technological change have been found to be critical in shaping the outcomes of change, and from management's point of view the success of their overall strategy. From the point of view of workforce and trade unions, implementation offers the best opportunity to influence change through consultation and/or negotiation. It is during the implementation stage then that the industrial relations implications of ICG systems come to the fore. In the cases studied here, two contrasting management approaches were in evidence. The first, adopted by ConsultantCo and BuildCo, involved the unilateral regulation of change. The second, adopted by MechCo and ShipCo, involved the joint regulation of change with trade unions.

Neither ConsultantCo nor BuildCo recognised trade unions. In both cases the approach of management to industrial relations was strictly paternalist in its orientation. In such circumstances it is not surprising to find that all decisions taken by management in relation to the implementation of the ICG system were made unilaterally. In the case of ConsultantCo, most decisions were taken by the three senior partners advised by the manager in charge of the existing CAD facilities. The role of this manager was extended to encompass responsibility for implementing and managing the operation of the new ICG system. Principal responsibility during implementation was for the selection and training of users. The approach taken was to train all eight existing draughtsmen [8]), of whom two were unable to adapt to using the system. No extra payments were made for training to use the system. In fact, according to the CAD manager, there had been little attempt to formally consult the staff about the change at all. In retrospect it was felt that more effort should have been made to keep staff informed, especially as the lack of information had fed rumours of potential job losses.

Unlike ConsultantCo, BuildCo was making its first venture into the introduction and use of CAD technologies. This lack of experience in managing change was reflected in a number of problems during implementation. First, the manager in charge of implementing the system had no knowledge of computer systems and it was envisaged that the terminals could be sited in existing drawing offices and would be used as required. However, after six months of trial operation with two terminals, it was realised that a centralised ICG department was required with its own CAD manager. This manager took subsequent responsibility for developing the system and staff training. Again, staff selection was of a 'trial and error' type, whereby all existing staff were given training and those who were unable to adapt were given the option to return to the manual board. However, in this case, a strong financial incentive (a 50 % increase in salary) was provided by management to persuade potential users to stay with the system. Moreover, there appeared to have been a relatively high level of informal consultation with the staff directly concerned with the use of the system, although the general approach to industrial relations in the company was, according to the CAD manager, of the 'like it or lump it' variety. As we shall see below, one novel feature of the operation of the ICG system in BuildCo was the use of a 24 hour three shift staffing pattern. In the view of the CAD manager the introduction of this shift system had 'quite succinctly' been 'cocked-up'. Management's inability to find an effective shift pattern, and problems in formally defining the jobs of the users, had meant that management had unilaterally made three changes to the users' conditions of employment, and two changes to their job definitions in the space of six months. Not surprisingly, there was some discontent amongst the system operators with regard to the way management had handled the introduction of the system.

The majority of the drawing office staff in MechCo and ShipCo were members of the principal British drawing office union, AUEW-TASS. In these two companies the introduction of the ICG system was subject to joint regulation by management and unions, although the extent of this varied between the two companies. AUEW-TASS, in similar fashion to other unions in Britain and in accordance with TUC policy, has published guidelines for local negotiators on the introduction of new technology the principal feature of which is the suggestion that a New Technology Agreement (NTA) should be reached with management. In the case of AUEW-TASS a 'model' agreement is suggested as a guide which contains, for example, clauses providing for no redundancies, no extension/introduction of shiftworking, and training on new systems to be offered to all those eligible [9]). Recently published research in Britain has cast serious doubt on NTAs as a viable means for unions to use in negotiating change [10]). More seriously from a union point of view, it has been suggested that even existing collective bargaining frameworks are inadequate for negotiating the introduction of new technology [11]).

The evidence from MechCo suggests strong support for these views. In this case all decisions about the introduction of the ICG system were taken by a small group of three engineering managers with no union involvement. This was a deliberate strategy on the part of management to avoid the creation of what they saw as unnecessarily large committees which would delay implementation. Thus, whilst staff were kept fully informed of management intentions through presentations and the like, the scope for unions to negotiate on issues raised by the introduction of the system was limited. No New Technology Agreement was therefore negotiated. In fact management offered a no redundancy undertaking to all drawing office staff (although contract draughtsmen were laid-off), training to all staff, but no extra payments for retraining or using the system. According to the CAD manager, the union had not pushed particularly strongly for additional money. If they had then training would have been restricted to specially selected groups who would then be 'dedicated' operators. The fact that no additional money had been secured appeared to be a source of some discontent with the union amongst the draughtsmen.

In the case of ShipCo the union, through a New Technology Agreement and existing collective bargaining mechanisms, was able to influence the introduction of the ICG system through joint regulation far more effectively than their counterparts in MechCo. First, members of the drawing office staff with management made up a joint working party to assess the various ICG systems available to the company. Second, a 'New Technology Agreement' was concluded between the AUEW-TASS and one other white collar union in the company with management to establish a framework to facilitate the introduction of new technology in general. Amongst the principal substantive points of this agreement were clauses agreeing to no redundancy, no compulsory shift working, and the requirement for consultation between management and union 'at the earliest stage' in introducing new technology. In the case of the ICG system, a joint monitoring committee, made up of management and drawing office staff, was established. This met on a six-weekly basis during implementation to monitor the 'impact' of the system on the 'individual'. However, according to the CAD manager, it also, on occasion, became a forum for collective grievances.

The substantive outcome of this process of joint-regulation was an agreement that all drawing office staff would be retrained to use the system. For this purpose the company established its own five-week training package administered by a newly created CAD department. In return for agreeing to being retrained, a 5 % increase in pay was granted. This was followed by an additional 2 % after six months experience using ICG was completed, and individuals were judged to be competent users. In practice though, the CAD manager admitted, most users were defined as 'competent' if only to persuade them to stay with the company whose rates of pay were not particularly competitive.

Management organisation and control of ICG systems

A number of case studies point to the problems raised for management organisation and control at supervisory level by the introduction of new computer-based technologies. On the one hand, there is evidence that an erosion of traditional supervisory roles can occur, leading to a 'control loss' on the part of management possibly in the direction of more autonomous work teams. On the other hand, there is also evidence to suggest new forms of management organisation are emerging with new supervisory roles specifically charged with managing the use of the new technology [12]). In short, a complex redefinition' of supervisory management appears to accompany the introduction of new computer-based technologies [13]). The data collected in this research suggests ICG systems are no exception.

As already indicated, in each of the cases studied, a CAD manager and associated CAD department existed. In the case of ShipCo and MechCo these had been created during the implementation of the new systems. In the case of ConsultantCo the responsibilities of an existing CAD department were expanded. Finally, in the case of BuildCo, a CAD manager and department were created after the first phase of implementation when it was realised that 'control problems' were resulting from relying on existing organisational arrangements. What then were the nature of the 'control problems' which prompted the managements in each case to develop new forms of organisation and new roles to manage their ICG systems?

Briefly, the crux of management's 'control problems' in each case revolved around the issue of system utilisation highlighted by senior management pressures for cost reductions. As has been pointed out in other discussions of 'CAD technologies', the high capital cost of systems tends to motivate managements to seek ways of making sure they are used to a maximum [14]). This utilisation problem expressed itself in the cases studied in two ways. First, there was a concern to maximise the productive use of the system by draughtsmen. Second, there was a concern to extend the amount of time out of normal daytime working hours where the system was used. Attempts to maximise utilisation also raised problems in relation to existing supervisory roles and the traditional individual autonomy enjoyed by draughtsmen. The pursuit of extended hours for using ICG systems raised the problem of staff and union resistance. Attempts to maximise system utilisation seemed to point to a tension between the cost-oriented 'strategic' and 'operating' objectives pursued by senior management, and the 'control' objectives of CAD managers as the latter are increasingly pressured to tighten-up their control of system utilisation.

In the case of ConsultantCo, the problem of maximising effort in the use of the ICG system had been approached by allocating dedicated operators to each terminal. These individuals worked exclusively on the ICG system and were fed work by project managers. In this way the terminals were kept in constant use, monitored by the CAD manager. A deliberate decision was taken not to group the terminals in a separate room or one area of the drawing office. Instead they were inter-mixed with manual boards. According to both the senior partner and CAD manager, this was to avoid the creation of a collective consciousness, a 'clique' or 'elite' mentality as they put it, amongst the CAD operators. One obvious benefit management might have obtained from this was a more compliant attitude on the part of the operators to their attempt to extend the time periods in which the system was used. To some extent this was achieved by using the system on an 'extended hours' basis with the operators working on an additional two hours per day as 'overtime'. Ideally, according to the CAD manager, a two shift system would be introduced, but at present the staff were resistant. Further, there was a problem amongst some operators of getting them to be more productive when using the ICG system. Some appeared to regulate their output to conform to what they were previously achieving on manual boards.

BuildCo had adopted a similar strategy to ConsultantCo in so far as they had also adopted a dedicated operator approach. However, as we saw, in this case a centralised CAD department had been created after realising utilisation problems were occuring by siting the terminals within the existing drawing office. In the view of the CAD manager, who had wide experience of ICG applications in the architectural sector, this was a common management error. Quite often investments were made in ICG systems without any management, direction, communication or allocation of responsibility on its use. As a result, the equipment stands virtually idle in a corner of the drawing office. This mistake had initially been made by BuildCo, and the appointment of the CAD manager and creation of a centralised CAD department with dedicated operators was seen as the means to resolve this. However, this did raise difficulties in relation to the existing drawing offices which the CAD department now served, since managers of these offices felt that their role was being undermined. The most striking aspect of system use in BuildCo, however, was the adoption of a 24-hour three-shift working pattern. According to the CAD manager, the volume of work to be done demanded this and in any case, 'the computer will work 24 hours a day so we'll work to it'. This pressure on increasing productivity and reducing costs by achieving maximum utilisation characterised the use of ICG in BuildCo. It was also evidenced by the working conditions in the CAD department. This was cramped and poorly lit and ventilated, with no attempt to control the environment or provide ergonomic workstations for users. The CAD manager explained, 'I haven't got the money, I can't extract the money out of the Managing Director'.

MechCo and ShipCo approached the problem of controlling system utilisation in a contrasting way to ConsultantCo and BuildCo. Here, a centralised CAD department was created but was provided on an 'open shop' basis to users from the drawing offices via a booking system. This in part derived from management's decision, influenced by union policy, to retrain all drawing office staff. One immediate consequence of this was that all draughtsmen were, in practice, subject to two sources of supervisory control; first that exercised by project managers and section leaders in the manual drawing office, and second that exercised by the CAD manager when using the ICG system.

In the case of ShipCo this led to particular problems. The CAD manager's formal role was to control the use of the ICG system in a purpose built CAD centre. He was not responsible however, for the individual work of the operators. In practice though he influenced the work that the draughtsmen did. This directly transgressed on the responsibilities of the drawing office section leaders who formally supervised the draughtsmen's work. However, since the drawing office section leaders had not been retrained in the use of the ICG system their role appeared to have been eroded in the face of the new 'skill superiority' of the draughtsmen. In the view of the CAD manager, the section leaders felt they had lost control over the operators because they did not understand the system. Moreover, they were antagonistic towards the CAD manager who had to some extent subverted their role. Similar, though not as pronounced tensions, appeared to exist in the case of MechCo.

For the CAD managers in both companies system utilisation, given the 'open shop' approach was a major problem. In ShipCo, problems revolved around a management and local union dispute over shiftworking. The national agreements covering the introduction of ICG systems in British Shipbuilders included, at corporate management's insistence to cost justify the investment, a provision for shiftworking. In the view of ShipCo management, this constituted an agreement to work shifts. In the view of the local union, it was merely a set of 'guidelines'.

In the absence of a formal agreement, ShipCo management had, in the interim, agreed with the local union that an overtime pattern would be worked to give approximately the same number of hours usage as would be attained via shiftworking. However, because the working of overtime was voluntary, as opposed to the compulsory working implied in shift-working, actual usage in recent months had fallen drastically. As a result, pressure was again being exerted by senior management to reach an agreement on shiftworking. This was currently being resisted by the local union because the premiums being offered were considerably below those being paid to other employees already working shifts in the company.

Interestingly, the CAD manager gave the strong impression that shiftworking, given the volume of work to be done and the numbers of staff available, was not required. One implication of the introduction of shiftworking, he claimed, would be to accomplish the finite amount of work there was to be done more quickly, and thus the ICG system would become idle faster!

In MechCo the 'open shop' approach raised problems of booking time on terminals to maximise their use. Individual draughtsmen, in liaison with project managers, decided on whether or not to use the system and then booked time with the CAD manager. However, this yielded only about an 80 % utilisation of the system in any week. In some instances, where bookings were cancelled or several holidays were taken at once, utilisation could be a lot lower. One attempted solution to this problem had been the adoption of 'extended working time' allowing additional hours to be worked voluntarily, as overtime in the evenings. However, this had not proved popular with drawing office staff. The management was now considering the introduction of a two-shift system, but union opposition and company unwillingness to be drawn into conceding large shift premiums, meant little progress had been made.

4. Conclusions

The observations reported in this paper are very much preliminary interpretations and call for further research in a number of areas if the managerial aspects of change involved in the adoption of ICG systems are to be fully understood. The data presented above suggests that motivations for introducing ICG systems are complex, varying according to management level, function, and over time. One thing that is clear is that cost-based justifications at the time of the decision to adopt do not tell the whole story. As in other studies of change which have focused on the adoption of new technologies within organisations, rather than general patterns of diffusion and impact, implementation sub-strategies appear to be critical. This is particularly so in relation to the scope for workforce and union influence. There were clear distinctions between the unilateral approach of the management in the non-unionised companies compared to the joint-regulation of change in the unionised companies. Finally, the emergence of CAD managers and CAD departments as the principal agents of management control in the use of ICG systems, suggests that many of the most significant changes within adopting organisations may well be occurring in the management function itself and perhaps not amongst drawing office staff.

Notes and References

1) This research was funded under the Economic and Social Research Council (ESRC) Post-Doctoral Fellowship scheme, hosted by the Department of Sociology and Social Administration, New Technology Research Group, Southampton University. The author is now Senior Lecturer in Industrial Relations, School of Industrial Relations and Personnel Management, Kingston Polytechnic, Kingston-upon-Thames, Surrey, England.

2) Groover, M.P., and Zimmers, E.W., CAD/CAM: Computer Aided Design and Manufacturing, Prentice-Hall, 1984.

3) For further discussion, see Kaplinsky R., Computer-Aided Design, Pinter, 1982.

4) See Arnold, E. and Senker, P., Designing the Future, EITB, Occasional Paper No. 9, 1982.

5) See Buchanan, D. and Boddy, D. (eds.), Organisations in the Computer Age, Gower, 1982.

6) See McLoughlin, I.P., Rose, H. and Clark, J., 'Managing the Introduction of New Technology' Omega 13(4) 1985.

7) Buchanan and Boddy op.cit.

8) In all four companies no women were employed as drafting staff in the drawing offices. Hence the term draughtsmen is used in the paper.

9) See New Technology: A Guide for Negotiators, AUEW-TASS, 1978.

10) Williams, R. and Steward, F., 'New Technology Agreements: an assessment' Industrial Relations Journal, 16(3) 1985.

11) Moore, R. and Levie, H., 'New Technology and the Unions' in Forrester T. (ed.) The Information Revolution, Blackwells, 1985.

12) See on both developments the case studies in Buchanan and Boddy op.cit.

13) See Dawson, P.M.B. and McLoughlin, I.P., 'Computer Technology and the Redefinition of Supervision', Journal of Management Studies, 23(1) 1986.

14) Cooley, M., Computer-Aided Design - its nature and applications, AUEW-TASS, 1971.

DECISION-MAKING ON CAD IN CONSULTING FIRMS IN DENMARK

Marianne Fodgaard
Department of Construction Management
The Technical University of Denmark
DK-2800 Lyngby

1. Introduction

Computer aided design has mainly been used in stationary industry so far. But within the last 3-4 years it has become more popular in the building industry, mainly in consulting firms and not very much in the architect firms (there is a rather sharp division of labour between those two professions in Denmark).

Some of the large consulting firms have purchased CAD systems while others are about to do it. These firms traditionally work on the international market and are therefore influenced by their international competitors. The smaller firms hesitate to buy CAD, and when they do, they buy smaller - and cheaper - systems, while the large firms buy big turn-key systems. In newspapers and magazines, at conferences and exhibitions and in the firms people talk about CAD and discuss whether the small-scale or the large-scale systems are the best for their purpose.

But the discussions begin and end with the question of the efficiency of CAD - how much money and time you save by using CAD in the design process. Here I will talk about the consequences for the organization (the working process, the division of labour within and between the professions in the design process, the skills) and for the product.

The best way to answer that question is to look at the intentions involved when introducing CAD. This leads back to the decision-making process, that is what kind of organization received the CAD system and what happened in the decision-making process. Through this analysis we can survey the tendencies how the implementation of CAD will take place.

2. The rational aspects of the decision

The rationality in the process is far the easiest to expose. The companies like to talk about these aspects and we traditionally accept them as true. They deal mainly with two subjects:

- If CAD is to be introduced, when shall we do it? And what do we want it for?
- What type of CAD system is to be chosen?

These questions cannot be asked separately as no one will decide to introduce CAD without believing in at least one system available. But in theory, the reason for introducing CAD is the question answered first:

- It is needed for rationalization and to intensify the design process, especially the draughting process.
- Corrections in and maintenance of the planning material are to be made easier.
- The planning material and the buildings are to be improved.

To this we can add the wish to control the production process, both as far as the employees and the other parties involved are concerned. Most companies are afraid to get left behind by their competitors. And as everybody is talking about CAD as the future tool in the design process, there is some prestige in having a CAD system. This alone has an effect on the number and the size of jobs the company will have.

This urge to introduce CAD is to be balanced against what the company's needs are and what is available at the right price.

3. The influence of organizational routines

If we make a closer investigation of a company it is evident that the rational and structural analysis does not explain everything. The decision-making process as well as implementation contain other aspects. A part of the explanation of this is provided by the structure of the organization and course of the process.

The organization has a certain inertia in its structure. Each part of the organization has its own tasks for which it has certain routines. This makes "standard" problems easy to solve, while new types of problems are either not even discovered or they cannot be solved by the routines.

In the case of CAD it is often quite accidental when and how this is realized as a problem to which the organization must respond. And therefore the needs in the company (if one can talk of "needs" when the company is not regarded as an entity with certain, common goals) are defined to the investigation of the market. Needs, goals, and actual possible solutions are very closely related.

4. The power struggles in the company

In the previous analysis the different parts of the organization were rather loosely related. But another aspect of the decision-making process is the struggles that are fought between the parts of the organization.

Most companies are very hierarchic. The management is the decision-maker while the departments collect and adapt information. Every department has its own interests which it defends against the other departments. The company cannot be regarded as a whole here either, and the decision is influenced by the mutual force of the departments. The initial goal for a department is to make the management interested in its problems, but the struggles must also be seen in relation to other struggles - both between departments, between professions, and between departments and management.

The positions of the competitors depend on the persons and their individual positions and goals, their alliances to other persons, departments, and the management.

5. An example: a Danish consulting firm

One of the big consultants can illustrate all three aspects of the decision-making process and its consequences for the implementation of CAD.

The company had for a number of years used computers for draughting. The computer department had developed the programs while at the same time it kept itself informed about the CAD market. But the serious change in the behavior of the company set in when the technical manager was introduced to Intergraph and was impressed by its possibilities.

From this moment a lot of energy was used to investigate the market (by the computer department). With the technical manager as an ally they convinced the board of directors to buy CAD. Intergraph was used as an example when the department investigated the company's needs, and finally Intergraph was bought.

6. Implementation of new technology

What happens in the decision-making process is often repeated later on while implementing the decision. The use of CAD does not necessarily reflect the rational aspects of the decision.

If the organization has difficulties in responding to new technology which does not fit into the routines, it is sometimes even more difficult to adjust itself to new working conditions. The changes in the working process and the design material that are promised by the vendor are rarely seen immediately. There have been both technical and organizational problems in implementing CAD. The needs of the company and the possibilities of the CAD system come closer to each other, but CAD is not developed to answer the needs of the Danish building industry, and many companies have had trouble because they purchased a general system without adaptations for their own needs. And there is no doubt that needs are different in the Danish and the American building industries - not to mention the U.S. Army.

Another aspect of the implementation is what people expect from design material produced on a CAD system. There is much prestige in having a CAD system in the company, but the material must not change too much to be accepted by other professions, owners and authorities.

CAD is often drawn into the process at the time when draughts are made. That means that some of the labour processes have changed, but not the division of labour, and the rest of the organization has remained unchanged.

Apart from the inertia of the organization there has also been a more conscious reaction influencing the development. The employees have not been drawn into the decision-making process except those who collected information.

The opponents of CAD have to a certain extent been able to refuse working with CAD. But in some cases the reaction has been almost the opposite: The employees have been very keen to work at the CAD system. This can be caused by several things. First of all CAD is a fascinating tool. Second, many people - especially draughtsmen - fear that they will become superfluous because of the use of CAD. By training to work with the CAD system this fear becomes weaker.

In return, this has meant a weakening of the employees as a group of professionals. Both the fascination and fear have led to rather individual reactions and not to demands on how to use CAD systems and what to use them for. This goes especially for architects and engineers who have weak traditions in looking at new technology in a broad perspective.

7. Conclusion

The rational and structural analyses cannot alone explain the introduction and the use of CAD systems in the Danish building industry. We also have to investigate the organization receiving the new technology, both with respect to its organizational routines and to the balance of power in the company (who has an interest in the new technology and who is against it).

In the light of these analyses we can say something about CAD's influence on the working conditions of architects, engineers, and draughtsmen:

- The division of labour has not changed very much yet, but the working process has changed especially for the draughtsmen.
- The efficiency effect has not been very clear yet. The use of CAD has meant more work rather than less, and even if draughting can be done quicker on a CAD system, the rest of the organization has difficulties in absorbing this saving of time.
- Those who are actually working at the CAD system are fascinated by it - and fear it. The natural breaks have disappeared, others have come instead when the system is too slow.

I can still conclude very little on my second question: What are the consequences of the use of CAD on the product. There has been a lot of talk about it. Some are fascinated by the possibilities, others fear the risks of standardization. But the changes have been almost invisible so far. That might be a part of the strategy but also caused by the difficulties of introducing CAD into the labour process.

This leaves the questions about what happens, when the initial difficulties are over:

- Does CAD change the buildings?
- Can CAD be used to make better buildings (and what is that?).

And this will probably lead me back to questions concerning the production process: At what stage in the process is CAD used and what for?

Does it change the division of labour (and by that the influence of the process and the product)?

8. Future work

Since September 1985 I have worked on a Ph.D. scholarship: "CAD/CAM in the Danish building industry".

The research project is being executed at the Department of Construction Management, The Technical University of Denmark, supervised by Kristian Kreiner, Ph.D., associate professor.

Reference

This paper is a summary of a report: Marianne Fodgaard: "CAD - beslutninger, teknologi, konsekvenser", København 1985.

NEW TECHNOLOGY IN VOCATIONAL TRAINING, MODELS AND REGULATIONS

Dieter Buschhaus
Federal Institute for Vocational Training
Fehrbelliner Platz 3
1000 Berlin 3

1. Introduction

An important part of the staff in engineering and planning departments are the draftsmen. Primarily these are mechanical/electrical draftsmen, civil engineering/architectural draftsmen, cartographical draftsmen and draftsmen for details. The statistics show that almost 135,000 gainfully employed draftsmen out of the total could be possibly affected by the introduction of CAD. As a handicap for a general solution to the problems, we have to consider that the introduction of CAD-systems into about 50 economic sectors where draftsmen are working is taking place with varying intensity.

The replacement of the traditional drafting machines by terminals is already well under way in the fields of aeronautical and automobile engineering as well as in printed circuit board development. But most of the firms in the remaining economic sectors have only just started to introduce CAD/CAM technology. These sectors include all mechanical engineering, the major field of activity for draftsmen.

In the past, technical change for industry could be integrated in the framework of conventional technology. For example, there is the use of new materials or new machines in the existing production process without basically new qualification requirements. Traditional basic and continuous training could be adjusted without any great difficulty. The introduction of information technologies in industry presents the companies and vocational schools with a completely new problem, which the methods of traditional training can hardly solve.

With a reorganization of the draftsmen, we have to consider not only the requirements of the work place at the design board, but also at the computer terminal. At present, we cannot stipulate training on CAD systems in training regulations, which apply to plants in all economic sectors. The handling of different CAD systems becomes obsolete rather quickly, as well. On the other hand basic knowledge on CAD and information technology remains stable. At this point we should therefore emphazise the training of basic knowledge and skills. In addition to new training material we have to examine the traditional material with regard to more analytical thinking. We should certainly try to train the apprentices directly at CAD terminals in order to make sure that their learning is both lasting and successful. The plants should go beyond the fixed requirements of training regulations. Because of the decreasing hardware costs, we can expect that more and more firms will be able to realize this kind of practical training. The reorganization of training regulations has already led to concrete results for the cartographical draftsmen where a CAD training section was adopted. For civil engineering and architectural draftsmen the design of the structure of the training has already been completed. A broad foundation training for one year consisting of basic craftsmen skills and knowledge should improve the understanding of practical problems. In the second year, the apprentices must learn within the frame of technical drawing to analyse the workpieces with regard to the basic geometrical elements and combine them with mathematical relationships. Learning edp for civil engineering and architecture should be dealt with throughout the third year of training. One of the tasks of the part-time vocational school will be to teach basic knowledge on information technology and how the CAD systems are able to work with geometrical problems.

The reorganization of the mechanical/electrical draftsmen is closely linked with the establishment of a further training regulation for a so-called "CAD detail constructor". This new occupation should open career possibilities for craftsmen.

At first only those draftsmen who complete their drawings schematically will be negatively affected by the use of the computers, whereas those who are themselves responsible for the detailing of designs will be less affected. Therefore, we have to ask if draftsmen with shorter training working on details are still necessary. To date, experience regarding CAD workplaces has shown that the draftsmen will have to acquire higher qualifications in the near future, because sophisticated working steps gain importance in comparison to schematical work. In future, training should stress the solution of problems in a more analytical way. Here manual drawing work should play a minor part.

2. Pilot schemes on CAD/CAM training of draftsmen

The series of pilot experiments on "New technologies in vocational training" organized by the Federal Ministry of Education and Science aims to provide solutions for the urgent qualification problems of firms caused by technological change. Technical support and coordination of the pilot schemes are provided by the Bundesinstitut für Berufsbildung (Federal Institute for Vocational Training), which is interested in passing on information and knowledge as quickly as possible so that it may be of practical use to the whole field of vocational training. The experiments are above all intended to develop direct aids for those involved in practical training, e.g. in the form of training curricula, didactic material, manuals or methodological assistance with regard to training methods.

This series of pilot experiments concentrates on CAD/CAM technology, i.e. computer-aided design combined with computer-aided manufacturing. The three firms of SMS Schloemann-Siemag AG, Krupp MaK Maschinenbau GmbH, and Mannesmann Kienzle GmbH are carrying out pilot experiments on the training of draftsmen, concentrating on different problems. Another experiment is planned involving a number of smaller firms and including also the field of further education. In order to utilize the knowledge and experience gained from these pilot schemes in other firms also, systematically planned and scientifically controlled experiments are required. Therefore each experiment is given scientific support which helps the firms carry out the pilot experiments and systematically evaluates the results. Like all other trainees in this occupation sector the future draftsmen have usually graduated from secondary general or intermediate school. The number of female trainees participating in the pilot schemes is about 50 % and corresponds to women's share of the total number of trainees for this occupation.

The firms involved in the CAD/CAM pilot experiment are characterized by customized manufacture with its high percentage of design work, which is typical of mechanical engineering. Their range of production requires CAD/CAM concepts with different job qualification requirements. For instance, different models of geometric processing within the computer (two-dimensional or three-dimensional internal representation) have an impact on the qualifications required for the processing and input of data.

The first CAD/CAM pilot experiment was started at SMS Schloemann Siemag AG in Hilchenbach in September 1984. There a scheme has been developed and is being tested for training draftsmen on 2D CAD systems. Scientific support for this experiment is provided by the Institute for Design of Siegen University. This pilot experiment includes the training of two age groups comprising 10-15 young people each.

The pilot experiment carried out by the Krupp MaK Maschinenbau GmbH in Kiel concentrates on training draftsmen for computer-aided design and drawing using 3D CAD systems. This experiment is supported by members of the Institute for the Teaching of Natural Sciences at Kiel University. The experiment covers four age groups with 10 trainees each.

The pilot experiment at Mannesmann Kienzle GmbH in Villingen-Schwenningen is designed to test a form of training which combines electrical and mechanical engineering including CAD/CAM technology. Scientific support is given by a member of the School for Precision Mechanics at Villingen-Schwenningen. Twelve adolescents per age group are being trained during the experimental period.

Under the auspices of the Federal Institute for Vocational Training those participating in the three pilot experiments have formed a working group with the aim of coordinating the different schemes and the new training contents as well as exchanging information and experience. So far, the firms involved in the pilot experiments have listed the qualifications to be acquired, described them in the form of learning objectives and have given them a didactic structure. On this basis they are now developing and testing training material such as exercises, work sheets and instructional aids. The working group unanimously stated that the new technologies required additional training phases for the draftsmen:

- basic training in information technology
- CAD training
- CAM training.

It is still essential for draftsmen to have a sound knowledge of manufacturing techniques and processes as well as skills and knowledge of drawing techniques. However, the traditional contents of training have to be reviewed and new priorities have to be established in order to gain time for the acquisition of additional knowledge. Furthermore it is necessary to develop mathematical and functional ways of thinking in order to create an understanding of geometric processing within the computer.

3. Basic training in information technology

The basic training in information technology included in the pilot experiments serves as a preparation for CAD and CAM training and provides a solid basis. Practical training on the other hand is at present frequently limited to a short-term training of skilled workers on CAD work stations to provide practical knowledge on the respective equipment and systems. However, a systematic CAD/CAM training as tested in the pilot experiments has to start from the basic knowledge of computer science and deepen CAD knowledge by adding the fundamentals of CAM technology.

Whereas a completely new curriculum has to be developed for CAD/CAM, there are a number of established EDP curricula for business training, the very approach of which may serve as model for the training of draftsmen. On this basis the firms involved have developed schemes on "Fundamentals of data processing in connection with CAD", "Contents of EDP training" and "Fundamentals of computer science". Following a division of labour it seems possible to provide this theoretical knowledge at part-time vocational schools. In two cases cooperation between firm and school has already started.

The present schemes intended to provide basic computer science training for draftsmen have been influenced by traditional models, which emphasize the value of extensive expert knowledge. However, there are also some approaches which focus on developing problem solution capabilities. On the whole these schemes comprise a large range of subjects which require considerable efforts by both teachers and trainees. During the pilot experiments it will be of major importance to critically review this range of subjects and examine whether they are relevant for the qualification or draftsmen, thus making it possible to establish adequate training priorities. Subjects such as the historical development of computers, the basic structure of EDP facilities and general problems of data protection are of universal importance and should actually be part of general education. Vocational training should above all provide knowledge on application-oriented computer science. Thus the trainees become in particular acquainted with the edp facilities, with their peripheral equipment, the characteristics of machine- and problem-oriented programming languages and the various operating systems. They acquire a background knowledge which enables them to better understand the whole in-firm data flow, going also beyond their CAD work station, and to assess the contributions they can make. Another priority of basic training in computer science is to provide the mathematical fundamentals of electronic data processing. In addition to the number systems used, the trainees learn simple logical operations and laws of switching algebra. It remains to be seen to which extent these demanding objectives - which are, however, of essential importance for a deeper understanding of computer science - can be integrated into the training of draftsmen.

In addition to theoretical instruction the trainees are supposed to draw up simple programmes in Basic, the main objective of which is, however, not to acquire programming skills but to analyze a problem and to draw up data and programme flow charts.

4. CAD training

The pilot scheme to be tested by the firms is based on the actual on-the-job situation, i.e. young people are trained to work with CAD systems they will have to handle later on in their jobs. Thus access is also provided to operational standards and rerun parts during the training phase in order to permit the solution of practical problems.

Training starts with a general survey of the function of CAD systems. This includes the major German and English technical terms related to computer-aided applications (CAD, CAM, CIM, etc.), hardware (bit, CPU, RAM, etc.) and software (2D, 2½D, 3D, etc.). The trainees learn about the structure of computers, their operating systems and data storage. They are familiarized with the visual display unit, the input units such as function keys, tracking ball and menue as well as the output units such as plotter, hard copy and printer.

In CAD training, much attention is given to the handling of the programme system and the survey of the possibilities and limits of the software used. Due to the various computer models and the varied computer-internal representation of technical objects, CAD training is a very comprehensive and complex task. With regard to 3D programme systems, for instance, a distinction is made between wire frame, area and volume representation which determine the range of application. Although a workshop drawing does not indicate the differences in software, the draftsman should know the characteristics of the different ways of representation. Handling a system requires knowledge of the working techniques such as translation, rotation, zooming or windowing. Using these techniques, the draftsman is able to make complex drawings also on relatively small screens.

The training of draftsmen is still based on acquiring skills and knowledge in the fields of metal engineering and drafting methods. Although CAD training already starts in the first or second year, handling CAD equipment and systems is mainly taught in the third and fourth years of training. Practical CAD training is provided systematically in the training department and, with regard to specific problems, in the design office.

5. CAM training

The results of the draftsman's work form the basis of product manufacture. The use of computers requires additional qualifications not only in the field of design but also with regard to manufacturing. The draftsman should have a sound knowledge of modern production engineering so that direct computer-aided processing of design data is possible. Workpieces, for instance, which are to be treated by numerically controlled machine tools have to be dimensioned in accordance with this process.

Basic NC/CNC training forms the central part of CAM training in the three pilot schemes. This includes the development, testing and execution of programmes. The basic knowledge comprises the technical terms of NC/CNC technology, the structural characteristics of numerically controlled machine tools, and programme structures as well as working with the coordinate systems of NC equipment. In particular, the draftsman should be familiar with the organization of numerically controlled manufacturing. The production process includes such tasks as accomplished by the process engineer, the NC programmer, the tool setter as well as the machine tool operator. Therefore the pilot CAM training schemes also include such fields as job and process planning. As edp is used more and more the knowledge and understanding of processes become increasingly important for the draftsman. Therefore training has to provide for an improved development of the ability to cooperate and communicate.

So far the schemes for a basic training in computer science as well as training in the fields of CAD and CAM have not provided any definite training curricula. However, they may now already help the interested firms to qualify their draftsmen for new technologies.

Employment Figures for Technical Draftspeople
(Berufsordnung 635: Technical Draftspeople, Construction Draftspeople, Detail Draftspeople etc.)

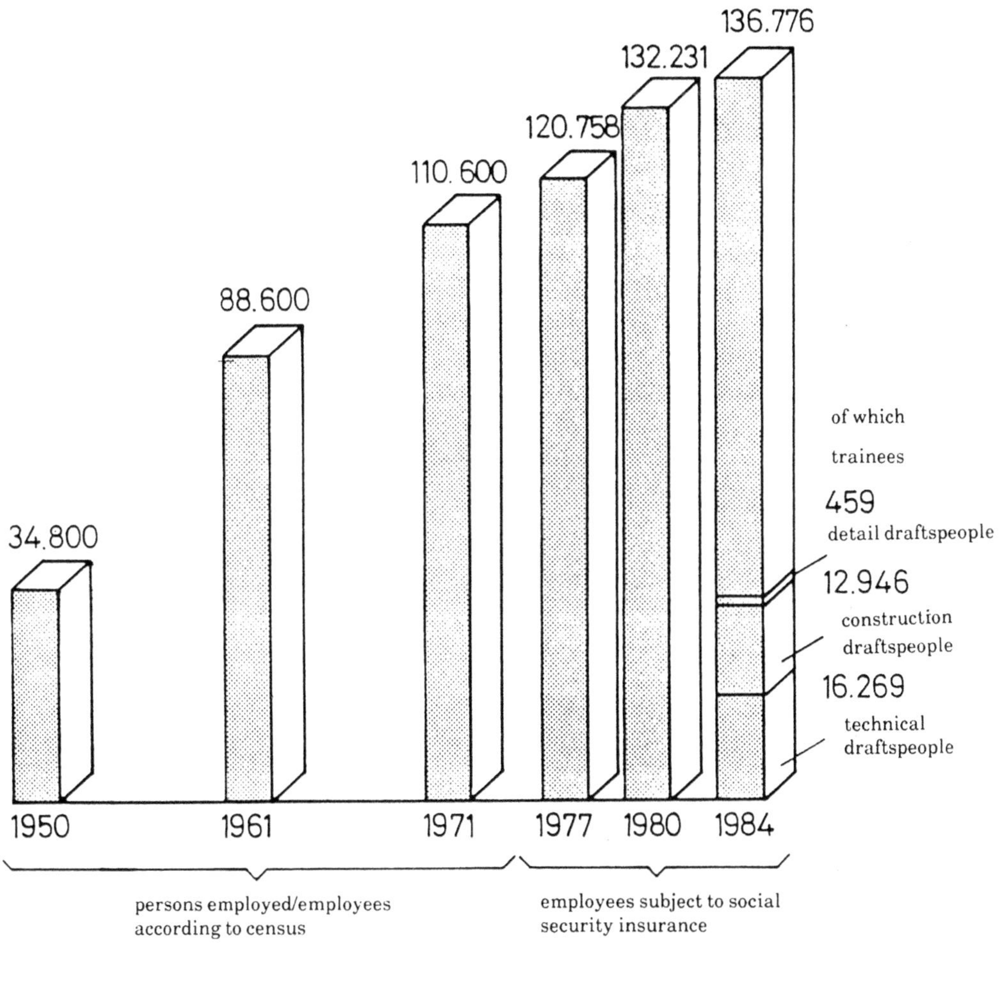

Source: Verzeichnis der anerkannten Ausbildungsberufe
Bundesinstitut für Berufsbildung

Training for technical Draftspeople

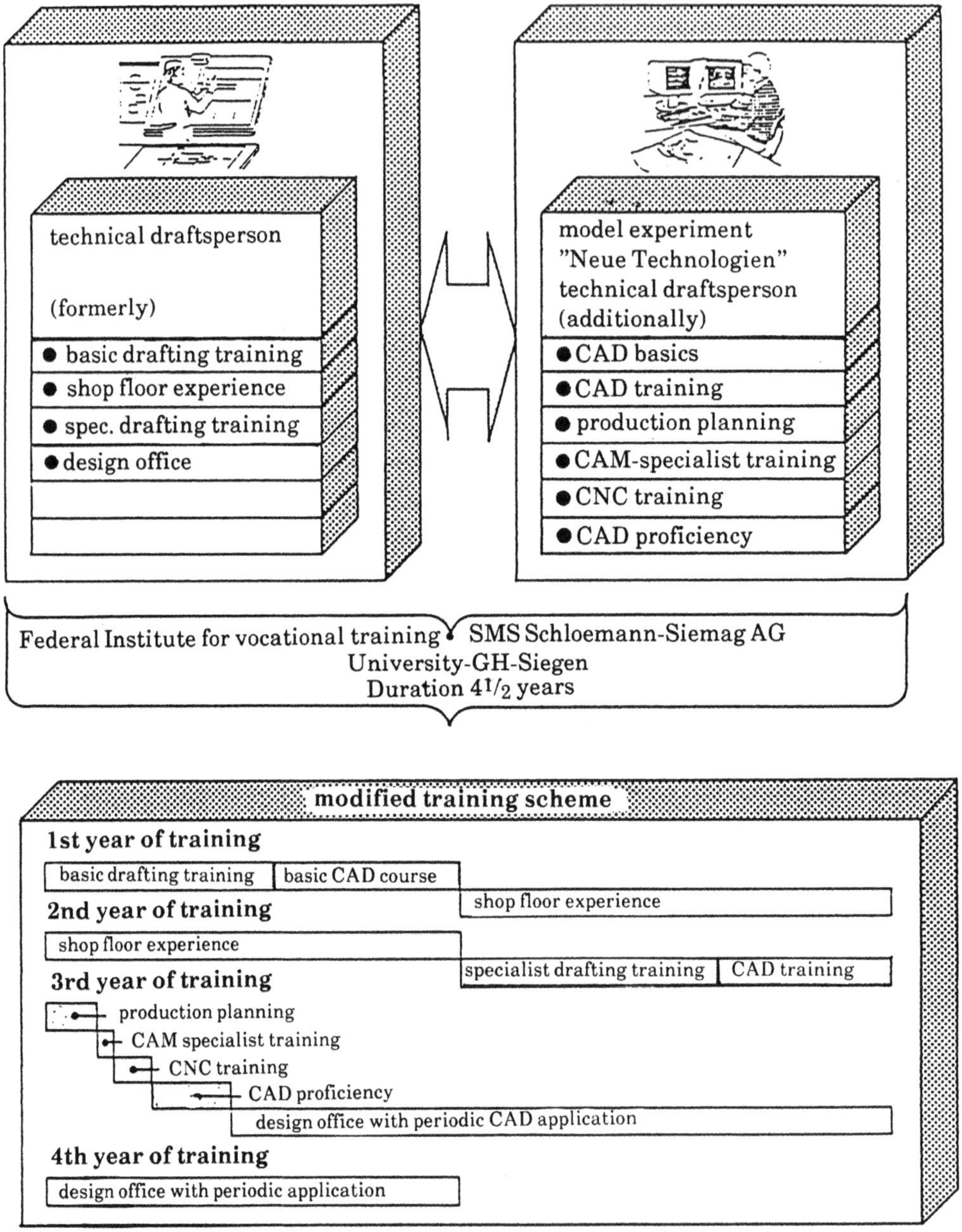

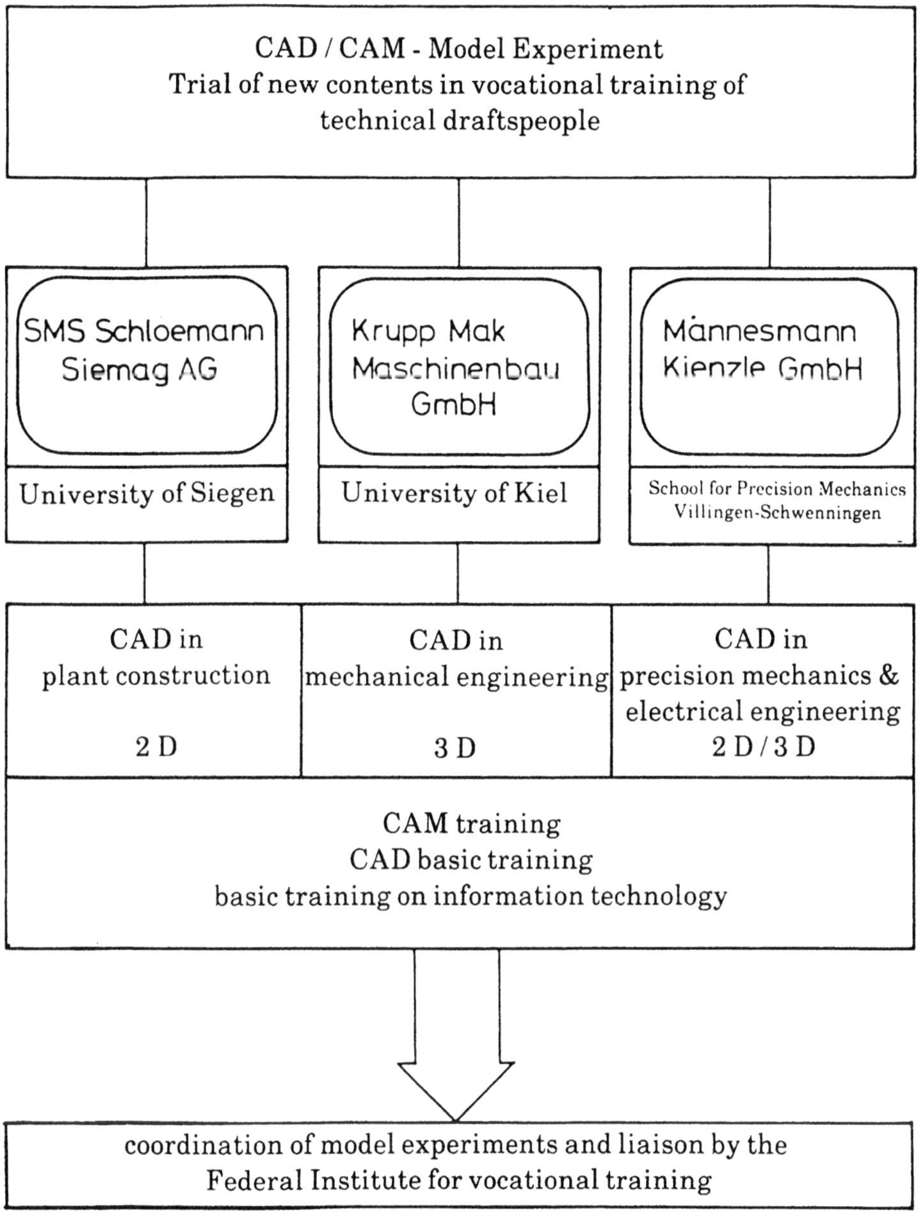
CAD / CAM - Model Experiment
Trial of new contents in vocational training of
technical draftspeople
SMS Schloemann
Siemag AG
University of Siegen
Krupp Mak
Maschinenbau
GmbH
University of Kiel
Mannesmann
Kienzle GmbH
School for Precision Mechanics
Villingen-Schwenningen
CAD in
plant construction
2 D
CAD in
mechanical engineering
3 D
CAD in
precision mechanics &
electrical engineering
2 D / 3 D
CAM training
CAD basic training
basic training on information technology
coordination of model experiments and liaison by the
Federal Institute for vocational training

CONCEPTION OF CAD/CAM TRAINING FOR TECHNICAL DRAUGHTSMEN IN A MODEL EXPERIMENT

Holm Gottschalch
Institut für die Pädagogik der Naturwissenschaften
Olshausenstr. 40
2300 Kiel
Federal Republic of Germany *)

1. Introduction

Following the introduction of the Ministry of Education and Science's Action Program: New Technologies in Vocational Education as well as the four model experiments with CAD/CAM training for trainee draughtsmen running in conjunction with this program, I would now like to outline the conception of educational and psychological research accompanying one of these model experiments in a large engineering firm, and also indicate initial experiences gained in the course of the training.

2. Domains of change due to CAD

The introduction of CAD technology in design departments and drawing offices will in future exert particularly severe rationalization pressure on the technical draughtsmen. CAD systems allow drawings to be produced and altered more quickly. With the appropriate software, special macros in the menu and facilities for product variant representation, parts design can work on a new computerized basis, i.e. the tasks which until now have been fulfilled by technical draughtsmen in design offices can in future be taken over by just a few CAD draughtsmen.

CAD is not, of course, used only to produce drawings or to work on existing drafts, but also to design or even conceive in a developmental process. It then, however, affects mainly the designers and technicians, with whom our model experiment is not concerned.

With the introduction of CAD technology the major skills involved in the qualification of technical draughtsmen are in danger of becoming devalued or redundant. This detracts both qualitatively and quantitatively from the long-term career prospects for technical draughtsmen.

---

*) Now with: Universität Bremen, Fachbereich Produktionstechnik, Bibliothekstraße, 2800 Bremen 33

3. Function of drawing, skills and careers

If technical drawing is regarded as a fundamental skill necessary for the general area of production planning, design, production control, programming and operations scheduling (areas in which technical draughtsmen can operate), then a strategy for retaining and developing this skill must be realized. The training course must be revised in order to compensate for loss of qualification.

Over the next few years, current trends in technical organization will lead to more integrated operational structures and processes on the basis of CAD/CAM technology. This development will affect all groups working in the area of production planning and preparation.

If technical draughtsmen are still to have a career perspective under these conditions, then not only must CAD technology be included in their field of operations, but they must also be introduced to new tasks which they can approach flexibly on the basis of their CAD/CAM training.

4. The necessity for CAD training

New technologies in the area of design, drawing and production must be included into the training courses (until now 3 1/2 years in firms and vocational schools, cf. charts), initially by means of model experiments. The traditional regulations governing the training courses, which will no doubt continue to hold for many years, must shift their emphasis. Many of the outdated elements, particularly those concerning the manual skill of drawing, could be greatly reduced. However, the CAD/CAM training (encompassing almost two months, i.e. 300 hours) should not be boosted at the cost of the basic training in drawing itself, as the examination regulations will continue to hold for all trainees for many years to come, and there will still be many firms which do not use CAD for design and drafting.

5. Research questions related to new CAD training and its evaluation

The support of the Federal Ministry of Education and Science has enabled us, on a trial basis, to extend, reorganize and change the emphasis of basic CAD/CAM courses in our model experiment with CAD/CAM instruction for trainee draughtsmen. I would now like to outline the major features of our educational and psychological conception of training in new technologies.

Outline
of a 3 1/2-year training course

1st 6 months	Introduction to use of instruments *Knowledge and skill in using drawing implements* Basic training in technical drawing *Knowledge and skill in representation, dimensioning, basic geometry, representational geometry* Reprography, documentation (microfilming) *Knowledge*
2nd 6 months	Basic workshop training *Basic skills in materials processing at workbench and machine, safety regulations* Measuring and testing *Knowledge and skills in measuring practice* Machine training, pneumatics and hydraulics *Knowledge and skills in cutting processes on manually operated machines*
3rd 6 months	Work process in a production firm *Mechanical production, surface treatment, materials testing, storage systems, part assembly, model joinery, foundry, electrical workshop, assembly sections* Basics of electronic data processing Machine training *Knowledge and skills in cutting processes on NC CNC machines*
4th 6 months	Revision and extension of basic training in draughtsmanship *Preparation for Chamber of Industry and Commerce intermediate examination* Specialized training in technical draughtsmanship *Production of drawings of individual parts, groups and complete structures confirming to workshop specifications, item lists, tolerances, (machine) fits, form and storage tolerances* Basic training in computer-assisted drawing and design *Work at CAD positions*
5th 6 months	
6th 6 months	Training in specialized departments *Specifics of the training firm (e.g. circuit diagrams, mains, knots etc.), Basic features of work sequences with design, operations scheduling, standard supervision, work at CAD terminals*
7th 6 months	Preparation for Chamber of Industry and Commerce final examination

Computers CNC CAD in context

The trainees are introduced to the new technologies in three units: a basic computer course (30 hours), a course in programming (60 hours) and application (60 hours) of CNC machines, a basic CAD course including practical work (120 hours), and a further CAD course for 3D modeling (30 hours) - a total of 300 hours.

The introduction of new technologies in the design activities of production firms necessitates an integration of operational structures and processes on the basis of information technology. In firms of the future, geared to CAD/CAM technology, technical draughtsmen should be in a position to assume tasks far beyond the scope of their conventional activities of drawing and (to a limited extent) designing. Potentially, they could be involved in CAD/CAM design and computer-assisted production planning on the one hand, or numerically controlled programming with computer-assisted production control and operations scheduling on the other.

By acquiring basic computer knowledge and familiarizing themselves with the application of computer systems in production and design, the trainees gain practical experience of the integrative effect of computerization. They learn to grasp their own tasks within the whole context of computerized operational processes.

Basic systematic knowledge

Basic systematic knowledge (with little specific reference to particular systems) of CAD technology and how it functions is provided. The aim of the training course is to produce technical draughtsmen qualified in CAD who can design and reproduce three-dimensional parts (geared to edges, surfaces or volume) on any CAD system, needing only a short time to become acquainted with the latter. They should be able to apply their basic skills rapidly, independently and reliably to other CAD systems, aware of the principles on which these function. We do not wish to restrict the training to that of simply a "producer of CAD graphics" or CAD system-user - and we particularly wish to avoid concentration on one type of system only.

Knowledge of operational processes

The trainees acquire comprehensive knowledge of operational processes and organization. They see their work at the drawing board or CAD terminal in its wider organizational context by getting to know a variety of departments.

In fact the technical draughtsmen of the future should be able to apply their CAD/CAM skills without being bound to any particular department. They will have to be able to recognize their own particular role (which may include any of a wide range of tasks) as part of a cooperative system integrated by new technologies acting competently and flexibly on the basis of this understanding. The basic technical and engineering knowledge necessary for computer-assisted design, together with the technological knowledge and experience required for CNC processing determine the scope of the work.

Understanding of rationalization

The introduction of new technologies, particularly CAD technology, in industry is represented as a process of rationalization in which organizational structures result from specific economic and strategic conditions. Examples are used to demonstrate how CAD systems may in various ways fit into the resulting structures. The trainees are shown how draughtsmen can play a role in the design process and an explanation of the legal basis for participation is given. The training course aims to demonstrate that the introduction of CAD/CAM technology has major consequences for technical draughtsmen in terms of their tasks and qualification requirements, and that this development has a lasting influence on the career perspectives in this field.

This topic affects the trainees directly and subjectively, reflecting problems they will encounter in their future careers. They learn to accept that they will be confronted with the introduction of new technologies in the firms where they work, and that in view of the mass unemployment they will be under pressure to achieve further qualifications.

Learning processes specific to CAD/CAM

The learning processes set out below are supported by specific didactic methods which cannot here be described in detail. In some instances we are still developing and testing these methods.

We promote the development of differentiated *mental models* of the structure, the complex inner systems and functioning of CAD information processing. We regard CAD draughtsmen as something more than simply program users and want to enable them to act competently and make decisions within the whole area of design.

We provide *in-depth knowledge* on the structure of CAD systems, their hardware components, their computer storage capacity, etc., as well as on how they function, with information on software and computer-internal representation of 3D geometry. The aim is for the trainees to see beyond the superficial representation of information processing on the terminal screen. The CAD system, which at first appears as a "black box" is to be made transparent.

We aim to *de-mystify* CAD technology through instruction which allows the trainees to "get to grips" - both metaphorically and literally - with the machines and systems, so that they no longer ascribe particular "abilities" to CAD or the computer, but instead see them as tools, fully aware of their limits and possible error sources.

The training course is intended to *dispel the fallacy* that CAD represents *technical perfection*. Problems of computer-assisted design are at times due to software deficiency, long reply times are due to inadequate storage capacity, computers can break down if the operators at the terminals make too many and too great demands on the system, data errors can be caused by contamination of disks, most CAD positions could be designed more ergonomically and more humanely - and so the list goes on. Information technology is a man-made tool and as such it has short-comings and begs improvement.

We are preparing a systematic acquisition of CAD techniques oriented to the *major characteristics of information technology* and the principles of its structure. At the three levels of computers, CNC and CAD, the essential structures of information technology and the basic principles of interaction between humans and computers are emphasized: the characteristics of programs and programming methods, software, command modes, menu trees, etc. From unit to unit in their training, the draughtsmen learn to grasp more exactly how their activities fit into the overall system, how information technology can be used and on what they must concentrate their learning processes.

The trainee draughtsmen familiarize themselves with practical working methods using CAD within a well-balanced and well-structured *combination of various training forms:*

- mental (cognitive and imaginative)
- observational
- verbal
- motor
- operative and
- explorative training.

The various forms of training alternate and are emphasized differently in the various phases of the course. Forms of mental, verbal and operative training take on particular significance for learning processes in information technology.

The learning processes are structured in phases of theoretical instruction and practical training at the terminal. Although we introduce practical work at the terminal from the start, most of the time at the beginning is devoted to theory and work on the basics. We adopted this *theory-practice structure* in order on the one hand to capitalize on the fascination which this medium (at first) exerts on young people, increasing their motivation to learn, and on the other to found the practical work at a CAD terminal using a graphic editor on sound, in-depth basic knowledge.

The CAD training provided in our model experiment is intended as a substantial step on the road to a *self-learning process*. In this process the teacher increasingly assumes the role of a guide leading towards independent activity and a helper in specific situations only.

- Learning takes place in groups of four, with two trainees per terminal. This concept requires cooperative learning, as well as mutual control and support during the drawing work at the terminal.
- Rather than asking the teacher for information and assistance, it is more important for the trainees to learn how to help themselves by consulting CAD textbooks, handbooks, operating instructions, and their own notes, or by calling up the information and help functions of the CAD menu.
- The concept of independent learning also includes self-controlled learning. The young draughtsmen can easily check their progress by consulting the geometry produced and plotted on the basis of the set tasks. The two pairs at the terminals can compare their results and help each other where necessary.

- During the course there is continual feedback of learning progress in the interaction between the four trainees and the teacher. The first exercises and examples are thus kept to a small scale and worked out so precisely that a gap in the learning process would be noticed at once.
- Finally, the self-learning concept also comprises participative learning, insofar as the trainees (in the first years of the project almost certainly more than in later years) can raise criticism, make suggestions, and contribute generally to the organization of the contents and material of the course (a task for which they, as technical draughtsmen are particularly qualified).

In a *contrastive work analysis*, the trainees learn to determine the characteristics of information processing in a CAD system and in the human mind. They are introduced to analysis of human-computer interaction and recognition of the (under certain conditions problematical) relation of the working person to computers i.e. recognition of the "interface" between them. There are certain questions to be answered, such as who is using whom, whether CAD is a tool and if so under what conditions, whether a division into programmer and program user or a polarization between CAD designer and drawer is unavoidable or dependent on particular conditions of organization.

New teaching/learning materials

The learning processes outlined briefly above require *special materials*: introductory texts, textbooks, overhead projector transparencies, German operating instructions, and manuals for the CAD system, worksheets for the trainees, and systematic practice exercises. These are not widely available and CAD teachers and trainees must therefore work out much of the material for themselves.

Our experiences with "user courses" offered by a manufacturer of CAD systems were by no means positive. The material provided is (almost) useless for the section of CAD training dealing with the specific system. The instruction manual and operating instructions, to some extent even the menu on screen and tablet, are written in - to the trainees - barely comprehensible English. Due to the continual development of software, a great deal of the information is outdated and ambiguous. The introduction to the editor of the CAD system is incorrect or misleading in many places. Rather than giving the name of this particular manufacturer I would prefer to ask instead which manufacturer *is* in a position to supply good learning material, together with the hardware and software for the system?

Parts of general basic instruction on CAD technology can use material from well-known German textbooks. A book which we have found very useful and which was conveniently published just as we were beginning our courses is the user reference book by EIGNER and MAIER (1985), which provides a good introduction for complete CAD novices.

But German literature helps us to realize only a part (albeit a most essential part) of our conception as described above: the general basics of CAD technology. Further instruction requires of appropriate material from literature in the area of sociology and work psychology, from recent information on CAD technology and CAD work provided by the trade union IG Metall. (The main problem facing educators and trainees here is not English but the specialized terminology of the social sciences.) This presents a task for social science research accompanying the model experiments: transposition of the information gained from empirical research in social science so that it can be applied at the level of practical vocational training.

6. Initial observations and experience

The model experiment is being conducted by a large engineering firm. The organizational structure of departments from design to production and the hierarchical structure within the departments is horizontally more separated and vertically more differentiated than is the case in small and medium-sized firms. For the technical draughtsmen this means that their field of activity is narrowed and that fewer demands are made on the CAD/CAM staff's flexibility and capacity for independent work, particularly in the area of parts design. This effect of the organizational structure on work content is also considered in several contributions to this workshop.

In the four design departments within the firm, the staff mainly involved in the introduction of CAD appear to be engineers, designers and technicians. After a short course for CAD users they independently acquire the CAD technique. In the future, drafting with CAD may be one of their auxiliary tasks. Although the technical draughtsmen also learn to work with the systems, their role appears to be restricted to the initial phase of a few years. At the latest when most of the drawings of the products are stored on CAD disks in libraries, the technical draughtsmen could become superfluous.

In our opinion, CAD/CAM technology restricts the scope of activity for technical draughtsmen in two ways. Designers and engineers have the appropriate qualifications to conceive and design parts and improve on them, whereas technical draughtsmen do not. Experienced technicians and master craftsmen can be promoted to operations scheduling, production control and programming. Technical draughtsmen have neither the theoretical knowledge of processing technology, nor the practical experience in the factory. Many CAD systems can be used for automatic CNC programming. It will hardly be the task of the technical draughtsmen to check these programs, to test and optimize them in the initial phase. Virtually insurmountable restrictions from two directions are gradually moving towards the work of the technical draughtsman.

I would now like to follow my description of these restrictions affecting our conception of the development of draughtsmanship with a rather paradoxical observation. It is highly improbable that any of the trainees will be taken on by the firm after completion of their training. Therefore, it is not only possible, but also highly recommendable to provide a broad-based fundamental training in CAD/CAM, avoiding the restriction both to a specific system and to the task of simply producing drawings. The training in the model experiment is not related to the firm's rationalization strategy. We can thus make use of ideal conditions, unaffected by the economic pressures under which the firm is currently operating. If the trainees were guaranteed a place in the firm after qualifying, they would have to be thoroughly familiar with the CAD system and able to produce drawings for the new disk library very quickly and reliably. If this were the case we would have to gear the training specifically to the firm's CAD system and its operation.

We have encountered no "acceptance problems" among the trainees. This is quite astonishing in view of the fact that none of them can envisage career opportunities with CAD. In their opinion, their advantage on the labour market with their knowledge of CAD is little more than negligible. On the other hand, we have not been able to ascertain any "fascination" with CAD which would explain the trainees' interest in work with computers. The young people accepted the units on computing, CNC and CAD in a manner completely free of illusions, even with indifference.

This reserve in the trainees' attitude towards new technologies does not mean, however, that their learning processes fall short of the required standard or that their independent learning capacity is reduced. All first-year trainees passed the three phases of the model experiment and acquired basic training in CAD/CAM. They wrote their own CNC program for parts they designed themselves, and produced the parts. They programmed CAD menu instructions themselves and, using the 3D edge-oriented model, also displayed and assembled a complex casing with many parts at the CAD terminal.

Reference

Eigner, M.; Maier, H.:
Einstieg in CAD, München/Wien 1985.

CHAPTER 4: Organizational Effects and CAD/CAM Integration

While most of the papers submitted for this session agreed that there is a certain amount of freedom of choice for organizational set-ups for the application of technology, there was disagreement on how optimistic one should be with regard to the possibility of taking advantage of this latitude. HOSS' paper outlines the broad alternatives and would seem to fall into the optimistic category, while both HIRSCH-KREINSEN and MANSKE et al. see forces at work to counteract any tendencies of De-Taylorization. FINNE shows that CAD/CAM tends to create organizational disturbances across the boundaries of individual departments which cannot, apparently, be removed by simple negotiation between these departments. HAYWOOD examines the role of computer-integrated manufacturing in securing the competitiveness of firms and points out factors he felt should be taken into consideration when integrating. Van WAGENBERG shows alternatives for the use of CAD and their possible effects on organization and task structure. Of his two development patterns, the one described as "vertical" looks more likely to have effect on the organization than that termed "horizontal". The effect is likely to be on the sequence of work and communication patterns rather than on the structure of the organization itself.

A large portion of discussion was devoted to the subject of Taylorism. It was pointed out by ARNOLD, that Taylorism is not simply exercised by instruction cards, but also by things like design information or computer programmes. The distinction made in France between "Dessin" and "Conception" in connection with CAD might be useful in that DAO meant computer aided drafting and might be employed as a Taylorist measure while CAO might be employed to enhance jobs. FINNE pointed out that Taylorism is a concept of relationship between people, not only on *what* they do but on *how* they do it. Previously, a designer would pass on a task to a draftsperson but give no instruction on how to do it. In fact draftspeople had highly individual styles. Computer aided drafting is, however, standardized and that is more like Taylorism.

POITOU pointed out that it is not sufficient to observe the individual plant when considering Taylorism. Firms often consist of several plants while large firms also have sub-contractors working for them. Renault is a company with somewhere in the order of 100.000 employees, with the design and job preparation divisions each consisting of around 4000 people. Each of these divisions has contractors doing draughting work and if one considers that 50 % of the draughting work is done by these sub-contractors and considers the average size of such firms, the magnitude of the effect becomes apparent. In addition, Renault has suppliers and each of these has its own design office. So while the effects in the central office might be interesting, this was far from the whole picture. On the subject of sub-contractors, there was some disagreement on whether a direct computer-link between the customer and the sub-contractor would increase the customer's dependence on the sub-contractor, enhancing the latter's position, or whether CAD/CAM might put the customer in the position of being able to dispense with the services of the sub-contractor. Empirical evidence cited by ARNOLD and others suggested that job loss was being suffered by the sub-contractors rather than the customers, so this would support the latter position. Also, attention was drawn to "technological imperialism", meaning that customers actually dictate to their sub-contractors which CAD-system they should use. HAYWOOD added some information on the situation of sub-contractors and the effects CAD/CAM has been having on it. The number of sub-contractors working for the individual customer was on the decline and they were being given longer-term contracts for 2 to 3 years rather than 3 to 6 months. Although there was a tendency to prescribe technology, the sub-contractors sometimes benefited from preferential rates offered the larger customers. Also, the greater security provided by longer-term contracts was enabling the sub-contractors to plan for longer periods, including rationalization measures. However, since the customers were able to assess costs of jobs done with the equipment purchased by their sub-contractor, they were able to apply pressure to cut costs, although they left some of the benefits to their sub-contractors.

POITOU raised another point as needing further research: in some cases plants are connected via a computer network designed to provide a large data-base. In some plants access to information is restricted through a very rigid hierarchy and it would be interesting to see if the network helped overcome the hierarchy.

RADER made a brief contribution on the professionalization of CAD project groups. He noted that a person variously termed as the "CAD expert" (WINGERT et al.), the "CAD manager" (ARNOLD & SENKER), the "CAD champion" or the "CAD mother" (Mc LOUGHLIN) had been found in almost every firm introducing CAD. While initially there tended to be a sole individual responsible for CAD, as time went on, groups with the same task were established. He felt that this was due to the strategy of starting with a small system requiring little outlay, sometimes even without official approval of the company's top management. Also, implementing CAD tended to require more effort than had been planned for. The groups responsible for CAD also seemed to achieve permanent status, which may be due to two factors: specialized staff is required to maintain and up-date the system; systems are not frozen, but expanded or replaced by new, more powerful systems.

McLOUGHLIN made several observations on the people termed "CAD experts". These had established themselves in the direct role of controlling CAD use, factually supervising work in the design office. In the traditional design offices, supervisors were located fairly high up in the hierarchy and were not usually being trained for CAD use, since they did no drawing. This had the effect that they no longer were able to judge what their subordinates were doing and so they lost control, leaving room for the CAD experts to move in. Developments of this kind were leading to tension between the section leaders (the traditional supervisors) and the CAD experts.

On the subject of the relationship between CAD system and organizational environment, RADER noted that you cannot improve an unsuitable system by skillful design of the organization but you can ruin a perfectly good system by inappropriate organizational design.

Still on the subject of the relationship between organization and technology, SPRINGER doubted HOSS' claim that the traditional division of labour between departments would disappear as a result of computer integration. While this might be true for large firms, in his experience the small firms tended to use EDP, and CAD in particular, to build up a division of labour between planning departments, the design office and the shop floor which had not existed previously. WINGERT reported that generally, there was a dialectic relationship between design and production, although the transfer of information might be rigid. In his experience, the geometry for the same part might be different in the design office from the geometry required to produce it on the shop floor, i.e. tolerances differ, different parameters or different terms are used.

Finally, KJELLBERG commented on what are described as "vertical organization" forms. These were introduced to adapt to changing market requirements, in particular to the switch to customer-ordered production. The need for sharp calculation of prices led to the idea of product families, each within the responsibility of specialized engineer-designers. There was a need to bridge the gap between production planning, design and manufacturing and this is where CAD/CAM was coming in. CAD/CAM was, in fact, being employed as a means to reorganize firms.

ALTERNATIVES FOR THE INTEGRATION OF CAD/CAM *)

Dietrich Hoß

Institut für Sozialforschung
an der Johann Wolfgang Goethe-Universität
Senckenberganlage 26
6000 Frankfurt/M. 1

1. Motives for an alternative model of implementation

The discussion of models and the available published experience on the use of integrated CAD/CAM systems make it clear that there are different organizational alternatives. If the integration follows the traditional pattern of Tayloristic "Scientific Management", the option of centralizing the structures of direction and authority as a result of the integration of data material and computer-based information and control systems is used to exclude human labour from the production process or to confine it to very limited residual functions which can not (yet) be substituted by technological means. If such an approach is pursued, CAD/CAM technology means an end to all qualifications and social relations which were previously indispensable to organize and maintain the production process. The new technology is viewed as an instrument to "expropriate" individual and professional knowledge and to absorb the social communication structures, which until now had been indispensable for the organization and maintenance of the production process. Communication and exchange among the workforce are no longer necessary. They even seem to obstruct the work of the individual worker. The control over the work performance is centralized and rests with senior management and there is a tendency for it to become more and more extensive as the frequency of the on-line dialogue, the use of computing times at the individual workplace and thus the time used to accomplish a work task is automatically recorded and can be checked at any time.

An alternative model of implementation sees the efficiency of new technology as being based on the fact that all accumulated data of an enterprise can be called in from the storage if required by individuals in the different departments. It thus becomes possible at each stage of the production process - from design to planning and manufacturing - to take account of the information of the preceding and following areas of the production process. This not only reduces the frictional loss of transfer, correction and adjustment processes, but also creates an unprecedented capacity to react to shifts in the market and customers' requirements and to

*) This paper is based on a study for the Rationalisierungs-Kuratorium der Deutschen Wirtschaft (RKW) executed in cooperation with the Fraunhofer-Institut für Systemtechnik und Innovationsforschung (ISI), Karlsruhe (see Hoß et al. 1984)

develop new products and process technologies. According to leading technologists this potential for integrating systems can only be given full scope by revising the existing principles of "Scientific Management": On the basis of a relatively broad definition of functions, the individual operator or the team and work-group respectively, must be given a maximum of responsible autonomy and a new chain of communication facilities stretching to other areas of the process. The work of the individual worker or employee has to split: on the one hand he has to function as an "operating" element responsible for a smooth functioning of already predetermined processes and on the other hand, as a "master" of technology, he must constantly attempt to improve and optimize these processes (BEDNARZ et al. 1984). This is why a revision of the existing "top-down" principle of industrial enterprises is thought to be inevitable. Complementary to the traditional structure, the introduction of consultations "from the bottom up" is said to be necessary. The abandonment of the existing way of thinking in terms of separate segments of operation is deemed decisive in the future. There will have to be a permanent exchange of information between design and the following lines of production. Without institutionalized cooperation between the different fields of activity, the extensive knowledge within the plant could never be completely activated (EVERSHEIM 1983).

With regard to the technical possibilities it has been argued that with decentralized data processing in local networks which is performed by one and the same information system, it would be possible at each stage of the production process to optimize this process by means of graphic simulation. The simulation of all machining operations by the designer would gear designing to the manufacturing process and thus avoid errors and costs in the following machining operations. In the planning department dynamic simulation could be a significant aid in choosing the correct machine tool or its constructive design. These "simulation runs" could also be carried out directly on the production machines by using shopfloor-programming. After a production-oriented check of the NC-information on the machine tool it could be corrected and the revised manufacturing program could be reported back to the planning and the design departments (SPUR 1983).

By referring to the example of the integration of CAD and NC-programming, the technical and organizational framework for decisions concerning the above-mentioned alternative organization variants will be described in detail in the following.

2. Alternative consequences of organizational decisions

The integration of CAD and NC-programming is of particular significance in this context because this is an especially advanced example for CAD/CAM integration at the joint between the engineering and the manufacturing departments of the company. The analysis of this step towards integration is directly concerned with the question of changes of conceptual and executive work tasks and the forms of their reintegration in the course of the implementation of new technologies which is the main issue of the current debate in industrial sociology on the reorganization of industrial work (KERN/SCHUMANN 1984).

The actual consequences of the integration of computer-aided design and computer-aided NC-programming for the involved groups of employees (designers, draftsmen, NC-programmers, workshop personnel), the way the division of labour is changing between design, planning, NC-programming and the workshop, which groups of the workforce experience an upgrading or downgrading of their previous work and which groups are possibly threatened by dismissal - all this is determined by decisions which are taken at different levels.

The following levels can be distinguished:

- As far as the *technical system* is concerned, the question is whether NC-programming is completely integrated into the CAD-system, i.e. the NC-punched tape is directly produced in the CAD-system or whether the workpiece geometry, a "source programme" or a "CL-data-file" is handed over to NC-programming.

  The choice of the technical system, however, by no means involves a particular organizational solution.

- The following *organizational variants* can be found:
  In the case of complete integration of NC-programming into the CAD-system, the NC-programmer can produce the part programmed on the CAD-terminal but his function can also be taken over by the personnel of the design department.

If the workpiece geometry, a source programme, or CL-datafile which has been produced in the CAD-system, is handed over to the programming system, again either the CAD-operator can produce a NC-drawing (or with the help of a NC-module the source programme or the CL-Datafile) which means an additional new qualification for CAD-designers and draftsmen to the detriment of NC-programmers, or, on the other hand, the geometry data can be handed over to the NC department and the NC-programmer isolates the required data and takes charge of their further processing which would maintain or even extend his qualifications. Finally, there is also the possibility that the data produced in the CAD-system can be taken over, processed further or at least optimized by the workshop personnel.

However, there are not only different possibilities for the distribution of the functions of data-production and data-processing between the departments but also regarding the task patterns within the departments. That means the CAD-jobs can either be assigned to the respective departments in a decentralized way or can be located in a "pool" where the staff working with the CAD/NC programming system is centralized. In case of the latter solution, this can easily entail that only a few CAD-specialists are trained and deployed on the new system. Due to unbalanced mental strain as a result of the abolition of routine tasks this can lead for them to a high level of stress whereas the rest of the employees are threatened by a progressive reduction of job requirements. In the case of decentralized deployment in the different departments there is a greater chance that "mixed jobs" with conventional and computer-integrated tasks are emerging, maintaining or even extending existing skills.

Looked at from the angle of the *communication structure* finally, it is decisive for the form of the work requirements of the different groups of employees in integrated computer-aided CAD/NC-systems, whether in connection with the merging hitherto separated computer systems, traditional, hierarchical structures of direction and competence can be overcome or if they continue or become even more accentuated.

If, according to the traditional patterns of hierarchy, the direction and control of production from design to machine operation is exclusively organized according to the "top-down" principle, the workshop only deals with subordinate operating, inspection and maintenance work, while the intermediate departments are faced with the risk of being thinned out and reduced to subordinate routine. Corresponding to the alternative "bottom-up" feedback-principle outlined above, it is, however, possible that entirely new communication structures are being established. Proceeding on the assessment, that it is decisive to integrate exactly those elements of knowledge and thinking which are not formalized ("tacit knowledge"), into the design and control of production, there are created new possibilities of a permanent exchange of experience among the employees in the departments. One can find already reports which emphasize from a company point of view, the positive experiences with such feedback- mechanisms in the integration of CAD and NC-programming. In a case, in which the NC-geometry was developed by CAD-designers and draftsmen and the other NC-data were determined by NC-programmers, the resulting new communication structures were seen as a particular advantage. Although the designer and the NC-programmer intervened in the process of producing the NC-tape at different interfaces, there was a close co-operation between design and NC-department after the geometry had been drafted. As NC-programming was reporting back to the design department after having tried the tape, something like a closed "feedback control system" had finally emerged (Pham 1982).

3. The chances of alternative solutions

To what extent the shown alternative orientations of CAD/CAM integration are taking effect in reality as well as the question, whether, and under which conditions, the chances for an upgrading of tasks for individual groups of employees which is inherent in the described design variants, lead to an improvement of working conditions will be investigated within the framework of an empirical project of the Institut für Sozialforschung which has just started. Studies on the evaluation of new forms of work organization (ALTMANN et al. 1982) established that their effects for the workforce depend to a high degree on their integration into the general personnel policy of the company. Instead of extending the autonomy within the work process the combination of "work enrichment" with new forms of incentive policy and control can lead to new strains and even to a limitation of autonomy. In the case of insufficient training measures new skill requirements can entail overstrain and stress due to working processes which are not clearly understood.

A centralized concept of deployment will be usually connected with training measures which only familiarize a limited number of persons with the system. Only the software specialists are being trained in several months' courses by the manufacturers. For the operation of the system, the departmental heads favour the recruitment of young people who are not too familiar with the conventional working process so that it can be expected that they create fewer problems regarding the acceptance of the systems. This labour force is only being instructed with regard to particular functions of the system. That means they are able to bring about changes in the system only in clearly defined situations with the help of a detailed guidance, according to a strictly regulated pattern of sequences. As for the rest, the system has the character of a "black box".

If, however, human labour in integrated CAD/CAM-systems is seen in its dual aspect of functioning, on the one hand, as an "operating" element and, on the other hand, as an element which "dominates" the process and optimizes it, this will be reflected in the selection of labour. In a "dialogue"-oriented model of computer use traditional craft knowledge and experience are sought after as a valuable element of correction and optimization. This refers to process-specific as well as to non-specific and general social qualifications. The qualified workforce must gain a comprehensive insight in the functioning of the system to be able to bring in their expertise into the system and to "play" with it.

Finally the question, to what extent a favourable personnel policy for the employees is being pursued,depends on the specific balance of power in the enterprises.

As a whole it can be assumed that solutions which are relevant in terms of humanization are found in those cases when new cooperation arrangements and latent or open alliance structures are emerging from the differentiated network of conflicting and converging interests of management and workers. Relatively favourable conditions will prevail in places, where the innovating management, in the interest of a smooth introduction and an effective utilization of the new technology, takes account of the interest of the workers in skill protection and extension of autonomy and renounces the possible advantages of new computerized systems for controlling performance.

References

Altmann, N. et al., 1982:
Grenzen neuer Arbeitsformen, Frankfurt/New York 1982.

Bednarz, K. et al., 1984:
CAD/CAM und Qualifikation - Auswirkungen integrierter Computersysteme auf Arbeitsprozesse in Konstruktion und Fertigung. Frankfurt a.M./New York, 1984.

Eversheim, W., 1983:
Arbeitsvorbereitung als Bindeglied zwischen Konstruktion und Fertigung. in: Vorträge des Produktionstechnischen Kolloquiums Berlin (PTK), 1983.

Hoß, D. u.a., 1984:
Die sozialen Auswirkungen der Integration von CAD und CAM. Eschborn 1984 (RKW-Projekt: Integrierte CAD/CAM-Systeme, Entwicklungstrends - Einsatzmöglichkeiten - Auswirkungen, Teil 2).

Pham, T.T., 1982:
Erfahrung mit CAD und der NC-Kopplung. in: Zeitschrift für wirtschaftliche Fertigung, 1982, Nr. 10.

Spur, G., 1983:
Aufschwung, Krisis und Zukunft der Fabrik. in: Vorträge des PTK, Berlin 1983.

INTEGRATED CAD/CAM-SYSTEMS AND ORGANIZATIONAL LATITUDES ON THE SHOP FLOOR - INITIAL FINDINGS AND HYPOTHESES

Hartmut Hirsch-Kreinsen
Institut für Sozialwissenschaftliche Forschung e.V.
Jakob-Klar-Straße 9
8000 München 40
Federal Republic of Germany

1. Concepts of CAD/CAM integration

Integrated CAD/CAM-systems are employed to achieve computer-aided integration in all production functions, from design and planning up to manufacturing and the assurance of quality standards. So far, however, overall integration of this kind has hardly been put into practice. This applies particularly to the medium and small batch production of the machine-building industry *). At present various concepts of CAD/CAM integration which complement or overlap each other, often to the extent of operating concurrently in the case of implementation, can be discerned. On the one hand, concepts are concerned with the integration of design functions with planning, controlling and programming functions (CAD/CAP). On the other hand, they are concerned with the integration of manufacturing functions with planning, controlling and programming functions (DNC). Overall computer-aided integration, from design through to manufacturing, has only been conceived for a small number of product elements and limited manufacturing processes so far.

It is hard to estimate to what extent the various concepts of integrated CAD/CAM-systems are presently being applied. So far, overall integrated CAD/CAM-systems only exist in a few large aviation and machine building companies (DÖPPER/ILZIG 1985). The integration of CAD with NC programming systems has been achieved in several machine building companies; this partial integration is likely to become increasingly widespread in the near future, not least due to massive government support (WINGERT et al., 1984, pp. 69 ff). The integration of the design functions with further planning functions as the creation of operation plans is still a dream of the future which is, moreover, confronted with considerable barriers in the field of information technology (LAY et al., 1984; FÖRSTER, 1985). However according to the opinions of a number of the experts interviewed, the use of DNC-systems, particularly in small and medium batch production in the machine-building industry, is likely to increase rapidly (Roland BERGER, 1984). Overall concepts of integration, from construction to production, have recently been presented for relatively simple lathe work, milling work and sheet metal machining operations (LEIBINGER, 1983).

---

*) An empirical project of the ISF Munich is currently focusing on this branch and is investigating the anticipated effects of integrated manufacturing technology on staff and skilled work. The project aims at defining conditions and possibilities of securing and expanding skilled work on the shop floor in machine-building companies. The project is carried out on behalf of the Ministry of Research and Technology (Projektträger Fertigungstechnik). The project runs from 1984 until 1988.

2. Current state of integration

Our definition of integration is: A process during the course of which various process functions can be rendered comparable and coordinated with each other by means of central process dimensions. The goal is to establish the most coherent overall production process possible (BRANDT et al., 1978). However strategies concerning the computer-aided integration of process functions are not only to be comprehended in terms of information technology - they also entail preliminary decisions and basic considerations in terms of organization. In the case of CAD/CAM integration the structure of the company's vertical organization is roughly determined as well as the scope of differentiation of the execution of functions between the areas of design, planning and shop floor. While the form of hierarchical work division between planning and execution is thereby pre-structured, the job structures are not; the relationship between the functions, which have been roughly defined by integration strategies, and the job structures on the shop floor remains ex-ante relatively undetermined.

The following is therefore a preliminary estimation of the possible development of basic structures of work division and hierarchy within a company and the scope of autonomous action on the shop floor connected when integrated CAD/CAM-systems are put to use. Our empirical foundations are based less on actual CAD/CAM use but to a large extent on CAD/CAM concepts being discussed in the field of engineering sciences and being developed by many computer and software companies. Large-scale introduction has yet to take place. Our thesis is that the majority of the integration concepts concerned with the vertical organization of companies are mainly oriented towards the traditional hierarchical patterns of work division between executing and planning which usually exist in companies. While the more recent developmental tendencies in information technology undoubtedly offer a large scope for organizational planning as opposed to traditional data processing, the possibilities of flexible organization are not generally made use of. The various concepts of CAD/CAM integration usually tend to the systematic coordination of separate process functions in design, work planning and the shop floor, all of which have been run in relative isolation from each other in the past. According to these concepts the shop floor is to perform solely executive functions. Concepts based on organizational structures which are not oriented towards work division but aim instead at the preservation or reintegration of planning and executive functions on the shop floor have only been recently gaining significance.

Without a doubt, the present restrictions of information technology are partially responsible for this. For the majority of the workpieces to be processed, the transfer of geometrical data directly from a CAD-system in the design department to a CNC-machine or a computer in the workshop, where it can be used in planning and programming, still remains a problem, since a transformation of the geometrical data of a workpiece as a product of the design process into production oriented data is necessary. In terms of information technology this transformation entails an intermediary step, with a workstation in the area of the planning department or in a programming office (MAIER 1985, p. 57). Of course these problems can be viewed as surmountable since relatively simple parts and processing operations do allow direct transmission between a CAD-system and the shop floor (EIGNER, MAIER, 1985, p. 314

ff), leading to the creation of various concepts which have been explicitly devised as "workshop CAD/CAM-systems" (HELLWIG et al., 1983; von ZEPPELIN 1985).

3. The objectification of production

The fact that the majority of concepts concerned with vertical integration lead to a greater extent of work division between the areas of planning and execution is mainly the result of mechanisms which do not belong to the restrictions of information technology. The attainment of a coherent overall process of production is dependent on the objectification of central process parameters concerning production structures and times. The precondition for this objectification is the existence of CAD-systems. They hold a key position in the process of integrated manufacturing since they generate system compatible data which can find unrestricted, repeated use. The elements of a product are designed in terms of compatibility with the conditions and possibilities offered by production ("production compatible designing"). Parts should meet the requirements of technically optimal, expense-saving production from the start; therefore optimal NC-programms are to be created on the basis of these CAD-data, thus enabling better monitoring and planning of capacities and time. This is to have the effect of reducing disturbances originating in the areas of construction, planning and programming as well as interruptions and unforeseeable situations in the manufacturing process. This implies reducing and restricting the necessity for and the possibility of autonomous action on the part of the shop floor personnel. Especially in the field of machine building, a great deal of the shop floor staff's scope and potential for autonomous action used to be based on production conditions which were difficult to precalculate; the conception of CAD/CAM-systems can therefore be regarded as the attempt to alter this situation. Furthermore the objectification of central process parameters is a basic requirement for the endeavor to reduce information loss and further delays between the areas of design, planning and production. In a further step, the objectification of central process parameters can be utilized to attain the highest possible degree of automatic transformation of CAD-data into work plans, NC-programmes and processing.

The objectification of production conditions which have been relatively non-transparent so far can be secured by the standards of quality and exactness in drawing diagrams and figures which CAD permits, the reliable automatic transfer of geometrical data and NC-programmes; and a more rational design of parts from the standpoint of production technology, leading to a simplified parts geometry or processing operations. Both aspects can reduce the complexity of manufacturing conditions on the shop floor, as in the case of tools. Furthermore, an improved standardization of parts by means of unitized construction, part families or a more transparent creation of part variations, is perceivable. In addition, a tendency to store technological processing data, like cutting data, material characteristics and tool features in data banks for systematic use in planning and programming can be observed (HAMMER, HERHOLZ 1983).

These possibilities implied by integrated CAD/CAM-systems are especially apparent in the concepts used by large computer and software manufacturers. As far as statements can be made on the basis of the previous findings, many manufacturers of integrated CAD/CAM-systems are oriented to the work divisional structures of large companies. There are probably several reasons for this: on the one hand the basic concepts of integrated CAD/CAM-systems mainly originate from the aviation and space industry in the U.S.A., while on the other hand larger manufacturers of integrated CAD/CAM-systems orient themselves mainly to their own manufacturing operations, which are relatively standardized and organized in terms of work division. As a number of interviews with experts have shown, the experience gained and the problems encountered in these areas are finding direct consideration in the development of new CAD/CAM-systems.

The concepts of DNC-systems usually having a central terminal, which should be situated before the production stage, are a concrete example of this. Although the functions of a central terminal, namely planning, programming and monitoring of the manufacturing process, could be easily performed at individual shop floor terminals (CNC-controlling, for example), these concepts often lead to a concentration of planning functions at the control post, as in the case of regulating access rights. The means by which the effectiveness of the NC-programmes generated in an office for work preparation can be increased and optimized are central components of integrated systems such as graphic simulation systems and in some cases technology data banks for materials and tools. In the instances where integration is extended beyond NC-programming and work preparation into the department of design, an "automatic" processing line reaching from the area of construction to the NC-machine is aimed for, at least as far as the software company's concept is concerned. DNC-systems are also designed as self-regulating circuits. The step-by-step transmission of NC-data from the process computer to the CNC-machine regulates itself according to the current stage of the processing procedure which is communicated to the process computer by automatic sensor and data-recording systems (HELLWIG et al., 1983). CNC-controlling mechanisms, which basically could easily be utilized for shop floor programming, fulfill the function of automatic data-recording stations here.

4. The introduction of implemented systems

The existing conditions in most companies do not allow immediate implementation of these manufacturer's concepts. Particularly in the machine-building industry, complex manufacturing conditions and the potential for resistance on the part of the skilled work force on the shop floor, who are interested in maintaining the status quo of work organization and working conditions, oppose the rigid implementation of such concepts, as has often been demonstrated. Moreover, elements within the company seeking to preserve or extend the existing structures of work division and hierarchy are not to be underestimated.

The way integrated CAD/CAM-systems are introduced is very important. Only rarely is an encompassing system implemented in a company in one step. The rule is step-by-step integration based on existing department structures and the data processing units given. If necessary, this is supplemented by the exchange of parts of existing systems, or by partial extension of existing data-processing systems (WILDEMANN et al., 1985, p. 69 ff). Applied to the implementation of CAD/CAP-systems, this means that the existing computer units in the area of work preparation and construction must be coordinated to each other, or that the introduction of a new part system (usually a CAD-system) has to be coordinated with another already existing system (NC-programming system) (LAY, MAISCH 1984). The introduction of DNC-systems, which are often installed between existing programming systems and various CNC-machines, is similar ("NC-Praxis", May, 1985). Furthermore, the introduction process, which is usually loosely structured and planned, is often characterized by deficient methods of planning and decision-making, leading to dubious economical and sociological results (KNETSCH, BAAKEN 1983, p. 68 ff). In all cases, this procedure implies the taking over of given structures and areas of competence. At last, an increase in the effectiveness of construction, planning and programming processes associated with the extension of these systems is likely to lead to a de facto increase of competence in the area of technical service as opposed to the shop floor, due to the progressive objectification of manufacturing parameters. This underlines the influential role played by engineers, technicians and data-processing experts in the introduction of integrated systems. The significance of these specialists undoubtedly grows with the increasing complexity of these systems. Indeed, they monopolize expert knowledge within the company which can be used to consolidate or extend their positions within the company's hierarchy. The interests of this planning group are fundamentally opposed to any reduction of work division or increase of autonomous action on the shop floor. This group of experts executes the conversion to and the implementation of integrated systems according to the exclusively global instructions given by top management. As an independent group of experts they are interested in developing proposals which not only promise a reduction of costs, but which also entail a minimum risk of disturbances and mistakes. It is therefore easiest to follow the tried and tested logics of rationalization. This means atomizing, mechanizing, dissecting - and whenever possible - predetermining the work processes on the shop floor. This logic is supported by a "technological" way of thinking leading back to Taylor's philosophy, according to which labor is regarded as an unpredictable factor of disturbance and risk, which should be restricted and prespecified to the greatest extent possible (BERGMANN, HIRSCH-KREINSEN, 1985).

These interests of monitoring and controlling the manufacturing processes find a suitable instrument in the monitoring potential of integrated CAD/CAM-systems. By systemizing and objectifying the paths of communication and information, any deviations from the projected course of work become easier to detect. The integrated processing of information provides the technical means of detecting alterations or access to data at all times. Finally, the increased scope of data-recording and the acceleration of data-processing - as is the case with DNC-systems - give the management the possibility of quicker and directed access to production times, quantities and other interesting features of the production process.

This becomes very clear in the case of so-called extended DNC-systems which integrate the functions of data-recording and data-processing. These systems can automatically record and process the length of an interruption of a running machine, to what extent and how often a machine operator influences the cutting values, to what extent an NC-programme is not fulfilling its function properly and to which operating function a CNC-control is currently linked (STORR et al., 1985). A significant reason for the foreseeable adoption of DNC-systems is to be seen in the potential for control entailed. An expert interviewed voiced the hope that, "the nonsense in the workshop" would "finally come to an end", with the implementation of a DNC-system; meaning that alterations of NC-programmes by machine operators, which were previously difficult to monitor, would now come under the control of the work preparation department.

Undoubtedly there will still be scope for the concrete structuring of jobs and activities on the shop floor. The actual distribution of tasks involved in complementary correction and optimization of the NC-programmes and the monitoring and supplementation of order sequences and dates as well as all monitoring and operating functions at the CNC-machines are not predetermined by the prevailing concepts of CAD/CAM-systems. It remains highly unlikely though that central planning functions such as the determining of sequences of parts to manufacture and the programming of machines will be performed entirely in the shop floor area. Under these conditions the shop floor will only fulfill complementary planning functions, primarily performed on the executive level.

5. Alternative integration strategies

Of course it is not to be overlooked that these centralistic concepts are increasingly hampered by objective conditions which demand more and more open forms of work in the shop floor area. On the one hand, the requirements of the market have become increasingly dynamic, demanding a greater flexibility of the company's operational capacity; even those centralistic forms of organization, whose efficiency is also enhanced by CAD/CAM-systems are likely to prove too inflexible. Delays and losses caused by faulty coordination as well as excessive bureaucracy remain the threatening problems. On the other hand, the problem of unimpaired, trouble-free access to, and utilization of, the increasingly expensive machines and manufacturing systems is becoming more and more important; increased availability of the complex machines and production systems is more likely to be guaranteed by an open and flexible use of skilled personnel than by work division and hierarchy. It is not least for these reasons and the resulting operational problems that an increasing number of CAD/CAM-systems are being developed for open work structures in the shop floor area. A central attribute of these systems is the fact that the objectification of central process parameters is not to be used to reduce the planning functions performed on the shop floor, but that it is intended to provide the shop floor personnel with more and better information. According to these concepts, CAD/CAM-systems are to be used as an information medium helping the shop floor personnel to perform preparatory, planning and programming functions with greater efficiency than before. Therefore such concepts contain explicit guidelines of work organization intended to utilize the personnel's skill, reliability and capacity to learn

(Projektträger Fertigungstechnik 1984). As far as can presently be discerned, these concepts are being primarily developed by smaller software companies and machine tool manufacturers, often with government support.

Thus shop floor oriented CAD/CAM-systems are intended to take over the geometrical data from the design department in order to create NC-programmes based on these data in the shop floor area, or else a systematic compilation is omitted to begin with. In this case the shop floor works independently of the design department; for example the shop floor personnel has the task of independently making part contours and then NC-programmes based on rough hand sketches (GANGL, n.d.). DNC-systems are usually used without a central terminal or a link with a central NC-programming system. The DNC-computer merely has the function of a "data-recorder" for the shop floor and the NC-controls. The individual CNC-machines perform the function of "intelligent" terminals where all the programming functions are executed (HELLWIG et al., 1983).

Whether such concepts will find widespread application in companies in the near future seems uncertain, particularly as far as large companies which have been using data-processing systems over a longer period are concerned. These concepts will probably only find limited application in such companies due to the persistency and the tenacity of the established structures and the interests connected therewith. It is probable that open job structures, like shop floor programming or manufacturing "islands" and matching CAD/CAM-systems, will only find specific integration in structures which are hierarchical and are based on work division seen on the whole. In these cases the growing objective demands made on the companies' flexibility are to be met without seriously jeopardizing traditional structures.

In smaller companies however, without an active work preparation department, the implementation of integrated CAD/CAM-systems is likely to be easily used for the stabilization or the extension of open work forms in the shop floor area. Shop floor oriented CAD/CAM and DNC-systems are being especially developed for such companies ("NC-Praxis", September 1985). As a number of findings demonstrate, such concepts readily find acceptance in companies with little previous use of data-processing in the area of manufacturing. Moreover, in these instances, the establishment of groups of experts who can use their specialized knowledge of the use of computer technology to the advantage of their position within the company has only just begun. It is significant that these conditions can be found in many machine building firms with small and medium size batch production, which means that the prospects for the preservation or the extension of forms of skilled work on the shop floor will be relatively good.

6 The future outlook

The concepts of integrated CAD/CAM-systems and the conditions under which they are applied give little occasion for speaking of a "fundamental change of manufacturing concepts" (KERN/SCHUMANN) or a general process of "De-Taylorization" in connection with the introduction of new technologies ("Blick durch die Wirtschaft", 8.10.1985). This is due to the fact that an extremely stable constellation of interests, firmly intent on maintaining centralistic technical and organizational concepts and structures, prevails within most companies. However, we are not only dealing with the persistency of established structures, hierarchy, work division and the associated interests of technicians, engineers and information specialists in such cases. Their influence is also increased by the influence of external groups also oriented at the traditional patterns of rationalization such as traditional as well as large manufacturers of data-processing equipment who continue to control the manufacturing information market. In addition the influence of a presumably larger number of management consulting firms on machine building firms, which usually lack the necessary know-how, is not to be underestimated.

Furthermore, many engineers are encouraged by the perspectives once again offered by technical developments to foster new hopes of finally achieving viable forms of automation. The use of artificial intelligence, expert systems and their connection to extensive data-bank systems will, so it is hoped, lead to an exclusion of the faults that current production systems are still laboring with (SPUR 1984). From this perspective personnel and skilled work will become superfluous to a large extent; their only remaining task is to set self-regulating systems in motion and to monitor them from a great distance.

References

Beitz, W.:
Entwicklungszwänge für den Konstruktionsprozeß, in: ZwF, Vorträge des Produktionstechnischen Kolloquiums Berlin, Sonderdruck 1983.

Bergmann, J.; Hirsch-Kreinsen, H.:
Arbeitsorganisation an CNC-Maschinen. Wirksamkeit von Positionen und Interessen im Umstellungsprozeß, in: Werkstatt und Betrieb, 118 (1985) 8.

Brandt, G. et al.:
Computer und Arbeitsprozeß, Frankfurt/New York 1978.

Döpper, W.; Ilzig, F.:
Einsatzverfahren mit CAD/CAM-Systemen in der spanenden Fertigung, in: Kolloquium: Automatische Produktionssysteme, hectograph. paper, TU-München 1985.

Eigner, M.; Maier, H.:
Einstieg in CAD, München/Wien 1985.

Förster, H.-U.:
CAD/PPS-Kopplung - ein Meilenstein auf dem Weg zur rechnerintegrierten Fertigung, in: CAD/CAM Report, 1,2/1985.

Gangl, P.:
Praktische Gesichtspunkte beim Einsatz eines CAD/CAM-Systems im Werkzeugbau, paper, Darmstadt n.d.

Hammer, H.; Herholz, B.:
NC-Programmierung und DNC-Betrieb, in: tz für Metallbearbeitung, 77 (1983) 3.

Hellwig, U. et al.:
Die Kopplung von CAD und CAM, in: VDI-Z, 10,11/1983.

Knetsch, W.; Baaken, Th.:
Veränderungen beruflicher Qualifikation durch neue Technologien am Beispiel CAD/CAM hectograph. paper, VDI-Technologiezentrum, Berlin 1983.

Lay, G. et al.:
Wirtschaftliche und soziale Auswirkungen des Einsatzes von integrierten CAD/CAM-Systemen. Untersuchungsteil I: Technische Entwicklung, Diffusion und betrieblicher Einsatz, RKW-Projekt A 148/83, hectograph. paper, Eschborn 1984.

Lay, G.; Maisch, K.:
Vernetzte Programm-Module, in: NC-Fertigung, 2/1984.

Leibinger, B.:
Zukunftsperspektiven für die Klein- und Mittelserienfertigung, in: ZwF, Vorträge des Produktionstechnischen Kolloquiums, Berlin, Sonderdruck 1983.

Maier, H.:
CIM-Expertise, unpublished paper, Leopoldshafen, Oktober 1985.

NC-Praxis:
NC-Praxis, Landsberg, Mai 1985, Sept. 1985.

Projektträger Fertigungstechnik (ed.):
Autonome Fertigungsinsel. Flexible Fertigungsstrukturen für die Einzel- und Kleinserienfertigung, KfK-PFT 79, Karlsruhe 1984.

Roland Berger & Partner GmbH:
NC-Technik. Stand und Entwicklungstendenzen, hectograph. paper, München, Oktober 1984.

Spur, G.:
Über intelligente Maschinen und die Zukunft der Fabrik, in: Forschungsmitteilungen der DFG 3/1984.

Storr, A. et al.:
Numerische Standardsteuerungen in verketteten Fertigungssystemen, in: wt - Z. ind. Fert., 75 (1985) 6.

Wildemann, H. et al.:
Strategische Investitionsplanung für CAD/CAM, hectograph. paper, Universität Passau 1985.

Wingert, B. et al.:
CAD im Maschinenbau. Chancen, Wirkungen, Risiken, Berlin etc. 1984.

von Zeppelin, W.:
Rechnergestützte NC-Programmierung und Betriebsorganisation, in ZwF 80 (1985) 8.

TAYLORISM AND CAD/CAM. REMARKS ON THE POTENTIAL IMPACT OF NEW TECHNOLOGIES IN DESIGN AND PRODUCTION PLANNING AND ON A PARADIGM SWITCH IN INDUSTRIAL SOCIOLOGY

Fred Manske
Soziologisches Forschungsinstitut Göttingen (SOFI)
Friedländer Weg 31
D-3400 Göttingen

1. Paradigms in industrial sociology and the reality of industrial life

If one examines the production of industrial sociology for committed convictions concerning the quality of a paradigm, prime position belongs to the mainstream interpretation of the development of labour in capitalism: the opinion that labour is being ever-increasingly subdivided and de-skilled by Taylorism, the "basic conception of capitalist rationalization". In the words of Kern and Schumann: "Until now every form of capitalist rationalization was based on a notion that regarded human labour as a barrier for production, to be overcome by a maximum of technical automation of the production process. Residual human labour was regarded as a potential source of disruption to be eliminated and controlled by restrictive job design" (KERN/SCHUMANN 1984, p. 19).

As far as the impact of Taylorism was concerned, the two authors were rather cautious: they restricted their statements to actual producers and subscribed to the well-known polarization thesis (KERN/SCHUMANN 1970). It was left up to others to propose a secular de-skilling not only of labour of actual producers, but of labour in general, e.g. even the work of employees in the design office or production planning [1) 2)].

In the meantime, there are signs of a paradigm switch in industrial sociology: Kern and Schumann's discovery of a possible "End of the Division of Labour" - the authors recognize "new production conceptions", new management strategies, no longer banking on total automation and further subdivision of labour, but on the "integrated" use of work, albeit within highly mechanized production processes (KERN/SCHUMANN 1984, cf. CORIAT/ZARIFIAN 1986 for France).

Debate on the possible paradigm switch in industrial sociology is of particular importance in an article dealing with the application of CAD and CAP in mechanical engineering: research on the application of these technologies (and on PPS [*)]) in mechanical engineering reveals that the mainstream interpretation hid the fact that there are significant segments of work not yet rationalized according to Taylor's recipe. In fact, in the words of Lutz, these were able to resist "Tayloristic temptations" (LUTZ 1986).

---

*) PPS: computer assisted production planning and control.

The following theses will be discussed in this contribution:

1. Concentration on Taylorism, and perhaps even the equation of division of labour with Taylorism, has led to the almost exclusive examination of a single segment of work: work of actual producers in mass production industries.
2. Conclusions reached in this segment of labour have tended to serve as moulds for the interpretation of research on work in general. As a consequence, the fact was ignored that there are significant segments of work which may by no means labelled Taylorized work. Or these segments were viewed as being at an "interim" stage: sooner or later they too would be Taylorized.
3. According to our present knowledge, the application of new technologies like CAD, CAP, CNC etc. in these segments of work does not lead to Taylorism. The prophesy (see 2) does not appear to be fulfilling itself.
4. If one takes Taylorism as an approach for the centralized control of the production process seriously, something new does indeed seem to be emerging: a *change in the form of control* by management which explains why an end of Taylorism in capitalism was possible. This change in the form of control is of significance for technical employees in design departments equipped with CAD and CAP.

"Taking seriously" is meant as an allusion to the fact that Taylorism has, up to now, been viewed mainly from the angle of "skill". Although reference is made to the workers as a "disruptive factor" and to power relationships, this was generally on the fringe of "mainstream discussion". It was the labour process debate which first introduced this theme into West German discussion (cf. for example DÖRR/HILDEBRANDT/SELTZ 1983; DÖRR 1985; SELTZ/HILDEBRANDT 1985).

2. Taylorism = division of labour. An inadmissable equation and its consequences

Taylorism is (originally) aimed at the actual process of production: the work of the actual producers is to take place according to a previously set plan, which was derived from "scientific" analysis and for the workers "prescribes in detail and compulsorily the best possible method of production" (cf. TAYLOR 1967). This sentence contains the main principles of Taylorism, e.g. the principle of the separation of preparatory and executive tasks, the principle of the centralization of knowledge on the production and labour process as well as the principle of the compulsory prescription on the ways and means of executing tasks (cf. BRAVERMAN 1974, p. 112 to 121).

As a *general* conception of rationalization, Taylorism has obviously had very specific consequences, or, to put it another way: in order to realize Taylorism as a definite approach towards centralized control of the production process, a number of preconditions have to be established that are, at the same time, to be regarded as specific consequences of Taylorism. And when these impacts on the structure of industry and labour are examined closely, it would appear as if Taylorism, in its consequent application, was simultaneously producing its own restrictions.

One of the consequences is the development of production planning staffs in the design and production planning departments (throughout industry), the root of which is contained in the principle of separating planning form the execution of tasks. By means of Taylorism, the structure of tasks in industry has grown significantly more complex, and in design and production planning, segments of work have emerged, which at least up to the present, put up barriers against a "Taylorization of mental labour" (cf. on specific details LITTEK/HEISING 1986; WINGERT et al. 1984; MANSKE/WOBBE-OHLENBURG 1984 among others).

The application of Taylorism both enhances and requires the development of mass production industries. The production departments of mass production industries are by consequence the area at which Taylorism as a rationalization and division of labour strategy is actually aimed. The conversion of living labour into Taylorized labour requires a maximum of standardization of labour processes which may be repeated massively in exactly the same manner: Taylorized work is repetitive work.

The minute sub-division of mass-production processes according to Taylor's (and then Ford's) recipes leads to the need for the production of highly specialized machines. This - as division of labour at the societal level - has led to the emergence of *mechanical engineering* as an important branch of industry whose net output, so to speak, is the specialized machines required for mass production. These specialized machines are, however, generally produced as one-off runs or in small batches and this may be regarded as the reason why the work of actual producers in mechanical engineering was not able to be Taylorized, in the same way that work in design and production planning has been spared.

However, there have been approaches to Taylorization in mechanical engineering as may be recognized from the establishment of production planning departments, mainly in large and medium sized plants and from time-and-motion studies conducted to pre-plan work. In other words, approaches did exist to divide planning from the execution of tasks. However, results were most unimpressive: effective centralized pre-planning and control of the production process were not achieved. The dominant type of work in the production divisions of mechanical engineering is by no means de-skilled, Taylorized work but rather skilled, specialized work, characterized by the inclusion of both the execution of tasks and above all planning functions. For this reason, the type of division of labour to be found in mechanical engineering cannot be termed Taylorism (on details cf. MICKLER 1981 or LUTZ 1986).

In all, Taylorism as a definite conception of the division of labour and rationalization has, on the one hand, led to the emergence of significant sectors of deskilled work in mass production industry, to which the predicate of a secular tendency towards loss of meaning in work really applied. On the other hand, other significant segments of skilled work were created [3]. Within these segments, attempts have been made at a division of labour which cannot, however, be termed Tayloristic: the types of work under review are all characterized by varying degrees of planning functions - in these domains there is no strict application of the Tayloristic principle of the separation of planning and executive task functions.

3. Computer applications in design and production planning: The Taylorization of mental work?

Thus Taylorism has its, to some extent, ironic aspects: it has at least contributed to the emergence of a kind of "necessary coexistence" of various kinds of division of labour and of work, a fact not sufficiently recognized by industrial sociology before now.

The "rationalizers" in industry are now faced with a dilemma that they themselves are largely responsible for: although mass production has emerged as a zone where labour may be planned and controlled with comparative ease, other segments of labour have been created almost as a by-product that are far less susceptible to control.

The question arises, whether the Taylorization of mental labour in design and production planning has merely been delayed: will the immanent rationalization in these areas by means of C-technologies adhere to Taylor's principles and will de-skilling of the "mental labour" required in them take place?

The current status of development and diffusion of computer applications in these areas does not permit more than a first hypothesis, but there is some evidence that there will be no Taylorization of mental labour in design and production planning.

Two preliminary remarks are necessary: first, because of the "integrative" character of computer technology, it might be dangerous to examine certain C-technologies, e.g. CAD, in isolation and to pursue their consequences for certain groups of employees in isolation - this could produce - mutatis mutandis - similarly inaccurate results to those criticized in mainstream industrial sociology.

Secondly, one should be wary of adopting the term "reintegration": all too frequently (usually with an eye on the actual production process) statements are made to the effect that an integration of formerly separated functions - by means of Taylorism - is taking place in the introduction of new technologies: previously separate functions are being tied together in "integrated" bundles of tasks. This picture is inaccurate in as much as the application of the computer may change these functions beyond recognition. A considerable portion of a sociological research programme is thus devoted to assessing the potential of the new technologies: which functions are changed, are new ones created, which functions remain for the human and which do computers take over in the "computerized" factory?

CAD and design

The cautionary remarks just made by no means invalidate several theses on the relationship between CAD and design tasks. However, these theses require expansion in the near future.

In most design offices in manufacturing industry, such as mechanical engineering, the initial situation is characterized by a division of labour between designers, detail designers, and technical draftspeople. According to completed studies, even the technical draftspeople located at the bottom of the hierarchy perform tasks which by no means may be termed Tayloristic.

Among the possible consequences of CAD in design, the following two are, in my opinion, of particular importance (cf. in detail: SPRINGER/WOLF 1986; MANSKE/WOLF 1986; on CAD cf. WINGERT et al. 1984; MUGGLI/ZINKL 1985).

(1) Conceptions for the application of CAD appear to be determined largely by the *type of production:* batch producers, whose construction process is largely de-coupled in time from the production process, tend towards an application of CAD "from the top", i.e. they apply CAD in design in the narrower sense of the term. Producers of individual units or of variants, where the design process is an integral part of the total production process, usually start with the production of drawings and other documents in order to cut the length of the production process. In both cases, the existing division of labour seems to dissolve in such a manner that the functions of detail drafting changed by CAD are gradually transferred either "upwards" to the designers (in the first conception of application) or "downwards" to the new type of CAD draftsperson.

In the second case, it would appear that the skills of the CAD draftsperson are broadened and elevated when compared with the technical draftsperson. It is, however, also conceivable that the functions of CAD drafting will be taken over by former detail designers.

(2) A new group of employees is emerging on the scene in the shape of the so-called *CAD-experts*. Up to the present, their tasks include the implementation of CAD, training for CAD etc. In future, however, the development of application programmes should be an extremely important function required in the firms (presently most CAD users learn to use the standard potential of CAD and are still a long way from creative further development).

This new function largely determines the future status within the firm of CAD experts: will it be the CAD experts, externally recruited newcomers, who will fulfill this function or will a kind of "design group" composed of experienced designers (with pertinent knowledge on design) and of CAD specialists (with system and programming knowledge) emerge to jointly adapt and further develop the CAD systems in a practical-theoretical process according to the firm's requirements? There is much in favour of cooperation since the CAD experts can scarcely do without the experience-based knowledge of the designers and since, on the other hand, designers will hardly be in the position to acquire the system knowledge required for extensive programming.

If this roughly outlined scenario is correct, CAD will be responsible for new forms of the division of labour. But as a whole, a tendency towards the enhancement of skills is more likely than a reduction.

CAP, NC programming and tasks in production planning, design and production

In conventional production planning instructions for the work in production are prepared on the basis of design drawings. For this purpose, the main task is to determine the manufacturing technologies and their sequence (planning the job sequence) and processing times (calculation of job times). In cases where NC machines are available, planning the job sequence also determines which further steps are to be done by NC programming: in the early days of NC technology, the customary bi-partite division of labour between *work planners* and *time calculators*, was expanded by the addition of *NC-programmers*.

This is a widely diffused division of labour in production planning encountered in practice. To get a job in production planning is regarded as the classic case of promotion for the (specialized) workers in mechanical engineering; tasks in production planning are to be viewed as skilled and non-taylorized.

CAP and changes in NC-programming (in addition to PPS) could have the following effects on production planning:

(1) For a variety of reasons, calculation of times is likely to be eliminated as a human task: in general, it is fairly simple to determine job times by means of calculation programmes or the like once the job sequence has been determined. In addition, the time calculator (as the embodiment of Taylorism) will be required less in the future since the piecework rate system in mechanical engineering appears to be growing obsolete for a variety of reasons (one of which is the introduction of PPS and BDE *); BDE is also an alternative means of determining standard times rather then by the classical time study).

(2) As an independent task, NC programming appears to be threatened by two developments: first, the increasing link-up of CAD with NC programming (cf. the description by Lay et al. 1986, which is well worth reading) and, second, the tendency to relocate programming (or what is left of it) or programme optimization on the shop floor.

(3) Finally, automatic job planning (CAP), which is however still at very early stages, could jeopardize the function of job step planning; a tendency towards the relocation of this job in the design office cannot be discounted (cf. LAY et al. 1986).

As may be recognized from the above, the object of research requires a broadening of perspective: CAD, CAP, NC programming, in addition to PPS and BDE, have connections which set restraints for the isolated examination of one of these C-technologies and also for the isolated observation of one group of employees. The brevity of this contribution also exerts forces, in this case to sketch out more scenarios; how may tasks in work planning be designed in future and what will be their position between design and manufacture?

If all future work planning functions were computerizable, work planning would simply flow into an extended CAD system in the shape of CAP and NC modules.

---

*) BDE = Betriebsdatenerfassung = Shop data registration

All existing experience contradicts this scenario: it is likely that some form of "translation" will always be necessary "between" design and the finished product as an output of a certain configuration of CNC machines. Thus, one may observe that automatically produced NC-programmes, even those from the latest CNC machines, generally require alterations and are "optimized": CNC operators draw upon their experience-based knowledge, that would principally appear to enable them to be that little bit "better" than "theoretically" determined programmes. In practice, a kind of cooperation between NC programmers and machine operators develops in most firms.

Could the part of the NC programmer in this not be played by someone from the design office? In general, this also seems unlikely: the NC programmer happens to be largely a practical person with a large amount of knowledge on the method of production - and he is also a practical person with regard to the application of the NC programming system. The idea of instructing a designer or a technical draftsperson in this role in addition to his tasks in computerized construction, will probably prove largely dysfunctional (as it should also prove dysfunctional to make the CAD a "super-designer" or a designer a CAD expert: cooperation should also prove more fruitful in these areas).

In all, the (shrinking) work planning department of the future - whatever it may be called and wherever it is located in the firm, it may, for instance, formally be a part of the design department - will thus be composed of skilled CAD planners and of NC programmers.

4. Computer applications in design and work planning: Non-Taylorized but controlled mental work

It is likely that job and established departmental structures will be disrupted as a result of the infiltration of design and work planning by C-technologies. There is much evidence against the assumption that the application of C-technologies will lead to a Taylorization of mental work.

So, probably no Taylorism but also no idyll of integrated job structures, since a strong increase in controls over design and work planning seems likely. This statement is largely a conclusion drawn from the results of a research project on PPS in mechanical engineering (MANSKE 1986, MANSKE/WOBBE-OHLENBURG 1984).

In mechanical engineering, one may observe a switch in the approach towards centralized control of the production process: while the traditional approach à la Taylor was a direct approach to central process control in as much as the *nucleus of the work process* was to be exposed by means of the time study, the new approach is *indirect,* since the idea is, in a manner of speaking, to centrally organize and control around this nucleus.

The main components of this new approach are:

- an improved "outfield";
- assignment of relatively small volumes of tasks to the workers (for about one or two days' work);

- the tendency to determine the times required per job in almost real time and most precisely by means of "BDE";
- the tendency to register all possible disruptions and their causes by means of BDE in order to eliminate them;
- abandoning the piecework wage system.

This new means of control aims, on the one hand, at eliminating a wide range of organizational flows which were in part responsible for the lack of transparency for management of production in mechanical engineering: Thus attention is paid to ensuring that documents, materials and tools are at the workplace at the time when they are required. A most important component of the "outfield organization" is ensuring that job documents are complete and correct.

The assignment of relatively small volumes of tasks represents a break with ancient tradition in mechanical engineering: previously, the workers were given assignments to last weeks, if not months, that they were relatively "free" to complete at their own discretion. Reducing the dose of assignments to a matter of days, increases control over the process in a simple and thus "genial" manner.

Of equal importance is the registration of disruption data and the determination of time used close to the event.

The, in effect, tighter control over workers is ensured by abandoning the piecework wage system which is compatible with neither the now customary small assignment volumes nor with "BDE".

Management's control is increasing enormously - although attempts are no longer made to break through to the nucleus of the work process by Tayloristic means using time studies. A new method of setting times shows that management has in fact acknowledged that the nucleus of the work process is obscured in a manner not fully defined: times registered by various methods via BDE are quasi processed into time goals by statistical methods. Registered times are thus transformed into a new type of time goal - which I shall term surrogate time goals - which nonetheless have the quality of enabling planning, steering and control of the production process. This method of time registration can do without the time study à la Taylor, and leaves a veil largely obscuring the way in which the labourer works.

Therefore, it is correct to speak of a change in the form of control by management: management surrenders in part its claim to directly planning and controlling the actions of the individual worker at work and retires to the position of increasingly perfect planning around the nucleus of the work process. Relationships between management and labour are subject to a decisive change. To put it very bluntly: the approach to direct control à la Taylor is superfluous since management is far more effectively able to centrally control the process indirectly by means of the new technologies.

The very specific abandonment of Taylorism sketched out above obviously owes much to the fact that relevant components of experience-based knowledge exist, which cannot be exposed by any amount of planning and computerization management may bring to bear: the official or unofficial optimization of programmes for "their" CNC machine practised by the machine operators is a case of the "tortoise and hare" game, in which the "expert" at the machine is always a bit ahead of the "theorist" who is responsible for advance planning of his work. There is doubt whether it will, firstly, ever be possible to close this gap in practice by using expert systems and, second, whether this is at all in the interest of firms acting in accord with the need to expend capital: whoever is attempting to cut back opportunities to form experience-based knowledge "on the job" fails to recognize that this would be laying waste a significant productive resource. The existence and permanent new formation of experience-based knowledge is probably the systematic reason why cooperative divided labour structures with types of non-Taylorized work are being created or preserved at all levels of the production process (from design down to actual manufacture) in the computerized factory.

On the other hand, we cannot discount the possibility that exactly the types of work in computerized design and work planning will be subjected to closer control by means of the new approach to the control of the production process, that work in these areas will remain skilled, but that it will be controlled skilled work.

Surrogate time goal determination would appear to be the method required to more exactly determine time goals for jobs in design and production planning: the method of taking advantage of the potential of information technology to approach "bulky" processes and to indirectly determine steering and control values without revealing the nucleus of the work process concerned. However, circumstances were undeniably far more favourable for indirect process control on the shop floor than is the case in an area like design. Therefore, it is a relatively open question whether approaches taken by technicians will prove effective in practice. However, it is reasonable to assume that these approaches will not be without impact and that the formula adopted by technicians "What's good for the shop floor is good for design" will prove technically feasible [4].

References

Abendroth, P.:
Planung, Steuerung und Überwachung von Entwicklungs- und Konstruktionsprojekten am Beispiel M.A.N. - Roland Druckmaschinen AG, in: PPS '80, Tagungsband des Kongresses: Produktion, Planung, Steuerung 1980 in Böblingen.

Bravermann, H.:
Labor and Monopoly Capitalism: The Degradation of Work in the Twentieth Contury, New York/London 1974.

Brödner, P.:
Fabrik 2000. Alternative Entwicklungspfade in die Zukunft der Fabrik, Berlin 1985.

Coriat, B., Zarifian, Ph.;
Tendenzen der Automatisierung und Neuzusamensetzung der Lohnarbeit, in: Prokla, Heft 62, Jg. 16. (1986) Heft 1.

Dörr, G.:
Schranken betrieblicher Transparenz, Schranken betrieblicher Rigidität - eine Problemskizze zum Umbruch der Arbeitsformen im Maschinenbau, in: Naschold, F. (Hrsg.), Arbeit und Politik. Gesellschaftliche Regulierung der Arbeit und soziale Sicherung, Frankfurt/New York 1985.

Dörr, G., Hildebrandt, E., Seltz, R.:
Kontrolle durch Informationstechnologien in Gesellschaft und Betrieb, in: Leviathan-Sonderheft 5/1983.

Düll, K.:
Industriesoziologie in Frankreich, Frankfurt 1975.

Junghanns, W.:
Pro - Besser, schneller, rationeller durch verstärkten EDV-Einsatz, in: PPS '84, Tagungsband des Kongresses: Produktion, Planung, Steuerung. 1984 Böblingen.

Kern, H., Schumann, M.:
Industriearbeit und Arbeiterbewußtsein. Frankfurt 1970.

Kern, H., Schumann, M.:
Das Ende der Arbeitsteilung? Rationalisierung in der industriellen Produktion. München 1984.

Lappe, L.:
Technologie, Qualifikation und Kontrolle, Die Labour-Process Debatte aus der Sicht der deutschen Industriesoziologie, in: Soziale Welt, 37. Jg (1986) Heft 2/3.

Lay, G., u.a :
Vernetzung betrieblicher Bereich, Teil I: Technischer Stand, Verbreitung und arbeitsorganisatorische Arbeitsformen vernetzter Systeme, Schriftenreihe der Bundesanstalt für Arbeitsschutz - Forschung - FB 449, Dortmund 1986.

Littek, W., Heisig, K.:
Rationalisierung von Arbeit als Aushandlungsprozeß. in: Soziale Welt, 37. Jg. (1986) Heft 2/3.

Lutz, B.:
Wie neu sind die "neuen Produktionskonzepte"? in: Soziologische Revue, 9. Jg. (1986) Heft 3.

Manske, F.:
Auswirkungen von Produktionsplanungs- und Steuerungssystemen in Klein- und Mittelbetrieben, will be published 1986 in the Schriftenreihe des Kernforschungszentrums Karlsruhe: KfK-PFT Berichte.

Manske, F., Wobbe-Ohlenburg, W., u. Mitarbeit von Mickler, O.:
Rechnerunterstützte Systeme der Fertigungssteuerung in der Kleinserienfertigung - Auswirkungen auf die Arbeitssituation und Ansatzpunkte für eine menschengerechte Arbeitsgestaltung (Endbericht zum Projekt), KfK-PFT Berichte, Bd. 90, 1984.

Manske, F., Wolf, H.:
Organisation Form and Work Sequences in CAD Usage, in: Brödner, P. (Hrsg.), Skill Based Automated Manufacturing, Proceedings des IFAC WOrkshop, Karlsruhe 1986.

Mickler, O.:
Facharbeit im Wandel. Frankfurt/New York 1981.

Muggli, Ch., Zinkl, W.D.:
CAD in der Maschinenindustrie und im Architektenbüro. Zürich 1985.

Seltz, R., Hildebrandt, E.:
Produktion, Politik und Kontrolle - Arbeitspolitische Varianten am Beispiel der Einführung von Produktionsplanungs- und -steuerungssystemen im Maschinenbau. In: Naschold, F. (Hrsg.), Arbeit und Politik, Gesellschaftliche Regulierung der Arbeit und soziale Sicherung. Frankfurt/New York 1985.

Springer, R., Wolf, H.:
Rationalisierung mit CAD/CAP. VDI-Z Bd. 128 (1986) Heft 13.

Taylor, F.W.:
Principles of Scientific Management. New York 1967.

Teschner, E., Hermann, K.:
Die Taylorisierung technisch-geistiger Arbeit, in: Leviathan, Sonderheft 4, 1981.

Wingert, B. u.a.:
CAD im Maschinenbau, Wirkungen, Chancen, Risiken. Berlin/Heidelberg/New York/Tokio 1984.

Wood, St.:
Neue Technologien, Arbeitsorganisation und Qualifikation: die britische Labor-Process-Debatte. In: Prokla, Heft 62, Jg. 16 (1986) Nr. 1.

Remarks

1) Braverman went furthest in his interpretation as may be surmised from the subtitle of his work: "..The Degradation of Work in the Twentieth Century" (Braverman 1974). In *English-speaking countries*, he triggered off the "Labour-Process-Debate", in which his theses are now judged rather skeptically (cf. Lappe, 1986; Wood 1986). In the *Federal Republic of Germany*, discussion was greatly influenced by the polarization thesis proposed by SOFI and picked up by other institutes even though these each favoured different approaches to the analysis of the development of labour. The polarization thesis is well within the mainstream interpretation of the development of labour under the regime of Taylorism. The division of labour and Taylorism are also prominent themes of *French industrial sociology*. Within it, there were repeated attempts to theoretically determine the future development of work as "integrated" (cf. Düll 1975).

2) Many authors have claimed that Tayloristic job design in the field of technical employees, a "Taylorization of mental labour", was likely. Cf. recent works by Teschner/Hermann 1981, Brödner 1985 who argues against a Taylorisation of design work, but nethertheless thinks it possible.

3) Besides tasks in design and production planning in addition to specialized labour in the production area of mechanical engineering this also refers primarily to areas of "secondary specialist work" (cf. Mickler 1981).

4) An indicator for this are approaches towards control of design, such as systems like CAPOSS-MPT or TERMIKON (cf. Junghanns 1984; Abendroth 1980 a.o.).

ORGANIZATIONAL ALTERNATIVES IN THE INTEGRATION OF CAD/CAM

Håkon Finne
Institute of Social Research in Industry (IFIM)
N- 7034 Trondheim, NTH

1. Introduction

The present paper concerns organizational changes related to the development and interconnection of computer aids for design and manufacturing in the metalworking industries. The topic is particularly interesting because such computer systems now will tie together activities of design and planning departments in ways quite different from what has been established practice. These integrated CAD/CAM systems will tend to create organizational disturbances across boundaries of departments that probably cannot be sorted out by intradepartmental measures alone.

I will present some general trends and alternatives, along with empirical material from two cases. But first it will be useful to take a look at the functions of design and planning, their organization, and the development of computer aids for these functions.

2. Design, planning and CAD/CAM integration

In an industrial setting there is a sharp departmental division between designing and making products. There is also a division between the planning of making and the actual making. The locus of this latter division is not definite, however. Over the last decades planning personnel have increased in numbers and their plans have given the workforce more and more detailed instructions. This holds in particular for complex products in large firms and certainly for those having tried CAD/CAM integration so far.

When a mechanical component has been designed, the design is usually documented as an engineering drawing. This drawing is the basis for a process plan, in which it is decided on which machine(s) and by which method(s) the component will be manufactured. The process plan may also estimate machining time, etc. The next step is to work out an operation plan determining sequence of operations in the machine, selection of tools, and cutting data. If the component is to be produced on a numerically controlled machine, an NC program must be prepared that contains control information in numerical form for the machine tool. Process planning and operation planning (including NC programming) are together termed technological planning, as opposed to production planning which is concerned with resource allocation, time scheduling, and similar aspects.

Computer aided manufacturing systems cover a number of technological planning functions and, in some cases, the actual control of the machine tools. Some authors also include production planning systems under this heading. Because CAM systems usually are confined to activities prior to manufacturing itself, I find the term rather misleading. In engineering circles, however, manufacturing seems to be understood as planning of manufacturing.

Most frequently CAM is identical with computer aids for NC programming. Systems for generation of process plans do exist, but they are usually highly company and product specific. Somewhat more general systems exist for automatic selection of cutting data, but they have had little diffusion so far. On the production planning side, a host of general systems are available.

By CAD/CAM integration is normally meant that the data created via the CAD system either are used directly by the CAM system or the transfer of data between the two systems is taken care of by computerized means. Functionally, there are two different types of links. One is a means of connecting parts lists etc. generated by the designer in the CAD system to systems for production planning (including purchase planning). This type will concern us less here. The second type is a way of transferring the geometry of components and other manufacturing data to systems for technological planning. In particular, most CAD/CAM integrations to date consist of making geometry data from a CAD system available to an NC programming system. This link will do away with the double work in translating a drawing from a CAD system into a new numerical model, and the errors associated with this operation will disappear as well.

3. CAD/CAM integration philosophies and hidden organizational assumptions [1)]

Since most CAD/CAM integrations are effected on limited product ranges in highly specific situations, it is difficult to generalize. In the more commercially oriented work, however, two distinctly different philosophies of integration can be found.

The first philosophy is to integrate as many functions as possible into one system that can be operated by a single person. At present this means attempts at automating NC programming. For simple parts there now exist automatic tool path generators that can be operated from the designer's terminal after he has completed the design. Much work is being done to expand the range of routines that can be automated and hooked on to existing CAD systems.

The second line of development aims at making systems for each of the separate functions of design, process planning, and NC programming. The integration is then done by facilitating data transfer between the systems, e.g. by using common data bases and data carriers.

The two ways of integrating CAD and CAM systems have vastly different effects on the division of labour if work is organized according to the assumptions of the systems developers. If successful, the first philosophy will wipe out the separate job of NC programming and later that of process planning. It is also counteracting the possibilities of reintegrating the programming and execution tasks into the job of a skilled metalworker. The second philosophy maintains the present division of labour. Figure 1 illustrates the two different patterns.

Now consider the designer's job. In the first instance, he will be required to operate the automated routines for creating process plans and NC programs.

As a final state this would perhaps be acceptable. The routines would be sufficiently good to grant the required quality regardless of the technological planning capabilities of the designer. Until then, however, there would be a number of programming and planning tasks that would require skilled intervention. The division of tasks between designer and planner would be extremely complex, the designer might need a lot more technological competence, and the two groups would be competing, normally with negative organizational effects.

It is worth noticing that the same final state of a common CAD/CAM operator using highly automated routines can be reached either way (provided it can be reached at all). Going along the second route, this would happen by integrating the tasks into one job only when an extremely high degree and scope of automation had been achieved. What would be different, though, was the situation from now and till then. In fact, it seems that the second line of development grew out of problems in progressing sufficiently fast along the first path.

Neither hidden nor overt assumptions about the organization of work around specific technologies do always get across, however. There is often a discrepancy between the actual work organization, which is rooted in old technology and traditions, and an organizational pattern that would be better suited to the potential of new technology. In the following I shall present some actual cases of organizational adaptations to CAD/CAM integration.

4. Case A: Uncoordinated plans and redirection

In 1981 I did a case study of planned CAD/CAM integration in a large company developing and manufacturing highly complex products to order. The company had just purchased its second generation CAD system with possibilities of linking up to existing systems for NC programming, and with some routines for automatic tool path generation. At the time of my interviews, no integration had yet been accomplished, but all prospective stakeholders (except for the process planners) were expecting it to begin in the near future. Their expectations as to the goals and outcomes of the integration varied immensely, however. The expected division of labour between designers, process planners, and NC programmers (who also did operation planning) is listed in Table 1. From that list it is by no means clear that they are all talking about the same CAD/CAM system.

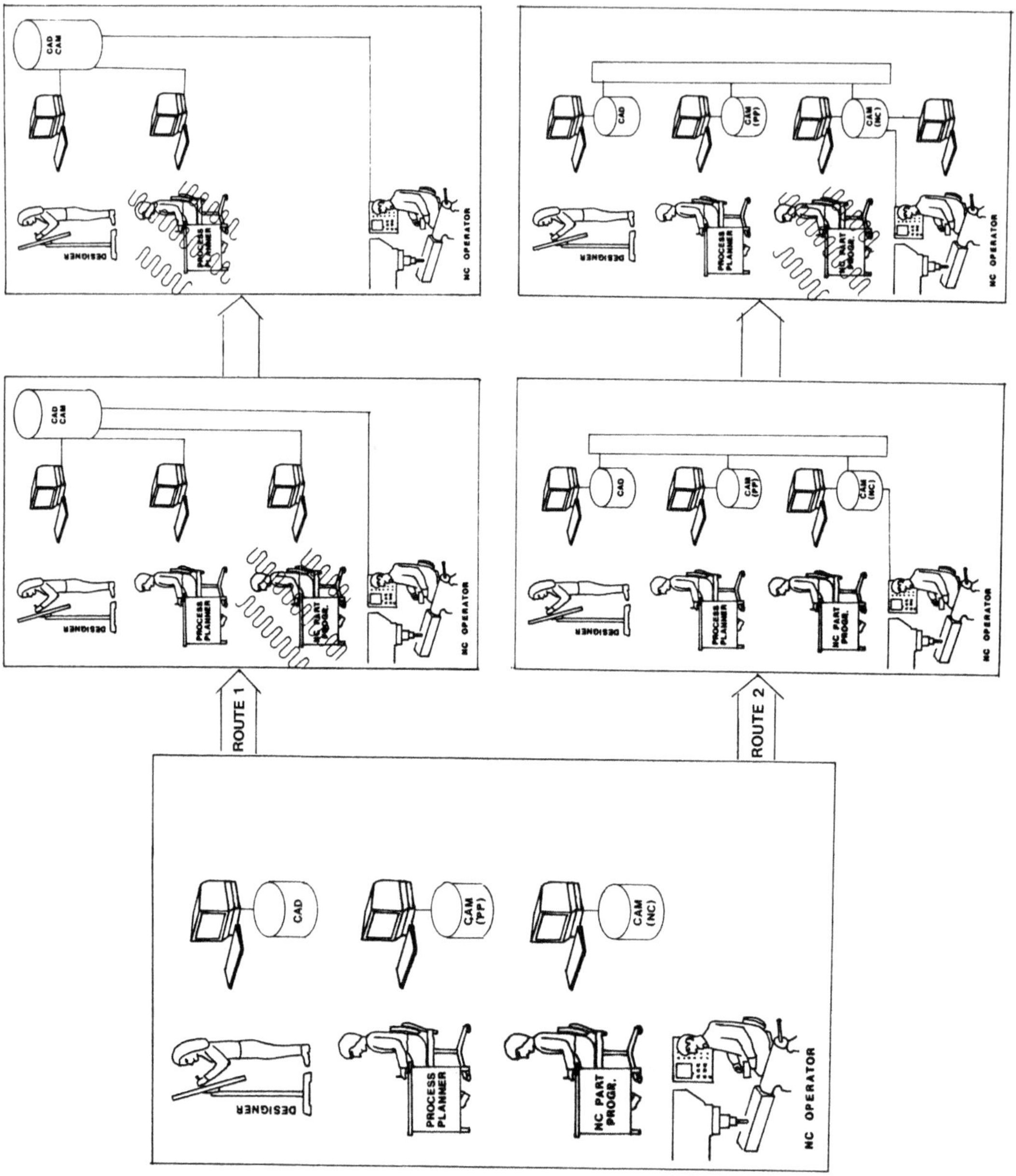

Figure 1: Two routes of CAD/CAM integration

Note: ∫∫∫ means partial deletion of job

Organizational patterns corresponding to the assumptions behind the two philosophies of integration are both visible behind the different statements in Table 1. Many people in the user organization expected CAD/CAM integration to support the present division of labour, but reduce duplicate work and potentiate the work of each profession. (More precisely, they did not consider the possibility of altering this organizational pattern.) Several reasons were given for this. The designers thought it hard enough to keep up with developments in their own field. The process planners thought the other strategy would be impossible because of the importance of locally acquired experience for making good process plans.

Table 1: Views on division of labour in integrated CAD/CAM systems operation

Whose view	Change in tasks for:		
	Designer	Process planner	NC part programmer
Manager 1 (step 1)	no change	no change	works directly on CAD database
Manager 1 (step 2)	dimension control	less help to designers	no such job
Manager 1 (step 3)	remaining process planning	no such job	no such job
Manager 2	produces process lists	reduced	works directly on CAD database
CAD expert	dimension control	no change	operates auto-NC
Chief designer	no change	works directly on CAD database	works directly on CAD database
Designers 1 & 2	operates auto-NC	no change	no such job
Designers 3 & 4	no change	no change	more controlled by machine
Process planners	no change	no change	no change
Chief NC programmer	operates auto-NC simple programs	no change	complex programs semimanually

Note: auto-NC means an automatic computer routine for tool path generation.

The people expecting to concentrate all functions in the design office either saw this as a long term goal or they (in the case of two designers) obviously had learnt this at the CAD system supplier's introduction course. The intention of the CAD/CAM vendor was clear: Much effort was being put into expanding the range of geometries that could be automatically transferred into NC programs from the designer's console.

It was clear that although aims and expectations existed and in some instances were fairly specific, they were not generally known. At least seven different departments would be effected by the planned integration and, significantly, the same number of unions. Yet in my interviews I found only two persons who were even vaguely acquainted with the expectations of others.

A closer look at Table 1 reveals a pattern, however. Most of the views on NC programming can be classed into one of three categories:

1. The NC programmer works (semi)manually on the CAD database.
2. The NC programmer operates (and tests) the routines for automatic NC part programming.
3. The designer operates the automatic NC programming routines.

Furthermore, these views may be seen as relating to different stages of maturity of the automatic routines. Hence the disagreement boils down to one of the time it will take to reach these stages of systems and organizational development.

Similarly, three categories appear if one looks at the views on the relation between designer and process planner (although in this case people were more hesitant in suggesting future developments):

1. The process planner works as before, possibly with computer aids independent of the CAD system.
2. The designer takes over some process planning, the process planner does some work directly on the CAD database.
3. Both designer and process planner operate automatic routines for process planning, with a gradual shift of functions towards the designer, who will eventually do it all.

Also these categories may be seen as consecutive stages in a process expected to take much longer time than the automation of NC programming.

When confronted with these syntheses, most of the persons involved accepted them as reasonable scenarios. Four years later, however, not even the short term expectations have been fulfilled, and the development is taking an unpredicted direction. In Table 2 the present pattern is compared to the previous expectations in a condensed format. The specific competencies of various departments have been acknowledged, but in the case of complex parts, there is now a considerable degree of cooperation between the process planners (who are also complex part NC programmers) and designers both in the design phase and at the programming stage. This cooperation takes place before the screen of the designer or the process planner's screen, respectively, according to the phase of work.

Table 2: Consensus views and actual development regarding division of labour in integrated CAD/CAM systems operation

Consensus view 1981	Change in tasks for:		
	Designer	Process planner	NC part programmer
Short term	no change	computer aids indep. of CAD	works directly on CAD database
Medium term	some process planning	works directly on CAD database	operates auto-NC
Long term	operates auto-NC + some auto-PP	operates auto-process planning	no such job
Very long term	operates auto-NC and auto-PP	no such job	no such job
Situation 1985			
Simple parts	no change	no change	works directly on CAD database
Complex parts	process planner helps designer design for ease of NC programming, programs directly on CAD database		

5. Case B: Shop floor concentration

The other case of CAD/CAM integration I would like to present has not been studied in detail. The company's effort is centered around a NC flamecutter and involves a substantial job enrichment for the operator of this particular machine.

In the company one envisages a number of different data systems to be integrated. The organizational solution one is aiming at has one striking feature: a number of planning tasks is to be integrated into one particular job on the shop floor.

The NC flamecutter is a critical point in the production because a substantial percentage of the parts produced first have to be cut from steel plates of various thickness. This involves firstly a problem of materials planning and administration. A data system is being developed to keep track of steel sheets from need assessment via purchase and stores to flamecutter. By operating this system from the point of production, one hopes to get better material administration and lower overhead costs than by letting production planners do it all.

Secondly, there is the problem of maximizing steel sheet utilization. This is primarily a geometrical problem suitable for a type of software called "nesting", which is lined to the NC programming system. However, since this optimization problem also involves the priority of parts to be cut, the availability of steel sheets, etc., it is believed to be better to let this task also be performed at the point of production.

Thirdly, since computer aided design of the parts to be cut is feasible, it would be advantageous to do this and to let NC programming and nesting be performed on the data base of the CAD system, again by the flamecutter operator.

Thus by coupling a CAD system with an NC programming system and a nesting program, integration has been achieved on the technical side. On the planning side, there are links between this CAD/CAM system and the materials and production planning system in the sense of identification of parts and plates and of quantities of steel required and used. One also gets more accurate cost estimates at an earlier time.

And in the center of this, one expects to find a skilled metalworker with additional training in planning, NC programming, and use of the various computer systems. This organizational solution seems almost the diametrically opposite of the one where all tasks are seen to move upstream. Refer to Figure 2 for a visualization of this third philosophy.

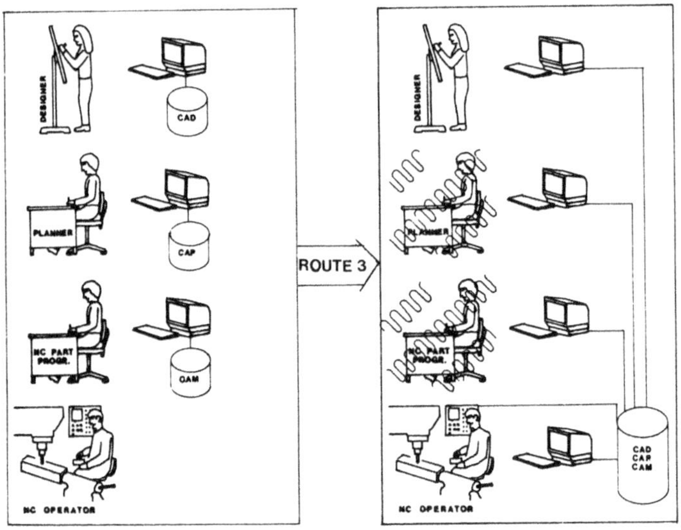

Figure 2: Third route of CAD/CAM integration
Note: means partial deletion of job.

Two cautions should be taken. One is that neither the systems nor the organizational solution have been fully implemented yet. Transfer of more tasks to the operator depends on acceptance of this in the involved departments and is limited by the time it takes to learn how to handle all these systems. At the moment the operator does about half the programming.

The second caution is that one is trying to automate a number of the tasks to be performed from the operator's terminal. This is particularly true for the programming of the individual part to be cut. Parameterization is the keyword and hence the actual programming task becomes practically clerical. More complex programs will still have to be done by experts. Nevertheless, this case shows the possibility of organizational choice and CAD/CAM systems developed to support this choice.

6. CAD/CAM integration: Functional organization or organization by product?

With the two cases in mind it is reasonable to assert that a complete concentration of tasks either at the design end or at the shop floor, based on a high degree of automation of intermediate tasks, belongs to the far future if anywhere. On the other hand, most CAD/CAM integration efforts can be seen as attempts at overcoming the problems of coordination and communication that were introduced with the growing specialization of tasks in the manufacturing industries. The millwright who erected his mill on the basis of a small number of requirements from his customer never had the problem of communicating his design to the planner and the plan to the immediate producer: it was all in one person. Not only have tasks been specialized, however. The tasks have been organized according to function. Everywhere in industry (except in very small firms) there are separate departments of design, planning and production.

This organization according to function has been instrumental in developing the individual tasks, but it has been dysfunctional in terms of growing overhead costs and, significantly, the time and effort it takes to design a product and get it produced. This holds particularly for products made to order.

I propose that CAD/CAM integration would seem to give greater benefits if design, planning and production were organized according to product and not to function. In the extreme, this would mean that a department consisted of all the people involved in designing, planning and producing a particular product. All these people would be in the same physical space, they would have the same supervisor, they would have breaks together, and they would work together on the same product.

I do not think of this as a viable, general organizational model (except perhaps in very small firms). Tradition alone would forbid it. Also, one would have great difficulties in defining appropriate product related boundaries between the departments. There is also the question of numbers as some categories of specialists might be too few to cover all departments. But as a general source of inspiration this alternative model has its value.

For example, the basis organization could be functional with frequent use of project groups including not only white collar personnel but also the shop floor workers who would actually be making the thing. This kind of a matrix organization is becoming more frequent in engineering firms but here it does not make for a good integration between preparatory work and the actual production. The extension of such organizational forms to production would give a much better basis for utilizing the potential of CAD/CAM integration.

In case B above one is actually trying this in a rudimentary form in one phase. Experienced workers are involved in preconceiving how to process particular types of customer orders. If successful, this will result in the individual customer orders being processed by designers, planners, and producers in a preconceived way. Both drawings, time estimates and production plans for a specific type of product will be quickly produced by insertion of the appropriate values of a number of parameters. The preconception is done in a product-specific project group, the actual orders will be processed in the functional organization.

In case A above, the differences in practice between the handling of complex and simple parts also point in the direction of organization by product, although production is kept outside.

A reasonable conclusion then would be to request more thinking to be done in the direction of organizing according to product and not according to function when one speaks of CAD/CAM integration.

Note

1) Sections 3 and 4 of this paper are in part based on H. Finne: Mellom tegnebrett og terminal, IFIM, Trondheim 1982, and H. Finne: "The designer and his job in the face of integrated CAD/CAM systems", in T. Martin (ed.): Design of Work in Automated Manufacturing Systems, Pergamon Press, London 1984.

CAD/CAM INTEGRATION: FLEXIBLE MANUFACTURING SYSTEMS IN THE U.K

Bill Haywood & John Bessant
Innovation Research Group
Department of Business Management
Brighton Polytechnic
Brighton, BN2 4 AT, United Kingdom

1. Introduction: The trend to computer integrated manufacturing

The introduction of computers in the U.K. - as in all other countries - has tended to be rather fragmented in the past. There was little of it, it was expensive, it was physically energy and space consuming, there were few people who knew how to run it effectively, and it was devoted to specific functions such as salaries or tool stocks. All these factors are now rapidly changing and the integration of all of aspects of manufacturing is growing from the receipt of orders through design, planning, production, assembly, despatch etc. This can be visualised by reference to a model offered by KAPLINSKY [1]).

However, integration does not stop there, for increasingly companies in the U.K. are looking at links, both with their customers and their suppliers. In both cases they are examining their relations at the technical level where CAD/CAM can be so important, and the links that exist organisationally with other companies. In the latter case this is what Oliver WILLIAMSON [2]) has called "obligational contracting", put more bluntly it's a relationship that American economist Robert SOLOW [3]) described in a labour relations context as "More like a marriage than a one-night stand". This is the common form of contracting in Japan. In these new terms therefore, an expanded version of the Kaplinsky model is needed.

Figure 2 below offers one way in which these issues might be considered. For example, while Kaplinsky offers us a picture of integration within the firm, we anticipate growing links between firms as well. If this is the case then there will also be a growing need to establish an overall communications system which would allow common standards within Open Systems Interconnection networks; and examples of such developments would be the current General Motors initiative - Manufacturing Automated Protocols (M.A.P.) -, and the Initial Graphics Exchange Specification (I.G.E.S.).

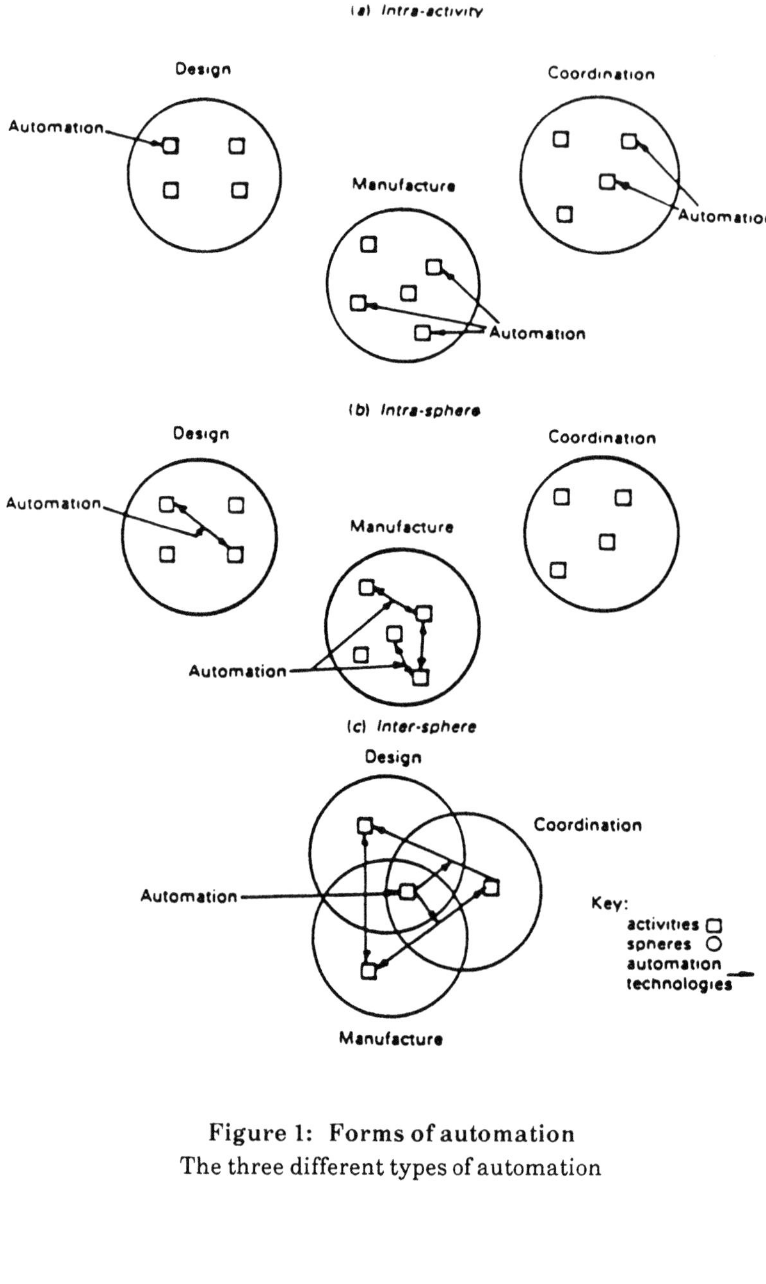

Figure 1: Forms of automation
The three different types of automation

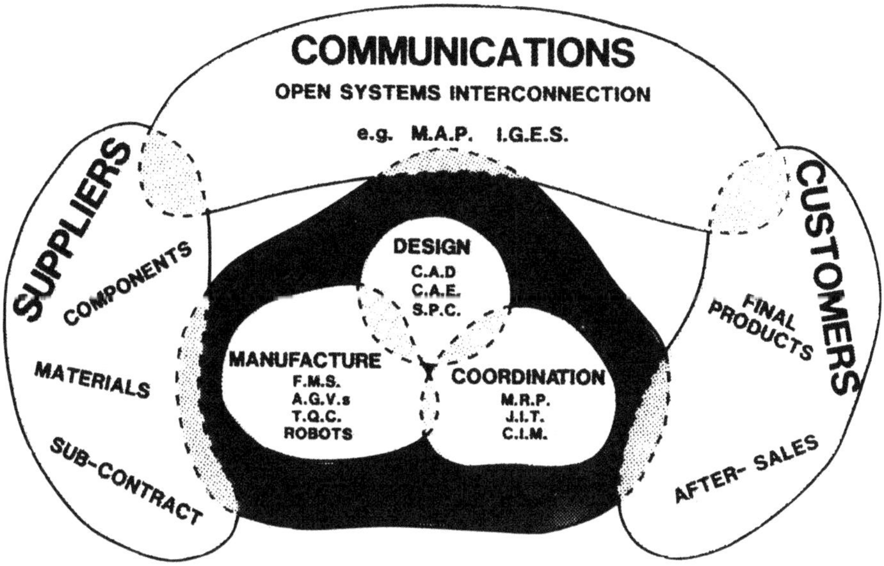

Key

M.A.P. Manufacturing Automation Protocol
I.G.E.S. Initial Graphics Exchange Specification
C.A.D. Computer Aided Design
C.A.E. Computer Aided Engineering
S.P.C. Statistical Process Control
F.M.S. Flexible Manufacturing Systems
A.G.V.s Automatic Guided Vehicles
T.Q.C. Total Quality Control
M.R.P. Material Requirements Planning
J.I.T. Just-in-Time
C.I.M. Computer Integrated Manufacturing

Figure 2: Organization in the "Factory of the Future"?

2. The diffusion of Flexible Manufacturing Systems

In an interim report in April we noted twelve FMSs either installed or planned, and another thirty cells. Currently we know of at least seventy systems or cells in the metal removal sector and around twenty others in the furniture, castings, sheet metal, assembly, and rubber and plastics sectors. In terms of actual installations (as against planned installations as well, e.g., the ninety noted above) this can be seen by reference to the following diagram.

Graph 1: Growth in FMS installations (U.K.)

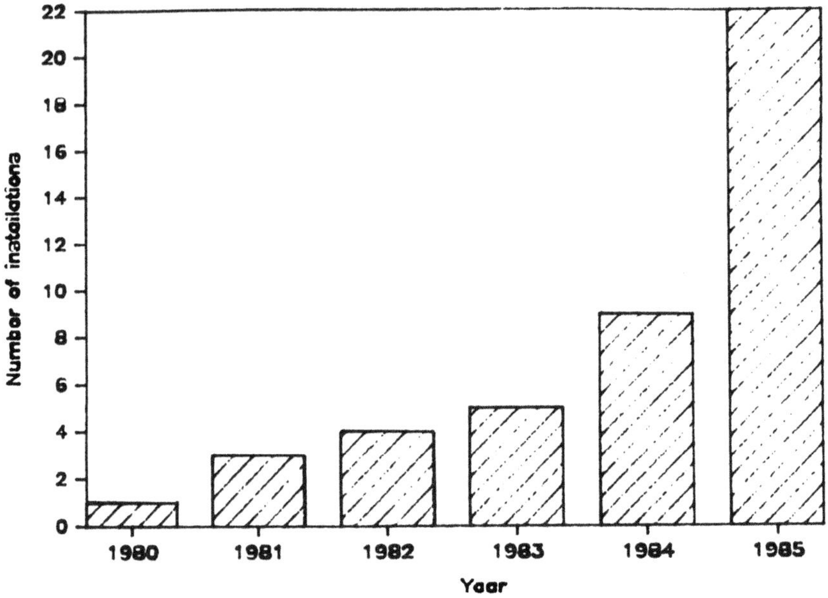

Obviously therefore, there has been an extremely rapid recent growth of interest in such technologies. This was something that we forecast as likely to happen but we were less sure how quickly this would occur. However, despite this rapid growth, only an international comparative study would reveal if this represents a closing of the gap between the U.K. and Japan, the U.S.A., and West Germany. It may well be that similar or even more rapid growth rates are being experienced in these countries, and starting from a higher base than the one that existed in the U.K.

3. The benefits of Flexible Manufacturing Systems

Having said this, what are the potential benefits of FMS style technologies? Fifty of the systems/cells covered by our research are listed in Table 1. Although some of the measures which we wished to include were not obtained at the time that the table was compiled, it provides sufficient data to illustrate the changes that have been occurring in the past few months - both in terms of the cost of such systems and cells, and of the potential benefits, e.g., reduced lead-times and work in progress, increased machine utilisation, etc.

We can see that there have been quite dramatic changes in a whole series of important manufacturing criteria, such as:

Lead Times	- 74 %	(n=23)
WIP	- 68 %	(n=22)
Stock Turnover	+ 3-4 Fold	(n=17)
Machine Utilisation	+ 63 %	(n=16)

(Up from say 50 % with CNC to more than 80 % with FMS)

Given that an estimated £ 20B is currently tied up in stock lying around on the shop floor in U.K. manufacturing engineering the benefits for the average company are obviously very considerable.

4. The configuration of Flexible Manufacturing Systems

With regards to the definitions imposed by us, these reflect the fact that even now there appears little consensus as to what a F.M.S. or F.M.C. is. Our definition encompasses batch sizes, size of part families, and configurations of systems or cells. Figure 3 indicates this range of choice.

However, we have also discovered that the parameters of FMS and FMC are changing somewhat in the U.K..

Before:
(a) Such systems cost around £ 5M.
(b) They could only deal with fairly large batch sizes.
(c) They could only deal with fairly small family of parts.
(d) They were nearly always installed in large companies.

Now:
(a) The average cost has halved to around £ 2.4M.
(72 % of systems/cells we know of cost less than £2m)
(b) 58 % now normally deal with batch sizes of 10 or less.
(c) 22 % of systems now cope with over 100 different parts.
(d) 69 % are in companies with less than 1000 employees.
(41 % in 500 n or less.)

Interestingly a new group of users is also emerging, e.g., companies manufacturing electric motors, pumps, marine components, valves, hand-tools, switch gear, etc.; compared with vehicles, aerospace, engines, agricultural machinery, and machine tools, which have dominated the market in the past.

We can see these parameter changes more clearly from the set of four graphs that follow.

Graph 2: Distribution by size (employees)

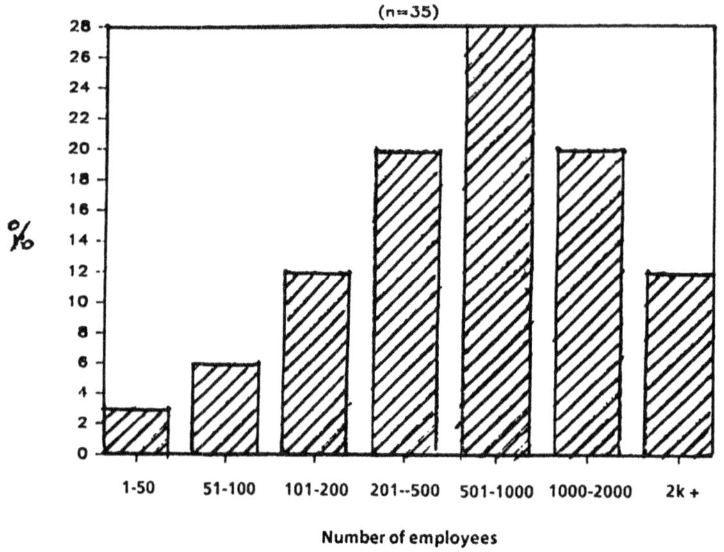

Graph 3: Average cost per system

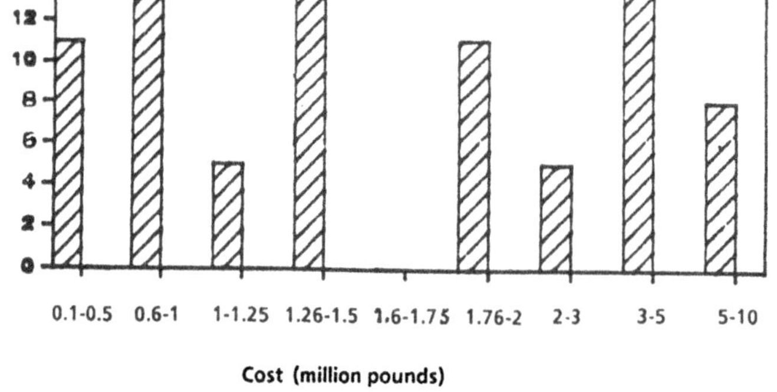

Graph 4: Average parts family

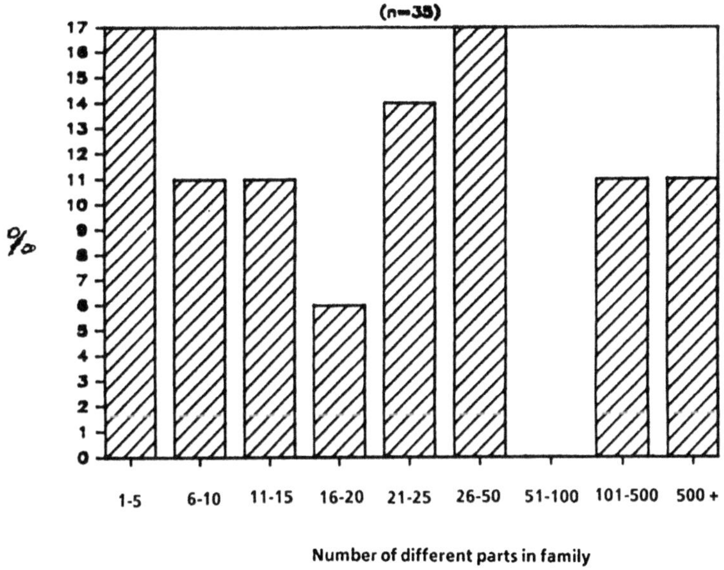

Graph 5: Batch sizes

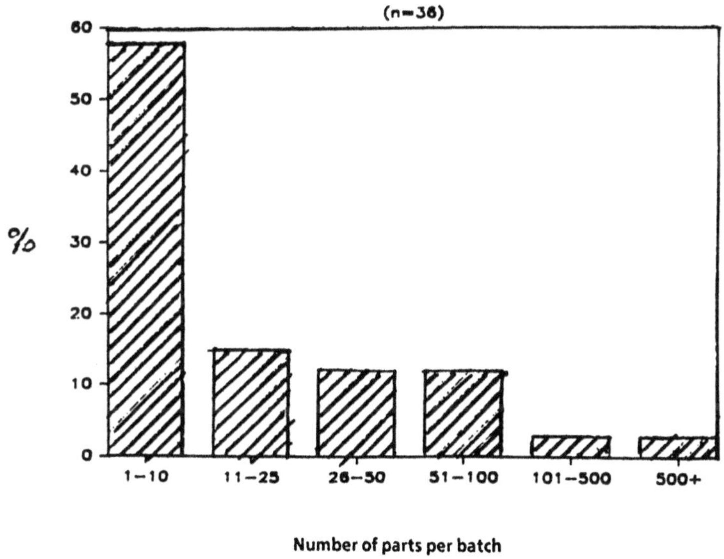

Table 1:

SECTOR	A DEFINITION	B COST	C EMPLOYED	BATCH SIZE	PART FAMILY	LEAD-TIME	WIP	D TURNOVER	E MACHINE UTILISATION
MINING	DEDICATED FMS	£6.5	1850	2	14	- 81%	- 70%	x 5 FOLD	v
VEHICLE	FMS	£10.0M +	16000	x	1000+	x	x	x	x
MACHINE TOOL	FMC	£2.0 M	240	2	7	x	x	x	x
AEROSPACE	FMS	£10.0 M	8000	1	2000	- 85%	x	x	x
POWER	DEDICATED FMS	£5.0 M	90	100	4	x	x	x	x
MACHINERY	FMS	£1.5 M	950	1	500	- 75%	- 60%	x	x
MACHINERY	DEDICATED FMS	£0.5 M	180	1	2	- 80%	- 70%	x	x
ELECTRIC MOTORS	FMC	£0.8 M	200	10	5	- 60%	-60%	x 4 FOLD	+ 50%
PUMPS	FMC	£1.5 M	200	50	20	x	x	x	x
MACHINE TOOL	FMC	£0.7 M	700	2	13	x	x	x	x
ENGINES	DEDICATED FMC	£2.0 M	50	100	2	- 80%	- 40%	x	x
ENGINES	DEDICATED FMC	£0.7 M	580	1	8	x	x	x	x
MARINE	DEDICATED FMC	£0.5 M	250	3	20	- 60%	x	x	x
MINING	DEDICATED FMS	£2.5 M	400	15	27	- 83%	- 70%	x 4 FOLD	+ 35%
COMPONENT	DEDICATED FMS	£5.0 M	900	2000	25	x	x	x	x
GEARS	FMC	£1.1 M	550	50	30	- 60%	- 60%	x	+ 50%
ENGINES	DEDICATED FMS	£4.5 M	1000	x	x	x	x	x	x
VALVES	FMS	£4.2 M	x	2	700	- 50%	x	x	+ 50%
VALVES	FMC	£1.1 M	320	1	30	x	- 70%	x	x
VEHICLE	DEDICATED FMC	£0.3 M	10000	100	2	x	- 25%	x 0.5 FOLD	x
MACHINERY	DEDICATED FMS	£3.5 M	120	5	24	x	x	x	x
MACHINE TOOL	FMC	£0.8 M	370	5	x	x	x	x	x
COMPONENT	FMC	£1.3 M	500	50	6	x	x	x	x
VEHICLE	DEDICATED FMS	£2.0 M	1500	5	23	- 40%	- 40%	x 4 FOLD	x
ENGINES	FMC	£0.8 M	2000	50	15	x	x	x	+ 50%
ENGINES	FMC	£1.0 M+	2000	125	320	x	x	x	x
ENGINES	FMC	£1.9 M	1000	x	25	x	x	x	x
AEROSPACE	DEDICATED FMS	£1.5 M	2000	20	14	- 88%	-80%	x 3 FOLD	+ 40%
ENGINE	DEDICATED FMS	£2.5 M	3500	20	2	x	x	x	x
AEROSPACE	FMC	£1.5 M	2000	25	27	- 85%	- 80%	x 3 FOLD	+ 100%
PUMPS	FMC	£1.0 M	950	8	50	x	x	x	x
TOOLS	FMC	£0.5 M	260	100	6	- 65%	- 60%	x 5 FOLD	+ 50%
AEROSPACE	FMC	£1.0 M	2000	25	1000	- 85%	- 70%	x 2.5 FOLD	+ 40%
MINING	DEDICATED FMS	£10.0 M	x	10	23	- 75%	- 90%	x	x
SWITCH GEAR	DEDICATED FMS	£1.5 M	70	10	50	x	x	x 2.5 FOLD	x
PUMPS	FMS	£1.5 M	950	8	480	x	x	x	x
PUMPS	FMS	£1.5 M	950	8	480	x	x	x	x
AGRICULTURAL MACHINERY	DEDICATED FMS	£1.3 M	1200	20	15	- 90%	- 85%	x 5 FOLD	+ 20%
SWITCH GEAR	FMC	£0.4 M	50	50	49	- 50%	x	x	x
MACHINE TOOL	DEDICATED FMS	£3.0 M	720	25	150	- 92%	- 70%	x 3 FOLD	x
AGRICULTURAL MACHINERY	DEDICATED FMS	£1.5 M	1200	20	9	- 92%	- 90%	x 5 FOLD	+ 15%
AGRICULTURAL MACHINERY	DEDICATED FMS	£1.6 M	1200	1	8	- 55%	- 80%	x 5 FOLD	x
AEROSPACE	FMS	£8.0 M	8000	15	4000	x	x	x	x
VEHICLES	DEDICATED FMS	£3.0 M+	1650	1500	9	x	x	x	x
AEROSPACE	FMS	£1.0 M+	5000	30	WIDE	x	x	x	x
TRANSMISSIONS	FMC	£1.3 M	1100	45	8	x	x	x 4 FOLD	+ 35%
VEHICLE	FMC	£1.5 M+	16000	1	25	x	x	x	+ 100%
ENGINES	DEDICATED FMS	£2.0 M+	2000	1000	15	x	- 70%	x 3 FOLD	+ 50%
ENGINES	FMS	£10.0 M+	2000	1	100	- 75%	- 75%	x	+ 100%
ENGINES	FMC	£0.8 M	2000	40	100	- 85%	- 80%	x 4 FOLD	+ 50%
AVERAGE		**£2.4 M**				**- 74%**	**- 68%**	**x 3.5**	**+ 63%**

KEY:

(A) Constitutes a definition imposed by authors depending on batch size, part family and system configuration,

(B) Is the cost of the system. These are figures provided either by the companies or derived from published material.

(C) Numbers currently employed at these companies at time of research.

(D) Represents increase in stock turnover.

(E) Machine utilisation shows increases over previously installed equipment, e.g. company number 8 (Electric Motors) improved machine utilisation from 60 % with conventional machine tools to 90 % with its FMC configuration.

NB Where a cross has been positioned this does not mean that the information is unobtainable, merely that such figures have not yet been obtained.

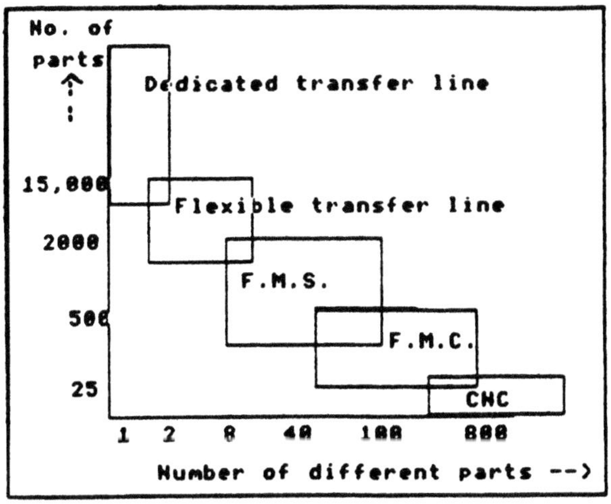

Figure 3: (Source: ISI)

In other words there is proliferation of choice; flexibility is becoming more widely available. One result of these changes is that the diffusion has, as forecast, already started to occur down to the smaller firms; and more flexible, cheaper, more standardised systems/cells are becoming available.

5. Manpower and skill implications

With regard to manpower requirements, at this early stage of diffusion we found that there was little evidence of significant job-loss as a result of the introduction of FMS/FMC. Although many firms have looked for "Unmanned production" in the past, the difficulties posed have meant that "having people in the system" has been the practical experience. While there was evidence of some reduction in the "direct labour" content, there has also been some growth in "indirect support". Job-loss in the companies interviewed has been quite considerable (averaging 37 % in the last five years), however, much of this was attributable to low demand in the economy, lack of competitiveness, and to poor infrastructural support. This is not to suggest, of course, that job-loss might not be considerable in the future as FMS/FMC diffuse more widely.

In terms of skill, theories based on the division of labour and economies of scale seem to be becoming supplanted by multi skilling and economies of scope. These are much more relevant to production requirements that in batch manufacturing, for example, show that around 70 % of output in metal manufacturing lies in batches of less than fifty.

FMSs and Cells, which answer many of these production problems, call for multiplicity of skills, e.g., setting, programming, simple maintenance, diagnostic skills, etc., rather than employing a wide range of specifically skilled people. In other words there may be less "direct" skilled labour but demand has tended to be for a higher quality of labour. The "indirect" element is harder to quantify, but most firms appear to have used increased levels. For example, Driscoll [4)] found that in Japan, while only six people were employed directly on running the now well known Yamazaki installation, ten times more were employed in support of it, e.g., for programming, for swarf removal or parts movement, button pushers, etc., and that while direct labour saving might be quite high, overall levels of employment were much less dramatically affected.

However, these direct/indirect structural changes require detailed examination since obviously not all people in these categories are similarly affected. For example, a simple matrix could be used to show general changes from the F.M.S. study.

	Labour	
	Direct	Indirect
Employment	-	+
Quality of Life	+	-

This FMS study shows job-loss amongst direct labour as a general trend, but that job-growth and quality of life improvements have probably occurred in the other three quadrants. In the past, most emphasis has been put on this direct labour impact - with good reason given the social implications - but this may as a result distort the overall picture. However, we define "quality of life", e.g., less division of labour, health and safety improvements, enlarged job opportunities or skills, etc., it appears that at this stage of the diffusion process, the impact has tended to be positive. We should keep in mind though, that quality of life changes *within* a group might well vary. For example, within the direct labour/quality of life quadrant, some jobs for men might possibly be degraded, while some job opportunities for women *might* possibly be enhanced.

Overall in the U.K. there is strong evidence to suggest that there are insufficient numbers of the wider skilled personnel that are being called for - not so much the people running the systems on the shopfloor - but of good electronics and production engineers with "hands-on experience", and of skilled software personnel. What in fact was repeated to us time after time was the need for good "systems" people.

Much of the preceding discussion has been in respect of the technological problems and opportunities posed, but in almost every interview carried out the importance of methodological routes to improved efficiency were also stressed. When accounting for overall improvements in efficiency, estimates of the importance of methodological change varied between 40 % and 70 % of the total improvement. Clearly around half of the improvement tended to come from these methodological changes. One company, which had not introduced FMS/FMC, had reduced the level of stocks held by 60 % and increased output by 30 % just by adopting "good management and methodological practices". An investment of £ 5m in the following three years in CNC standalone equipment was undertaken, and turnover was trebled from £ 20m to £ 60m (1981-84). This was during a period when employment declined on average by over 30 % in many other companies in the study who were introducing FMS/FMC, yet employment grew in this non-FMS company by some 14 %. In other words what was important here was not so much the technology but the adoption of good management and production practices.

Thus the rethink required encompasses both the hardware and the software elements of production, right through to the methodologically efficient management of production. In some instances simply conducting a feasibility study into the implications of FMS had been enough to convince companies that substantial improvements could be made to efficiency by an overhaul of their production processes. This is highlighted by the following two figures. The first offers two options for approaching some concept of the "factory of the future". The second while perhaps being an over-simplification of production engineering opportunities prior to the introduction of microelectronics, provides a framework for considering the impact of both technological and methodological factors on current opportunities.

It is becoming increasingly clear that such factors as: Just in Time Production; Total Quality Control; Supplier and Customer relationships; etc., are all extremely important in improving efficiency, and that it is not merely the technology that we should consider. Significantly, it is precisely in these areas of organisational and methodological techniques that the Japanese are strongest; and which are somewhat belatedly attracting the attention of the West. There is growing interest in these areas in Australia [6)], America [7)], and the U.K. [8)]. No doubt there are many similar experiences that could be highlighted in other countries.

Many people have talked of the cultural reasons why such "Japanese" style methodological developments are inappropriate for Western countries. However, it would be difficult to think of many "Japanese" production methods which do not have their roots in Western ideas, taken and developed by the Japanese in the 1950s and 60s. Theorists such as Taylor, Sloan, and particularly Deming and Juran, have been extraordinarily important to the Japanese, and as SONBERGER [5)] has pointed out. "The Japanese have had little trouble learning our techniques, and we will have little trouble learning theirs".

6. Conclusions

In conclusion, given the above findings, in the successful implementation of FMS emphasis needs to be placed on a number of factors.

a) A need for the integration and compatibility of hardware and software. A major constraint in the past has been the problem of developing hierarchical controls that could cope with the demands of truly flexible systems. It is now clear that most companies have identified Local Area Network systems as the answer to many of these problems.

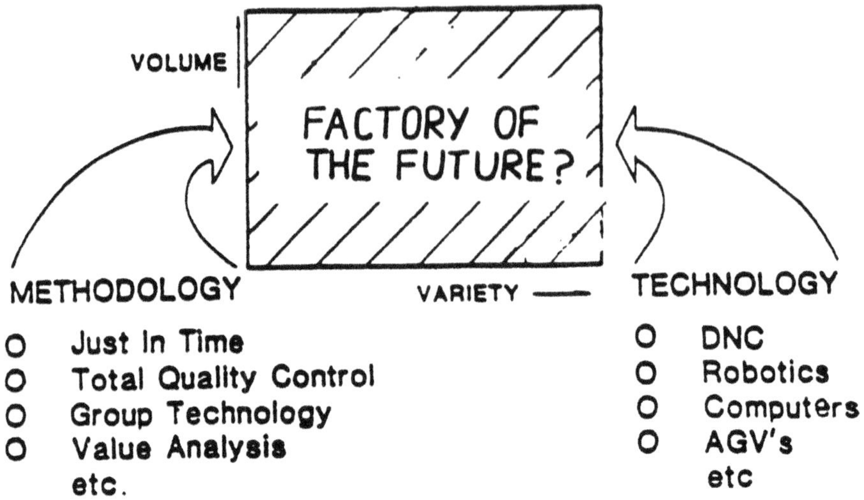

Figure 4

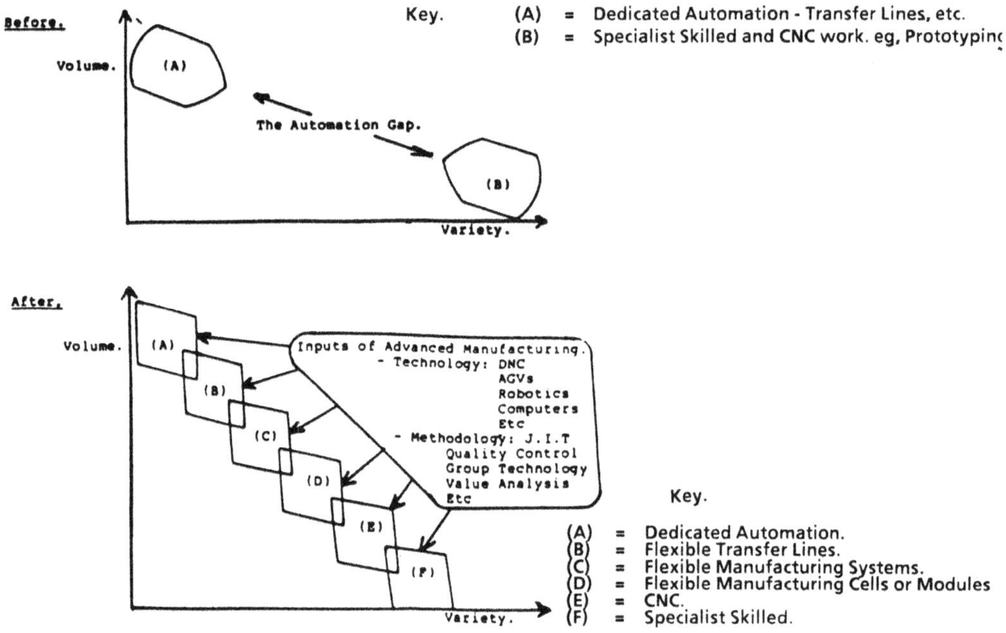

Figure 5: The impact of advanced manufacturing technologies on choice in production engineering

b) The need to examine both the technological and the organisational structures within the company. In many instances the view has been expressed that over half the benefits of introducing FMS/FMC arose, not from the system itself, but from a reappraisal which covered such aspects as planning, design, materials, management organisation, and long-term overall objectives.

c) The efficient integration of manpower and skill resources; and an increased awareness of the longer time perspective for this at both the company and the national level. This approach is also needed with the important issues of industrial relations that FMS raises. Clearly a much less demarcated job structure emerges with FMS requirements, and there is an increased need for personnel with skills that combine operating, setting, diagnostics, programming, and maintenance abilities. While recognising this trend towards a much less "division of labour" orientation, it would appear that few U.K. companies have as yet come to terms with these problems, and the efforts of people such as ROSENBROCK [9]), and COOLEY [10]), to promote technology as supporting the efforts of workers rather than the other way around, have yet to bear substantial fruit.

d) Considerable benefits might also be gained by companies establishing closer links with their sub-contractors. This holds the key to: strengthening the infrastructure of manufacturing industry, and offers opportunities to reduce costs and improve quality of components and final products. Such moves would result in lengthening the time horizons of the sub-contract industry; create improvements in the production processes employed, and reduce costs to the customer. Already a number of companies interviewed in the U.K. have indicated moves towards such a system of fewer suppliers with longer term relationships, and have highlighted the considerable benefits that are already arising, such as, Just-in-Time deliveries, improved component quality, reduced costs, etc., which as we have noted has tended to be the norm in Japanese companies. In a number of forward thinking U.K. companies this trend appears to have strengthened in the last year.

e) FMS also pinpoints the need for closer collaboration within the firm, e.g., between marketing, production engineering, and manufacturing engineering, in order to identify, develop, and produce the appropriate goods in the most economical and human manner. One example of this is the need to make sure that goods for which markets have been identified, can be designed and proven to be "makeable"; economically viable rather than over-engineered or merely another competitor in an already over-subscribed market; and, which enhance the skills of labour and are not destructive of them.

f) The fact that longer term planning and investment profiles are needed which keep/make companies internationally competitive. There are indications that in the U.K., links between industry and the academic world are growing, e.g., the Applications of Computers in Manufacturing Engineering programme sponsored by the Science and Engineering Research Council [11]); venture capital is slowly becoming more readily available [12]); major firms are investing more heavily in FMS and employing cellular logic as our research shows [13]); and small to medium sized firms are adopting increasing levels of FMCs and standalone CNC equipment. However, a recent report by ROTHWELL & GARDNER [14]), once more emphasises the ways in which product innovativeness is hampered by a lack of long-term city investment in the U.K., and the problems that arise from the failure of the financial institutions to support engineering in the ways that are seen in Japan, and West Germany, etc..

Finally, while the use of new technology is absolutely vital to continued competitiveness, what is even more important is *how* it is used, and this ultimately depends on the modernisation of organisational structures and managerial attitudes in companies which allows and plans for the efficient introduction of new technology in both economic and human terms.

References

1) Kaplinsky, R.:
Automation: The Technology and Society.Longmans. London, 1984.

2) Williamson, O.E.:
Transaction Time Economics: The Governance of Contractural Relations. Journal of Law & Economics. Vol. 22, No ii, 1979.

3) Solow, R.M.:
On Theories of Employment. American Economic Review. Vol. 70, i, 1980.

4) Driscoll, J.:
The Use of Flexible Manufacturing Systems. Industrial Studies Dept., Liverpool University, 1984.

5) Schonberger, R.J.:
Japanese Manufacturing Techniques. The Free Press. New York, 1982.

6) Report:
How Australian Industry points the Way on Kanban. Production Engineer. June 1984.

7) Report:
Just in Time: On the Move and Out of the Aisles in America. Manufacturing Engineering, June 1984.

8) Report:
Could the Kanban Production Control System Work here? Production Engineer. June 1984.

9) Rosenbrock, H.H.:
Seeking an Appropriate Technology. I.F.A.C. Conference. Austria, March 1983.

10) Cooley, M.:
Architect of Bee? Langley Technical Services. Slough, U.K., 1980.

11) Applications of Computers in Manufacturing Engineering. A body within the Science and Engineering Research Council devoted to establishing close links between industry and academia.

12) Pauley, R.:
Lawson Hails Success of Venture Capital. Financial Times. 20 August 1985.

13) Bessant, J.R. & Haywood, B.W.:
Flexible Manufacturing Systems as an Example of Computer Integrated Manufacturing. Innovation Research Group, Brighton Polytechnic, 1985.

14) Rothwell, R & Gardner, P.:
Innovation: A Study of the Problems and Benefits of Product Innovation. The Design Centre. London, 1985.

THE ORGANIZATIONAL IMPACT OF CAD IN ITALIAN FIRMS
- MAIN PROBLEMS AND KEY FACTORS FOR SUCCESS -

Olimpio Brivio - MAIN S.r.l., Via G. de Grassi 3, 20123 Milano, Italy
GianCarlo Cainarca - University of Padova and MAIN S.r.l.
Marco Mutinelli - Politecnico di Milano, Piazza Leonardo da Vinci 32, 20133 Milano, Italy
Claudio Roveda - Politecnico di Milano and Cestec S.p.A.

1. Introduction

The qualitative analysis is based mainly on the findings of two empirical investigations on the process (from decision to actual implementation) followed by a certain number of industrial firms (both large and small-medium sized) for the introduction of a CAD system. Special attention is given to the factors (economical, cultural, organizational, etc.) that create in some way a barrier for the access of small-medium size firms to the technology of CAD.

Finally a brief overview is given on industrial relations involving CAD, particularly on the attitudes of trade unions towards this new technology.

2. CAD applications in large firms

The decision-making process

The way in which the reasons/determinants presiding over the introduction of CAD into companies may be reduced to a limited set of options, emerges from the empirical investigation. The main reasons are:

- the attempt to reduce drafting/design times, both at the local level of function, and, more generally, at the company level, in order to counteract the reduced life-cycle of products and increase the overall market competitiveness of the company;
- the technological productive and qualitative restraints set by the market and by client companies;
- the need to reach output levels scarcely achievable with traditional instruments. It should be stressed that such motives have been encountered in nearly all the cases analyzed, both when dealing with "high-tech" sectors such as electronics and aerospace, and with those sectors traditionally defined as "low-tech", such as footwear and the production of dies;
- a process of technological up-grading, understood in its double meaning of adapting existing production processes to higher standards and restyling the market image.

The companies studied had resorted to a fairly roundabout set of approaches in evaluating the introduction of CAD, there being basically two: firstly, "costs/benefits", and secondly, "systemic".

The first approach reflects an essentially economic type of analysis. Although this was the most frequent approach, it should be pointed out that the level of sophistication of the evaluation methods employed was still relatively low. Apart from a few exceptions, the analysis of advantages and disadvantages was limited to direct consequences alone, ignoring "indirect" effects such as the qualitative improvement of the final product and the impact on the whole of the design-production cycle.

In the second case, the evaluation of the introduction of CAD was above all centered upon the possibility of using the technology to define new "routines" capable both of promoting the utilization/diffusion of the instrument, and of rendering the organization as a whole more efficient.

It is interesting to note, in the cases examined so far, how the "systemic" approach corresponded to situations in which CAD already represented a widely-used technology, and how it could be seen as the result of the progressive perception and transformation of such technology in terms of success factors and, consequently, the way in which it was used. An example of such dynamics, which could be called "feel-by-using", may be witnessed in the course of action undertaken by a company operating in the telecommunications sector. Following an initial "piecemeal" diffusion of CAD, an integration process of the various systems was launched within the division analyzed. Besides fulfilling the need to link distinct phases of the process, such integration corresponded to the realization that various kinds of competitive advantages could be obtained (organizational, productive, etc.).

Implementation strategies

The cases analyzed have given certain clues to the factors that favor the success of new technology implementation. It emerged, as confirmation of what had been indicated in more general terms by the literature of this field, to what degree the involvement of top management levels is of fundamental importance in determining, at all organizational levels, the correct perception of the strategic values of CAD and the support of its application. In short, other more important factors that emerged were:

- A systemic vision of the introduction of CAD, which is to say, the ability to perceive and follow through advantages in all aspects of the specific areas of drafting and/or design, and, where necessary, redefine the division of tasks among the various phases. With respect to this, the innovations introduced should be taken into account when evaluating the output of areas of CAD application.

  For example, as is demonstrated in the case of an aircraft company, it is no longer possible to continue the evaluation of CAD areas only on the basis of drafts produced.
- The availability of internal resources able to "personalize" the software packages with respect to the needs of the company's productive processes and the specific utilization. Such needs are not exclusively of a technical nature (specifically concerning the sector's basic problems), being also linked to pre-existent organization "routines", and satis-

factory solutions are not always to be found among the packages available on the market, or with suppliers' post-sales services.

- The involvement of the entire organizational structure of the interested areas (from those responsible to the operators). The course of action seen in certain of the cases analyzed has demonstrated how the widest possible involvement plays a double role in preventing a possible rejection by the operators and in promoting research into the most efficient configurations of the system. Generally, the most frequently pursued path towards the involvement of systems users is training. With respect to this, it should be pointed out that training is rarely directed towards management, despite the decisive role it plays in contributing to the success of CAD introduction. Certain large industrial holdings in Italy, such as the IRI, are moving in this direction.

With more specific regard to the implementation strategies enacted within the companies taken into consideration, two complementary tendencies have merged.

A first approach, centered upon the delegation of choice to operational levels, has, to an equal extent, shown both merits and defects. The "bottom-up" process has allowed for CAD introduction as a result both of technological interest and of specific production needs faced by management, although at an operational level this process has been unable to bring about innovations in organizational structures and to allow for a homogeneous diffusion of CAD. The experience of a telecommunication company gives an illuminating example of this. The germination of automation "islands" in design led to the co-presence of differing CAD systems, which later necessitated seeking solutions that would make them compatible.

A second approach, centered upon the co-ordination of CAD introduction, showed that it could allow important results to be obtained.

The above-mentioned case of the telecommunications company is of great interest because it demonstrates how this second approach may form itself as a development of the first. To be specific, in the case of the telecommunications company, it could be seen how success linked to CAD introduction was above all consolidated from the moment when, in 1982, abandoning the spontaneous "piecemeal" germination, the company decided to create "project groups" with the aim of integrating and up-dating the various CAD and CAM systems operating within the company, and to introduce, as an evaluation level of new systems, a clause relating to their compatibility with those already existing.

Organizational effects

A consideration based only upon the effect of CAD on the company's organizational structure risks creating a static idea, omitting the opportunities offered by new technology and the choices available. With this in mind, only the most important aspects that have emerged from the empirical investigation are pointed out in the following:

Effects on professionality:

A reduction in the professional qualification level of operators has not generally been a result of CAD introduction. Within the kind of situation described for the telecommunications company differing consequences may co-exist. The example mentioned before has demonstrated how, for the operators at certain stages, CAD introduction has brought about no change in their professional profile, while for those at other stages it has meant the development of new professional contents.

Operators do not always perceive the opportunities for professional requalification; the case of the aircraft company has shown how, in the presence of an organization possessing a rigid product definition for every function (therefore separating the drafting and the mathematical model of a component), operators saw the utilization of CAD as a reduction of their own professional qualification.

Effects on organizational integration:

At the organizational level two integrational trends have emerged from the cases studied: a "vertical" one and a "lateral" one.

The trend towards a "vertical" integration, favored by the technological integration of CAD and CAM, is justified by research into the advantages created by linking the various phases of the production cycle, from design to drafting to production. By pursuing this tendency, important results have been obtained by the aircraft company, which managed to considerably reduce adjustment times during the final phase of component assembly.

The tendency toward a type of "lateral" integration is linked to the partial overlapping created between various functions by an information system. In both the aircraft company and that of telecommunications, CAD has, in fact, allowed the development of lateral relationships between the equivalent levels of the various functions involved. In other words, in the experiences examined CAD and CAM have, to echo Galbraith, represented "liason tools" in the real sense.

3. CAD applications in small and medium size firms

The decision-making process

The aims that SME's try to pursue with the utilization of CAD are rather similar to those of large firms (in this sense, these aims reflect the benefits that vendors of CAD systems claim in their marketing effort). The main issues appear to be the following:

- to increase short term productivity in the design and drawing office (in terms of output/manpower input);
- to rationalize and standardize product design in terms of components and subsystems;
- to reduce the need for new drawings by using again past drawings;
- to shorten design and drawing time;
- to achieve higher quality standards for the final product;

- to increase marketing capability, through a quicker response to customers' demands for a supply offer.

It is interesting to note that the aim of reducing the number of draftsmen is not given priority (and is often not even mentioned).

The approach followed by SME's for the evaluation of the convenience to introduce CAD, is mostly based on a rather simplistic "cost-benefit" analysis: one usually compares the productivity of CAD in terms of, say, "number of drafts/hour of manpower" (evaluated through the data supplied by CAD vendors) with the productivity of traditional drafting systems. Little use is made of more sophisticated criteria (i.e. return on investment, etc.). Even less frequent is the use of a "systemic" approach, which takes into consideration the overall impact of CAD on the firm and not only on the technical department: almost no attention is paid to the "indirect" effect of CAD, especially in a longer time perspective, such as design of entirely new products for new market segments, new manufacturing techniques, etc. The emphasis is on short term operational results in a substantially static framework (inside and outside the firm).

The feasibility study which precedes the decision to buy a CAD system, is largely based on a somewhat lengthy investigation carried out with internal professional resources: it includes talks with vendors, visits to existing installations, participation in demonstrations, etc. Practically no use is made of external expertise because, for one thing, small entrepreneurs generally mistrust consultants, and there is also a substantial lack of independent expertise (in this field one is usually faced with the problem of "experts with hands off experience").

Implementation strategies

Once a small entrepreneur has decided to introduce CAD into his own firm, the way this is accomplished reflects largely the rather simplicistic approach followed to make the decision. It is believed that the implementation process starts and ends with the act of buying the equipment (as any other piece of hardware) and giving some training (almost always provided by the vendor) to the person(s) going to operate the CAD system; and positive results must follow in the short term. This last requirement stems mainly from the size of the financial investment for a CAD system, which often is larger if compared to the limited financial resources of SME's.

This approach at implementing CAD, typical of SME's, is lacking mainly in the following respects:

- the absence of an overall master plan, which considers and takes advantage of all the links of CAD with the firm's functions and activities, mainly in a strategic (i.e. structural change) framework;
- there is no precise responsibility for implementing CAD successfully (no internal vendor of the CAD project);

- no provision is made for internal programming resources to adapt the CAD system as supplied by the vendor to the specific needs and conditions of the firm;
- limited attention and resources are given to the problem of training the CAD operators.

This aspect turns out to be one of the most critical for the success of the implementation of CAD, as well as of all other advanced automated manufacturing technologies. In fact, the evolution towards CIM (Computer Integrated Manufacturing), of which CAD is a major component, requires a substantial expansion of training programs, which are going to become a continuous activity of a firm. This implies a remarkable increase of a firm's resources, like time and money to be devoted to training programs: the new computer based manufacturing technologies are not only very sophisticated but also very expensive (as much as 10-20 times the cost of traditional equipment for the same job) and require highly specialized operators. These are usually not available on the labour market, due to the novelty of the technologies, and must be drawn from existing personnel through training; but the high cost of the new equipment and its complexity make its use for training (instead of production) very expensive, as there also is a definite risk of a break-down due to errors of the operator under training [1]).

Usually SME's are ill equipped to face all these requirements: their organization is "slender" and lacks any back-ups; the difficulty of finding external solutions (specialized and reliable organizations) and the impossibility of setting up an internal training department are going to push them towards an increasing utilization of training services provided by vendors of computer based equipment, with some obvious and well known limitations about their quality and respondence to SME's needs. In fact, vendors usually provide training courses on their operational system and their application software, but are unable to take care of the specific application problems of any of their customers, as this would require setting up specialized technical service departments capable of handling problems from a large variety of sectors.

Results from the application of CAD

Given all these deficiencies and faults in the decision-making and the implementation of CAD in SME's, it is not surprising to find that in many cases the first results of its application are well below the expectations.

The CAD system, put immediately into "production" after its installment and a short period of training of its operator (who has traditional skills and usually very little knowledge and practice with the new information technologies), turns out to be (much) less "productive" than the traditional methodology: i.e. it takes longer to make a draft.

A possible consequence (maybe after some tentative interventions, which put even more pressure on the CAD operator to achieve positive results quickly) is the mistrust of the entrepreneur for the new technology, leading him eventually to abandon CAD and to switch back to the tradition.

The negative evaluation of CAD performance is derived not only from "objective" facts and data, but also from the often widespread resistance to changes by the personnel (which turn out to be not only local, i.e. in the technical office, but throughout the whole firm). They see CAD as a threat to their routines, skills and well known and safe environment and try to blame all the misfunctionings of the firm on CAD.

It requires strong motivation on the part of the entrepreneur for technological innovation, or at least the desire to save the investment made so far, not to cancel, or delay, the CAD project and to try to overcome all the mistakes made in the implementation process. These often include:

- the search for external expertise through consultants, including for training;
- the appointment of someone responsible for the CAD project;
- the acquisition of programming capabilities for software development;
- the introduction of changes in the organization and management techniques, especially in the factory, and the integration of CAD with the existing information system;
- eventually, taking the CAD system out of the "production" line, so that training is properly done and also to enable adjustment to the company's requirements, so that the full benefits of CAD are achieved.

4. Some general remarks

Based on the findings of the empirical investigation on cases of the application of CAD within SME's in Lombardy, one can draw some general conclusions on the constraints and problems to be faced in the diffusion of this advanced production technology among SME's: the recognition of these problems can be the trigger for public intervention aimed at overcoming the main obstacles that SME's meet in their effort to utilize advanced technologies in order to be competitive in the international market [2]).

The roots of all these problems lie in a mismatch between the requirements (in terms of management, organizational and financial resources, professional skills, education, etc.) of a successful implementation of CAD and the corresponding characteristics of a typical SME.

In fact, on one side, the implementation of a CAD system requires:

- a large investment;
- a remarkable capability to assess the overall convenience of an investment in new technology;
- an open-minded management and an attitude to master radical technical changes, if not using them for strategic aims.

On the other side, the decision-making process in a typical SME is characterized mainly by:

- the identity of ownership with management;
- a very simple organization structure;
- few formalized liasons within the organization, poorly defined responsibilities and little delegation of power from the entrepreneur to the executives;

- a step by step approach to tackle innovation (including technological) and reluctance to make radical changes;
- an emphasis on the solution of "day-by-day" problems and lack of a strategic, long-term view;
- distrust of outside consultants and suppliers of advanced technologies.

Beyond this, SME's usually have some remarkable weak points, such as:

- limited range of functions performed inside the organization;
- low level of standardization;
- low level of culture in information technologies;
- poor capabilities to evaluate benefits;
- poor capability of providing training;
- (last, but not least) limited financial resources.

Notwithstanding all these drawbacks and barriers, the empirical investigation showed that there is a growing interest of SME's in CAD and that quite a number of them (as shown also by the data on the Italian situation of CAD) have undertaken, with varying degrees of success, the difficult task of installing a CAD system.

5. CAD implementation and industrial relations

Generally, it should be born in mind that specific clauses on the regulation and protection of workers faced with technological innovation do not exist in Italian contractual rules, except in the cases of employees of newspaper editing and printing companies and those of press agencies [3]). Legislation in such matters is equally absent.

At present, Italian unions encounter considerable difficulty in discussing new technology bargaining, even if a great deal of attention is given to it in the union press. Such difficulty owes its origin both to the traditions and characteristics of Italian unionism, and to the present situation of industrial relations in which little willingness on the part of employers, especially in the private sector, may be seen. Furthermore, it should be remembered that Italian unions, being organized not on the basis of professions but of sectors, are often poorly represented at technical and white-collar levels. There is at present a fierce debate in progress on whether, when and in what way intervention should take place in new technology as early as the planning phase. At the same time, unions have launched activities, both in research (Cesos and the Foundation "P. Seveso" mentioned before are both union-linked organs) and training.

As far as CAD applications are specifically concerned, in the cases examined in this research project - all of them in private industry - unions have played a marginal role in the choice and planning phases of new technology, although in certain cases the company has kept unions informed of the project from the beginning. In other cases, examined in the literature on engineering, unions have to some extent intervened with respect to organizational choices and, particularly, in the choice between open-shop and closed-shop solutions and in the redefinition of professional patterns.

Other problems dealt with in negotiations are those of working hours in the event of a request for the introduction of shifts, and the regulation of the amount of time spent seated at video terminals and for breaks.

In more general terms, what emerges from the cases examined in this research project and those reported by other researchers, is the absence of a preconceived opposition to the diffusion of new technology and, indeed, the expectancy, not always justified, of positive changes, especially in terms of the professional development of the employees.

Data that would allow for generalizations on the occupational effects of CAD have not been collected to date.

Notes and references

1) This, by the way, indicates that there is a great potential for equipment simulators for training purposes.

2) In this framework one has to mention that Cestec is setting up a specialized Center promoting CAD applications within SME's; the Center, which is supported by several large firms, which have gained quite remarkable own experience with CAD, and some R&D centers, is going to provide SME's with a variety of services in the areas of demonstration, consultancy and training.

3) G. Della Rocca, "Technological Innovation and Industrial Relations in Italy", Quaderni della Fondazione Adriano Olivetti, No. 5, 1985.

CAD IN PETRO-CHEMICAL PLANT DESIGN.
THE DEVELOPMENT OF CAD WITHIN DIFFERENT ORGANIZATIONS AND THEIR CONSEQUENCES FOR THE ORGANIZATION AND TASK STRUCTURE

Maurits van Wagenberg
Studiegroep CAD en Organisatie, Singel 159 A
1012VK Amsterdam
The Netherlands

When describing the effects of CAD on organizations and task structures, it is important to have an insight into the context (environment) in which organizations operate. This specific context will influence the development and implementation of CAD applications. Thus, the context relates to

- the conventional organization,
- the expectations the organization has, when applying CAD,
- the further development of CAD.

And as a result, it has, in interaction with CAD, an influence on the changes in the organization and task structure. In the paper I will comment on the following aspects:

1. A short description of the design process and the possible process and the possible use of CAD;
2. Different organizations, working on the same design;
3. The development of the CAD configuration;
4. Possible effects on the organization structure;
5. Possible effects on the task-structure;
6. Concluding notes.

1. A description of the design process and the possible use of CAD

The design process for petro-chemical installations is extremely labour-intensive and elaborate. More than 1000 manyears of engineering are not uncommon. It can be divided into two principal stages: basic design, in which the chemical process is developed and detailed design, in which the installation is designed.

Basic Design: the design of the chemical processes, usually developed by the chemical company: it consumes 20 % of all the design effort	──────►	Detailed Design: the design of the installation and further preparation for the construction, usually performed by a contractor: it consumes 80 % of all design effort.
t 0 year	1/2 year	4.5/7 year in total

(Sietz in Montfoort, Dilworth 1979)

Before we look at the different possibilities of CAD within this design process, I would like to define CAD as all graphical and non-graphical applications that support the design process. Therefore, engineering - as well as administrative programs - are seen as a part of a CAD system. Also, communication and database-applications will be regarded as a part of the CAD system.

Basic design

The different support possibilities of CAD in basic design are primarily engineering (calculation) programs. Some are very complex and some of those programs are directly developed and used by the process-engineers themselves. In the later phase of the basic design process, more and more emphasis is laid on the graphical representation of the process (in Process Flow Diagrams or PFD's); for that purpose 2 D graphical applications can be used. These are usually operated by draftsmen. This is illustrated in Figure 1.

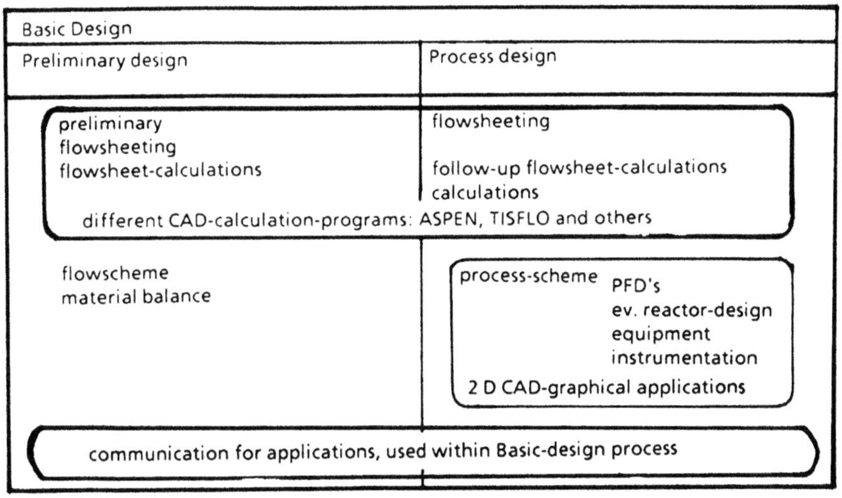

Figure 1: Basic design

Basic design

The possibilities of CAD support in detailed design are manifold. This process is time-consuming. It is rigidly structured. Many different functional areas of design can be named:

- piping design,
- mechanical design,

- design of electro-technical installation,
- design of process control and instrumentation,
- administrative support, purchase,
- project-management support.

The P & ID's (piping and instrumentation diagrams), the electrical diagrams, the civil designs may be produced with a graphical 2 D CAD application. Since most of the design activities in these fields are put down in diagrams, very much attention is spent on the development of macros. The macros are standard representations of elements, like valves. Thus, the draftsman calls up a macro of a valve, and does not need to care about the graphical aspects of the valve. In some cases, even alphanumerical information is automatically added to the design.

However, the most important area in which graphical programs can be used is piping design. In some cases the piping design can represent 50 % of the detailed design. Thus, piping design may represent 30 to 40 % of all design activities. For piping design activities, 3 D CAD-applications ("plant design applications") are appropriate: one can actually build the piping structure and in fact the whole plant in a 3-dimensional database. Since piping design is such an important activity, it is also the key activity within the organization, toward which other design activities are balanced. Piping studies are carried out and a plastic model is built to achieve a more optimal layout and design. The use of 3 D plant design application may lead to a central database in which the whole installation is graphically built up, and from which all kinds of administrative information can be derived. In the near future, even NC-programs for automatically bending pipes might be derived.

Since piping design fixes a larger part of the costs of the total construction, the design is closely controlled by the project-management. Therefore, administrative - and planning - programs are used in this area of design.

To conclude this short introduction: CAD is used in two basically different design processes with two different needs for CAD applications. During basic design, engineering programs and some 2 D programs are used.

During the labour-intensive detailed design, 2-D programs, some integrated with administrative programs, and 3-D programs are used. In general, administrative programs are widely used. These applications can be illustrated in figure 2.

2. Different organizations working on the same design

The two stages of the design process are so different from each other that one may speak of two processes, as we have done. The first is a less structured, a more heuristic design process, performed by a small team of highly skilled engineers. They develop new chemical processes. They work on alternative solutions and choose those which will show the best cost/benefit performance, given the projected capacity. Investment costs of the installation will play an important role, thus emphasis is put on cost-estimates and cost-oriented choices between alternatives. However, detailed costs of parts of the installations play a less important role, since they are minor, compared to the costs of material and processing (energy for example).

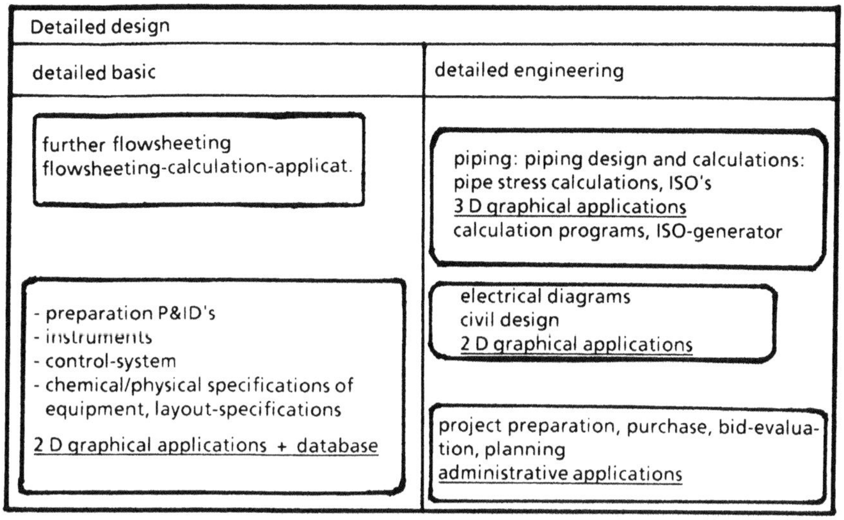

Figure 2: Detailed design

The development of new processing principles is usually connected with the development of new chemical materials/products and done by the (petro-)chemical company, named: the owner. The owner employs the process-engineers who possess all the know-how on the materials to be processed. The owner's engineers can also rely on experience the company has built up with processing equivalent materials in the past. And, they have know-how on operational aspects of plants.

When the process-design is outlined, the more labour-intensive and organizationally demanding detailed design process can be handed over to the contractor. The contractors have the organization able to handle the enormous bulk of design and drafting. They have the relations with sub-contractors to allocate work; the contractors have specialists, familiar with the local environment and governmental bodies. They can handle project-management, sometimes even the management of the construction of the plant. They can prepare all the purchase documents and delivery-schemes.

The organization of the contractor is strictly geared to minimize design cost, to have control over the planning and the quality of the design. The relationship between the petrochemical company (the owner) and the contractor is strictly cost-oriented, since engineering bids are usually evaluated by costs.

However, there is not always a division of labour between owner and contractor. In some situations, the owner organization performs the basic design as well as the detailed design.

Thus, all the design-activities are in one hand. The chemical (non-oil) companies especially seem to have an interest in performing the basic design process as well as the detailed design process.

To end this description of the different organizations, attention should be drawn to an important item which influences the corporate strategies of the owners and which may have an important impact on the design process, the division of labour between the owner and contractor. Nowadays, the chemical industry is facing major changes. Bulk-chemicals are more and more produced in East-European, Middle East countries and Mexico.

Thus European and American chemical companies are increasingly oriented towards the development and production of specialities with a high value added. The development of these specialities is "the" strategic item for the Eighties. Therefore, more and more owners have an interest in strict control of the development and design-process and are less tempted to contract out the complete detailed design process. However, time-consuming piping design activities will probably still be handed over to the contractors. Besides the strategic aspects of control over know-how, owners have an interest in a short lead time for the whole product development and installation development cycle. They will try to shorten both processes by organizing design activities in parallel instead of sequentially. This will require a stricter management and often a strict control over enhancements in different functional areas.

A second important strategic item is the quality of the installation. More emphasis is laid on energy-saving and flexible refineries, which are marked by a more complex instrumentation and control system. This will lead to some very intensive labour and complex design-orders, which may exceed two million engineering manhours, or more than 1000 manyears of design labour. In this case, we may also see more emphasis on shortening lead times, this to reduce investment risks and interest. The use of CAD may change the design possibilities, so that the process will fit better with these goals.

To recapitulate items of corporate strategy which may influence the design process and division of labor between the owner and the contractor:

- a changing pattern of design-orders in fewer medium-volume, more specialised contracting orders for chemical companies (plants) or very high-volume all-in orders (for oil-companies);
- more specialization;
- shorter lead times;
- more lump sum contracting in specialized areas like piping;
- pressure on the prices of contractor services.

These changes have a direct influence on the adoption and implementation of CAD within owner-organizations and contractor-organizations.

3. The development of the CAD configuration

As we have seen, one may recognize two types of organizations, which will be interested in buying CAD: the owners and the contractors. They have, however, different motives for applying CAD. Probably, the difference in goals is of importance to understand the development of CAD within the organization.

To start with the description of the development, the different possibilities of several CAD applications are compared.

	price of application	costs change work methods	reduction of labour costs design	improvement quality	reduction investment risk	shortening design lead time	revision possibility	flexibility organization	improvement control	reduction of operational costs	reduction of construction costs	profit selling application
calculation programs basic design				X						X		X
calculation applications construction			X	X		X	X			X		
administrative applications			X	(X)	X		X	(X)	X		X	
word processing			X				X		X			
database/ communication	X	(X)	X	X		(X)	X	X	X		(X)	
2 D graphical applications	X	(X)	X	(X)			X		(X)		(X)	
3 D graphical applications	X	X		X	X	X	X	X	X		X	

Figure 3: A scheme of the advantages and disadvantages of different applications

There are two different types of graphical applications. The 2 D graphical applications provide a less complicated and more cost-oriented type of benefit; 3 D graphical applications have more advantages such as shorter lead times, but are less cost-efficient, if focused on the productivity-ratio (PR). The real advantages may occur on the site, where a better design of all the pipes and interference checking may lead to fewer contingency spare parts and fewer construction- and management hours. Sometimes this may lead to 1 -3 % less piping material, which can be equivalent to millions of DM, dependent on the size of the installation.

If one compares the possibilities of CAD with the (strategic) goals of the companies using CAD, one may conclude that the owner/oil company will be less interested in CAD; they may, however, have a 2 D system for the PFD's and P&ID's.

However, the owner/chemical company may be interested in 2 D as well as 3 D systems, in order to design both the process and the installation. The company may thus have all the advantages: shorter lead times, better control, more possibilities to check alternatives and better control of material and assembly work on the site. Thus, these owners may be interested in highly integrated CAD systems, as a strategic tool to cope with changes in the marketplace.

The contractor is in a difficult position since his relationship with the owners is cost-oriented. The market is characterized by ample engineering capacity and is thus even more cost-oriented. For these organizations it is very difficult to invest in applications other than those which improve production. The 3 D applications may be of less interest since they show benefits on the site. And this benefit will probably be experienced by the owner or the builder of the plant, and not by the contractor. However, some of the larger contractors have heavily invested in 3 D applications. This may be explained by assuming that they are aiming at other relationships with owners, for example:

- contracts which include the management of construction on the site,
- contracts in which a price is paid for the 3 D database, which can be handed over to the owner
- contracts with chemical companies, in which only the design of piping is done by the contractor and in which lead times are shortened.

The difficult market and the difficult financial position is reflected in the diverse development of the implementation and growth of CAD-applications within various organizations. Some contractors have started with a very cost-oriented investment program and the implementation of a 2-D application and may, as a next step, have integrated these with administrative applications.

Besides the 2-D system, other contractors and owners have installed a 3-D system in the piping design department. This 3-D application can also be used in other departments. The first development of the implementation of CAD is horizontal; the second development and implementation is vertical. These two different developments of the implementation and integration of CAD in the detailed design process will lead to different patterns of effects. This is illustrated in Figure 4.

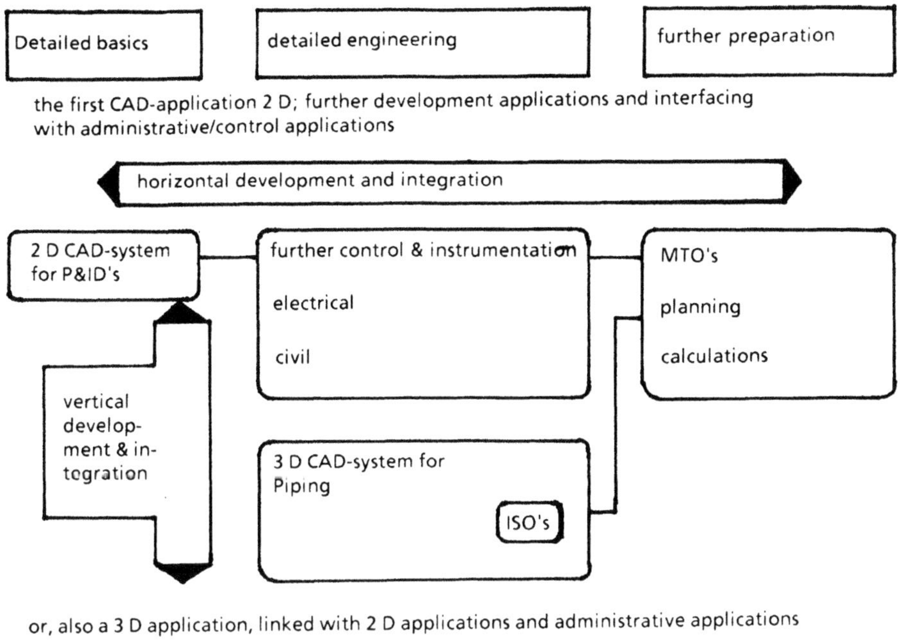

Figure 4: The development of the implementation of CAD-applications

4. Possible effects of CAD on the organization structure within the engineering process

The description of the effect of CAD in the detailed design process on the organization structure causes some problems. With the implementation of CAD, new work methods may be hidden within the CAD programs or may be implemented at the same time as the CAD system. An example of new design methods is modular plant design. Methods, hidden within CAD programs, are planning and control principles, the use of macros, etc.

Before the effects of CAD are discussed, some characteristics which mark the conventional organization should be mentioned. They mark both the owner and the contractor organization.

- A design is usually considered as a project on which the organization as a whole will work for more than a year.
- The quantity of design labour has such a level, that a relatively high division of labour and specialization is feasible.
- The design process is usually closely cost-controlled.
- The choices within the design process are limited, because of all kinds of safety and other demands. The coherence of the design with demands and limitations must be checked over and over.

- The design process is very control-oriented; much of the drafting and listing of data supports this control.
- During the design process, constant interaction takes place with the owner manufacturers and government bodies, and this may result in redesign.

These different demands may lead to relatively fixed organizational structures. Most organization structures are functional: the departments are set up on the basis of technical disciplines; within the departments different levels of qualified personnel can be found. This organization is efficiency-oriented. However, it is difficult to control the stream of information between the departments. This structure is illustrated in Figure 5.

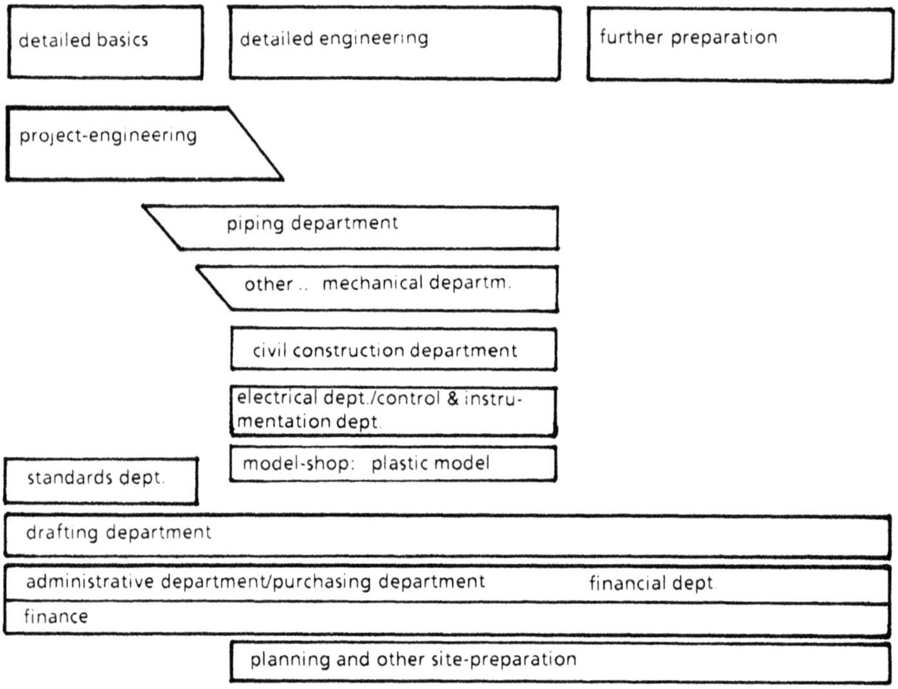

Figure 5: The functional organization within the detailed design process

Some organizations have a project structure and within that project structure, a functional structure. All the personnel working on one project, may be put together in one building and placed under complete project supervision, in order to realize strict planning and control.

A few organizations have, however, selected a modular structure. The plant to be designed is divided into logical geographical partitions, on which multi-disciplinary teams work. This division of labour should lead to stricter control and a better fit between disciplines which may lead to a more integrated design. It will also shorten lead times. This structure will, however, show a lesser degree of specialization. This structure is illustrated in Figure 6.

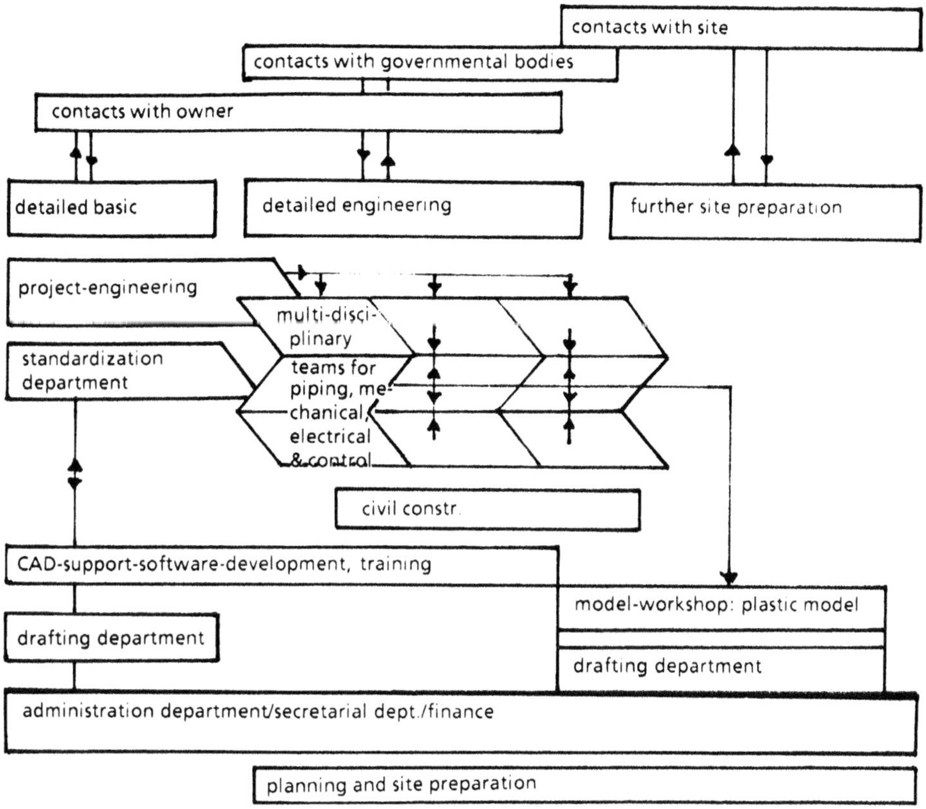

Figure 6: The modular structure within the detailed design process.

If one returns to the functional organization, one may mention characteristics which are of importance to understand the organization as well as the possibilities of applying certain CAD applications. The first thing required is strict formal co-ordination, built up in procedures. These procedures (or co-ordination methods), are developed over the year, to minimize construction mistakes, which may cause disasters.

As far as the design process is concerned there is a strict hierarchy of what can be freely chosen/designed and what has to be designed within limitations set by another department, the owner or by governmental rules. Thus, design activities belonging to a more creative design process are limited and strictly set aside from the more methodical design activities. Creativity is especially needed for the set up of the piping structure (piping studies) and in another dimension for the set up of the control and instrumentation system (P & ID's).

However, most of the work is very methodical. This provides a good basis for diversity of technical specialization and hierarchical levels.

If one looks at the possible use of CAD within these contexts, one has to take into account two different developments, the horizontal and the vertical development.

The horizontal development of CAD in the detailed design process

As illustrated in Figure 4, one can see that the integration of graphical and administrative applications may lead to one stream of information, from P & ID's up to drafting and final administration (listing, planning). Thus, one might be tempted to form a new department, where these activities are brought together. However, there are some aspects which have not yet led to an integration. In some cases, the contrary is the case: most of the organizations already worked with administrative applications on a conventional computer embedded in the conventional organization. The new CAD system was installed in a newly set up CAD department, sometimes as a sub-department within an automation department (closed shop - for raw graphics copying), thus leaving the conventional organization structure intact.

But the first examples of integration can be seen at the stages of development: communication chains and interfaces are developed; next databases are connected, then procedures are streamlined. Development with this kind of integration will have an impact on the control structure. It would be logical to expect that the control structure can be simplified. However, this will only be possible if project management understands the new procedures and takes responsibility for the new situation. In practice this is not the case. Thus, this development is hampered.

Another change is the role of the standards department. This department will become more important as it becomes involved in the development of the macros. To conclude: this horizontal development has an impact on the procedures and control and task structures. This may cause personal conflicts within and between departments. However, the fundamental structure of the departments will remain the same.

The vertical development of CAD in the detail design process

The vertical development starts in the department in which the 3 D application will be installed, i.e. the piping department (see Figure 4). The use of this application will fit in the conventional structure. Thus, piping engineers are trained to work with the 3 D applications. The training will take a very long period (sometimes more than a year in all). After this period of different time-consuming experience, organizations are less tempted to redesign the work content/structure. However, after a few years, companies working with these applications actually integrate electrical design or wish to do so. Even 2 D applications P & ID's can and will be automatically linked with the 3 D applications, thus creating a link between 2 D and 3 D applications (horizontal and vertical development).

This development leads to a direct possibility of merging departments and of working on a modular basis. The plant will be divided into several geographical areas. Each of these areas will be designed by a team of electrical and piping engineers. In the near future, an integration of other activities such as civil and structural steel construction will be seen as well. This vertical integration will diminish the need to control different functional activities. The computer program can partly carry out geometrical controls (clash reports).

What will bring about greater change is the simplification of the design process itself. This change is not so obvious because it does not affect the departmental or hierarchical structure. Within the piping department, the design process starts with piping studies. The use of CAD will probably diminish the need to carry out these studies. Another important activity during piping design, the construction of the plastic model, can and will be simplified. It will stop being a key activity, since piping engineers can model and change a real plant layout. These changes may have an impact on the task contents and interrelations between piping engineers.

But here as well as with the horizontal development, possible changes are dependent on the attitude of the project management/project engineer responsible for the design. If he feels insecure, he will prefer a low rate of CAD use and CAD control. But if he uses CAD as a new control tool and plans and manages accordingly, changes will be experienced in all activities and at all levels. Different companies are now at this development-stage. In the next two or three years a pattern will emerge.

As illustrated in Figure 6, it will be logical for organizations to change to a modular design structure. In this structure, piping will be the most important activity. Drawing activities and administrative activities will diminish drastically. These changes may lead to a design process in which it will be easier to carry out changes in the design, even at a later stage. In this way it will be suitable for those projects which need a short lead time and of which the basic design is not yet conclusive.

Another aspect may be, that a new relationship between the contractor and the owner, other (sub-)contractors and equipment manufacturers will emerge. In the last case, a direct link with NC piping-manufacturing will be feasible.

To conclude: the impact of the development towards a 3 D application within all major engineering departments will lead to a more integrated, less functionally oriented design process. It will lead to another control structure and another engineering process structure. Some activities can be dropped, some can be independently done such as the plastic model. However, the changes do not yet display a fixed pattern. In our opinion, the outcome will be dependent on the demands which are put on the organization. If one designs specialized chemical plants, vertical development and integration may be feasible right away. If one designs standard refineries integration may be less important. The organization may be tempted to implement the CAD system, and develop it in a horizontal way.

5. Consequences for work content

The description of the development of the organization shows differences in outcome at the department level, which, in turn, will lead to a differentiated pattern of changes in task-structure. Since the implementation of CAD is still at a transient stage, it is yet too early to describe an exact set of new functions. But on the basis of interviews, carried out among owners' and contractors' organizations in The Netherlands, a short description of two functions can be given. It should be emphasized, however, that these descriptions will probably be invalid in a few years from now.

The first function is a draftsman or a highschool graduate without additional training, who works in a closed shop environment with a 2 D system. The second function is a mechanical engineer working in a mechanical department.

The draftsman

As far as the working conditions are concerned, the ergonomic conditions are dependent on the quality of the system and the office environment. In some of the companies this seemed rather poor: the system was too slow, software unfriendly, the screen too dark (low brightness) and light in the office environment was not well dispersed. Another problem is the change in working hours. Till now only a few of the organizations have taken the step of working in two shifts, not always with success.

In one case, the implementation was aimed at lowering drafting costs through untrained draftsmen, two shifts and a closed shop. This failed and the program was abandoned.

The changes in the task structure of draftsmen seem very predictable, if no additional provisions are made. They seem

- more methodical, and
- more manipulation and combination-oriented.

In some organizations, a senior operator function has been created whose task structure also contains programming and the development of new routines (macros).

The relationship with the superior will be intensified and will be more productivity and quality-oriented. The superior may also plan work more carefully than in the past, but this is not the case in every organization. Also, relationships with colleagues and other departments will probably be diminished.

Training: The closed shop and drafting oriented use of 2 D systems will lead to a less demanding function. However, this qualification will probably be inappropriate in some years from now, at least probably in those organizations which have to deal with a new, strategically more demanding environment. Thus a different function will emerge, which demands other, not necessarily lower qualifications in the future.

To conclude: from a functional point of view, the function will be embedded in a more closely co-ordinated and controlled organizational environment. The product of the draftsman will be more predictable and will have a higher quality. From a quality of work point of view, the environment may be very poor. However, some organizations are faced with changes in the design process which do not necessarily lead to a context in which functions show a diminishing quality.

The mechanical engineer working with CAD

The office conditions for the mechanical engineers are dependent on the set-up of the system, usually in a normal engineering department. Since this software requires experienced and trained engineers, who work on a more part-time/short period basis with the system, changes are less negative. Since this software cannot be applied strictly efficiency-oriented, there is a slight chance of cuts in pay or lay-offs of labour.

The task structure, however, may change drastically. Probably, drafting and design functions will be integrated. Calculation programs can be more easily applied. This will result in a broader set of tasks. What will change as well is the sequence of the engineering process, which may be more fixed with more possibilities to change one's own engineering product. This change in task structure has some consequences for co-ordination. The engineer must closely plan his own activities within the limits set by his superior.

The relationship with colleagues may intensify: they may have discussions on software problems and the definition of interfaces between two geographical design areas etc. Disfunctional contacts, however, may decline.

To conclude, the engineer makes a more functional contribution towards the engineering process, which should advance the importance of his position. But this will be traded off with tighter planning and a more demanding task structure. From a quality of work perspective, some changes may be positive. Good personnel management may minimize negative effects.

6. Concluding remarks

In this article, several aspects are traced leading to the concluding remark, that one cannot speak of *the* impact of CAD on organization- and task-structure. First, CAD can be used in separate parts of the design process. Secondly, different organizations may work on the same design process. These different organizations may be faced with a different set of contingencies, even when working on the same part of the design process. This aspect may lead to alternative choices during the implementation of CAD applications and thus to different development patterns of CAD applications within those organizations.

Two different patterns have been described: the horizontal and the vertical development. The consequences have also been described. We concluded that, especially within the vertical development process, fundamental changes can be expected in the organization, however, not so much in the organization-structure, but in the sequence of work and communication between engineers.

As far as changes in task-structures are concerned, the different development-patterns have not yet led to a clear picture of new job contents. Some of the present situations can be described as negative, some as positive. In several years from now, when organizational changes show a clear pattern, a more coherent picture may emerge. We expect that within some organizational settings, which are aimed at cost efficiency, from the perspective of quality of work, changes will be less positive. However, organization settings which are aimed at shorter lead times and more innovative design will probably show alterations in the organization which do not necessarily lead to negative changes in the task content of engineers and draftsmen.

References

Cherry, D.H., Grogan, J.C., Knapp, G.L., Perris, F.A.:
Procesontwerpen met databases; Pt/Procestechniek 38 (1983) 2, pp. 28-33.

Computervision:
The CAD/CAM handbook, ed. by Machover, C., Blauth, E.; Bedford Mass. 1980.

Diegelmann, E.:
Erfassung, Beschaffung und Montage von Rohrleitungsteilen; Chem.Ing.Tech. 54 (1982) pp. 303-313.

Dilworth, P.J.:
The design of pipework for chemical plants; Current design thinking, Symposium Aston University, September 12-14, 1979.

Gelbe, H.:
Rohrleitungstechnik und Verfahrenstechnik; Chem.Ing.Tech 54 (1982) pp. 649-654.

Leesley, M.E.:
Computer Aided Process Plant Design; Gulf Publ.Comp. 1982.

Montfoort, A.G.:
Dew chemische fabriek, Ia; M17, 1983, TH Delft.

Peters, R.A.:
Computer Aided Engineering (part II); Chem.Eng. July 9, (1984).

Schermann, P.S.:
Ervaringen met CAD; Pt/Procestechniek 38 (1983) 9, pp.57-59.

Sietz:
see Montfoort.

Wolski, H.R.:
Einführung eines CAD-Systems unter besonderer Berücksichtigung von Wirtschaftlichkeitsüberlegungen; Chem.Ing.Tech. 55 (1983), pp. 584-586.

CHAPTER 5: The Development of CAD/CAM Systems

This chapter is being added in hindsight and assembles two papers originally included in other sessions. To some extent they do deal with the mutual relationship between the organization and the CAD system, but in this case the main focus is on the system. George KOVACS' contribution, the other part of a longer paper included in the national reviews section, describes the situation in a firm having a CAD/CAM system tailored especially to its own requirements. In the case described, this is more out of necessity than by design, but the situation may have been comparable in the early days of CAD in Western countries. Jean-Pierre POITOU's paper is a novel contribution in that it traces the histories of selected well-known systems, originally developed for in-house use and then widely marketed. It also shows some of the forces at work in economics which may enhance or obstruct the development of technology under certain circumstances. While the work behind this paper is somewhat removed from the mainstream of social science research into CAD/CAM, it stands up as a model for contributions in a direction where work should most certainly be done while people still remember.

WINGERT wondered whether national origins of systems might account for the degree of their effectiveness if applied in a country other than that of origin, e.g. if systems developed in countries with Tayloristic traditions of rationalization and division of labour could be effective in countries alien to this tradition. In reply, POITOU drew attention to different British and continental European traditions in drafting and geometry. Technologically Britain had a lead over the rest of Europe in the 18th century and at this time there was little training other than apprenticeship. When the other countries recognized Britain's lead, they tried to stop the gap with mathematics and scientific methods. Even now, the very term "engineer" has a different meaning in Great Britain and continental Europe.

With regard to CAD/CAM POITOU remarked that this had started earlier in the USA than in Europe and that the software was something like patchwork and deeply rooted in firm culture. Europeans tended to take a different approach to solving a problem like the geometry of objects being designed. Thus different traditions lead to different kinds of solution for a problem.

CAD/CAM: WHY, WHEN, HOW? SOME EXAMPLES IN THE FRENCH INDUSTRY

Jean-Pierre Poitou
Technologies, Idéologies, Pratiques
CNRS - Université de Provence
13621 Aix - France

1. Introduction

In the sixties and seventies, several major French companies recognized a need to improve the effectiveness and accuracy of their design and drafting methods, to shorten the length of their product design and job preparation cycle.

The then emerging computer controlled equipment, plotters, graphic screens and NC machine-tools, provided various possiblities for developing aids for the designer and the draftsman. Furthermore, in the late sixties and early seventies, CAD/CAM programs and/or systems became available from aircraft and electronics companies in the USA.

French companies were then faced with the basic questions about CAD/CAM: to develop or to buy, when, and what for? If the choice is made to develop a system, should it be sold to other firms, or kept in-house and, if so, why?

I will report various case studies on CAD/CAM development as evidence for various answers to the foregoing questions. Such cases are not merely of historical interest. They also give understanding of what CAD/CAM is really about: a sophisticated electronical drafting board, or a technology of strategical interest for the firm, with a potential for overall restructuration of the work-process?

2. Automotive industry

French automotive engineers, namely Casteljau at Citroën and Bezier at Renault were among the first to develop methods for computer aided geometric representation of complex curves and surfaces such as those involved in the design of car bodies (BÖHM et al., 1984, POITOU, 1984). As early as 1958, Casteljau, was asked by la Boixière, head of the numerical controlled milling department (service de fraisage numérique), where he worked as a mathematician, to design a method for a numerical definition of dies. Within two years he succeeded in having NC tapes for milling produced out of a purely mathematical model and numerical definition of the surface to be worked out. The method was taught to draftsmen from 1963 on and a full car body for the Citroën model GS was designed in 1968, with the SADUSCA/SPAC-CAR System, developed at Citroën out of Casteljau's method (KRAUTTER & PARIZOT, 1971).

Notwithstanding this success, the company executives considered that developing a CAD/CAM system was not becoming for a car company, and that they would rather turn to suppliers from the market place. As we will see later COMPUTERVISION was to be selected in 1978. Industrial secrecy being a tradition at Citroën, Casteljau was not permitted to publish his theory until 1985 (CASTELJAU, 1985).

Among the reasons for renouncing the development of a system, were the severe profit losses the company had to face by 1974, which resulted in Citroën being bought by Peugeot. We will return to this point after considering early CAD/CAM development at Renault.

At the end of the fifties, Bezier was in charge of the Renault machine-tool subsidiary R.M.O. (Renault Machine Outil). He suggested to Renault head-quarters that R.M.O. invest research money in numerical control. His proposal was turned down, and as a consequence, Bezier was discharged and given a very loose assignment (BEZIER, 1982). He then occupied himself with what he considered a special case of numerical control: computer-aided design for tooling car-body models, dies and casts. Beginning in 1960, Bezier attached himself to the same problem which Casteljau had set out to solve two years earlier, and by 1966, had breveted a system called UNISURF. The solution he had come to, which he presented at the Society of Automotive Engineers in Detroit in 1968, was quite similar to Casteljau's, though less aptly formulated (BEZIER, 1982).

Bezier did not meet much understanding from his top management. In 1966, however, when Renault and Peugeot signed an agreement for cooperation in research and development, some engineers from the latter company got greatly interested in UNISURF and contributed substantially to further developments of the system. In 1968, they achieved the design of the whole body of the Peugeot model 204, using UNISURF.

However, in 1974, Peugeot broke with Renault, and bought both the Citroën and Talbot companies, thus becoming under the name of Peugeot S.A. (P.S.A.) the premier group in the French automobile industry. Surprisingly enough, as far as CAD/CAM was concerned, Cirtroen's policy, instead of Peugeot's, prevailed in the group. That is: giving up home-made developments, and buying a turn-key system. As mentioned earlier, COMPUTERVISION was selected. In order to improve CV's limited capacities in surface design and solid modeling, parts of Casteljau's and Bezier's results were incorporated into what was to be named the "CV+" system.

As for Renault, we have first to consider the story of the EUCLID system before finding what has become of UNISURF.

In order to understand the Peugeot S.A. decision, one has to consider a difference in CAD/CAM concept between Renault and P.S.A. Bezier worked on the idea of a direct method in computer aided body design, while at Citroën and Peugeot, an indirect approach prevailed. According to the former, each step in the design process should be under computer control. Styling, modeling, drafting, tool-making should be computer-aided. This radical approach takes full advantage of CAD/CAM, thus the company should take the greatest care in keeping complete control over such a powerful tool, the best way of control being in-house development. In the other companies, the car was fully styled, designed, and modelled by conventional methods. Only then were the complete draft and tape model for tooling prepared with CAD/CAM. In such conditions, self-development of a system was of less strategical importance, and a turn-key system more acceptable.

3. From university to aerospace: EUCLID

UNISURF was to end up melted into another program: EUCLID. A word or two on this latter system is in order, for it shows another company strategy toward securing control over a CAD/CAM system.

J.-M. Brun and M. Theron, two fluid-dynamicists working for the Centre Nationale de la Recherche Scientifique (CNRS) at L.I.M.S.I. (Laboratory of Data processing for Mechanics and Engineering, at Orsay, near Paris), developed a language for the simulation of hydro- and aerodynamics flow over a solid mobile. By 1970, they proposed EUCLID, which appears as one of the earliest solid modeling programs (THERON, 1980, 1984). EUCLID needed further development in order to become a fully fledged industrial product. Nevertheless D.B.A., an automobile part-maker company, became interested in what promised to be a very good CAD system. Unfortunately, the American main stock-holder decided that DBA, its French subsidiary, had to cut down on R&D expenditure: EUCLID had lost its industrial father. For several years, governmental agencies nursed the orphan, looking in vain for an industrialist to take care of its development. In 1979 Brun and Theron decided to resign from CNRS, and to found their own company, DATAVISION. Among the first four clients of the new company, was the Military Department of the MATRA Group (cars, aerospace, city transportation, electronics). People in Matra understood the help they could get from a good CAD/CAM system, and the importance of having control over its development. They proposed to buy 51 % of DATAVISION capital. Brun and three associates needed assets to improve their product. They also understood that a CAD system has to be tested at each step of its development in a real industrial environment. Matra could provide both capital and testing grounds. In 1980 MATRA-DATAVISION was presented to the public. MATRA paid the governmental agencies about seventeen times what they had spent for "nursing" EUCLID from 1976 to 1979. The CNRS was never paid back for the basic research it had supported up to 1976. EUCLID has become one of the best selling systems in Europe, with subsidiaries in the USA and Japan. It is not certain whether MATRA foresaw the returns they got from their investment. It is clear however that they gave CAD/CAM enough consideration to buy not only a system, but also the company that was developing it. In 1985 Renault and MATRA-DATAVISION came to an agreement to merge EUCLID and UNISURF. More precisely UNISURF was up-dated and re-written into EUCLID on the one hand, and on the other, EUCLID was completed with SURFAPT, the NC tooling language for UNISURF.

4. Aircraft industry

There are two major companies in French aircraft industry: AEROSPATIALE, a government-owned group, with an airplane division based in Toulouse and a helicopter division, in Marignane near Marseille and AVIONS MARCEL DASSAULT-BREGUET AVIATION (AMD-BA), a private company. AMD-BA concentrate on designing, assembling and selling planes, and sub-contracts the manufacturing itself. Aerospatiale is by far the main subcontractor for AMD. For historical reasons, Aerospatiale divisions are fairly independent of each other, and the authority of the head-office in Paris over them meets some limits in orienting their technological choices. By 1972, the influence of Bezier's work on UNISURF reached Marignane and then Toulouse. Both the helicopter and the aircraft divisions decided to start designing and developing a CAD system for helicopter or plane bodies. However, for the sake of their independence, as illustrated by the fact that Marignane had IBM, and Toulouse CONTROL DATA equipment, each division developed its own system, though along very similar lines.

By the mid-seventies, both systems were operative, SDS at Marignane, and SIGMA at Toulouse. The question rose then whether to keep them for internal use, or to have them commercialized. In Toulouse, management opposed investing into the costs of marketing and maintenance. It was decided to leave to CONTROL DATA, their hardware supplier, the burden of selling SIGMA, whenever someone wished to buy it. The same attitude "we are here to sell aircraft, not software" prevailed among Marignane Directors. However, the head of the design department, who was responsible for initiating SDS, succeeded in persuading management to have it commercialized by the Battelle Institut in Geneva. Thus, under the name of SYSTRID, the program brought royalties to Aerospatiale. Later on, CISI (Compagnie Internationale de Services Informatiques) a subsidiary of the French Nuclear Energy Agency (Centre de L'Energie Atomique, CEA) took control of the Aerospatiale System, and is presently selling it quite successfully under the name of STRIM 100.

Up to 1968, AMD-BA, curiously enough, had no home-based data processing. Scientific calculations were sub-contracted to either IBM or Control Data. However, the cost of such services, on the one hand, and the appearance of the IBM 2250 graphic terminal on the other roused the interest of design executives for CAD. One of their US competitors, LOCKHEED had already developed the CADAM system. So, in 1972, the question was raised: buy or develop? The answer came from the Directors: both. It was decided to buy CADAM from Lockheed, in 1974, because CAD was considered an immediate necessity in order to keep pace with competitors. It was also decided to develop a system, because CAD was considered of strategic importance to keep a technological lead, and thus to maintain the position of "maitre d'oeuvre" over cooperating firms. Accordingly AMD-BA bought from Lockheed the source language for CADAM, in order to develop its own version under the name of DRAPO. Furthermore, CATI, an entirely home-made program was developed for the years to come (NEUVE EGLISE, 1981). In 1982, CATI was fully operational and considered a good CAD/CAM program. Should it be sold to other companies, including competitors?

It was considered that competitors were also co-contractors in national or European projects, and that having them using the AMD-BA systems would help to ensure the company a key position of project-leader. On the other hand, being the designer of this system would maintain for AMD-BA a superiority over ordinary users, and thus help it preserve its know-how. Thus the CAD/CAM department was made a subsidiary of the company, under the name Dassault Systèmes, with a manpower of 150 persons in charge of developing CATI, re-named CATIA for the circumstance. IBM, the supplier of AMD-BA hardware, and already seller of CADAM for Lockheed, was also happy to sell CATIA.

5. Conclusion

The various cases reported here show that major companies may fail to grasp the importance of CAD/CAM, and thus suffer loss of time, and strategic positions. Other companies considered that investment in CAD/CAM was a necessity, in order to keep abreast with the changes that technology will produce in manufacturing and work-organization in the times to come. As reported here, these cases do not show what these changes are or will be. Fortunately so, for this leaves room for social studies of CAD/CAM.

Bibliography

Bezier, P., 1982:
Petite histoire d'une idée bizarre. Bulletin de la section d'histoire des usines Renault, 1982, 4,, 24, p. 256-268 et 4, 25, p. 319-331.

Böhm, W.; Farin, G.; Kahmann, J.; 1984:
A survey of curve and surface methods in CADG. Computer Aided Geometric Design, 1984, 1, p. 1-60.

Casteljau, P. de Faget de, 1985:
Formes à Pôles, Paris, Hermes, 1985.

Krautter, J.; Parizot, S.; 1971:
Système d'aide à la définition et à l'usinage des surfaces de carrosserie (SADUSCA). Ingénieurs de l'Automobile, 1971, XLIV, 10, p. 581-587.

Neuve Eglise, M., 1981:
De l'idée à l'objet: un système intégré de CFAO. Gadz'arts 81, 1981, p. 25-34.

Poitou, J.P., 1984:
Le cerveau de l'usine, Rapport S.T.S., Aix-en-Provence, Université de Provence, 1984, Multicopié.

Theron, M., 1980:
CAO et PMI, EUCLID interactif dans un secteur d'activités traditionnelles. MICAD 80, s.l., s.d.

Theron, M., 1984:
L'algèbre des solides et la CFAO en mécanique. Un exemple: le système EUCLID. MICAD 84, Paris, Hermes 1984, Vol. 3.

SOCIAL EFFECTS IN THE RELATIONSHIP BETWEEN USERS AND SUPPLIERS OF CAD/CAM SYSTEMS IN HUNGARY

George Kovács

Computer and Automation Institute
Hungarian Academy of Sciences
Budapest, Hungary
H-111 Kende utca 13/17

1. Introduction

CAD/CAM developments and investments have effects on almost everybody involved.The international literature deals mostly with the purchaser side, i.e. the impact of CAD/CAM on the organization. The main questions are:

- What are the benefits?
- How are the investments justified?
- What is the role of management and specialists like programmers, users/operators?
- Problems of job security?
- Effects on staff morale?

In the Hungarian circumstances it is not enough to deal with the acceptance of CAD/CAM systems, the development of the systems having equal importance.

It is basically due to the fact that we do not yet have a wide market of CAD/CAM systems, as imports from developed countries are restricted and home development is not independent and not fast enough.

2. New CAD/CAM systems in Hungary

New CAD/CAM systems are developed in most cases on contracts between the end-users (e.g. factories) and the programmers-developers (e.g. research institutes).

This way, if a factory understands the needs of a new system (e.g. a professional draughting system or a sophisticated surface design system) generally there is no way of buying it on the home market, but there are two ways to proceed:

- to try to import a system. It may take 6-12 months to get a negative answer from the vendor, or it may take 1-3 years to get all the home and foreign permissions and to get the necessary - or a similar - system at a very high price, and one is then faced with the problem of a unique hardware-software system (nothing is similar in Hungary, it is hard to understand and difficult to maintain).
- The other way is to find an organization in Hungary capable of developing the necessary system and to make a contract with it. This way, the development may be very long and

expensive, but because of the close cooperation between the vendor-developer and the purchaser-user the system will most probably cover the real needs.

As recently the second way is more common, let us make some remarks on the personal interests and problems of people involved.

3. Personal interests in CAD/CAM diffusion

Three levels of hierarchy are examined:

- HM: high level management (managers, directors)
- MM: medium level management (heads of departments or divisions, leaders of 5-30 persons)
- W: programmers, users, operators.

The following abbreviations are used:

- HMV: vendor's manager
- HMP: purchaser's manager
- MMV: vendor's head of department
- MMP: purchaser's head of department
- WV: vendor's program developer
- WP: purchaser's programmer (user, operator).

The relationships between these people are roughly shown in Figure 1.

Generally the idea of having or developing a new system first appears at the 2nd level (MMP or MMV), but sometimes the first level or even the third level may initiate.

The 2nd level informs the first level about results and problems and orders the 3rd level to work on the tasks and to inform him about achievements and problems (feedback of all levels).

Some problems are worth examining.

Who is interested in a new CAD/CAM system? To what extent?

- *Developers:*
  - HMV wants to secure income for his organization, but does not necessarily understand the technical problem and he is afraid of the risks of the unknown new work (60-90 %)
  - MMV exactly knows the problems, he is scientifically and materially interested, he pushes the work, he is personally involved in the preparations for the contract (80-100 %)
  - WV depends on his boss, MMV. He is interested in working on a new, interesting problem. He knows that if the system is sold, he will get a license fee, and during the work he may have scientific benefits as well (75-95 %).

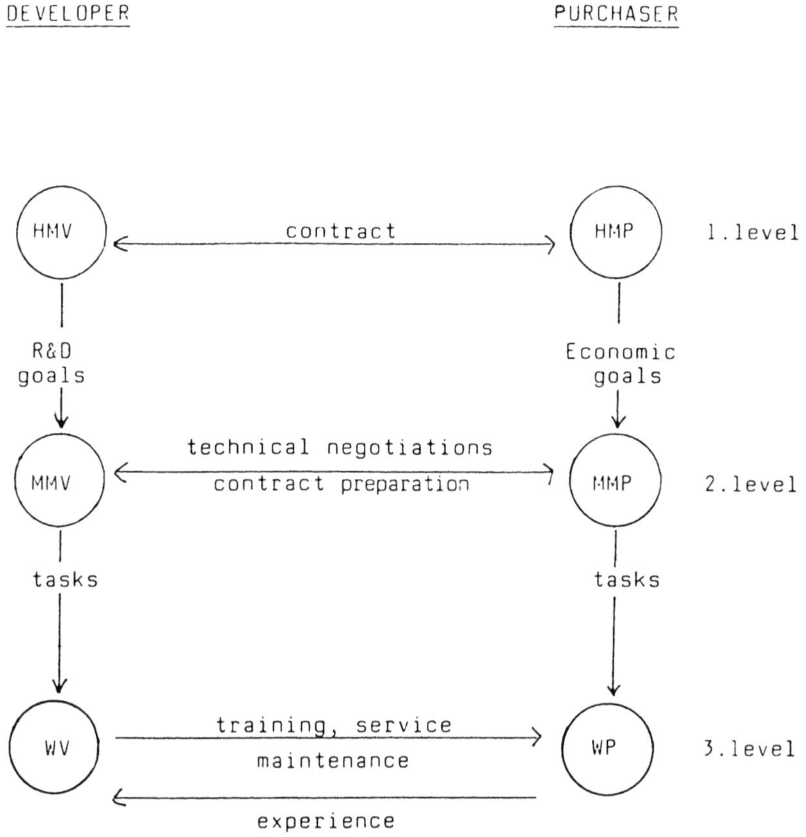

Figure 1

- *Purchasers:*
  - HMP is not really interested in a new CAD/CAM project or investment as it is hard to see its benefits and he is afraid of the risks of any changes, if the factory works well enough. In several cases HMP is a real enemy of new CAD/CAM systems (10-50 %)
  - MMP is well informed, he understands the problems, and he negotiates with MMV to prepare the contract and he informs his boss (HMP). If real benefits are to be had from a CAD/CAM system, he is really interested, however if errors occur, he is responsible (80-90 %)
  - WP is the most problematic. A programmer may believe that he could do the same work, or if the system is bought he will not like to cope with it, however he may understand that a new system gives new interesting tasks as well (20-40 %). An operator/user may hope for the improvement of his performance but may be afraid of the

new expensive hardware and of the familiar work. Most users (e.g. designers) have to continue their traditional work as well, thus instead of looking for advantages they prefer to look for flaws and weaknesses of the new system (10-40 %).

Should we develop a new system or adopt an existing one?

- Ten years ago there was only one answer. There were only a few software-houses run by the government and some university faculties and research institutes, which had the experts to work on CAD/CAM problems and the computers to use.
- The last five years have changed the Hungarian situation. The new economic system made it possible to form small private company-like software groups which exist almost completely without overheads (e.g. 5-6 programmers working in the flat of one of them having no administration). They started offering contracts at lower prices than the big institutes, as the work was done on the computers of the contractor. Lately the price drop and greater power of professional personal computers made them available for the new small firms to develop software on their own.
- At the same time a brain-drain started from big professional institutes/software houses to small software-making enterprises. This is caused by the increasing income of people working without overheads and an expensive background, but having all the professional knowledge acquired while working with the big institutes. Small software houses became partners for all kinds of end-users, however mostly for smaller tasks.

Recently there is a certain equilibrium, under which long term (2-5 year) sophisticated problems should be solved by big professional firms which often use small firms as sub-contractors. This may cause problems between similarly qualified programmers who formerly worked together in a software house, but with one of them now with the small firm, doing the same job for double salary. When there are short term jobs or adaptation problems, the small firms are at advantage and they get this kind of contract.

Who should use a new CAD/CAM system?

- If a new system is implemented in a factory where computers are rarely used, the main problem is the acceptance of the system. As we mentioned earlier the average user is not very enthusiastic, as he is forced to use the new technique, while he has to continue his traditional work as well. For example a car-body designer knows his job (perfectly), but has never seen an interactive workstation although he is advised to use one. He will try not to do so.
- Management may try to employ new people, who are more familiar with computers on the one hand, but on the other hand they are beginners in engineering problems (e.g. car-body design). They will like to play with the workstation but no new car-bodies will be designed.

Recently this has been a real controversy to be solved. Old specialists have to be convinced to use new techniques and new computer people have to learn special engineering knowledge. If management is good enough, a smooth conversion can be done towards CAD/CAM systems. Otherwise the investment will never pay off. Some examples for both cases are already known.

References

Gaál, B.; Várady, T.:
Experiences and further development of the FFS system. Proc. of the 9th IFAC World Congress, Budapest, 1984.

Andor et al.:
GRECO, User Manual Computer and Automation Institute, Budapest, 1984.

Kovács, G.:
Displaying Tool Paths IKM'82, Vortrag 39, Leipzig, 10.12. March 82.

Böhm, W.; Farin, G.; Kahmann, J.:
A survey of Curve and Surface Methods in CAGD-Computer Aided Geometric Design, Vol. 1 (1984), pp. 1-60.

Fenyves, F.; Licskó, I.; Kovács, G.:
Translation Surfaces in the 3D Subsystem of the COMECON NC Programming System, ICED'83, Kobenhavn, 15-18 August 1983.

CHAPTER 6: Utilization of Results and Cooperation between the Disciplines

Although research for its own sake is, of course, perfectly legitimate, most scientists level their findings at some kind of audience. In the cases of the projects represented in the workshop this meant a variety of audiences:

- One's own scientific peers;
- developers of CAD/CAM systems;
- state policy makers;
- CAD consultants;
- firms employing or considering CAD/CAM, in-house decision-makers;
- unions and employee representation.

In most cases, there is the problem of communicating one's results in a manner and language to get the intended audience to take notice. A similar problem exists in multi-disciplinary projects involving engineers and social scientists. To some extent, this may be solved by involving persons with qualifications in both fields, but since this is an exception rather than the rule, the more common course is to involve scientists from both disciplines. While it seems a good idea to involve all disciplines with equal rights, in practice and depending on the accents of the project, one or the other discipline tends to dominate, involving the scientists from other disciplines as "pets".

McLOUGHLIN reported on what he described as the second interdisciplinary project in Great Britain next to ROSENBROCK's widely known example. This was carried out at the University of Southampton and McLOUGHLIN was among the social scientists involved. He stressed three points:

1. Although it might sound desirable to provide the disciplines with equal influence in defining the focus and area of research and in leadership of the project, this doesn't work out in practice. To have real influence, one has to take the lead. In ROSENBROCK's case at Manchester, the engineers took lead, at Southampton it was the sociologists.
2. Disciplinary synthesis could lead to a new body of knowledge. In such projects, people from various disciplines would work on common problems, although with different accents.
3. Engineers could be employed by social scientists as interpreters to help them understand technology and the work being observed in the field or as consultants on technological matters.

In the Southampton project, collaboration helped to broaden the data base. However, since the contracts awarded for such research work are not particularly attractive compared with those offered by industry, there were problems of fluctuation, leaving too little time for scientists to accumulate some kind of working knowledge in the other disciplines involved as suggested by WINGERT. The latter suggested long-term cooperation between engineers and social scientists to achieve a change of perspective for both sides. FINNE supported Mc-LOUGHLIN's suggestions for roles for engineers, adding a third: that of a kind of bridgehead to diffuse social science ideas into their own profession.

BERCKMANS remarked that the impact of social scientists in Belgium was about zero and underlined this by pointing out that while there were many programmes to stimulate the diffusion of technology, none of these involved social scientists. Interdisciplinarity had to be one-way, in that social scientists had to draw engineers into their projects. BERCKMANS also remarked that, in his experience, the trade unions were often not interested in results because these were too long-term. Thus there was a need to convince the unions that social science research work was truly useful.

In their paper, Langaa JENSEN et al. outline strategies for the utilization of research results by employees. Commenting on this, ARNOLD remarked that the legitimate role for social scientists in Scandinavia appeared to be in association with the trade unions, while in Great Britain, social science research was directed towards policy makers. Interesting though the approach of viewing workers as the "victims" of technology may be, this ran the risk of adopting a static perception of work, the structure of industry and of the role of technology in this pattern. One of the features of capitalism were periodic upheavals in production and these were more often due to new products than to processes. If research is focused on a process like CAD it runs the risk of looking at a dying industry and of overlooking the restructuring of industry taking place at the same time. Langaa JENSEN agreed on the necessity of taking such a long-range view, but argued at the same time that it was difficult to interest people in the long-range effects of technology. In Denmark, policy makers were simply not interested in understanding technology as such, but oriented towards its economic aspects, for instance, in terms of numbers of jobs.

HOSS remarked that in the discussion on the possible alternative use of technology, the fact that the working environment was seeking to obstruct autonomy was often neglected. The remedy was to allow workers to participate in the design of technology and the chance to do so did really exist. In this context, HOSS singled out the IG-Metall-Technologieberatungsstellen (metal workers' union technology advice centres) which supply knowledge on technology to works councils. While not violently disagreeing with HOSS, Langaa JENSEN claimed that participation in design was no solution but more of a trap. He elaborated on this by saying that, in Scandinavia at least, a new management type seemed to be emerging. This new breed of manager was involving the work force in all kinds of projects, leaving no time to formulate a cohesive new policy on technology. In a slightly different vein but on a similar note, Langaa JENSEN remarked that funds in Denmark were provided for social science research directed towards action and not towards analysis.

Besides the contribution by JENSEN et al., this chapter includes contributions by FINNE on the subject of feeding back results of social science research, a short paper by Elsebet Frydendal PETERSEN on the effects CAD is having via changed prefabricated products on the safety of construction workers on the site plus a provocative piece by Wolfgang JONAS, a CAD consultant, stating his demands on social science.

UTILIZATION OF RESEARCH RESULTS BY THE EMPLOYEES *)

Niels Møller, Per Langaa Jensen

Institute of Technological Development and Working Conditions
Building 301, The Technical University of Denmark
DK- 2800 Lyngby

1. Introductory remark

In the last 10-15 years there has been a general increase in research on the social implications of introducing new technology at the workplace. In the Scandinavian countries, social scientists have had different strategies for utilizing the results of this research.

2. Three strategies for utilizing results of research

One strategy is to concentrate on the legislative system. The research results are here produced for the state apparatus to form an "objective" basis for legislation and regulation. In the field of occupational health and safety this strategy has been dominant. But many social scientists have found that only a few of the possible paradigms of research were suited for legislation.

Another strategy is to concentrate on the people involved in developing the new technology. Often social scientists identify these people with the technicians at the research institutions or in the companies. The main aim of this approach is therefore to establish a cooperation with these technical experts in the hope, that they will recognize the importance of taking into account not only the technical but also the social system involved in or affected by the developing process. The main problems in this approach are to establish a mutual cooperation with experts within other disciplines, and to present the research results in a manner understood by and useful for the technical experts.

A third strategy is to concentrate on the employees who will be affected by the introduction of the new technology. They are potential victims of the negative consequences of the new technology. In this approach the role of social science is often defined as delivering results on the social implications of new technology with emphasis on the working conditions. Sometimes it may be acceptable for social science to point out demands to be followed by the unions and the federations in their activities.

---

* This paper is based on a study by Jesper Holm, Per Langaa Jensen and Niels Møller. The results will be published in a book in Danish: Fagbevaegelsen og alternativ teknologi (Labour Unions and alternative technology), publ. by Teknisk Landsforbund, Copenhagen 1986. References to the Scandinavian research mentioned here can be found in this publication.

In this paper we will demonstrate that social science within this strategy has greater potential than this interpretation suggests. We will present tentative results from ongoing studies in which we are involved, and finally we will discuss how the utilization of research results must be seen in this broader interpretation of the role of social science within this third strategy.

3. Employees and the cooperative system

Throughout the history of industrialism employees have experienced problems connected with the introduction of new technology to the production process. One reaction to this situation has been to demand a democratization in the sphere of production. The main idea behind this reaction is, that if democratic bodies were established at the workplace it would be possible for the employees to ensure that their interests are taken into account.

In the Scandinavian countries the employers and the legislative system have complied with this demand from the labour unions by making agreements or passing legislation on cooperative bodies in different fields of society, including the individual firm. These bodies have among other issues the right to discuss the use of new technology. Even though the bodies don't injure management's prerogative they do make it possible for the employees to influence decisions concerning technology. But are they able to make use of these possibilities?

Research on the functioning of these bodies shows that, in general, they have very little - if any - effect on fundamental matters related to the efficiency of the production process and the working conditions related to this. But within the last decade, there has been research on how these cooperative bodies can be used by the local unions to pursue the interests of the employees in matters of new technology. The researchers have entered the process of influencing decision-making in the firms by using their resources on the workers' side. By analyzing the reports on these research activities it is possible to give a first answer to the question: Can local unions and other employees use research results on potential social implications of the introduction of new technology for their work in the cooperative bodies?

In the following we will refer to these activities as "technology-activities" which means activities meant to influence the choice of technology and its implementation.

4. A description of the study

A literature study of 15-20 mainly Swedish and Danish research projects was conducted to answer the question. These projects were chosen because they all were concerned with the possibilities of involving employees in questions related to technological change.

There have been several research activities on this question. The greater number of these studies have focused on the functioning of the cooperative system in general. Only a few have studied the limitations and possibilities of the system seen from a pure wage-earner- and union-perspective. It was among these studies the 15-20 studies for close examination were chosen.

The main criteria for choosing the studies were (1) we knew of them in advance, (2) we had the impression that they had contributed to the development of knowledge in the field and (3) they illustrated different ways of coping with technological changes from a union point of view. The different ways are:

- engagement in the cooperative system purely at the level of local union activities;
- engagement in the cooperative system in cooperation between the local union, the associated federation and researchers;
- activities facilitated by special forms of ownership (i.e. owned by the state or owned by the employees);
- activities directed towards the choice of product rather than towards the choice of production process;
- activities directed towards the design of the new technology rather than towards the implementation of new technology;
- activities seen in a regional context rather than within the context of the single firm.

The result of our study gives an approximate idea of the context in which employees and their union will be able to use research results on social implications of new technology.

Our findings concern five main questions:

- What is 'new technology' in the context of production processes?
- Is it possible for unions and employees to influence the new technology?
- What preconditions for union-based technology activities play an important role in the success of the activities?
- How do union and employees engage in the activities?
- What are the potential results of the activities?

5. The concept 'new technology'

It follows clearly from all the studies, that defining technology as "the means of production" is too narrow a definition. It is neither possible with this definition to identify most of the potential problems connected with the changes in the production process nor is it possible to identify actions that can reduce or eliminate these potential problems.

The implementation of new technology is not only the implementation of a new means of production. The concept 'technology' includes:

- the materials in work
- the means of production
- the organization of the process, and
- the capacity to perform the work.

Changes in one or more of these elements have effects on the working conditions, and solutions to the workers' problems in the production process must focus on all these elements. Therefore union and employees must include all elements in their definition of a new technology. Their assessment and their demands and solutions must be based on that definition.

6. The determination of new technology in production

It is evident from all the studies, that neither general economic laws nor the actual technological situation determine totally the introduction of new technology. The economic situation sets limits for the choice of technology, and there are some technical constraints which have to be taken into consideration. But within this framework there is a margin for choice. While management and the technical experts are conscious of this range of possibilities, the employees are only rarely aware of it. But activities in the field of new technology provide them with an understanding of this margin for decision making.

7. Preconditions for union-based technological activities

The examined studies reveal a set of conditions of importance for establishing union-based technology activities with a degree of success. The conditions can be grouped under five main headings.

Conditions external to the single firm. These include:

- The general economic and competitive situation of the firm: Union-based activities will have a better chance for success if the firm is not in a crisis, if it is in a situation of monopoly or if it is protected by state regulations.
- Legislation and agreements on negotiations or cooperation: An elaborated body of regulations gives legitimacy to union-based activities.
- Technological alternatives: The existence and knowledge of possible alternative techniques and work-organizations give a better chance for union-based activities to take advantage of the margins.
- The labour market: A favorable labour market, seen from the employees' point of view, provides a better position in negotiations and cooperative activities.

Conditions related to management. These include:

- Ownership, general policies and management attitudes: A positive attitude of management to bargaining and cooperation makes it easier to establish union-based activities. Different types of ownership often lead to different general policies which affect management attitudes.

- The knowledge of management on the production process, and the necessity of a skilled workforce: Limited management knowledge on the production process is often connected with dependence on a highly skilled workforce. This situation provides a better basis for union-based activities.

Conditions internal to the individual firm. These include:

- The flexibility of the process: A process easy to rearrange gives better possibilities for meeting demands.
- The division of labour: A production process characterized by a work force composed of people with different highly specialized qualifications makes it difficult to formulate and pursue union demands.
- The working conditions: A production process with inspiring work and 'acceptable' physical strains gives a better chance of establishing union-based activities on technology.

Conditions related to the local union. These include:

- Previous experience with and traditions for participation in decision-making in the firm give naturally better possibilities for leading union-based technology activities to success.
- Consciousness of the role of unions and collective action and technical knowledge also give better possibilities for leading union-based activities to success.
- Time and money earmarked for technology activities also support the development of these activities.
- Internal support from the union and the employees is of course also of importance.

Conditions related to the structure of the central trade union. These include:

- External support from other parts of this structure (among them the affiliated federation) is of importance.
- External support from consultants, through information, and educational programmes are important in this context.
- Established policies of relevance for local union-based technology activities. Their existence gives support to local activities. They may even include different types of financial support.

These five groups of conditions are a summary of the conditions found in different studies. In a given case, not all have to be fulfilled to ensure success. Instead, we see this list as a basis for a check up on the actual situation for a union before entering technology activities.

But favorable preconditions do not ensure success in union-based technology activities. The structuring of the activities plays also an important role in establishing successful activities.

8. The progress of union-based technology activities

The examined studies do not only reveal a set of nreconditions. They also contribute to our knowledge on how to establish and conduct technology activities. The contributions concern:

- *How to get started*

  Several of the studies used with success the same procedure to prepare the unions and the employees for bargaining and cooperative activities with management. Group activities are fundamental for this procedure. First, the group sums up the problems in working with existing technology. Next they formulate the characteristics of the ideal job. Through visits to production units using (elements of) the new technology, through reading and through contacts with consultants, researchers etc. they build up knowledge on the new technology, potential associated problems and possible solutions to these problems. On this basis, they formulate demands for the new technology and its implementation.

- *Different types of objectives for the activities*

  An overview of the studies shows three dimensions to include in objectives:

  - The ecological dimension, i.e. emphasizing the assessment of the technology and the production system as components in an ecological system.
  - The socio-economical dimension. i.e. emphasizing the assessment of the 'productivity' of the technology, but from a humanistic, social point of view, and not only from a traditional producer's point of view.
  - The dimension of general living conditions for members of society, both in work and in leisure.

All these dimensions do not necessarily need to be included in a given set of objectives. The point is that all the objectives are formulated within these dimensions.

- *Cooperation versus bargaining?*

  The studies show a series of problems connected both with strategies based on cooperation and with strategies based on bargaining. While the problems are evident, the studies unfortunately do not provide any solutions. They conclude that one cannot choose just one of the strategies, but that both forms of relations to management must be included in a good strategy. Management strategies must be taken into consideration by the employees, but none of the studies elaborate these aspects of determination of a worker strategy.

- *Type of arguments*

  In the studies, three types of arguments on the side of the employees can be identified:

  - a rational, micro-economic argumentation trying to show the superiority of the alternative technology;

- a 'workers' control' argument, where the development of the production process is seen as only determined by consideration of profits. This development will never be in accordance with the demands and objectives of the workers. An alternative 'utopian' technology must be conceptualized, taking into consideration the resources of the workers, the potential of the technology and the demands on working conditions and employment. While the first type of argumentation may result in some changes in technology, this second type serves mainly to mobilize the rank and file;
- a socio-economically based argument, where main focus is on the consideration of the development of local society. This type of argument has especially been used in situations where there has been a threat of a close-down of a factory.

It isn't possible to point to one of these types as the best. The types must be mixed through assessment of the situations.

- *Tools applicable in the activities*

In all of the studies a series of different tools to be used at various times in the procedure are presented. These tools can serve as inspirations to develop tools for actual activities in a union.

9. Results of union-based technology-activities

Finally, the examined studies show what kind of results to expect from union-based technology activities. None of the studies report a fundamental change in the plans formulated by management. But a series of modifications were accomplished. They include:

- changes in the organization of work, i.e. changes in both the horizontal and the vertical division of labour;
- educational arrangements to secure a proper education for the people confronted with the new technology;
- man-machine-system changes, primarily in the field of ergonomics;
- the decision processes are in general affected so that more alternatives are taken into consideration and workers take more part in the decisions.

These may be modifications, but they have an important impact on the working conditions of the new technology. Certain issues are very difficult to approach, typically the introduction of shift-work, the utilization of the machines and the intensification of work.

Also the available machinery presents limitations on union demands. Only rarely a technology complies with all union demands. This is an important reason why the activities only result in compromises, manifested as modifications to the technology originally planned by management.

Besides these modifications all of the studies show changes in attitudes and consciousness of the people involved. Typically they get:

- a more fundamental knowledge on the process of production and the forces determining its development;
- more consciousness of the role of unions at the local level;
- more active at participating in decision-making, and
- more active in union activities internally and with other trades.

It is not possible to judge the long range effects of this change in attitude and consciousness on the basis of the examined studies.

One conclusion is, that even though the general effects of the bargaining and cooperation system are limited, there are recommendations on how to use this system from a union point of view. These recommendations do not at the present stage form a contingency theory on union influence in matters of technology. But a number of concepts and strategical choices are uncovered.

10. Once more: Utilization of research results by the employees

Our study shows that it is possible to establish union based technology activities having a certain effect. It also shows that there is a general need for research results on how to carry out the process. But if social scientists define their role as suppliers of analyses of social impact and eventually proposals for demands, the effects of their research activities will be limited.

Our study shows that scientists working in the field of new technology and working conditions - a field including both parts of social and parts of technical science - can contribute with results on many other subjects of relevance to union based activities. Examples are: Concepts to explain important choices and thoroughly analyzed experience in technology activities. In the longer perspective this research can contribute to the development of "alternative industrial engineering" based on union goals.

But to accomplish this, more experience has to be analyzed, assessed and discussed with the people concerned. An important issue in this context is to evaluate the role of the researcher in the process. The prime obstacle to progress in this kind of knowledge is economic. While traditional industrial engineering receives massive financial support under the impression of the challenge from Japanese industry, worker-based industrial engineering receives little or no financial support. As opposed to traditional industrial engineering, which is viewed as based on "real science", this body of knowledge is considered "pure politics".

It is therefore of importance to utilize every possibility to initiate research within this field. At our department we are involved in studies to develop knowledge within the field.

One study is concerned with the possibilities of establishing self-supported technological activities within a federation and its affiliated unions. Many of the examined studies demonstrate that an external support is of central importance for local union-based technology activities. This external support has often been based on contacts with researchers. To establish widespread activities within a federation, another type of external support has to be established.

In Denmark the Federation of Technicians has in the last five years developed activities in the field of technology (focusing on CAD technology) to promote local activities. The federational activities have resulted in leaflets, videos and courses on CAD-technology and working conditions, and in establishing technology as a subject continually discussed in articles in the magazine for the members of the federation. With this material, the federation tries to pass on the latest results in science and information on some of the experience had with CAD by its members.

We are conducting a study to assess the effects of these activities. We expect to identify some of the factors of importance in establishing self supported activities in the field of technology within unions. The study is financed by the Technical University.

Another study is trying to improve our knowledge on industrial engineering and the possibilities for workers' influence in this connection. In the labour unions' discussions on new technology, the role of industrial engineering is only seldom discussed. This is remarkable because the concept "industrial engineering" covers most of the decision-making determining the new technology. At the same time we find the existing knowledge on the functioning of the industrial engineering very poor.

Therefore this study is trying to develop an understanding of actual practice within industrial engineering, to evaluate the existing recommendations for workers' influence on new technology, and to develop new more adequate recommendations. This study is a part of a Ph.D.-study also financed by the Technical University.

The last study to be mentioned will analyze the opportunities for worker - representatives elected to cooperative bodies. Previous studies have shown that these representatives have difficulties in utilizing the rights laid down in regulations. This implies that successful activities by the representatives are never covered in these studies. Therefore this study will try to analyze and describe these more successful activities, and bring them into the discussion with other representatives. The study is focusing on the safety-committees and the safety and health representatives. It is financed by the National Foundation for Occupational Health and Safety.

11. Conclusion

In this paper we have tried to elaborate on one of the possible strategies to utilize research results on the social implications of new technology. We have demonstrated that the 'traditional' role of social and technical scientists as suppliers of analyses of social impacts and eventually pointing out possible demands is limiting the possibilities for scientists. The perspective within a strategy based on bringing research results to the use of unions and employees is to establish a 'worker-based industrial engineering'. The difficulties of getting financial support for the development of this body of knowledge stresses the importance of finding alternative ways to develop this knowledge, and of informing others on recent results and actual plans. We have in the last pages briefly described ours. We hope to hear from others within this field of research, so that worker-based industrial engineering will be developed.

HOW DO WE FEED OUR FINDINGS BACK INTO THE DESIGN PROCESS?

Håkon Finne
Institute of Social Research in Industry (IFIM)
N-7034 TRONDHEIM-NTH

What social scientists find about the effects of CAD systems, they cannot themselves apply to the redesign of such systems. Software and engineering scientists do systems development and hence a cooperation is called for between two widely different disciplines. This is not an easy task as those will know who have attempted cross-disciplinary research with closer scientific relatives than the two in question.

With a background in both fields and an interest in using social science to redirect technological development, I have put together some experience and some speculation as to the pre-requisites for a fruitful cooperation. This paper is intended to stimulate discussion rather than answer the question borne in its title.

1. The organization of research projects

Cooperation between disciplines in a project can be classified according to the degree of integration between the two fields of knowledge. A multidisciplinary project will attack a problem from various angles or even separate problems. No findings or theories on either side will influence what is done on the other. As opposed to this, a cross-disciplinary project will contain regular exchange of theories and results across the disciplinary boundary, and the exchange will in part determine the actual development of new knowledge on each side. But only when the two types of knowledge are fused into a new type, possibly followed by the development of a new discipline, shall we speak of a disciplinary synthesis.

If the research done by the two groups of people is organized as separate projects, only a multi-disciplinary approach will be possible. A prerequisite for a cross-disciplinary approach is at least an umbrella project which provides for a common source of funding, a common (and commonly understood and accepted) project goal, and the provision of time and resources to communicate. A disciplinary synthesis is in my view only possible if the two groups of people form one group and work together (physically and mentally) most of the time in a common project. Table 1 illustrates possible combinations.

It is clear from the outset that, if social science is to influence systems development, a multidisciplinary approach will be inadequate. In a later section I shall show some very serious problems in attempting a cross-disciplinary approach in the design of software (or other machines) and hence the question becomes how to proceed for a disciplinary synthesis.

Table 1: **Possible degree of disciplinary integration with different types of project organization**

disciplinary integration	project organization		
	separate	umbrella	common
multi-disciplinary	X	X	X
cross-disciplinary		X	X
disciplinary synthesis			X

2. Motivation for cooperation

The motivation for cooperation between social and engineering sciences has generally been low on both sides. Engineers have seen little need for equipping their teams with social scientists who would probably slow down development anyway. Social scientists have been afraid to be without influence in development projects, while at the same time losing the possibility to criticize the product.

External incentives now exist as some funding bodies for the social sciences expect their projects to be in the forefront of technological development and not mere criticism after the fact. This comes as an opportunity to social scientists who have wanted to influence technological development but without the possibilities of establishing projects.

The motivation on the engineering side is still low. KJELLBERG (1983) rightly treats this as a pedagogical problem. The first question is how to make engineering scientists aware of the importance of quality of working life (very broadly meant). It is reasonably simple to convince engineers as persons that they should care about this - compared to the task of convincing them that their work as research engineers has consequences for other people's working lives. For one thing, the myth of the neutrality of technology is a tough one: 'It is the way technology is used in the firm that decides the outcome, not what the technology looks like.' Of course it is impossible to set a uniquely defined border between pure and applied knowledge and hence research engineers developing new technology are also contributing to the eventual outcome.

3. The nature of engineering knowledge

My hint at the need for a disciplinary synthesis implies an antithetical relationship between knowledge of the engineering science type and the social science type. Let me consider engineering science first by trying to use some concepts introduced by KUHN (1962).

KUHN describes how a scientific discipline is embedded in a largely consistent matrix of theory, equipment, methods, problem definitions, social organization, ontological assumptions etc. - summarised by the well-known term paradigm. Different paradigms are largely incommensurate, i.e. transfer of elements (for example theories) from one paradigm to another would not only be considered erroneous, but would in fact be meaningless.

While KUHN's concepts are hardly directly transferable to the description of an engineering science, let me at least consider a couple of aspects to illustrate a point.

Within a paradigm, there exist a number of preferred models. These may be of a heuristic kind, i.e. they are shown to be useful but hardly 'true' analogies. One example is how cognitive psychology works by modelling its experiments on the assumption that the brain functions on the same basic principles as the digital computer. This allows the treatment of mental processes as data processing (see DREYFUS 1979 for an expansion of this theme). Models may also be of a more ontological nature, and sometimes heuristic models develop over time to become de facto ontological assumptions (as in the case of the computer brain).

One important preferred model in all engineering sciences should be mentioned. In the heuristic version it is stated as the usefulness of treating the world as if it were composed of independently existing small components or units or atoms. This atomist assumption has certainly been important in scientific and technological development. The atomist assumption is not only heuristic but ontological, however, as will appear if you suggest that a machine should be designed as a whole with no attention to its details.

Systems thinking may seem to have surpassed this stage. By a systems approach one can consider systems effects, i.e. changes in global system characteristics attributable to the interaction of its elements. The elements themselves remain unchanged by this interaction, however. This is different from systems concepts found in biology, linguistics, and social science, where elements (species, words, or actors) develop simultaneously with their global system (ecotope, language, or society, respectively) and the part is unthinkable without the whole.

Another aspect of a disciplinary matrix or a paradigm are the values that distinguish good work from bad work and disciplinary from irrelevant knowledge. Only two values will be mentioned here. The first one concerns what counts as an explanation of a phenomenon. If one speaks of engineering, only causal explanations are allowed. Or who has heard of an intentional machine? And think of a bridge that was governed by teleological principles instead of Newtonian physics! Although causality practically is abandoned in modern physics (but not replaced), this is not so for the engineering sciences.

The second value I will mention is that explicit knowledge is a candidate for acceptance as scientific but tacit knowledge has no recognized place. In fact, an important side of scientific work is precisely to objectivize knowledge and make it independent of the personal knower.

It is important to note that I am not speaking of the values held by individual engineers. Engineers vary in their personal values as much as other people. These are the values of engineering knowledge, and they are - together with the preferred models - integral to the working methods of engineering scientists. Even if an engineer saw negative effects of working this way, there would be no engineering methods available to do it in another way!

History shows us that this paradigm has proven extremely useful in developing machinery. There can be no doubt about that. It is equally clear, however, that tacit engineering knowledge has been crucial in designing all the new technology (including software). POLANYI (1958) originally developed his concept of the tacit dimension to underline the crucial role of personal knowledge in the presumably least personal discipline of all, physics. More recently COLLINS (1985) has supported this empirically. Tacit knowledge is important to creativity, which is valued in the designing engineer, but not in engineering knowledge! In a way, engineers deny their own existence in the engineering sciences.

4. Engineering paradigms and social science paradigms

Now try to understand human social activities in the context of an engineering paradigm.

I have already sketched the dialectical relationship between the actors and their society. Admittedly, much social science research has a conception of this relationship that is structurally more akin to the engineering definition of a system. These are the approaches that still hope to base their science on the positivist model now largely abandoned by physics. But definitely the sociology of BERGER and LUCKMANN (1967) has this dialectical concept, and so has Marx, of course.

While social science puts high value on explicit knowledge it is also capable of recognizing the existence and importance of tacit knowledge. The problem of reaching a good understanding of the nature of the tacit dimension does not result in its rejection as a real phenomenon. (Again there are differences between approaches, of course.)

A good example is to look at how the activity of design is conceived by software scientists making a CAD system and a social scientist. The following remarks relate to Figure 1.

At the outset, design is an ill-defined activity with unclear boundaries (a). The social scientist will try to understand this activity as a set of acts informed by the actor's explicit knowledge, his subsidiary awareness of details in considering the problem to be solved, his subsidiary awareness of the whole when focusing on the parts, his reliance on social interactions with other competent designers for learning, cultural and structural constraints on how to define and attack a problem, economic and other criteria for what counts as a solution, the importance of routine work for creative behaviour, the existence of a tacit framework that allows the designer to find a meaningful pattern in all his "sense data", and so on. (Unfortunately I have no illustration of this.)

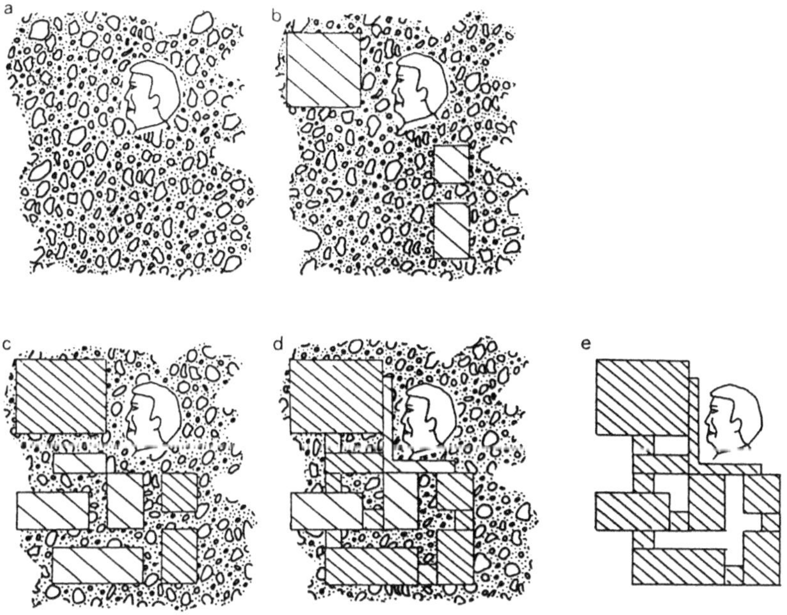

Figure 1
From design to CAD

The software scientist, on the other hand, will first concentrate on the explicable elements of the design activity. These will be delimited, defined, broken down into micro-elements and reconstituted in a shape that lends itself to computer programming (b). Even with "artificial intelligence" programming techniques this is necessary if one is to make software.

Gradually the area of design knowledge thus reconstituted is expanded (c). But the designer still has to tie it all together and this integrating function is scrutinized by the software people. They focus on how to tie together the reconstituted elements of design and the integrative function is achieved by the means of interfaces (which are not actually faces but objects, i.e. new elements of software). The interface towards the designer (or user) is a more or less transparent barrier towards the newly explicated logic of design (d).

Hence the wider the software developers analyse and reconstitute design as an activity, the narrower their perspective gets until they have finally re-realized design as a system (e), which is of course continually refined.

It is not the engineer who chooses to do it this way. It is engineering (or computer) science that requires software to be developed in this way.

Then my question is: How can the social scientist's understanding of the design activity become useful in the engineering scientists' work on a design system? I think it can be so only if the engineer manages to reinterpret that understanding in an atomist conception that makes it meaningful within the engineering paradigm. But if he manages to do this, then the holist perspective, which somehow was the reason for bringing in the social scientist in the first place, gets lost.

Nor is a solution to rely solely on those social science disciplines which are more akin to the engineering way of thinking and working. This would be the case for current cognitive psychology, which seems to work very well with software science once a working relationship has been developed.

An evident conclusion is that the paradigmatic differences between a holist social science and an atomist engineering science are too great for a cross-disciplinary cooperation to be possible in a research project. If this seems countered by the experience of such cooperation running well in developing, say, work organization around new technology, then this is because both sides, but particularly the engineers, act in ways that are antithetical to their disciplinary knowledge proper.

5. Social science in for a change

It would of course be absurd to simply let social scientists design CAD software. Their main problem is not that they do not master programming, this is rather a benefit. Two problems have to be faced. One is that social scientists have very little experience in designing - it simply is not part of a social science brief. The other one is that to the extent that social science knowledge is a suitable basis for designing social systems, this is not applicable to technical systems. Let me offer two general examples to illustrate the shortcomings of social science on the design side.

The first example concerns degree and scope of specification of the design. One of the few generally accepted - but also very general - design principles for good jobs is that they are to be designed so as not to constrain the jobholder in his or her personal adjustment of the job. This is the criterion of minimum critical specification (HERBST 1974). Compare this to the design of a machine and you will find that engineering knowledge prescribes not only maximum, but total specification. After all, you cannot expect the parts of a machine to sort out things between themselves the same way that people can!

This leads us to the second example: design of machines require positive design criteria. It has been relatively easy to derive these from studies in natural science. In social systems, however, norms (which in turn could be reinterpreted as design principles) are only discovered when violated, and from this stems a negative teint to the social science knowledge that might be applicable to design.

In other words, social science seems to lack the synthetic capacity that has made engineering science a successful design discipline. The question now is whether it is possible to fuse the analytic strength and holist perspective of social science with the synthetic strength of engineering science into a design activity and design knowledge.

Unfortunately there is no answer to that yet. On the question of logics of design, HERBST (forthcoming) is suggesting that the aggregate and modular design logic of simple and systems engineering is subsumable under the more general and non-Aristotelian logic of contextual systems (as developed by SPENCER-BROWN 1969). This latter logic permits the existence of non-reducable wholes and as such could be used to understand social systems.

Hence social science would have to be the leading part in the development of a synthesis with engineering knowledge and one would imagine that the engineering way of fine-tuning details would have to be related neither to a single goal of local efficiency, nor to a composite function of weighted (but commensurable) goals, but rather to a changing set of partly contradictory goals contingent on the local and global context of use of the systems.

Of course, one could imagine a division of labour where social science was used to specify a system and software science used to realize it. But this concept overlooks precisely the kind of problems I have discussed above: The findings of social science would have to be reinterpreted into something meaningful within the frame of reference of software engineering.

6. Steps towards a new technology?

One final aspect of a paradigm is to be mentioned here. In the case of physics, KUHN speaks of an exemplary case that in a condensed way embodies the whole field. Newton's own works, for example, embody in a nutshell the kind of problems that can be attacked by Newtonian mechanics, how to approach their solution, and some of the theories involved. Kuhn himself argued that these exemplary solutions to standard problems, which are paradigms proper in a narrow sense, serve an important function in the transfer of scientific knowledge to new members of the scientific community. The function is that they teach students the (hidden) analogy between a specific problem and the master solution. An example is that by learning to concentrate on identifying variables that fit into the $F=ma$ scheme, students learn to reproduce the Newtonian paradigm.

There can be no doubt about the powerful influence of concrete and acclaimed solutions on the future solutions engineers make to similar problems. A machine that is successfully used in production serves as a model for future development. Along with its explicit features, the model also transfers its hidden assumptions to the new solutions, for example the atomist world conception and the preference for causally determined contexts that I have discussed above. Elsewhere I have argued that today's machinery still embodies the potential for deskilling that was a prime mover for the design of machinery when it first emanated during the industrial revolution - carried over from generation to generation of technical solutions and not easily erased from the technological paradigm (FINNE 1983). My point here, however, is that if a holist technology developed as a synthesis of social and engineering science is to gain momentum, it is absolutely necessary to produce a good exemplary case that can serve model for further development by others.

References

Berger, Peter L. and Thomas Luckmann:
The Social Construction of Reality. Allen Lane (Penguin), London 1967.

Collins, H.M.:
Changing Order. SAGE Publications, London 1985.

Dreyfus, Hubert L.:
What Computers Can't Do. Harper & Row, New York 1979 (revised edn.).

Finne, Håkon:
Teknologiformidlet dekvalifisering og kontrollkapitalens krav eller ingeniørens tenkemåte? In Olav Fagerlid (ed.): Historiske og samfunnsvitenskapelige perspektiver på teknologisk utvikling. University of Trondheim, Trondheim 1983.

Herbst, Philip:
Socio-technical Design. Tavistock Publications, London 1974.

Herbst, David Philip:
Contextual Design: Towards the Development of Socio-Technical Learning Networks. Journal of Applied Behavioral Science, forthcoming.

Kjellberg, Ann:
Beteendevetenskap i verkstadteknisk tillämpning. The Royal Institute of Technology/Dept. of Manufacturing Systems, Stockholm 1983.

Kuhn, Thomas S.:
The Structure of Scientific Revolutions. International Encyclopedia of Unified Science, Vol. 2, No. 2. Univ. of Chicago Press, Chicago 1962.

Polanyi, Michael:
Personal Knowledge. Routledge & Kegan Paul, London 1958.

Spencer-Brown, I.:
Laws of Form. Allen and Unwin, London 1969.

FOR A MORE COMPREHENSIVE VIEW OF CAD.
SOME REFLECTIONS, EXPERIENCE, AND QUESTIONS FROM A CAD-CONSULTANT, AWARE OF THE IMPLICATIONS OF THE TECHNIQUE

Wolfgang Jonas
SYSTEM CONSULT GmbH
An der Rehwiese 28
D-1000 Berlin 38

1. Why these reflections?

Vendors of CAD-systems describe an almost ideal state: The immediate route from the idea in the designer's imagination, via the coloured three-dimensional model in the computer and on the screen - delivering, if necessary, the exact drawing as a by-product - to fully-automated production. Fig. 1 shows a snapshot from a CAD-designer's every-day work.

Figure 1: Design work with CAD

But this way of representation is not a real description of the situation. Everybody involved in the business knows that it is only wishful thinking, just advertisement that can be disproved immediately by every-day experience. Nevertheless CAD-advertisement is quite amusing, see Fig. 2.

Bei einem guten CAD/CAM-System muß morgen die Kuh auf dem Fahrrad zum Bäcker fahren können.

With a good CAD/CAM system, tomorrow the cow will be able to ride a bike to the baker's.

■ Warum ist die Banane krumm?

Why are bananas crooked?

Mit unserem CAD/CAM-System sehen Sie mehr als drei Dimensionen.

With our CAD/CAM system you can see more than three dimensions

Die Wirklichkeit ist dreidimensional

Reality ist threedimensional

Wir haben mehr Lösungen als Sie Probleme

We have more solutions than you have problems

Grafik in der 4. Dimension

Graphics in the 4th dimension

Über CAD muß man nachdenken. Aber nicht ewig.

One has to think about CAD. But not for ever.

Anschließen, einschalten und vergessen.

Plug it in, switch it on and forget it.

Glauben Sie über CAD nichts, was Sie nicht selbst gesehen haben.

Don't believe anything about CAD you haven't seen for yourself

Figure 2: From the wonderful world of CAD

More important - in my opinion - is the resistance against a way of thinking which is propagated with power, less by "serious" CAD-experts than by advertising and marketing experts. Weizenbaum very appropriately calls it the "Imperialism of Functional Violence" (I hope the retranslation is correct!) 1).

An example for this reduced way of thinking is the motto of a well-known consulting-company, active not only in the area of CAD:

> **Denken was machbar ist - machen was denkbar ist?**
> *Thinking what can be done - doing what you can think of*

Here thinking seems to be nothing more than the necessary prior condition for making. There is no examination whether things that can be thought are desirable or not. That means, more honestly but less sophisticatedly, the motto should be:

> **Doing what can be done**

But thinking (of engineers) must no longer provide only the prerequesites for doing things that can be done. It has to take into account the social, ecological, and moral criteria for doing or not-doing the things that can be done, (e.g. SDI). Otherwise this thinking is mechanical and inhuman and can in fact be done more effectively by machines.

2. The problem

The simplification and distortion of concepts

The Designer's way of Thinking

The designer's way of thinking, at the moment, seems to be a matter completely at the disposal of the vendors and their marketing experts. This is annoying because of the extremely unhistoric view, and it becomes almost painful, when engineers or marketing experts start to reflect the question whether designers think "2D or 3D". If a 2D-system has to be sold, designers think 2D, as design drawings have always been two-dimensional. If a 3D-system is offered, designers think 3D, of course, as the real world is three-dimensional too.

The sales manager of a leading vendor says: "What Leonardo da Vinci was able to do, that is to design in perspective, and what a designer had to be able to do up to 1930, namely to design a perspective view on a drawing - this of course without CAD - a modern designer should certainly be able to do - of course with CAD."

Of course designers, like all people, think three-dimensional. Otherwise they would not be able to create plane views of real objects. But does thinking have dimensions? And if so, why only three?

However, this train of thought is not to the essential point. More promising is the question of the manageability of systems, irrespective of the external or internal dimensionality of model representation.

An important prerequesite for the formulation of the problem is the clear intellectual separation of designing and drawing 2). In the design process there are the tasks design (inventing, creating a new product in the imagination) and drawing (representing, elaborating an existing idea of a product). Design work requires phantasy, creativity, and a total and simultaneous way of thinking, whereas drawing work requires discipline, subordination to fixed standards, renouncing initiative, reduction of view onto details that may be unimportant for the whole complex. CAD-systems of today, even if they are called modellers, support the drawing process rather than the modelling process.

The way of thinking in design and construction is mostly unexplored. There is no generally accepted theory of the design and construction process. Activities are very complex, happening mainly unconsciously and simultaneously. There is no linearity or obvious clear algorithmic structure as in analytic processes. Results will not be achieved in small consecutive steps but in larger changes that form qualitatively new levels of the problem solution process 3).

In a CAD-system there is a formal language level between thought and its realization which interrupts the natural flow of thinking. CAD is a qualitatively new level of estrangement between the draughtsman/designer and his work (drawing/construction) as shown in Fig. 3.

Task: Construct a tangential line from a given point to a given circle.

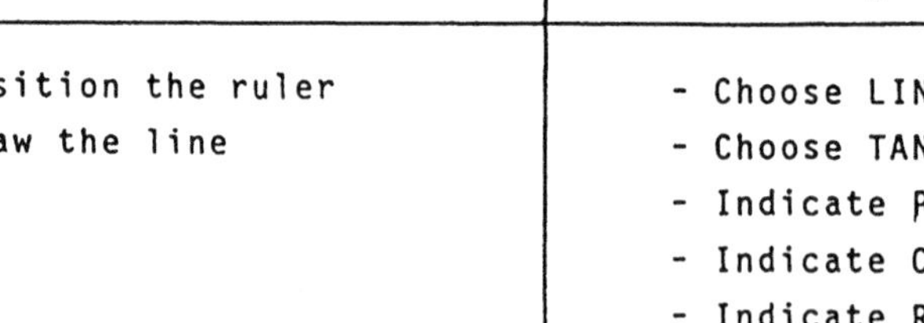

Conventional way	Using CAD
- Position the ruler - Draw the line	- Choose LINE - Choose TANGENT - Indicate POINT - Indicate CIRCLE - Indicate REGION (- Trim LINE)

Figure 3: Conventional and computer-aided design/draughting

Terms like "tool", "dialogue", "communication", "partner", etc. conceal the real facts.

Tools

A very clear and impressive presentation on the improper use of the term "tool" in connection with CAD can be found in [4]). The authors show that work with a CAD system has the character of operating a complex system rather than handling a tool like a pencil or a ruler.

CAD is not (yet?) a tool!

Communication

Two tendencies are remarkable in this context. On the one hand the development of mechanistic models of man as an information processing system, on the other hand the application of terms of human communication to the interaction between man and computer. This is no contradiction, as it might appear at a first glance, but the former is a necessary condition for the latter. See e.g. the IFIP-model of communication interfaces [9]).

A very comprehensive description of the whole problem is given by Bammé et al. [5]), who say that the interface between man and machine, in course of historical (technical) development, has shifted more and more towards man. That means that man (and especially the male species of man), in the course of past centuries, has adopted mechanical structures of acting and communicating.

CAD-designers learn very quickly the effective use of the system by internalizing the required mechanical sequences instead of the conventional actions. In many cases one can observe an identification of a user with "his" system/machine which is equivalent to taking over inhuman machine structures into the human psyche to a certain degree. Thus the interface is shifted into man indeed and is no longer tangible, no longer describable, and even no longer a matter for discussion as an element to be influenced. This turns out to be a considerable problem in discussions with CAD-users about requirements concerning man-machine interaction.

The former is not at all to be understood as criticism. This unconscious adaptation is the user's only chance of survival in this process of rapid change in their work. The necessary adaptation to CAD-systems will support the development of reduced mechanical interaction structures even between people.

Creativity

"Creativity, creative thinking, production of original ideas which lead to the recognition and solution of problems" [10]).

Vendors and CAD-researchers declare that CAD promotes creativity, as it relieves the designer of routine work. Even if it is correct that CAD relieves him of certain kinds of routine work, is this equivalent to an increase in creativity? Maybe creativity even requires certain portions of "noncreative" (stupid) work, that can be done almost automatically, where thoughts can deviate.

On the other hand, the operation of the present unflexible and clumsy systems requires a great deal of creative energy (to find a solution compatible with the system's capabilities, to by-pass the system's defects, etc.), which does not serve the actual purpose, which is the product design.

As a "proof" for the effectivity of a system one can often hear: "We succeeded in designing this well-known part (formerly designed conventionally) with our system." And there is often pride, that they were able, despite all obstinacy of the system, to reconstruct the desired part in laborious work, at least approximately.

Much more plausible to me appears VOLPERT's thesis [8]), that algorithmic, mechanical routine work, and that is what we encounter in operating a CAD system, paralyses creativity in the long run.

And how does the thesis of increasing creativity by the use of computers match with the statements of the most extreme advocates of future expert systems [6]), who claim that the task of elaboration of the world's future knowledge should be transferred from men's mind to machines?

CAD-systems do not support creativity. At best they will not hinder creativity!

"Ordinary" CAD-consulting

The scheme in Fig. 4 shows the schedule of a standard SYSTEM CONSULT CAD-introduction consulting. We know, that it can only be a framework, but the client wants (and needs) a rational scheme like this.

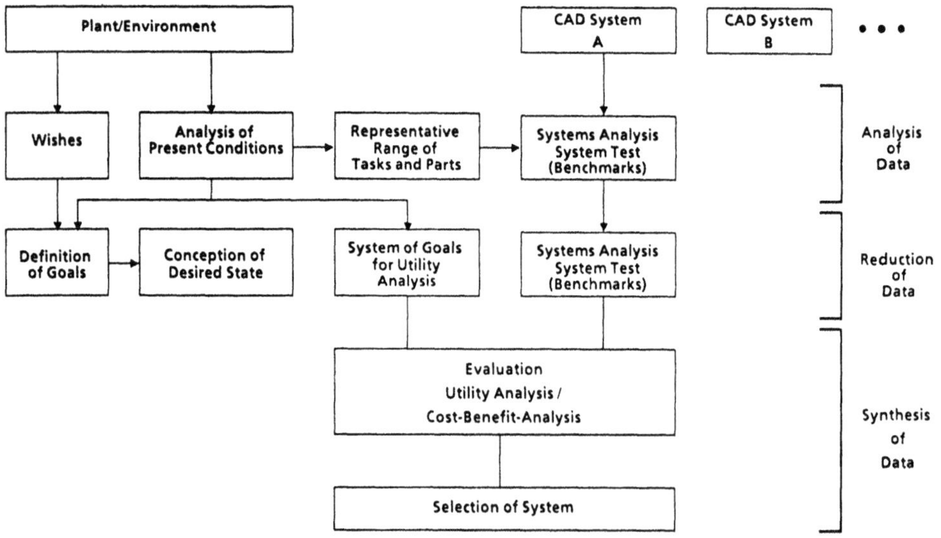

Figure 4: The CAD-decision process

Influences on the decision process

Company Internal Aspects

In both important cases, CAD-introduction as well as modification or extension of an existing installation, there are certainly optimal solutions with regard to technical or organizational efficiency, but these will most likely be at odds with the actual company internal constellation of interest and power. Consultants are often expected to confirm such decisions "scientifically", as were fixed in advance at entirely different levels.

An important aspect in this context is the difficulty or even impossibility, mentioned in [7]), to revise a decision once fixed in a hierarchy because of the very fragile balance of powers related to it.

The Competition among Vendors

The rather stiff competition among vendors often leads to the consequence, that systems or new components are offered, which are far from being fully developed. Every new release will certainly bring extensions in functionality, but not normally improvements in stability, manageability, or response time of the functions. More international standardization efforts might bring a chance for a stronger promotion of qualitative rather than quantitative growth of systems. But I have my doubts ...

Competition among the Users

Companies are exposed to the pressure of being up to date with new technologies like CAD, even if immediate improvements can not be expected to be caused by the introduction. This argumentation is realistic indeed, as current CAD-systems are no new tools, simply to handle, but extremely complex systems. Their introduction normally means a considerable expense of time and money and often even a certain risk. A two year phase of introduction (not of amortization!) is quite usual.

The evaluation of "user-friendliness"

The optimal CAD-system should meet the demand:

Do what I mean, not what I say!

Ruler and pencil immediately do what I mean. I don't have to say what I mean, because there is no formal level (language) between the thought and its realization. A CAD system often will not do what I say, even if I say what I mean, because I don't say it in accordance with the rules.

In my attempt to deal with the problem of "user-friendliness" in a better way I tried to include all completely or partially quantifiable aspects on the check-list and to examine them during the functional system tests. Fig. 5 shows a part of the section concerning man-machine interaction.

	- problem-free linkage with external application	
	programmes	
2.2.6.2	Learnability/Self-explanation	
	- no knowledge of edp required	
	- Learnable without users' handbook	
	- on-line users' handbook available (Text + Figures)	
	- within a command	
	- within a string of commands	
	- Guidance of user in accord with context of design	
	- HELP function within a command	
	- HELP function adaptable to user's knowledge	
	- HELP function adaptable to context of design	
	- availability of knowledge-based explanatory components	
	- system state transparent at all times	
	- uniform format of all speech elements (Syntax)	
	- mnemotechnically appropriate command language	
	- uniform, memorizable lists of parameters	
	- systematic, memorizable abbreviations	
	- clear separation of graphical area, menu area	
2.2.6.3	Controlability/Reliability	
	- Echos (prompting) after all inputs	
	- unambiguous distinction between all inputs	
	- reporting of interim results of complex operations	
	- interim messages during lengthy operations	
	- option to interrupt dialogue steps	
	- no occurrence of situations without solutions	
	- critical functions (such as deletion) safeguarded	
	- analogous behaviour of system in analogous situations	
	- messages always appear in some location and in the	
	same format	
	- response times not too long	
	- no "aggressive" system behaviour	

Figure 5: Part of a CAD-check-list, not suitable to examine "user-friendliness"

This method very quickly turned out to be a failure, as the dynamic process character of the aspect can not at all be regarded in this way. To my opinion a reliable judgement can only be based on practical experience over a longer period of time.

A system satisfying most of the criteria mentioned in the list may nevertheless be extremely clumsy and inflexible to handle. On the other hand a system satisfying only a few of the criteria may have a very pleasant man-machine interface. I am still searching for reliable criteria, which can be examined during a system demonstration.

There is no doubt that techniques as realized in the LISA user-interface, or pattern-recognition techniques as in the BRAVO CAD system present an important step forward, compared to the "communication"-techniques of most CAD systems. But this is still a first step, and I don't even know if the direction is correct.

Promising (not in the near future) seems to be VOLPERT's suggestion [8]), to attempt the creation of a model which describes the differences rather than the conformitics between man and machine more clearly, and based upon this, to define requirements concerning the design of man-machine interfaces.

3. What to do?

Consequences for CAD-Consultancy

There has to be a stronger accent on the non-quantifiable, subjective aspects of the problem. Consultants must not hesitate to emphasize, that analytical decision techniques applied to a mixture of quantifiable and, to some extent, non-quantifiable criteria are an excellent means of manipulation (in a way which may still appear "scientific").

But the share of "classical" CAD-consultancy will decrease. CAD will be in general use in the near future. The current BMFT-support-program for the manufacturing industry will cause a considerable increase in the number of CAD-installations among 2300 companies in this branch in West-Germany [11]). An increase from about 2-3 % in 1983 to more than 50 % in 1986 is expected.

Further consulting activities will concern the areas:

- Integration of CAD into general edp-concepts,
- Communication between different CAD-systems,
- Databases and CAD,
- Special applications of CAD, etc.

"User-friendliness" will play a minor role in this context, compared with functional aspects.

More Interdisciplinary Efforts

More meetings like this one will be necessary. But where are the vendors and where are the users? And where are the system-designers?

Sometimes one can get the impression, that "social studies on CAD" is sort of a well-guarded playground. Well guarded and even sponsored by those who guide the development and who might say: "Let them play, their influence is too small compared to the powerful dynamics of the market. They cannot do any harm". Meetings like this run the risk to be abused as an alibi to justify uncontrolled development.

And maybe some of us have similar feelings, even if they seem to express the antithesis [7]: "... Thus, today every technology appears to be possible and malleable. The continuing discussion on options and forms of technology design feeds on this realization. In the historical perspective this is a consolation since it demonstrates the changeability of technology and it is important as an impulse to participate in the design of technology."

Compare this to:

Thinking what may be done - doing what is thinkable!

Consequences in Education

Interdisciplinary efforts will only have a chance of producing effects in the future, if they lead to comprehensive consequences in education.

A new discipline has to be created to deal with the *design of design aids* common to all traditional areas like architecture, mechanical engineering, civil engineering, etc. Whereas the essential mode of communication in science is mathematics, and in the humanities it is language, the essential mode of communication in design is *modelling* - through drawings, physical analogues, and increasingly, through CAD software. And compared to mathematics or language, modelling is still in the stone age of its development.

Design may emerge as the intellectual discipline common to all branches of engineering and technology.

The Role of Trade-Unions

Concerning CAD, the question if or if not is no longer a matter for discussion. But we have to look at things in a more comprehensive way. The problem is not as much technical (CAD is a technique just at its beginning) but the organizational aspect. CAD is one step on the way towards the realization of large integrated information systems, and information means power.

I won't presume to give any advice to trade-unions. But I want to express the wish that they should interfere in decision processes wherever possible (sorry, if this sounds too naive). The management's seeming advantage in knowledge about a new technology often turns out to be nothing more than an advantage in taking possession of a new terminology.

References

1) Weizenbaum, J.: Die Macht der Computer und die Ohnmacht der Vernunft, Frankfurt, 1978.

2) Wingert, B.: Werkzeugerfahrungen und Qualifikationsveränderungen beim CAD, Sonderheft "Office Management", 31. Jahrgang, Baden-Baden, 1983.

3) Bach, K.: Denkvorgänge beim Konstruieren, Konstruktion, 25. Jahrgang, Heft 1, Januar 1973.

4) Wingert, B.; Riehm, U.: Computer als Werkzeug, Anmerkungen zu einem verbreiteten Mißverständnis. In: W. Rammert und G. Bechmann (Eds.), Technik und Gesellschaft, Jahrbuch, Bd. 3. Frankfurt, Campus 1985, S. 107 - 131.

5) Bammé, A. et al.: Maschinen-Menschen, Mensch-Maschinen. Grundrisse einer sozialen Beziehung, Hamburg 1983.

6) Feigenbaum, E.A./McCordruck, P.: The Fifth Generation, Reading, Mass., 1983.

7) Wingert, B. et al.: CAD im Maschinenbau - Wirkungen, Chancen, Risiken. Heidelberg a.o.: Springer 1984.

8) Volpert, W.: Computer und Denken. Machen wir uns selbst zu Maschinen? Proceedings 7th International Congress on Data Processing in Europe, Wien, 19. - 23.3.1984.

9) Dzida, W.: Das IFIP-Modell für Benutzerschnittstellen, Sonderheft "Office Management", 31. Jahrgang, Baden-Baden, 1983.

10) Fischer-Lexikon, Frankfurt, 1975.

11) CAD/CAM-Journal, München, 3/85.

CONSEQUENCES ON THE WORKING CONDITIONS ON SITE WITH INCREASED USE OF CAD/CAM IN CONSTRUCTION

Elsebet Frydendal Pedersen
Department of Construction Management
The Technical University of Denmark
Building 115
DK-2800 Lingby

The Danish Parliament has established a technological development program running from 1984 to 1987, designed to support the Danish trades' and industries' change-over to high technological systems, production and product development. The program is divided into several smaller programs, one of which, "The program for overall technological assessments", supports the following research project. In construction today, CAD/CAM systems are used in connection with technical calculations, for instance strength, quantity and energy calculations, cost accounts, management and drafting.

1. The purpose of the project

The purpose of the project is:

To analyze and assess the consequences on the working conditions for the employees on site when advanced technology (CAD/CAM) is introduced into construction.

To work out recommendations for the use of CAD/CAM in order to minimize negative consequences of this technology. This includes investigations of the preconditions required to assure that the technology will result in better working conditions for the employees.

To spread knowledge of prospects and consequences on the working conditions on site when introducing CAD/CAM in construction. This includes the design of a checklist for the systematic overall assessment of choice and use of CAD/CAM.

2. Project background

The following characteristics of the construction sector are of importance in connection with the purpose of the project:

- generally, construction work is characterized by craftsmanship, small firms and the complexity and variety of the products,
- the building process - from planning to the final result - is dominated by the need for efficient exchange of information between architects, engineers, different construction wor-

kers and others. This exchange of information has to assure both that the construction work proceeds according to schedule and that the result meets the demands of the owner and the authorities.

In regard to health and safety questions the working conditions on site are dominated by many accidents, strained postures, time pressure, problems related to the weather and increasing problems with chemical products.

The local health and safety groups are not established until construction work has started. They are limited in their function due to problems of applying experience from one site to another and to the fact that many construction workers are only hired for relatively short periods.

3. The technological development in construction

After the Second World War technological development in the construction sector has resulted in the increased use of mechanized cranes, excavators, motor-driven tools and so forth.

An increased part of the work on site has also been transformed into prefabricated products, produced in factories, where the use of CAD/CAM is considerably more common than it is on sites.

4. The future use of CAD/CAM in construction

Several circumstances support the assertion that CAD/CAM will be introduced widely in the construction sector within the next 10 years. Among others to be mentioned is the international competition in the construction sector.

As far as CAD/CAM hardware is concerned, systems have been developed which can handle large amounts of data. The systems can compete in price so that even small firms are able to purchase them. Furthermore, today's systems are easy to work with. However, at present only few Danish construction firms have any experience in the use of CAD/CAM.

5. Consequences for the construction sector due to the use of CAD/CAM

Research on the consequences of introducing CAD/CAM to the construction sector has until now been very limited. Research funds have mainly been used to make the systems work technically. Interest has been concentrated on the economic consequences for the firm.

In 1984 a medium size engineering firm estimated that with increased use of EDP 40 % mantime could be saved, distributed with 15 % on drafting, 15 % on text editing, and 10 % on other functions among which are technical calculations.

The consequences for the division of labour between architects and engineers and between consulting and contracting engineers respectively have been debated and so has the question of the new qualifications that CAD/CAM systems will require. It has also been emphasized that use of CAD/CAM in construction will increase the influence of the users and will allow increased use of construction workers' practical experiences.

Research on the direct or derived consequences of use of CAD/CAM for the employees on site is very sparse. In an ongoing Swedish research project [1)] the following possible consequences are emphasized:

Better planning will diminish the number of unforeseen events and errors in connection with the building process.

For the construction workers the working environment could be improved in the following respects: less physical and psychical strain, reduced risks of diseases and wear and tear, fewer accidents, increased information and general knowledge on the work processes on site.

At present there seems to be general agreement that the use of CAD/CAM in construction will imply several advantages of both qualitative and quantitative character: for instance more effective planning and execution of the building process through better time planning and management.

Better service to the involved parties through a more flexible design process will make discussions about alternative wishes and claims possible.

Finally, a number of working environment problems on the building site can be expected to be solved more efficiently, among other things through easier access to general databases which contain up-to-date knowledge about these problems.

Studies of the *consequences* of introducing *information technology* in other sectors have shown that it is essential to involve those who are going to use the technology as well as those who will be affected by the technology in the choice of technology. A number of negative consequences related to the introduction of information technology should then be reduced.

The execution of the research project

The research project will be executed in two phases:

Phase one: By visiting firms which have experience in CAD/CAM in Denmark as well as abroad (i.e. Sweden and Great Britain), existing experience in and knowledge of CAD/CAM in the construction sector will be collected and analyzed. Contact with a consulting firm and a contracting firm in Denmark has been established. Further, studies of literature and discussions with researchers will be carried out.

---

1) Ranhagen & Jägbeck: "Den framtida Byggarbetsplatsen - datoriseringens konsekvenser för arbetsorganisation, arbetsmiljö och medbestemmande". Stockholm 1983

The use of CAD/CAM in construction will be compared with the use of CAD/CAM in other sectors - for instance the shipbuilding industry. Proposals for desirable trends of development related to the introduction of CAD/CAM in construction will be given. Knowledge on the possibilities and consequences of CAD/CAM technology on working conditions on the site will be spread through articles, a leaflet, slides and work-shops in which the various parties from the construction sector will participate.

Phase two will include monitoring the development in a construction firm, which introduces/applies CAD/CAM.

The research group will take an active part in discussions with the involved parties on the basis of the introduction of CAD/CAM. This means that the consequences of the new technology not only will be passively registered but also actively influenced. Working conditions on the site will be registered before and after the introduction of CAD/CAM with regard to the effect of the new technology.

The relevant groups which the project aims to reach are first and foremost construction workers and engineers employed in both consulting firms and contracting firms. Other relevant groups are architects and technical employees.

7. Research group

The research project is being executed at the Department of Construction Management, The Technical University of Denmark.

Researchers are:
Margit Velsing Groth, assistant professor, sociologist.
Elsebet Frydendal Pedersen, research worker, occupational therapist.
Kristian Kreiner, Ph.D., associate professor.
Steffen Goth, associate professor, civil engineer.

GPSR Compliance

The European Union's (EU) General Product Safety Regulation (GPSR) is a set of rules that requires consumer products to be safe and our obligations to ensure this.

If you have any concerns about our products, you can contact us on ProductSafety@springernature.com

In case Publisher is established outside the EU, the EU authorized representative is:

Springer Nature Customer Service Center GmbH
Europaplatz 3
69115 Heidelberg, Germany

Batch number: 10726298

Printed by Printforce, the Netherlands